Lawrence Moonan was formerly Senior Lecturer in Philosophy at Bolton Institute.

Divine Power

DIVINE POWER

The Medieval Power Distinction
up to its Adoption by Albert,
Bonaventure, and Aquinas

LAWRENCE MOONAN

CLARENDON PRESS · OXFORD
1994

Oxford University Press, Walton Street, Oxford OX2 6DP

Oxford New York Toronto
Delhi Bombay Calcutta Madras Karachi
Kuala Lumpur Singapore Hong Kong Tokyo
Nairobi Dar es Salaam Cape Town
Melbourne Auckland Madrid
and associated companies in
Berlin Ibadan

Oxford is a trade mark of Oxford University Press

Published in the United States
by Oxford University Press Inc., New York

British Library Cataloguing in Publication Data
Data available

Library of Congress Cataloging in Publication Data
Divine power: the medieval power distinction up to its adoption by
Albert, Bonaventure, and Aquinas/ Lawrence Moonan.
Includes bibliographical references and indexes.
1. God—Omnipotence—History of doctrines—Middle Ages, 600–1500.
I. Title.
BT133.M66   1994   231'.4—dc20   93–30542
ISBN 0–19–826755–X

1 3 5 7 9 10 8 6 4 2

Typeset by Selwood Systems, Midsomer Norton
Printed in Great Britain on acid-free paper by
Bookcraft (Bath) Ltd. Midsomer Norton, Avon

BT
133
.M66
1994

TO
JOHN GEORGE MOONAN
AND
MARY MOONAN

ACKNOWLEDGEMENTS

The present book is part of a much wider programme of research, pursued over many years. I acknowledge early encouragement from E. F. Jacob, L. Minio-Paluello (both now dead), and M. Caren Berry, now of London; and shrewd observations from Professor Geach in a brief exchange of letters following the published articles mentioned in the Introduction below. A valuable sabbatical at the Mediaeval Institute, Toronto, permitted a systematic survey of later medieval uses of the Distinction, and by way of a bonus, a pleasant discussion with Professor Courtenay at Madison. At a later stage, tools for a more explicit appreciation of the Distinction were sharpened in discussions with Friar Herbert McCabe OP and Dr György Geréby, following a series of lectures in Oxford, arranged through the good offices of Dr A. Kenny. For a couple of terms in Oxford, I am indebted to the research fund of Bolton Institute of Technology (now Bolton Institute), and to my colleagues there in the Philosophy Section: especially Drs Peter Caldwell and Suzanne Stern-Gillet. When the present book was already in draft, I was able to have a number of discussions with Dr Randi during his short visit to Oxford. Our exchanges of drafts and criticisms continued, but in a tragically short time Dr Randi died: a greatly respected colleague, and already a friend. During later revisions I have benefited from related discussions with Mr David Melling, of Manchester Metropolitan University (where I also held a visiting fellowship for a time), and Mrs Julie Jack, of Oxford. For an interest in serious medieval philosophy more generally, I thank Prof. Fernand Van Steenberghen, and my colleagues of many years ago in the seminar of the De Wulf-Mansion Centre in Louvain.

The whole of the book in its present form is from a time when my wife was not only providing the support commonly acknowledged in these places, but acting as a one-woman CNRS. This is Pat's book, and without her it could not (*de potentia ordinata dei*) have appeared.

CONTENTS

Contents

Introduction

Can God save my family from the plague? If he knows that I shall be damned, or that my lover is going to reject me, can I avoid rejection, or damnation? These are not academic questions, but they had academic counterparts—just as sharply personal to many of the medieval academics who faced them—which took a challenge to the heart of the thinking Christian's world-view. If God has disposed this or that mode of redemption, the schoolmen were asked, could he nevertheless have ordered otherwise? If he has disposed this or that mode of redemption, is it possible in any way that precisely this or that mode of redemption will not be punctiliously executed, no matter how terrible that might sometimes seem?

THE CHALLENGE—AN ENDURING CHALLENGE?

The *opus redemptionis* was at issue, and theologians were precisely as theologians concerned. But the issues of theory which lay behind the challenging questions were not so narrowly theological, and put schoolmen in perplexity not only as working theologians, but as reflecting Christians, and indeed as reflecting human beings, considering how ultimately the world is, or is not.

On the one hand, the schoolmen could hardly deny out of hand that, say, God could save my family from the plague, or could have disposed redemption otherwise. How could such a denial have been rendered consistent with their view that we live in a universe ordered by God? To deny a God-ordered universe— would it not have been to leave the way open for the position that there is no infinite God and no universe; nothing more than a sum of things, in which whatever happens happens by necessity, and can appear to recur indefinitely many times?

On the other hand—and it is crucial to give weight to this—

many of the schoolmen could not claim to say anything intelligible about what God may have it in him to do, but does not do. Most if not all of the schoolmen examined below, for example, maintained or sought to maintain a rigorously negative theology on the nature of God: a view to the effect that nothing we can understand may be affirmed properly and with truth of the divine nature. The views of Albert, Aquinas, and Bonaventure, to mention only the most famous, were all as stark as that on the point, as will appear.

Schoolmen persuaded of such views could not escape from their perplexity simply by asserting without commentary such things as 'God has freely decreed this, but might have decreed something else.' They certainly used formulas to that effect, but were able to use them to good purpose only by understanding them rather carefully. For the faith of their Church also taught them that 'God has sworn and will not repent' (Ps. 109/110), that the actual order of things is by God's free disposition to be the only order of things, maintained punctiliously and in perpetuity. From this further point a number of more subtle perplexities arise, as will appear, from difficulties in reconciling the point with others which the schoolmen typically wished to maintain: not only in order consistently to pursue the theology of the theology faculties, but in order to pursue a genuinely scientifical inquiry—scientifical, by the received (Aristotelian) standards of the time—into the natural world.

THE DISTINCTION MENTIONED IN THE TITLE

A remarkable generation of schoolmen sought to dissolve their perplexities by (1) a distinction and—in the period covered below—by (2) a regularly followed manner of using it.

The distinction is the one which for convenience I am calling the Power Distinction, or sometimes simply the Distinction; made typically in such locutions as:

> Even if God cannot *de potentia ordinata sua* save my family from the plague, or dispose some mode of redemption other than some mode mentioned, he nevertheless can *de potentia absoluta sua* do so; *or*

Neither *de potentia ordinata sua* nor even *de potentia absoluta sua* can God be said to be able to do some other thing you mention, or purport to mention.

The regular manner of using it will appear. So will the point of being able to do so, which is not always immediately obvious to sophisticated modern readers; for reasons which have to be looked for.

In the meantime I note a further fact which appears below about the earlier medieval Power Distinction; as it opens up horizons today, of a kind which not every idea important in its own day necessarily does. It appears that the Distinction is addressed to complications arising from a concern to maintain both a rigorously negative view on the divine nature, and a specific view of the things around us as being providentially ordered in particular ways. The negative theology view in question is at bottom a metaphysical view, not necessarily implying further views (e.g. concerning worship), in which its users were no doubt interested for reasons of a different kind. The view of the ordered world—though the schoolmen examined below indeed accepted it on grounds of a narrowly theological kind—appears as understood below to be itself not necessarily dependent on narrowly theological premisses or any supposed Revelation, but is a view of things which can be argued (for or against) on more neutrally scientifical or metaphysical grounds, not necessarily implying any commitment for or against religious or narrowly theological positions. The Distinction is thus in principle "portable" to contexts of use significantly different from those in which it was first developed.

Yet it is in a domain not too distant from that of its early development that it could be timely to be able to adapt and apply the Distinction in our own day.

It could be, at any rate, if a need for something very like the Power Distinction as isolated in this book arises (as can be argued) wherever there is call to render (1) a rigorously negative theology on the divine nature consistent with (2) at least an important and typical core of the theology of the theology faculties, or indeed of views of a type canvassed by some leading philosophers of religion. This was not called for in the heyday of Deism, when negative theology was disregarded. It is not

much called for today among many proponents of "theism", as
they focus on the coherence of divine "attributes" (attributes
being understood as what putatively significant predicates are
supposed to designate), or the coherence of a divine "nature"
identifiable with a bundle of such attributes.[1] But if we are
convinced by the destructive arguments of Hume and Kant
against Deism, or by the destructive arguments raised against
the "theism" of more recent times—against "the God of the
philosophers"—then the whole scene is shifted.[2] What then
returns to centre-stage among thoroughgoing inquirers of intellectual integrity is whether the bare assertion that some God
exists—'que nous entendons nuement qu'il y a quelque Dieu',
as Calvin put it—can be true, whether we can understand it or
not, and whether we wish to respond in worship or not.[3] What
then follows is that the analytical move encapsulated in the
earlier medieval Power Distinction resumes its crucial concern
for honest and "scientifical" theologians: the working theologians
of the theology faculties, and their counterparts in certain reaches
of philosophical theology or philosophy of religion.

For as long as some form of Deism could be defended, or if
"theism" and "the God of the philosophers" can be salvaged,
then philosophical theologians, if not historians, could or can

---

[1] The intended content of "theism" is described in the opening pages of R. W.
Swinburne, *The Coherence of Theism* (Oxford, 1977), 302 pp., which also contains systematic
defences of theistic positions. For a Bundle Theory of the divine nature (my description,
not Prof. Plantinga's) see A. Plantinga, *Does God have a Nature?* (Milwaukee, 1980), 146 pp.

[2] Critiques of "the God of the philosophers" are to be found in J. L. Mackie, 'Evil
and Omnipotence', *Mind*, 64 (1955), 200–12, and *The Miracle of Theism: Arguments for and
against the Existence of God* (Oxford, 1982), 268 pp.; and A. Kenny, *The God of the Philosophers*
(Oxford, 1979), vii + 135 pp. Contrasting ways of situating the issues in philosophical
theology can be seen in F. C. Copleston, *Religion and Philosophy* [Dublin, 1974], x + 195
pp.; J. Owens, 'God in Philosophy Today', in *Towards a Christian Philosophy* (Washington
[1990]), x + 332 pp.; and the title essay in A. Flew, *The Presumption of Atheism, and Other
Philosophical Essays on God, Freedom and Immortality* (London [1976]), 183 pp., 13–20.

[3] The allusion is to a passage in Calvin, *Institutes*, Bk. 1, ch. 2: 'Or i'enten que nous
cognoissons Dieu, non pas que nous entendons nuement qu'il y a quelque Dieu mais
quand nous comprenons ce qu'il nous appartient d'en comprendre, ce qui est utile pour
sa gloire, brief ce qui est expédient. Car a parler droictement, nous ne dirons pas que
Dieu soit cognu ou il n y a nulle religion ne piété.' (1560 Fr. text, ed. J.-D. Benoît, *Jean
Calvin: Institution de la religion chrestienne* (5 vols.), 1 (Paris, 1957), 55.) Note that Calvin does
not dispute either the truth or the fundamental importance of the bare (metaphysical)
assertion 'qu'il y a quelque dieu'. What he insists is that merely to be able to assert it
(even with truth) is not eo ipso to be accounted as "knowing God", in the context of
pious instruction.

continue with equanimity to ignore the medieval Power Distinction. (Historians have long suspected that it could provide a key to some of the origins of modern European thought, if only we could rub off the verdigris of the centuries.) If for whatever reason the negative theology on the divine nature which even Hume allowed to be untouched by his own destructive arguments, returns to centre-stage, then the case is altered: and the alternatives opened up by the model of the earlier medieval Power Distinction return to centre-stage with it. If they do, it will have to be as an alternative to post-Deistical debate, not as a possible contribution to it. Neither the Power Distinction not indeed a rigorously negative theology itself may be expected to fit without travesty into the mannered and sanitised drills of move and counter-move into which so much recent discussion at times appears to be locked.

Not that any such substantive applications are argued through in the present book. This is a book of intellectual history: *verstehende* intellectual history, in case there is any other kind. It provides the first analytic exposition in detail of the medieval Power Distinction, as understood and used in its formative period (*c.* 1215–*c.* 1280). The analysis is pursued to the point where anyone who can read books of modern philosophy or theology with understanding should be able to make use of it, without any particular knowledge of medieval disciplines. But it is not arrived at without such knowledge, and I have "shown my working" to a considerable extent: showing how the analysis has been tested against the texts, and may be tested further.

The book takes the analysis further in some crucial respects than has been attempted hitherto: most fundamentally, if undramatically, by explicitly situating the Distinction within a strategy to permit certain kinds of theological discussion, consistently with maintaining a negative theology on the divine nature; then by recognizing explicitly that both of the Distinction's contrasting determinants (*de potentia ordinata dei*, *de potentia absoluta dei*) are to be understood only on a reading of *potentia dei*, 'God's power', as being 'systematically misleading' in specifiable ways.

To formulate what can be specified in an understanding of the Power Distinction so as to exclude all damaging vagueness or ambiguity calls for an initial mistrust of the schoolmen's idiom, and will eventually call for a systematic use of technical means.

But the specifiable elements themselves are not especially technical, and the importance of the Power Distinction must not be
imagined to be that of some rigorously technical device—some
Solomon's Mine of modal logic, perhaps—which the medievals
somehow hit on, and then lost. The Distinction is indeed to be
seen as a quasi-technical device, but one from the incompletely
analysed level appropriate to dialectical discussion: eventually,
when we are clear enough about what was intended, and needs
to be caught in our analyses, we should be able to formulate the
results better than the original users of the Distinction were
placed to do.

The real difficulty is in being clear enough and comprehensive
enough about what has to be caught in our analyses. That is the
difficulty addressed in this book, and that is what has called for
the means chosen: outlining a working notion of the Distinction,
and ancillary working notions in philosophical logic and in
metaphysics (Ch. 1); testing the working notion in a comprehensive range of contexts of use from the Distinction's formative period (Chs 2–8); refining the notion as used and
understood in that period, and situating what may be detachable
from the understanding current in that period, in a broader
context (Ch. 9).

CHRONOLOGICAL LIMITS

The medieval story of the Power Distinction falls conveniently
into three broad stages. The first, the concern of this book, takes
it from the earliest extant witnesses, from around the time of the
Fourth Lateran Council in 1215, or from the establishment of
the Theology Faculty of Paris University, in the same decade, to
the time of the Second Council of Lyons in 1274, or that of the
Parisian condemnations of 1270 and 1277. In this stage the
Distinction is being elaborated, is winning acceptance, and its
terminology is settling; and most of this is happening within
Paris's Faculty of Theology, whose importance within the culture
of the time can hardly be exaggerated. A second stage takes it
to the Black Death of the 1340s, and (at Paris) the shifts of
emphasis coinciding with Jean Buridan's academic reforms. This
is a stage of enormous expansion in popularity and range of

application. It is also a stage during which much of the excitement moves from Paris, to Oxford and Cambridge. A third stage takes it to the time of Luther, and thence into modern times. With systematic and philosophical theology generally, the Distinction seems to fade in academic attention. The formulas are still used, but a common understanding of them can no longer be presumed, even in academic users.

Both conceptually and historically developments of the Distinction in the second and third stages mentioned are certainly of great interest. But without an analysis of the Distinction in its formative period for comparison, it would seem difficult if not practically impossible to do them justice. My own interest in the Distinction was roused by suggested applications to fifteenth-century issues, and issues that led well beyond the schools of theology. By working back—to slightly beyond Aristotle, when in search of a prehistory of logical and metaphysical issues involved in the problématique to which the Power Distinction was addressed—I was led to the choice of the formative period covered in this book, not only as being of interest in its own right, but as probably providing the fairest core positions for comparison, whether with the later developments, or with elements from its own historical ancestry.

Historical periods rarely begin and end neatly, without some arbitrary determination of boundary problems. The period of this book is no exception. The cutting-off point is determined by the completion date for the then academically obligatory lectures on the Sentences. Schoolmen doing this after Bonaventure and Aquinas—after 1257, therefore—are excluded from consideration in the present book, whether or not they outlived those two, who both died in 1274. But all works composed by schoolmen included are examined, even if composed by them after 1274.

POLICY ON QUOTATIONS FROM MEDIEVAL AUTHORS

The schoolmen examined below wrote in a regimented form of Latin, a professional jargon whose nuances may escape us, especially when—as is inevitable in a study where quotations can hardly but be numerous—the original contexts cannot be more than sketched. Translation, and interpretative translation at that, becomes unavoidable.

My policy is that (1) a reader who is content to accept my interpretations and formulations of the medieval texts will be able to follow the overall historical argument without any particular knowledge of either Latin or the other disciplines (e.g. text-criticism, palaeography...) used in preparing the book; but that (2) when a medieval academic's position is open to more than one reasonably arguable interpretation (which is perhaps the usual case rather than not, in a topic of the present kind) the subsidiary exegetical arguments at those points will certainly require a number of ancillary disciplines, including Latin, in a reader who would wish to contest the matter. To make the work of such readers easier, so that they may take such discussions further where they think it useful, I "show my working", giving key terms in parenthesis, where they are not necessarily obvious, and providing the original in the notes.

PUNCTUATION AND WAYS OF SPEAKING

In the quotations of medieval Latin texts, the punctuation and "modern" spelling are from me, failing indication to the contrary. Forms of *deus* have lower-case initials: partly, as in editions of patristic texts, from the frequency of such forms; partly, to respect the views of most if not all the medievals examined, to the effect that such expressions as *deus*, referring to God, ought not to be understood as proper names of an individual, but rather analogously to mass terms such as 'cream' or 'sugar'. I have not been so bold as to do likewise in English (but cf. Mackie 1982, as at n. 2), though only because 'god', so used, still looks odd to me.

'We', when unrestricted by the context, is intended to include those who speak English and have understood the argument up to that point, whether or not they have been persuaded by it, or think its assumptions to be true. I try not to smuggle the readers' collusion in judgements which are mine but not necessarily theirs, in uses of 'we'. In particular, I try not to smuggle collusion in substantive judgements, especially in metaphysics or in theology, in which I might be inclined to agree with this or that medieval, but in which many modern Christians, say, or philosophers might not. But for some obviously contentious points which were not especially in contention among the schoolmen examined, I omit explicit reminders of the contentiousness: sometimes speaking of God's existing or the Sacraments' giving grace, rather than God's supposedly existing or the so-called Sacraments purporting to give what was called grace, or whatever. Let the godly bear with me in some of those places, and the ungodly bear with me in others.

ACKNOWLEDGEMENT OF THE CRITICAL LITERATURE

The interpretation offered in Chapter 9 is based on first-hand examination of a comprehensive range of academic texts from the period: a would-be exhaustive range, for the earliest users. Specific debts are acknowledged in the appropriate places, but I would like to record here a more general debt to the substantial body of work done on the Power Distinction in the present century. It is not least from interpretations which have been found insufficient, by myself or others, that my own interpretations have gained. What follows here is no more than an acknowledgement of this. A critical appreciation of the earlier interpretations of the Distinction—often given only sketchily, or tangentially, or in a distorting context—would require a longer book than this one. More to the point, it would need much of the present one as a prolegomenon, if it should be able to do justice to the diversity of valid points to be made about the Distinction.

The Distinction was never quite forgotten. In its general bearing it continued to be understood in at least some quarters long beyond the Middle Ages themselves. More interestingly, other uses came to be found for the terminology, and the notions or related notions came to be detached more strongly from their earlier theological settings. This is most striking in the 'absolute power' of despots, in post-medieval political discussions. But in Newton, Leibniz, Descartes, and even Hume some important discussions are still in need of clarifications which a better appreciation of the medieval distinction(s) can provide. Through the post-medieval scholastics too, some residual understanding of the medieval Power Distinction lasted into the nineteenth-century revival of interest in medieval thought, and in scholastic philosophy and theology. In a widely used manual of Kleutgen's, from the later nineteenth century, a brief but sober account of the Distinction is given; but not all neo-scholastic accounts were so sober.[4] In the twentieth century, interest in the Distinction revived after Grzondziel's historical study, which also paid much attention to earlier anticipations of the Distinction; and after Borchert's impressive appeals to the notion, as found in a variety of medieval users, to clarify an understanding of some doctrinal issues important in later medieval theology.[5]

After the 1939–45 War the Distinction or its close relatives began to interest historians of medieval thought more widely. Professors Leff and Oberman, in series of studies in later medieval thought, began to wonder whether emphases or shifts perceived in the ways the Distinction seemed to be being used in the later Middle Ages, might serve crucially to explain some acknowledged movements in culture and society more broadly, towards the origins of modern times.[6] Historians of science followed the

---

[4] J. Kleutgen, *Institutiones theologicae in usum scholarum*, 1. *De ipso Deo* (Ratisbon, 1881), VIII + 752 pp., § 645–7; and cf. § 639. But see Ch. 9, n. 24 below.

[5] H. Grzondziel, *Die Entwicklung der Unterscheidung zwischen der potentia Dei absoluta und der potentia Dei ordinata von Augustin bis Alexander von Hales*, diss. (Wrocław, 1926). E. Borchert, *Der Einfluss des Nominalismus auf die Christologie der Spätscholastik nach dem Traktat De communicatione idiomatum des Nicolaus Oresme: Untersuchungen und Textausgabe*, esp. III, ch. 1: *Der Begriff der potentia absoluta et ordinata*, in *Beiträge zur Geschichte der Philosophie und Theologie des Mittelalters*, 35/4–5 (Münster, 1940), XVI + 153 + 44 pp. Remarkably similar views, in addition to passages cited, can be seen to an extent unusual in a successful thesis, in R. Desharnais, *The History of the Distinction between God's Absolute and Ordained Power, and its Influence on Martin Luther*, diss. C.U. (Washington DC, 1966); which also contains other matter of value, notably on Albert the Great.

[6] G. Leff, notably in *Bradwardine and the Pelagians: A Study of his 'De causa Dei' and its Opponents* (Cambridge, 1957), xiii + 282 pp.; *Heresy in the Later Middle Ages: The Relation of Heterodoxy to Dissent c. 1250–1450* (2 vols.; Manchester [1967]), x + 800 pp., in 2 vols.; *William of Ockham: The Metamorphosis of Scholastic Discourse* (Manchester [1975]), xxiv + 666 pp. H. A. Oberman, notably in *Archbishop Thomas Bradwardine, a Fourteenth-Century Augustinian: A Study of his Theology in its Historical Context* (Utrecht, 1957), xii + 422 pp., *The Harvest of Medieval Theology: Gabriel Biel and Late Medieval Nominalism* (Cambridge, Mass., 1963), xv + 495 pp. Consideration of the Distinction in connection with political thought especially can be seen in a series of studies by F. Oakley, including 'Jacobean Political Theology: The Absolute and Ordinary Powers of the King', *J. Hist. Ideas*, 29 (1968), 323–46; and *Omnipotence, Covenant and Order: An Exercise in the History of Ideas from Abaelard to Leibniz* (Ithaca, NY, 1984), 165 pp.; also in W. Courtenay, 'The King and the Leaden Coin: The Economic Background of "Sine qua non" Causality', *Traditio*, 28 (1972), 185–209; in A. de Muralt, 'La Structure de la philosophie politique moderne, d'Occam à Rousseau', in *Cahiers de la rev. de Théol. et Philos.* 2 (1978), 3–84; in E. Randi, 'La vergine e il papa: Potentia Dei absoluta e plenitudo potestatis papale nel XIV seculo', *History of Political Thought*, 5 (1984), 425–45; and in A. Pacchi, 'Hobbes e la potenza di Dio', in

example of Duhem, to at least the extent of looking seriously to possible medieval roots or precedents for modern ideas.[7] Critics of medieval literature began to speculate that this or that literary text might be illuminated by some of the more "exciting" accounts of the Distinction which had been suggested. At this period some of the views entertained for attribution to fourteenth-century schoolmen—Holcot, Woodham, and Buckingham were among the favourites—could be little short of wild. Yet the result of study after study was to cast increasing doubt on the applicability of the wilder interpretations.

In Germany especially the interest in how later medievals' ways of understanding the Distinction or something related to it might throw light on doctrinal shifts in other matters, continued: notably in studies by Auer, Dettloff, Bannach, and Hamm.[8] If anything, however, the effect of this work was to emphasise that a more specific understanding of at least some medievals' own understanding of the Distinction was needed, before the ulterior

---

A. Vettese (ed.), *Sopra la volta del mondo: Onnipotenza e potenza assoluta di Dio tra medioevo e età moderna* (Bergamo, 1986), 186 pp., 79–91.

[7] See E. Grant, 'The Condemnation of 1277, God's Absolute Power, and Physical Thought in the Middle Ages' (1979), repr. *Studies in Medieval Science and Natural Philosophy* (London, 1981), No. XIII, 211–44. See also K. Tachau, *Vision and Certitude in the Age of Ockham: Optics, Epistemology and the Foundations of Semantics* (Leiden, 1988), xii + 422 pp.; M. J. Osler, 'Providence and Divine Will: The Theological Background to Gassendi's Views on Scientific Knowledge', *J. Hist. Ideas*, 44 (1983), 549–60; A. Funkenstein, *Theology and the Scientific Imagination from the Middle Ages to the Seventeenth Century* (Princeton, NJ, 1986), xii + 421 pp. More than one history of science contribution conflates the perceived danger from non-Christian thought in response to which the Power Distinction can be seen to have its place, and the (different) perceived dangers to which the 1277 condemnations have been seen to be addressed. And it is a great misplacement of emphasis to see God's option-neutral power as the 'central idea' of the 1277 condemnations (E. Grant, *Much Ado about Nothing: Theories of Space and Vacuum from the Middle Ages to the Scientific Revolution* (Cambridge [1981]), xiii + 456 pp., 109). Discussion and further references are at A. de Libera, 'Le Développement de nouveaux instruments conceptuels et leur utilisation dans la philosophie de la nature au XIVe s.', *Acta Philosophica Fennica*, 48 (1990), 158–97, 178–84.

[8] Notably J. Auer, *Die Entwicklung der Gnadenlehre in der Hochscholastik, mit besonderer Berücksichtigung des Kardinals Matteo d'Acquasparta*, I. *Das Wesen der Gnade* (Freiburg i.B. 1942), xv + 362 pp.; II. *Das Wirken der Gnade* (1951), XIII + 216 pp.; W. Dettloff, *Die Lehre von der acceptatio divina bei Johannes Duns Scotus mit besonderer Berücksichtigung der Rechtfertigungslehre* (Werl, 1954), XVIII + 233 pp., esp. 72–4, and 204–10; and (for the later period) *Die Entwicklung der Akzeptations- u. Verdienstlehre von Duns Scotus bis Luther, mit besonderer Berücksichtigung der Franziskanertheologen*, in *Beiträge*, 40/2 (1963), xx + 318 pp.; K. Bannach, *Die Lehre von der doppelten Macht Gottes bei Wilhelm von Ockham: Problemgeschichtliche Voraussetzungen und Bedeutung* (Wiesbaden, 1975), 423 pp. B. Hamm, *Promissio, Pactum, ordinatio: Freiheit und Selbstbindung Gottes in der scholastischen Gnadenlehre* (Tübingen, 1977).

appeal to the notion in connection with other matters could be carried through properly. A similar effect was produced by some comparative studies.[9]

Increasingly, more cautious notes were being sounded, not least in a series of studies by Prof. Courtenay.[10] Two studies primarily concerned with individual users (Aquinas, and Peter de Trabibus) also provided something of a working notion of the Distinction, but seemed content to eliminate some of the wilder suggestions of the terminology, without seeking to penetrate much below the surface.[11] An effect of the increasing caution was that the Distinction was in danger of looking so harmless as to make readers wonder why even some well-informed medievals had been disturbed by uses of it which, increasingly, were being seen as essentially no threat to the doctrinal orthodoxy of the time. Any complacency on the matter was soon under threat from a series of related arguments from Prof. Geach. These may not have unpicked the issues quite so clearly as their author might have wished, but they were enough to show that more than a harmless triviality had to be involved in uses of the Distinction, if the Distinction itself was not to be confounded with something bogus. The real force of the arguments was not fully addressed by replies made at the time (my own included).[12] In the present book I attempt to take the force of Geach's difficulties into account; even though an explicit examination of his formulation of the difficulties would be out of place here.

---

[9] M. A. Pernoud, 'The Theory of 'potentia Dei' according to Aquinas, Scotus and Ockham', *Antonianum*, 47 (1972), 69–95.

[10] Most notably in 'Nominalism and Late Medieval Religion', in C. Trinkaus and H. O. Oberman (eds.), *The Pursuit of Holiness in Late Medieval and Renaissance Religion* (Brill, 1975); 'The Dialectic of Omnipotence in the High and Late Middle Ages', in T. Rudavsky (ed.), *Divine Omniscience and Omnipotence in Medieval Philosophy: Islamic, Jewish and Christian Perspectives* (Dordrecht [1985]), lix + 299 pp.; and in vol. 7 of the Ritter *Wörterbuch*, s.v.

[11] G. Gál, 'Petrus de Trabibus on the Absolute and Ordained Power of God', in R. S. Almagno and C. L. Harkins (eds.), *I. C. Brady Festchrift* (St Bonaventure, NY [1976]), 283–92. L. Moonan, 'St Thomas Aquinas on Divine Power' in the *Atti* of the international congress *Tommaso d'Aquino nel suo VII centenario* (Rome and Naples, 1974), 3 (Naples, 1977), 366–407 (= *Atti* 1974).

[12] P. T. Geach, in 'Omnipotence', *Philosophy*, 48 (1973), 7–20, and 'An Irrelevance of Omnipotence', in pp. 327–33 of the same volume; largely repeated in *Providence and Evil: The Stanton Lectures 1971–72* (Cambridge [1977]), xxii + 153 pp. Among replies, L. Moonan, 'Why can't God do everything?', *New Blackfriars*, 55 (1974), 552–62; P. Helm, 'Omnipotence and Change', *Philosophy*, 51 (1976), 454–61; M. MacBeath, 'Geach on Omnipotence and Virginity', *Philosophy*, 63 (1988), 395–400.

Something of a new phase in historical studies of the Distinction was marked by the important *Il sovrano e l'orologiaio* of Dr Randi, which provided both the sweep of historical coverage needed for a wide enough context, and the accurate study of an impressive number of uses of the Distinction, including not a few from sources still available only in manuscript. The same author's selected bibliography, in another volume, served around the same time to focus attention helpfully.[13] For focusing attention on certain issues, Courtenay's 'The Dialectic...' from another volume of related studies, has also been of particular value (see n. 10), and the same author's concise historical account in volume 7 of the Ritter *Wörterbuch* will be of use to many. In the same period both Prof. McCord Adams and Dr McGrath provide attempts to get below the surface of the Distinction;[14] though perhaps without always giving enough weight to the differences between some medieval ways of conducting philosophical analyses and ours. (For relevant differences see Ch. 1 below.) The period also sees some re-evaluations of historical antecedents which have often been alleged, rightly or wrongly, as contributions either to the Distinction itself or to the problématique to which it was addressed.[15] At the time of his death Dr Randi had temporarily put aside a more comprehensive work, and Prof. Courtenay has more recently provided a further historical account.[16]

[13] E. Randi, *Il sovrano e l'orologiaio: Due immagini di Dio nel dibattito sulla "potentia absoluta" fra XIII e XIV seculo* (Florence [1987]), XII + 191 pp.; 'Bibliografia essenziale', in A. Vettese (ed.), *Sopra la volta del mondo: Onnipotenza e potenza assoluta di Dio tra medioevo e eta moderna* (Bergamo, 1986), 186 pp., 175–83; the three articles listed there, and his contributions to the volume he edited jointly with L. Bianchi, *Le verità dissonanti: Aristotele alla fine del Medioevo*, pref. M.-T. Beonio Brocchieri Fumagalli [Rome and Bari, 1990], XVI + 194 pp., esp. 151–81, 'Armonia: Musica e teodicea fra XIII e XIV seculo'. But cf. the review of *Il sovrano* in *Rassegna di letteratura tomistica*, vol. 23, No. 755.

[14] M. McCord Adams, *William Ockham* (2 vols.; Notre Dame, Ind., 1987), xx + 1402 pp. in 2 vols. A. McGrath, *Iustitia Dei: A History of the Christian Doctrine of Justification* (2 vols.; Cambridge [1986]), vol. 1, § 11 and 13; *The Intellectual Origins of the European Reformation* [Oxford, 1987], viii + 223 pp., 19–21, 78–82; *Luther's Theology of the Cross: Martin Luther's Theological Breakthrough* [Oxford, 1985], viii + 199 pp., 167, 193.

[15] W. J. Courtenay, 'The Critique on Natural Causality in the Mutakallimun and Nominalism', *Harvard Theological Review* 66 (1973), 77–94; L. Moonan, 'Impossibility and Peter Damian', *Archiv für Geschichte der Philosophie*, 62 (1980), 146–63; and 'Abelard's use of the *Timaeus*, *Archives d'Histoire Doctrinale et Littéraire du Moyen Âge* 56 (1989), 7–90.

[16] W. J. Courtenay, *Capacity and Volition: A History of the Distinction of Absolute and Ordained Power* (1989), = Pierluigi Lubrina, coll. 'Quodlibet' 8, reported by L.-J. Bataillon at *Rev. des sciences philosophiques et théologiques*, 75 (1991), 508–9; which appeared, unfortunately, too

Studies not specifically concerned with the Power Distinction
are not considered here, though of course many contribute
indirectly to an understanding of it, or of its medieval users.
The more narrowly germane are acknowledged where they are
exploited. Materials and studies throwing light on the dialectical
practices received at the time occupy a special place, and are
chiefly noted in Chapters 1 and 9. Some of the best and most
apposite to present purposes, even when in English, seem to be
published in festschrifts or Continental journals rather than in
their English-language counterparts, either in philosophy or in
medieval studies; and are often by scholars from Nordic countries.
On the other hand, assistance is increasingly available in the
ordinary philosophy journals in English, from discussions of issues
raised by Frege, Quine, and others, and with little or no overt
reference to medieval precedents. This convergence of interest
in certain metaphysical or dialectical issues, as it appears to me,
is surely welcome.[17]

late to be of assistance in the present book. So did G. van den Brink, *Almighty God: A
Study of the Doctrine of Divine Omnipotence* (Kampen [1993]), xii + 316 pp., esp. 68–92. While
referring to wide ranges of the literature, the interpretations remain essentially within
lines set by earlier 20th-cent. historians, with the arms of the Power Distinction being
treated as true, if true, of the divine nature (and not as 'systematically misleading', in the
ways argued below); and assumptions behind post-Deistical positions are rarely if ever
fundamentally challenged, even when the author seems rightly uneasy about the positions
themselves (especially where they sit ill with Reformed stances). See a review forthcoming
in *New Blackfriars*, Sept. 1993.

[17] Much the most important contribution is the Cambridge History, or *LMP* 1982: N.
Kretzmann, A. Kenny, and J. Pinborg, with E. Stump (eds.), *The Cambridge History of Later
Medieval Philosophy from the Rediscovery of Aristotle to the Disintegration of Scholasticism 1100–1600*
(Cambridge [1982]), xiv + 1035 pp. *LMP* is important not only for what it provides but—
by providing a thematically encyclopaedic treatment and frequent reminders of diachronic
progression—for bringing into focus the kinds of study still needed, and the range of
topics to be taken into consideration. The first of its advertised companion volumes, *Logic
and the Philosophy of Language*, also ed. N. Kretzmann and E. Stump (Cambridge [1988])
is disappointing in a number of respects.

Modal notions and diverse interpretations of modal logics have been much canvassed
in connection with theological matters from the problématique to which the Power
Distinction was addressed. These will be exploited elsewhere, when the understanding of
the arms of the Distinction outlined in Ch. 9 below can be spelled out still further.
Indeed without an analytical framework of the kind provided below, it has often been
difficult to see how the analyses being offered by those already exploiting the modal
developments could be reconciled with the rigorously negative theology on the divine
nature, maintained by at least some of those to whose understanding of attributions to
divine power, the modal analyses were supposedly applicable. Ivo Thomas, 'Logic and
Theology', *Dominican Studies*, 1 (1948), 291–312 should still be consulted, as may G. Jalbert,
Nécessité et contingence chez saint Thomas d'Aquin et chez ses prédécesseurs (Ottawa, 1961), 256 pp.;

BIBLIOGRAPHY AND INDEXING

The would-be exhaustive list s.v. 'Power Distinction, uses' in the topical index provides in effect a precise bibliography of the primary sources for the Distinction within the period covered. The list of variant expressions for the contrasting arms of the Distinction, s.v. 'PD, related terminology', provides a convenient check-list for scholars with particular interests in the terminology, and has the advantage of being indexed to the original contexts.

For secondary literature, notes to the several chapters provide focused supplements to the Randi 'Bibliografia essenziale' (see n. 13, above), usually recalling the main studies relevant. Bibliographical details are given at the first explicit reference, itself to be found through the nominal index. Later references use abbreviated titles long enough to be of some mnemonic use.

and P. Duponchel, *Hypothèses pour l'interprétation de l'axiomatique thomiste* (Paris, 1953), 202 pp. More recently S. Knuuttila has been active both in providing and in encouraging relevant studies. See e.g. 'The Statistical Interpretation of Modality in Averroes and Thomas Aquinas', *Ajatus*, 37 (1978), 79–98, Knuuttila's own contributions to *Reforging the Great Chain of Being: Studies of the History of Modal Theories* (Dordrecht [1981]); and the studies by him and others discussed by A. de Libera at *Rev. sc. ph. th.* 69 (1985), 281–91. See now S. Knuuttila, *Modalities in Medieval Philosophy* (London [1993]), viii + 236 pp., esp. Ch. 3, 'Varieties of necessity and possibility in the thirteenth century'. One application is discussed elsewhere, in 'The Question of Unrealised Divine Possibilities', forthcoming, but the present book is concerned rather to build bridges from the medievals' texts, interpreted in their historical contexts, to analyses within which the various modal logics can be deployed to fuller advantage. More narrowly germane to the task of initially isolating the medievals' understanding of the Distinction as a dialectical device (as against the task of spelling out that understanding further, in our own terms) is work contributing to an understanding of their several rules for drawing inferences from *cum determinatione* or *absque determinatione* assertions. (Both arms of the Distinction are to be seen as implying *cum determinatione* assertions, as will appear.) This is harder to find, as here too philosophers have been prompter to formalise chosen analyses than to argue for what needs or does not need to be caught in the analyses. G. Klima, '*Libellus pro sapiente*—a Criticism of Allan Bäck's Argument against St Thomas Aquinas's Doctrine of the Incarnation', *New Schol.* 58 (1984), 207–19, is an important exception, but see Ch. 6, n. 14 below. Bäck's own *On Reduplication: Logical Theories of Qualification* (Tübingen, 1990), has still not reached me. For related activity in Arts in Paris during the period covered see I. Rosier, *La Grammaire spéculative des modistes* (Lille [1993]), 26 pp., and A. de Libera, 'De la logique à la grammaire: Remarques sur la théorie de la détermination chez Roger Bacon et Lambert d'Auxerre (Lambert de Lagny)', in G. L. Bursill-Hall *et al.* (eds.), *De ortu grammaticae: Studies in Medieval Grammar and Linguistic Theory in Memory of Jan Pinborg* (Amsterdam, 1990), x + 372 pp., 209–26.

I

The Power Distinction:
Working Notions

In reading discussions from the earlier days of the Distinction's use, before the terminology settles, it is not easy to be sure when it is the Distinction as understood later which is in use, or even a closely related one. For heuristic purposes a working notion is here provided (Sections 1–8). Even if you find an Indies you did not expect, it helps to have been sure about what counts as landfall. The working notion, of its nature provisional, often anticipates results established only much later. It will be corrected or further specified as the historical uses are progressively taken into account.

The second part of the chapter (Sections 9–17) has a different purpose. It draws attention to systematic but easily overlooked ways in which medieval users of the Distinction typically differed from modern philosophers; not only in matters of substance (in metaphysics, most notably) but in accepted ways of expressing and conducting "scientifically" serious arguments.

I add the section for philosophical readers especially. Increasingly, I have found that when the better modern philosophers are misunderstanding medieval texts like those containing the uses of the Power Distinction, it is from insufficient awareness of "false friends", both in the texts and in many modern reports or translations: words like 'proposition', 'predicate', 'subject', which may seem familiar but were often used within a very different scheme of things from ours.

A WORKING NOTION OF THE DISTINCTION

1. *Profile*

By 'the Power Distinction' or at times just 'the Distinction' I refer, for convenience, to (*a*) a (purported) distinction between two ways in which we may consider God's power (to do things extrinsic to his nature): (1) in its (supposed) actual effect (or manifestation), the actual created order (of those who maintain that there is such a thing), and (2) in abstraction from whether any such thing is to be instantiated or not in extra-mental reality, provided such a thing is susceptible of instantiation by an unrestrictedly active power (such as was, in one way or another, attributed to God);

(*b*) typically expressed in such adverbial modifications as *de potentia ordinata sua* and *de potentia absoluta sua*, when modifying *potest* or *potest F-ere*, when the grammatical subject of the verb is being understood to stand for the divine nature;

(*c*) and in essentially the sense(s) established in the medieval schools, and dominant if not unchallenged in the period covered by this book: from around 1215, to the decade of the condemnations of 1270 and 1277.[1]

Point (*c*) anticipates some of what is established only below. So, inevitably, do other elements of the working notion. It is by anticipation that I restrict the possible reference of 'the Power Distinction' to distinctions concerning only divine power and its effects. By 'the Power Distinction' I shall not be referring to analogous distinctions concerning creaturely agency, or imagined to apply indifferently to divine and creaturely agency, sometimes

---

[1] For concise orientation and context see A. de Libera, *La philosophie médiévale* [Paris, 1989], 128 pp., esp. chs. 1 and 2; and F. Van Steenberghen, *La philosophie au XIII*[e] *siècle* (Louvain-la-Neuve, 1991), 551 pp., 109–40 (philosophical teaching and writing in Paris towards 1240) and 158–68 (Oxford). Commentaries and materials are in *LMP* 1982; A. Maierù, *Terminologia logica della tarda scolastica* (Rome [1972], 687 pp., which often records earlier testimonies too; W. and M. Kneale, *The Development of Logic* (Oxford [1962]), viii + 761 pp.; I. M. Bochenski, tr. I. Thomas, *A History of Formal Logic* (New York [1970]), xxii + 567 pp.; G. Klima, *Ars artium: Essays in Philosophical Semantics, Mediaeval and Modern* (Budapest, 1988), 185 pp.; E. Stump, *Dialectic and its Place in the Development of Medieval Logic* (Ithaca, NY, 1989), x + 274 pp. (a collection of articles which importantly lacks a subject index); A. Broadie, *Introduction to Medieval Logic* (Oxford, 1987), 150 pp.; D. Henry, *Medieval Logic and Metaphysics: A Modern Introduction* (London [1972]), xiii + 133 pp. Works from which more specific materials are taken are noted where they are used. A select bibliography in J. Marenbon, *Later Medieval Philosophy (1150–1350): An Introduction* (London, 1987), xii + 230 pp., 207–9, can be expanded from *LMP* 1982. Current bibliography can be found in *Linguistic Bibliography for the Year*, § 'History of linguistics, medieval', as well as in the usual philosophical repertoires, esp. *Rép. bibliogr. de la phil.*, which now carries the additional titles *International Philosophical Bibliography*, and *Bibliografisch Repertorium van de Wijsbegeerte* on its title-page.

expressed in similar formulas. I do call attention to these, which begin to appear in the period covered, and sometimes throw contrasting light on the Distinction itself.

2. *Option-tied, Option-neutral*

Throughout I translate *de potentia ordinata* as 'in option-tied power', and *de potentia absoluta* as 'in option-neutral power'.

The "option" in question is the actual, concrete order of created things, seen as God's option or volitum. The "tie" is that in such assertions as 'God can in option-tied power____', what goes in the blank (say, 'make there to be grunting pigs') is being understood to stand for (*supponere pro*) some or other thing subject to God's actual ordering of things; in other words, to stand for some or all of the actual order of things. It will be true only if there are grunting pigs in the actual order of things; and the truth of the assertion, when it is true, is tied to there actually being the things referred to.

In such assertions as 'God can in option-neutral power____', what goes in the blank is being understood to stand for something envisaged by us, prescinding from whether or not it is ever going to be subject to God's actual ordering, from whether or not it will ever be any or all of the actual order of things. In such assertions as 'God can in option-neutral power____', what goes in the blank (say, 'make there to be flying pigs') is to be understood as referring to the "thing" in question in its abstract, intrinsic content merely, and prescinding from its actually being ordered into existence or not. The *suppositio* of the expression in the blank will thus be *absoluta*, as some of those examined below will say, and not restricted to things of the actual order of things. The assertion will be true, when it is true, in virtue of the intrinsic consistency of the content of the thing envisaged (flying pigs, perhaps), prescinding from whether or not such a thing is ever going to be actualised. God's option-neutral power is thus power to do things extrinsic to the divine nature, attributed or attributable to God, whether or not the envisaged 'power' in question is ever exercised in the actual order of things, and indeed whether or not God ever creates at all. For a distinction to be made in this way, attributions to God's power to do things extrinsic to his nature are going to have to be treated as systematically misleading: but how this is to be done will appear presently.

For convenience I speak of assertions such as 'God can in option-tied power make there to be grunting pigs' as 'option-tied assertions', or 'the option-tied arm of the Distinction', and such assertions as 'God can in option-neutral power make there to be flying pigs' as 'option-neutral assertions', or assertions made 'in the option-neutral arm of the Distinction'.

A reason for choosing 'option-tied' and 'option-neutral' is that they have not yet gathered the unhelpful associations of the most likely competitors. 'God's ordinate power', opposed to anything else, at least suggests that somewhere there might be an inordinate power at God's disposal, or even that God may be pictured as a Jekyll-and-Hyde figure raised to the *n*th. 'Absolute power' readily suggests the despotic coercive force of some post-medieval political discussions, and invites the horror evoked by

> the absolute paternal care
> That will not leave us, but prevents us everywhere.
>
> (T. S. Eliot, 'East Coker'.)

'Ordained' has less troublesome associations, but may yet call up a suggestion that in addition to what God has ordained to be done (including things which may be surprises to us),[2] there might be some uncovenanted ontological jokers.

A word on the choice of examples, since thirteenth-century schoolmen were not given to referring to flying pigs and the like. Aquinas, following the Pseudo-Denis, notes and commends the Scriptural practice of speaking of the things of God in lowly corporeal figures. Most notably, they make it more obvious that what we are saying when we use them, is not being said properly of God. More sophisticated or more lofty figures could more

---

[2] This is usually understood as arising merely from subjective ignorance of what is in store, but more radical grounds for surprise have sometimes been envisaged and even philosophers who themselves accept that 'absolute omnipotence, which can override logical contradictions, is an incoherent notion' have emphasised that the suggestion of such "absolute omnipotence" has been taken seriously by others. 'At least one great philosopher, Descartes, argued for absolute omnipotence; and ... I have frequently encountered Evangelical Christians who thought Descartes was right'. (P. T. Geach, *Truth, Love and Immortality: An Introduction to McTaggart's Philosophy* (London [1979]), 182 pp., 164.) As will appear, there is no appeal to such "absolute omnipotence" in the *potentia absoluta dei* of the earlier medieval Power Distinction; whether or not arguments for "absolute omnipotence" are justly imputed to Descartes.

readily mask their inherent impropriety or inapplicability.[3] In view especially of the importance which a negative theology on the divine nature will turn out to have, for the medievals examined below, it seems worth extending Aquinas's commendation to at least those examples which are more or less routine.

So where examples needed are illustrative rather than probative—and there is less to fear from a too restricted sample— I shall go out of my way to prefer mundane examples to narrowly theological ones. In addition to reasons analogous to those given by Aquinas for preferring lowly to lofty figures, it may be said that narrowly theological examples may carry ad hominem force of an inappropriate kind, may avoidably multiply contentious matter, and risk cheapening the *mysteria* of the ways of God with men, when these are mentioned lightly and repeatedly where mundane examples would serve exposition or discussion just as well.

3. *The questions to which the Power Distinction was addressed*

These were of the genre: Can God alter the past? Can he save my family from the plague? And so on. Within the genre, as will appear, they more specifically concerned elements of the *opus redemptionis*: It is (taken as being) revealed doctrine that God has chosen such or such means of redemption, but might he not have chosen others; It is (taken as) implied by revealed doctrine that this or that is part of God's chosen scheme of things, but might not things have been disposed otherwise by him? Even these questions are not merely academic, and they at least seem to concern an envisaged power in God to be able to intervene decisively in such affairs, whether he chooses to or not. When they are raised, the questioners are not to be fobbed off with the

---

[3] Aquinas gives three reasons, all of which would ideally merit comment. 'Manifestum enim apparet quod haec [vilia corpora] non dicuntur de divinis: quod posset esse dubium, si sub figuris nobilium corporum describerentur divina; maxime apud illos qui nihil aliud a corporibus nobilius noverunt.—Secundo, quia hic modus convenientior est cognitioni quam de Deo habemus in hac vita. Magis enim manifestatur nobis de ipso quid non est, quam quid est: et ideo similitudines illarum rerum quae magis elongantur a Deo, veriorem nobis faciunt aestimationem quod est supra illud quod de Deo dicimus vel cogitamus.—Tertio, quia per huiusmodi, divina magis occultantur indignis.' (*ST* 1/1/9 ad 3. The whole of 1/1/9 should be read.)

suggestion—sometimes canvassed among interpreters—that they "really" must wish to know something quite different: say, Will God save my family, Will I escape damnation, rejection; Will God damn Peter, save Judas... ? Those questions no doubt concern the questioners too, but they are not the same questions. The former questions do evince an interest in what God has it in him to do, or does not have it in him to do, whether or not he decides to take a hand. They at least seem to be on a par with 'Is that newly qualified surgeon equal to the task of operating on my child's tumour?' They ought not simply to be reduced to questions of the type, Will my child's tumour be successfully operated on?, important as questions of this latter type also are.

4. *Ensuing embarrassment*

Questions of the former type put a certain kind of theologian into embarrassment. But one of the keys to avoiding a misunderstanding of the whole approach within which the Power Distinction was of importance, is in understanding the nature of this embarrassment.

It was not the embarrassment of the Deists and their contemporaries, rightly concerned about the plagues or the Lisbon earthquake, but additionally anxious to draw a veil of 'theodicy' over their Father's supposed moral nakedness. The medieval users of the Power Distinction—generally speaking—did not have that sort of embarrassment, because they did not have the kind of view of God within which alone such embarrassment makes sense. Before taking that further, it is useful to see what the nature of the medievals' embarrassment was.

It arose because they held—at least when they were being careful and deliberate—a negative theology view on the divine nature. The nub of this view, as it concerns present questions, is put well enough in the assertion from Malebranche with which Hume's Demea documents the view:

One ought not so much (says he) to call God a Spirit, in order to express positively what he is, as in order to signify that he is not Matter. (*Dialogues*, 2, ed. Price 1976: 159.)

In terms closer to Aquinas, if we disregard Hume's irony, Demea had just put things thus:

The Question is not concerning the BEING, but the NATURE of GOD. This I affirm, from the Infirmities of human Understanding, to be altogether incomprehensible and unknown to us. The Essence of that supreme Mind, his Attributes, the manner of his Existence, the very Nature of his Duration; these and every particular, which regards so divine a Being, are mysterious to Men. (Same ref.)

Hume's Demea continues here in terms which the most pious of his Reformed contemporaries could scarcely have faulted:

Finite, weak and blind Creatures, we ought to humble Ourselves in his august Presence, and, conscious of our Frailties, adore in Silence his infinite Perfections, which Eye hath not seen, Ear hath not heard, neither hath it enter'd into the Heart of Man to conceive them [1 Cor. 2: 9]. They are covered in a deep Cloud [Job 22: 14 and parallels] from human Curiosity... (Same ref.)

The irony comes in because in Hume's view, and within the assumptions of the Way of Ideas generally, what cannot be seen, touched, and so on cannot be asserted intelligibly even to exist, and cannot be asserted on a scientific level of discourse, for any inference of significance to be founded on such an assertion.[4] A view statable without irony, in the very same formulas, was indeed (as Hume with only a little exaggeration says) the view of 'all the Divines almost, from the Foundation of Christianity, who have ever treated of this or any other theological Subject', up to the dawn of modern times; what I am calling the Negative Theology view, in short.[5]

The difficulty is that because the practitioner of Negative Theology indeed can assert nothing to 'express positively what [God] is', he cannot consistently with his Negative Theology give any crumb of an answer to a question about what God has it in him to do. There are no exceptions to the 'cannot'. The point about Negative Theology is not that it permits very little, or hardly anything, to be properly said with truth of the divine nature: even those working within a deistical tradition are often prepared to concede that much. It is that it permits strictly

---

[4] See Locke, *Essay*, III. ix. 3 and 4; Hume, Introd. to *Treatise*.

[5] In case readers might be inclined to understand 'negative theology' otherwise, I either spell out 'negative theology on the divine nature', or use capitals in 'Negative Theology' to indicate that what is intended is this sort of negative theology on the divine nature.

nothing of the sort. And in such cases, as with walking with one's head in one's hand, '*C'est le premier pas qui coûte*'. The embarrassment was thus not, and could not be—by contrast with the Deists—over any imagined defect in God. It was over the intrinsic limitations of a Negative Theology approach, in the face of human difficulties of a certain general kind. This should be marked.

For the central point of using the Power Distinction, or anything of its genre, was to permit a non-evasive answer to difficulties or questions of just that prima-facie embarrassing kind, by theologians who wish to maintain a rigorously Negative Theology. But how is that to be done?

5. *The expression 'God's power'*

A first step is to isolate two diverse ways of taking expressions such as 'God's power'. A second is to distinguish one of the two ways: that will give us the core of the Power Distinction.

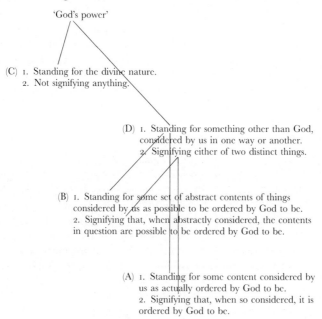

'God's power'

(C) 1. Standing for the divine nature.
2. Not signifying anything.

(D) 1. Standing for something other than God, considered by us in one way or another.
2. Signifying either of two distinct things.

(B) 1. Standing for some set of abstract contents of things considered by us as possible to be ordered by God to be.
2. Signifying that, when abstractly considered, the contents in question are possible to be ordered by God to be.

(A) 1. Standing for some content considered by us as actually ordered by God to be.
2. Signifying that, when so considered, it is ordered by God to be.

For convenience this will be referred to as the Waterfall Schema: from its shape, not from any suggestion of emanation from a source.

At (D) is represented what for convenience is often called 'God's power to do things extrinsic to his own nature, or power to do things ad extra'. Albert the Great calls it 'God's operant power (*potentia operans*)', but it is more helpful to think of (D) as a placeholder for (A) or (B) disjunctively. 'God's power', taken as at (A) and (B), is being understood as God's option-tied power (*potentia ordinata dei*) and his option-neutral power (*potentia absoluta dei*) respectively, the concern of this book. 'God's power' as taken at (C), is being taken to stand for that power which God may be held to be, and to be identified with the divine nature; of content unknowable to us, and not susceptible of being grasped for what it is in any understanding of ours.

6. *Systematically misleading expressions*

The key to the diagram is that no matter how 'God's power' is taken, whether in the manner indicated at (C), or in those indicated at (A), (B), and (D), it is to be reckoned a 'systematically misleading expression':

There are many expressions which occur in non-philosophical discourse which, though they are perfectly clearly understood by those who use them and those who hear or read them, are nevertheless couched in grammatical or syntactical forms which are in a demonstrable way *improper* to the states of affairs which they record (or the alleged states of affairs which they profess to record). Such expressions can be reformulated and for philosophy but *not* for non-philosophical discourse must be reformulated into expressions of which the syntactical form is proper to the facts recorded (or the alleged facts alleged to be recorded). (G. Ryle, 'Systematically Misleading Expressions', in A. Flew (ed.), *Logic and Language* (1st ser.; Oxford, 1963), 11–36, at 13–14, emphasis in Ryle.)

What makes the expressions related to (A), (B), and (D) to be systematically misleading, is that 'God's option-tied power', 'God's option-neutral power', and for that matter 'God's power to do things extrinsic to his own nature' all might seem to be suggesting a power somehow located in God, in the way my capacity to ride a bicycle may be thought to be located in me; whereas in each case it is something other than God which the expression, when analysed, must be understood to stand for. Out of context, the expression 'God's power' can suggest something analogous to 'Caesar's forces' in 'Caesar's forces began to fail him, as blood flowed from his wounds', or something analogous to 'McCaig's folly' in 'McCaig's folly was matched only by his impetuosity'. When taken in the ways indicated at (A), (B), or (D), 'God's power' has to be thought of rather on the analogy of 'Caesar's forces' in 'Caesar's forces crossed the river, while he remained on the near bank', or of 'McCaig's Folly' as the name of a large edifice constructed in obedience to McCaig's will.

What makes 'God's power', taken in the way indicated at (C), to be systematically misleading, is that it sounds like an informative designation of something; contrastable perhaps with 'God's wisdom', 'God's goodness', and so on. 'Stalin's power' suggests something analogous, and many might acknowledge that it had obvious application, in a way in which 'Stalin's goodness' did not. Yet within the assumptions of Negative Theology, expressed in the terms of the philosophical logic of users of the Power Distinction examined below, 'God's power' as taken at (C), if used successfully, stands for the divine nature, but signifies literally nothing of what it stands for. The same holds for 'God's wisdom', '. . . goodness', '. . . immutability', and indefinitely many more expressions capable of being taken in like manner. It may seem odd to say that 'Stalin's goodness' tells us something about Stalin whereas 'God's goodness' tell us literally nothing about God. But of course we are like Stalin in many respects, and are situated in more or less similar circumstances. If there is a God, we are not especially like God in any such respects, even the more admirable ones, and God—unlike Stalin and ourselves—is not situated in any respect. More on this will appear below: it is a view which most if not all the medievals examined will be found to hold.

7. *Mentions of the word 'God' in (expressions of) the Distinction*

In an analysis of either arm of the Distinction the word 'God' may appear prominently, though obliquely. Yet in a fuller analysis of either, it should be removed: precisely because the Distinction in itself is a matter not of religion, or philosophy of religion, but of metaphysics. In common usage, it is true, 'God' conveys and in typical uses is intended to convey the sense of being that which is worshipped, or prayed to, or cursed by, or the like. That is not the weight which it has to convey in an analysis of the Distinction. What is being referred to there, is the God of the metaphysicians: something both existent in extra-mental reality, yet not finite in any respect. Medieval users of the Distinction considered the God of their faith to be in reality nothing other than that, and for that reason had no hesitation in mentioning 'God' prominently in expressions of the Distinction.

Yet it is quite possible for someone to believe that there is something which exists in extra-mental reality, and not in any finite manner, without being in the least inclined to offer incense to it, or pray to it, or curse by it. As a fall-back position—in case he was mistaken about 'causes', 'order', and 'intelligence'— Hume was prepared to allow a stronger "theology" than this, and to continue: 'If this really be the Case, What can the most inquisitive, contemplative, and religious Man do more than give a plain, philosophical Assent to the Proposition, as often as it occurs; and believe, that the Arguments, on which it is establish'd, exceed the Objections, which lie against it?' (*Dialogues*, 12, ed. Price 1976: 260.)

When mentions of 'God' occur in accounts of the Distinction below, therefore, what is to be understood as being referred to is (at any rate) the God of the metaphysicians. Those who, like the medieval users (and I follow them in this), think that the God of Abraham, Isaac, and Jacob is nothing other than what the God of the metaphysicians is, may in addition take them as referring to the God of their faith. Anyone prescinding from information from such a faith, forming an opinion in the lights available to human inquirers as such—one *stans praecise in lumine naturali*, as would be said in later medieval times—and being unwilling to go further, may take them as nothing more than a shorthand for referring to the God of the metaphysicians: that which exists, but not in any determinate manner. This separates the metaphysical issues from the philosophy-of-religion ones, and in line with medieval views takes the metaphysical issues to be fundamental. In much modern discussion 'God' is taken from the outset to signify some object to which worship is due, if there is a God, or to which worship would be due, if there were a God (of whatever kind might be specified). By contrast, it can be coherent, when taking 'God' in the way in which it occurs in accounts of the earlier medieval Power Distinction, to say 'Some God exists (i.e. something exists, yet not in any determinate manner), but whether it is obligatory/permissible/possible... for anyone to worship it, is a further question; and not one which everyone who believes that God exists, need be troubled with.' This can seem a puzzling position for many modern 'theists', 'atheists', and 'agnostics' alike, who are not used to separating the metaphysical and the philosophy-of-religion issues in this way: a way not uncommon in ancient and medieval times. But it is a coherent position; and would presumably reflect the case where there was no creation, and hence no-one capable of believing anything. If God is not determinate in any way, he is no more capable of believing (as against knowing) things than of arguing stepwise or telling the time.

8. *Mentions of phrases like 'existing in extra-mental reality' in analyses of (expressions of) the Distinction*

Such phrases are to be taken as harmlessly pleonastic reminders, strictly equivalent to 'existing' sans phrase. To say that something exists in extra-mental reality need be to say no more than that it exists, sans phrase. No other kind of existence need be supposed. What may be said to 'exist intentionally' or 'exist as an object of thought' or 'exist in the mind' is not being said to exist sans phrase. In accounts of the Distinction, and more generally in accounts using the two-type analysis already noted, extra-mental reality (*esse in re extra animam*) is being opposed to fictions of the (created) mind (*esse intentionale*).

To say that something exists, is (1) not necessarily to say that it exists in the same order of things in which we do. (If the God of a Negative Theology exists, it does not exist in that or in any other order.) Yet the users of the Distinction did not have to suppose that there was or ever would be any other order of things. Those examined below did not dispute the doctrine that 'God has sworn and will not repent': that the scheme of things actually ordered by God is to be carried through punctiliously and without deviation, and is not in fact to be supplanted by any other scheme of things. What happens in the actual world, in other words, is not merely punctiliously executed, as any ordering of God's has to be. It is to be unique and ineluctably enduring, simply because God has ordered it to be so. We do not have to suppose that its being unique and ineluctably enduring is something built into the specifications of the order executed. So if we choose to consider that order only in its intrinsic specifications, and prescinding from its execution, or even from whether it is ever to be executed, then the fact (if it is a fact, as the medievals examined did not dispute) that our actual order is to be unique and ineluctably executed, can be left undisputed. It can simply be being left out of the current reckoning, when that current reckoning is not one which is to be taken to conclude to something in the actual order of things.

To say that something exists, is (2) not necessarily to say that it is willed by God. Again, the medievals examined did not dispute that nothing existed which was not willed by God. But to say that this rose is red is to say something about how things are in extra-mental reality. To say that it is willed by God is not to say anything comparable about the rose (in addition to implying that there is one there): being willed by God is not a descriptive feature of this (or any comparable) order of things, and to say of the rose that it is willed by God is in the view to be seen behind uses of the Distinction examined below, to make an assertion of a different type (as will appear).

All of that will be put more precisely, when there is call to do so. It is mentioned here in case anyone is disposed to imagine that accepting a doctrine to the effect that 'God has sworn and will not repent' has to make use of the Distinction nugatory from the outset. It does not, and medieval users of the Distinction, as will appear, regularly accommodated the doctrine with success.

FURTHER NOTIONS, AND "FALSE FRIENDS"

Helpful school dictionaries used to mark "false friends" like *cave*, or *grange*, to obviate the more avoidable kinds of mis-understanding. In the present matter some of the most pervasive and persistent obstacles to understanding the Distinction presented in the medieval texts are 'false friends' of a closely analogous kind. With even a modest knowledge of the history of French and of English, the connections between 'cave' and *cave*, 'grange' and *grange*, become apparent, and the expressions become less likely to play us false. The corresponding knowledge of the historical vagaries of the difficult words for modern readers of texts from the period of this book, is harder to come by than might be thought. This is not because the words are too strange, but because they are not strange at all. (The formulas, rather, are not strange at all.) The hard words are 'proposition', 'predicate', 'predicable', and the like. Since the days of Frege and Russell, these have come to be used with a fair uniformity (by careful writers). When writing departs from this established usage, the most natural assumption to take is that the writer is being careless, or is just muddled. When writing from earlier periods is ambivalent, and might be taken according to the established usage or not, the most natural thing is to take it as an attempt to write by our usage, and in "charity" to remember that the writer lived a long time before us. Thus Aristotle is regularly taken to be using 'predicate', 'predicable', and so on in the way we find natural, and we may even suppose that our way is in its essentials no different from his. Whatever may be the case for Aristotle, this "charitable" assimilation to ourselves could not always be relied upon to produce trustworthy interpretations of the writers examined below.

9. *Recognising terms of debate*

The difficulty is analogous to one isolated at A. MacIntyre, *Whose Justice? Which Rationality?* (London, 1988), 166–70:

When two rival large-scale intellectual traditions confront one another, a central feature of the problem of deciding between their claims is characteristically that there is no neutral way of characterizing either the subject matter about which they give rival accounts or the standards by which the claims are to be evaluated. . . . The attempt to discover a neutral, independent set of standards or modes of characterizing data which is both such as must be acceptable to all rational persons and is sufficient to determine the truth on the matters about which the two traditions are at variance has generally, and perhaps universally, proved to be a search for a chimaera (p. 166).

How, he continues, can genuine controversy proceed? It does so characteristically in two stages. In the first,

each characterizes the contentions of its rival in its own terms. [*I think he means the characteriser's own terms here*], making explicit the grounds for rejecting what is incompatible with its own central theses [*again, the characteriser's central theses, I think*], although sometimes allowing that from its own point of view [*the rival's own point of view, I think*] and in the light of its own standards of judgment, its rival has something to teach it in marginal and subordinate questions (p. 166).

If the 'own terms' are the rival's, the points I shall make about MacIntyre's stages have all the more force. In any case a second stage is reached,

if and when the protagonists of each tradition... ask whether the alternative and rival tradition may not be able to provide resources to characterize and to explain the failings and defects of their own tradition more adequately than they, using the sources of that tradition, have been able to do (pp. 166–7).

The difficulty in passing from the first to the second of the stages envisaged, is

for the protagonists of each tradition to be able to understand the theses, arguments and concepts of their rival in such a way that they are able to view themselves from such an alien standpoint and to recharacterize their own beliefs in an appropriate manner from the alien perspective of a rival tradition (p. 167).

One of the Scotsmen oddly omitted from MacIntyre's stimulating (and questionable) account of that country's eighteenth-century culture (MacIntyre's chs. 12 ff.) was reckoned sceptical, if I understand the little verse attributed to him, as to whether it can be given to 'see wurselles as ithers see us' (R. Burns, 'To a louse').

MacIntyre is concerned with rival intellectual traditions maintained by articulate contemporaries, and with conflicts in matters of substance, where even apparent conflicts are likely not just to appear but to leap to the eye. The difficulty in the present matter arises where the characteriser is a modern, heir to the tradition informed by Frege and Russell, and the rivals are long-dead medievals, some of them still only partially exhumed from the manuscripts. Moreover the "conflicts" with which I am concerned in the paragraphs are not on obvious matters of substance, but are on the understanding of "false friends" like (the Latin counterparts of) 'proposition', 'predicate', 'predicable', 'subject', 'attribute', and so on: on which, I would jalouse, the average modern, philosophically trained reader will either not notice a conflict, or will notice conflicts all along, and put them down to muddle on the part of the medievals. Medieval writers were sometimes muddled, just as writers in other times have been. But some of the more interesting difficulties in reading their texts arise from their expressing things clearly, in their terms, and our reading our "coding", not theirs, into their terms. My aim in the paragraphs which follow is not to controvert the medieval interpretations (or the modern ones), though that is often called for, and may be done elsewhere. It is only in some matters to get to the point where serious controversy can even begin, on the issues which divide the medievals and ourselves in post-Fregean times. But it is to indicate where there is room for controversy on a "false friend", on which no room for controversy may have been suspected.

10. *Beginning from speech*

When they wished to argue seriously, the medievals examined below were not disposed to start from a supposedly innocent inside and work outwards: to start from a formal language, assign meanings to its symbols or formulas, specifying a deductive apparatus and then hoping that what they were proving in their system might approximate closely enough to what they would initially have liked to have been able to prove. Their typical approach was to start from the theoretically tainted speech of their common conversations, regiment it, enrich it with words like *ly* or τοῦ for special purposes such as marking mentions off from uses, analyse it to varying extents, and hope that their progressive regimentations had been faithful enough to the starting-point to give them the assurance that if the starting-point was not bogus from the outset, then what they were proving was at least addressed to essentially the same problem they had set out to solve. The inside-to-outside approach has demonstrated its merits: yet the continuing debates over such exemplary arguments as that of Tarski on truth (or should we say 'fruth'?) show that it may not all be gain.[6]

---

[6] Tarski's concern was with 'the classical [conception of truth] (of which the semantic conception is but a modernized form).' (A. Tarski, 'The Semantic Conception of Truth', repr. L. Linsky (ed.), *Semantics and the Philosophy of Language* (Chicago [1972]), 13–47, 28.)

The advantage of the approach starting from speech is that the vehicle of discussion is visibly (or audibly) continuous with the interpersonal discourse—albeit unreflected—of our dinner conversations and our backgammon. An intersubjective dimension—albeit imperfect—is built in from the start, not tentatively added as a questionable extra.

The disadvantage of the approach starting from speech is that it is made within a language problematical from the outset. If, as in the less unfavourable case, the language is 'semantically closed', then it is a language in which truth cannot be defined without running into paradox. This is the less unfavourable case possible: Tarski sometimes hints that 'because natural languages are not formally specifiable, the question of their semantic closure cannot be answered' (S. Haack, *Philosophy of Logics* (Cambridge [1978]), xvi‑276 pp., 120). At best, therefore, there is 'a whole family of difficulties here', not least that 'natural languages are not static, but growing; and the prevalence in natural languages of such phenomena as vagueness, ambiguity, indexicality' (Haack, p. 121). Yet the disadvantages, in what concerns the present matter, ought not to be exaggerated.

For one thing, it is doubtful whether the medievals examined in this book would have attempted to 'define truth' unrestrictedly, in the manner thought at least desirable by Tarski, whether attainable or not. The very paradigm of truth in their views, 'the True' par excellence, was recognised not to be definable anyway.

Their clear division of labour between signification and *suppositio*, the insistence of many of them on a two-level treatment of propositions usable for scientifical purposes, and in particular the limits imposed by *confusio* (see under Albert the Great, Ch. 4 below), limited the possibilities of practical damage from vagueness of reference. In the case of God, vagueness or indeterminacy of reference was not even a possibility within their views. If some

His point is that he has explained what he had set out to explain, which he considered to have been of importance in philosophical discussions, regardless of what others might wish in the future to capture in the word 'true'. Many of us in philosophy are convinced, but others—by moving either to a less ambitious view of natural language, or by seeking to define a weaker notion of truth—in effect recognise a gap between what they concede that he has explained or maintained, and what they none the less think needs to be explained, or maintained.

God exists, they held, it exists unrestrictedly. There cannot be more than one of it to be referred to.

As for ambiguity, much of their dialectical industry was devoted to limiting possible damage from that quarter. Indexicality remained and remains a difficulty in need of particular attention in arguments carried on in regimented speech: but it is to the medievals' credit that the Power Distinction itself can be seen as a way of avoiding important ranges of difficulty on that head.

The unreflected nature of the interpersonal starting-point of the medievals may thus be less of a handicap than it might seem. And of course it was an attractive kind of starting-point for a medieval theologian: did not the most intellectual of the Gospels begin ἐν ἀρχῇ ἦν ὁ λόγος?.

In any case, the medievals examined below typically started from speech: from putatively significant utterances. The atomic utterance was the *dictio*, such as 'red', or 'runs', or 'immutable'. The molecular utterance, made out of *dictiones* (together with conjunctions and prepositions) was the *oratio*, like 'The cat is on the mat' or 'Oh! Gin I war whaur Gadie rins.' Some (like Abelard) used *dictio* only for the atomic utterances. Others (notably Aquinas) used *dictio* indifferently for atomic or molecular utterances; and so shall I below.

Utterances were taken—even out of context—as being putatively significant, "meaning something". 'Rose' could thus have the same signification in different contexts, or in isolation. Once provided with a context, 'rose' might be taken to stand for something or other. In 'This rose is red', for example, it stands for this rose. Each *dictio* could thus have or lack either of the two "properties": a signification (*significatio*) and "supposition" in the sense of 'sub-positioning' (*suppositio*) or 'standing for' some or other kind of thing.[7]

For certain ranges of use, and most notably for making assertions of "scientifical" import and drawing inferences from them, the relaxed standards taken from applicability to dining

[7] 'The Schoolmen distinguished between what a term "meant", i.e. its *significatio*, and its *suppositio* or what it "stood for" (*pro quo supponit*). What it means is fixed by usage, but once this meaning has been assigned, what it stands for depends on context.' (A. N. Prior, *Formal Logic* (Oxford, 1962), xi + 341 pp., 160, citing Peter of Spain's *Summulae*, 6.01–6.03.)

conversations and backgammon, were restricted. Typically, the restrictions did not concern the intelligibility of the utterances concerned: where there was intelligibility, that remained a property of the utterances. The restrictions concerned whether certain ranges of utterance (intelligible or not) were to be taken as apt for asserting something with truth, or for drawing consequences from.

This point is of importance for an appreciation of these medievals' strategy in philosophical theology. When 'God is wise' or 'God is powerful' is asserted (1) properly (non-figuratively) and sans phrase as something true (2) about the divine nature, it can be true only on condition of the predication in question's being strictly unintelligible to us. We can only know at most that it is true, if it is, when we thus say 'God is wise'. We cannot know which truth it is. Likewise for 'God is powerful', asserted similarly. They are different propositions, in the way the medievals examined below typically understood these (see Section 11 presently), because they are different utterances; but if true at all, they are not and cannot be different truths. How is this so, if we cannot know which truth either expresses? Very simply, because there can be at most one truth about the divine nature; at most one genuinely 'eternal truth', as Aquinas put it. Whether we say 'God is wise', in this way, and it is true; or assert the whole of the Athanasian Creed in the same way, and that should be true, it cannot be any other truth which is in question. It cannot, unless that other truth is about something other than God.

So the intelligibility of the utterances used for asserting things was not—as it was to be within the assumptions of the Lockean Way of Ideas—of particular importance for marking off discourse eligible to be used in scientifical arguments.

For medievals examined below, and especially for Albert and Aquinas, what was of importance was that utterances used in scientifical argument should be able to be true, and to sustain consequence. A way of meeting those requirements was available in what amounted to a requirement of analysability. Assertions acceptable for scientifical use had to be analysable disjunctively into propositions of two diverse types: distinguished by the type of truthmaker in virtue of which they were to be held true, when true. To understand this two-type analysis we must briefly consider 'proposition' itself.

11. *Propositions*

'Proposition' is one of the "false friends" mentioned above. The identity-conditions for propositions, inferred from the usage of a number of the medievals examined below, are not the same as any of the ones more in favour today. (To avoid awkward transitions, or a choice between systematic distortion and recurrent periphrases, I am following the same usage in the present book, save where a contrary usage is expressly indicated.)

A proposition, in the sense used below, is not to be taken for something like the designation of a type-sentence, and a fortiori not for the kind of *Satz an sich* associated with the name of Bolzano. Equally, a proposition is not simply to be identified with a type-sentence.

A proposition in the sense used below is to be understood as

(1) the token of an utterance (type-utterance)
(2) used to express, and normally to assert, some propositional content.

By condition (1) it has both the publicity of a formula and—putatively at any rate—intentional content (a signification). It is by having both of these, that its identity-conditions differ from those more commonly canvassed for propositions nowadays.

In the usage followed here 'There is a cat on the mat' and 'On the mat is a cat' are two propositions expressing the same truth; 'You have a bloody cheek', uttered by the barber and by the (descriptivist) Vulgar respectively are two propositions, if they are expressing different truths. Carnap, uneasy over some of Russell's usages (which possibly hark back to the medieval use outlined here), spoke of 'sentences in semantics, not in syntax', of a use which 'seems to go back to Aristotle' (R. Carnap, *Introduction to Semantics* (Cambridge, Mass., 1948; repr. 1959), 235–6, 236). In the medieval case it might be better to keep in mind that it is always utterances at bottom which are in question: corresponding perhaps to 'sentences in semantics', but only when the latter are uttered under certain pragmatic considerations.

12. *A two-type analysis*

Arthur Prior thought it worth opening his chapter on the logic of modality with the point:

A division of propositions which is given some prominence in the logic of Aristotle and the Schoolmen is that into (*a*) propositions simply asserting that something is or is not so, and (*b*) ones asserting that something must be, may be, need not be or cannot be so. The former are called in the Latin logics propositions *de inesse*, i.e. propositions simply concerning the predicates 'being in' or attaching to the subject; the latter, 'modal' propositions, or propositions *cum modo*, asserting the mode or manner of this in-being. (A. N. Prior, *Formal Logic* (Oxford, 1962), 185.)

Dr Bäck has spoken of 'an Aristotelian view of predication at odds with many current interpretations of Aristotle and views of predication', adding: 'Yet the advantage of this view is that it vindicates, or at least renders intelligible, certain doctrines and texts in Aristotle that appear baffling or careless from a modern standpoint.'[8] It seems to me that Prior and Bäck are correct there, and it is unfortunate that Prior did not indicate where the view has 'some prominence' in Aristotle; for Bäck—who does provide some important evidence for this—does not exaggerate when he speaks of the view being 'at odds with many current interpretations of Aristotle and views of predication'. Needless to say the view cannot be argued for here, but a brief, provisional statement of it is worth giving: if the medieval texts examined below are not likewise to appear, in certain places, 'baffling or careless from a modern standpoint', at least the following should be appreciated.

We should be prepared to find, in medieval texts, words such as 'proposition' and 'predication' sometimes to have a broad, sometimes a narrower sense. In the broad sense 'propositions' may refer to the unanalysed propositions of everyday speech, contrasting with the prayers, wishes, commands, etc. of everyday speech, and may or may not be susceptible of further analysis, and in need of it, if they are to be usable in arguments of scientifical importance.

---

[8] A. Bäck, 'Avicenna on Existence', *Journal of the History of Philosophy*, 25 (1987), 351–67, 351. Feys too had thought it worth noting that logicians of earlier times 'used modalities to express essential concepts, to distinguish between necessary laws and contingent reality or factual data, to evoke a realm of possibility contrasted with that of factual reality, and so on' (R. Feys, *Modal Logics*, ed. J. Dopp (Louvain, 1965), 5. For an account, however, which does not seek to accommodate a two-type analysis cf. N. Kretzmann, 'Medieval Logicians on the Meaning of *propositio*', *J. Phil.* 67 (1970), 767–87.

We might, for example, admit 'The average Scotsman drinks 2.3 measures of whisky each week' as a proposition in the broad, everyday sense, contrasting with, say, 'Would that the average Scotsman drank 2.3 measures', uttered by the whisky producer, or by the temperance campaigner, whichever might be more appropriate. The everyday proposition, however, even if true, will have to be at least susceptible of analysis in some less misleading way, if it is to be used "scientifically". Whisky is sold in unitary measures, and not many Scotsmen will leave two-thirds of a measure undrunk each week.

It is among the analysed propositions that we ought to look for Prior's division of propositions into two types: differentiated by the types of truthmaker in virtue of which they are true, when they are true.[9] Among medievals the propositions of the two types are named variously. The way Prior mentioned was one. Another was Avicenna's, whose 'absolute' propositions correspond to Prior's *de inesse* ones, and whose 'necessary' propositions correspond to Prior's *cum modo* ones. Avicenna emphasises that when he says 'necessary' here, he is thinking of the nature of the 'matter' in virtue of which they are true, if true; and that he does not mean 'necessary' as opposed to 'possible', 'impossible', 'contingent'.[10]

[9] The truthmakers for narrowly predicative and composing-apt propositions are respectively "things that are" and "things that are not, but may possibly be or not be". Cf. *De int.* 9, 19^{a}39–19^{b}4, tr. Ackrill (1963): 'what holds for things that are does not hold for things that are not but may possibly be or not be'. Aquinas remarks on this: 'Et dicit *manifestum* esse ex predictis quod *non est necesse* in omni genere affirmationum et negationum *oppositarum* alteram determinate esse *veram* et alteram *falsam*, quia non eodem modo se habet veritas et falsitas *in hiis quae sunt* iam de presenti et *in hiis quae non sunt*, sed possunt *esse* vel *non esse*; sed hoc modo se habet in utrisque sicut *dictum est*, quia scilicet in hiis quae sunt necesse est determinate alteram esse verum et alteram esse falsum, quod non contingit in futuris, quae possunt esse et non esse.' (Italics indicate expressions from the translation of Aristotle's text.)

[10] See A.-M. Goichon, *Lexique de la langue philosophique d'Ibn Sīnā (Avicenne)* (Paris, 1938), XIV + 496 pp., No. 586 esp. § 22, 35. A whole section of Avicenna's late and important *Isharat* is devoted to 'the modes of propositions and the difference between the absolute and the necessary proposition' (tr. Goichon, *Ibn Sīnā (Avicenne): Livre des directives et remarques (Kitāb al-'Išārāt wa l-Tanbīhāt)* (Beirut, 1951), 552 pp., 134–42, and see 134–52 generally). In the *Isharat* 'Toute proposition [*omit Goichon's gloss here*]: ou bien elle est absolue, d'une portée générale, et un jugement y est exprimé sans mention de sa nécessité, ni de sa durée, ni de toute autre situation en un temps ou selon la possibilité' (tr. Goichon 1951: 134). Citing a work of abbreviation made by Avicenna himself—*Najat*, 34: 'La (proposition) absolue ... est celle dans laquelle on ne saisit pas un mode de nécessité de jugement ni de possibilité de jugement, mais celui-ci est porté d'une manière générale, absolue'— Mlle Goichon comments '*Qaḍīya muṭlaqa*, proposition absolue (simplement attributive)

Avicenna's terminology has much to commend it, but to obviate at least some confusions involving other uses of 'necessary' and especially 'absolute' which are unavoidable in discussions of the Power Distinction, I propose to call the two types respectively 'composing-apt' and 'narrowly predicative'. The names have some mnemonic aptness. Both types involve combining (*compositio*) or dividing (*divisio*) of some kind or another, if they are to be used for saying something true; and in both types of proposition predicates (finite verbs) are used to significant purpose, at least in their unanalysed forms. But because the truthmaker for true propositions of the "necessary" type is an apt *compositio* or *divisio*, it can be thought appropriate that only those propositions should be called 'composing-apt' in what follows. And because the 'absolute' propositions alone retain a predicative expression even in their analysed form, it can be thought appropriate that only these should be called 'narrowly predicative'. But this rationale is given only to give the names some mnemonic force. The real reason for choosing them is to avoid at least some kinds of confusion.

Under whatever name, a two-type analysis, connected with what is to be allowed as assertible to scientific purpose, does appear to have endured. To appreciate just how far a systematic inquiry into its 'prominence in the logic of Aristotle and the Schoolmen' (Prior) might have to range, it is worth considering what appears as at least a sympathetic resonance, in an important place in the work of a philosopher with no great declared debts to either Aristotle or the medieval schools:

Reason is the discovery of truth or falshood. Truth or falshood consists in an agreement or disagreement either to the *real* relations of ideas, or *real* existence and matter of fact. Whatever, therefore, is not susceptible of this agreement or disagreement, is incapable of being true or false, and can never be an object of our reason. (Hume, *Treatise*, III. i. 1, TN 458.)

The analogies between the empiricist's 'relations of ideas' and the relations involved in apt composition or division, between his 'matters of fact and existence' and the truthmakers of narrowly predicative propositions, and between an 'object of our reason'

désigne une proposition non modale et sans indication de temps', *Lexique d'Ibn Sīnā (Avicenne)*, 313, s.v. 'QAḌĪYA', No. 22.

in his coding, and the truthmakers of propositions usable in scientifical arguments, in the two-type analysis, are at least worth noting in passing.

13. *Narrowly predicative propositions*

The first of the two diverse kinds of proposition into which our scientifically important assertions may require to be analysed are such as 'This rose is red'. They can be expressed in familiar *Fa* form, but that should not conceal (1) a difference in the way they were perhaps more likely to be analysed by medievals, and (2) a restriction which could be imposed by the underlying (metaphysical) theories.

The analytical point is that 'Some rose is red', for example, or its equivalent, when found in a medieval writer, may have to be analysed not as 'For some *x*, *x* is a rose and *x* is red', but rather as 'For some *x* of the rose kind, *x* is red'. (The differences appear in a square of opposition). For it has been argued that 'sentences such as "Every man is mortal", "Some man is mortal", "Most men are mortal" are not about all the things in the universe, but only about men, referred to by the common subject of these sentences'. It seems plausible, adds the writer quoted,

to represent these sentences by the introduction of a variable which takes its values not from the whole universe, but only from the set of men, the extension of the open sentence 'x is (a) man'. Let us say, therefore, that if 'x' is a variable, then 'x.x is a man' is a variable too, namely a *restricted variable* representing the subject term of the above sentences. (G. Klima, *Ars artium* (1988), 47–8, emphasis from Klima.)

Mutatis mutandis, an analogous approach can be taken for propositions. I am not concerned here to argue for the preference for a restricted-variables approach: but would wish it to be kept in mind when medievals' arguments are to be appreciated. Some arguments for the analysis are provided in Klima, and others could be found. Also, the approach allows for a view which some even in modern times have found 'simple and natural':

Aristotle's *De Interpretatione* recognised as belonging to the category of names not only proper names like 'Socrates' but also certain common names like 'man'. This simple and natural view was rejected by Frege and Russell, for reasons which I do not find convincing; and most

modern logicians have followed Frege and Russell in this matter...
(P. T. Geach, 'History of the Corruptions of Logic', in *Logic Matters*
(Oxford, 1972, xii + 335 pp. 61.)

The restrictions imposed by the underlying metaphysical theory
are more obvious; and prove to be more obviously important to
an understanding of the Power Distinction. Not every expression
permitted by the notation—not every declarative *oratio*—
expresses a narrowly predicative proposition which even can be
true, if true, in accordance with the underlying theory (about the
truthmakers). Cf. HO_2 and H_2O. Both can be expressed in the
notation, only the latter is permitted by the underlying theory
(about valencies).

The predicate-expression must be such as to signify a form
abstractly considered: being red, or being a rose. What is not an
integral form, cannot be signified in the predicate-expression of
a narrowly predicative proposition. 'Not being the Nine-o-clock
News' is not eligible. Neither is 'not knowing that he does not
exist in every possible world', which has been canvassed by some
philosophers as part of God's "nature". The medievals examined
below would not necessarily have been averse to allowing that it
is true of my bindweed, say, that it does not know that it exists
in every possible world. It is just that they would not have been
inclined to treat not-knowing-that-one-exists etc. as a positive
"perfection".

The subject-expression in a narrowly predicative proposition
is to stand for an individual of some kind to be found in extra-
mental reality.[11] If Platonic ideas are to be found there, then the
subject-expression of a narrowly predicative expression may stand
for one. But at least some of those examined below—most
notably Albert and Aquinas—repudiated this kind of Platonism,
and permitted no way of "talking about" forms abstractly considered, within a narrowly predicative proposition. In Albert
only structured *opera*, in Aquinas only individualised forms are

---

[11] So, apparently, does the *res propositionis*, 'this rose's being red'. In Aquinas's *De
propositionibus modalibus* (Leon. edn. 43: 419–22) the *res propositionis* is a linguistic item,
standing for the *res realis* (this red rose, an item in the world); and grammatical
transformation rules are given for getting between *res propositionis* and *dictum propositionis*
(that this rose is red). The *De propositionibus modalibus* covers not only modals strictly
speaking (*de dicto*) but also *de re* "modals", which are to be treated as propositions *de inesse*
are; and hence covers unanalysed 'modal propositions' as well as modals strictly speaking.

individuals of a kind to be found in extra-mental reality.

On the other hand, the narrowly predicative proposition of the medievals could permit 'is to the north of Avignon' as a one-place predicate, because 'being to the north of' somewhere identifiable is to be in one of the Aristotelian categories (of *situs*); and because 'Paris is to the north of Avignon' is true, if true, because 'is to the north of Avignon' expresses something in extra-mental reality, to wit, something of the situation of Paris. This is mentioned only as a way in which medievals might be inclined to think of certain propositions as narrowly predicative, which we might wish to treat differently. If there is a difference here, it is not one which appears to play a part in an understanding of the Power Distinction.

14. *Composing-apt propositions*

The second kind of proposition into which our assertions may have to be analysed, to be used to "scientifical" purpose, is the kind which, if true, is true in virtue of what "is the case" in the second of the two diverse ways for something's being the case: the way of 'any old object of reference concerning which an affirmative proposition can be formed, even if that object should be adding nothing to extra-mental reality' (*omne illud de quo affirmativa propositio formari potest, etiam si illud in re nihil ponat*; Aquinas, *De ente et essentia*, ad init.). The truthmaker here is some apt *compositio* or *divisio* in someone's actual judging thought.

Whereas, where narrowly predicative propositions are concerned, 'the true judgement affirms where the subject and predicate *really are combined*, and denies where they *are separated*, while the false judgement has the opposite of this allocation', it would seem that in composing-apt propositions 'it is another question, how it happens that *we think things together* or *apart*; by 'together' and 'apart' I mean thinking them so that there is no succession in the thoughts but they become a unity' (*Metaph.* E4, 1027b18 ff., emphasis added by me).[12]

---

[12] Cit. J. Owens, *The Doctrine of Being in the Aristotelian 'Metaphysics': A Study in the Greek Background of Mediaeval Thought* (Toronto, 1978), xxxv + 539 pp., 411. Cf. the comment at *Metaph.* Δ 7, 1017ᵃ31–35: ' "Socrates is musical" means that this is true; but "the diagonal of the square is not commensurate with the side" means that it is false to say it is' (Oxf. tr., ed. Barnes 1984, emphasis from me).

To assert 'Red is a colour', say, I com-pose my concept of being red and my concept of being coloured by means of some necessary relationship (class-inclusion, perhaps) envisaged to hold between their contents. If being red, as I understand it, is included (as I understand inclusion, if that is the relation) in being coloured, as I understand that, then my com-position is apt, and I have asserted 'Red is a colour' with truth: without being obliged to imagine "red's being coloured" to be in itself part of the furniture of extra-mental reality.

To assert 'Nothing circular is square' I 'divide' my concepts of squareness and circularity, largely as I 'composed' the others. If being circular indeed excludes being square, if exclusion is the necessary relationship needed here, my 'division' is apt, and I have asserted with truth that nothing circular is square.

That there should at least be a true *divisio* is necessary for there to be true affirmations at all, and hence true propositions (whether positive or negative in quality) of the composing-apt kind. A *divisio* of (my concepts of) squareness and circularity is possible, because squareness and circularity are severally intelligible. Such a *divisio* is quite literally a *contra-dictio* in the sense of *dictio* given above: there is opposition between the senses of the severally intelligible *dictiones*, which opposition the *divisio* recognises. An attempt to com-pose squareness and circularity results only in a *confusio* of the two forms, and a *confusio* is not distinct enough to permit sure reference, and hence the possibility of truth and consequence. Where there is *confusio* of forms, as will appear, there is no *ens* of any kind for God to be able to be said with truth to be able to bring about.

A putative *divisio* between squareness and bligs blags blugness is no *divisio* at all, because 'bligs blags blugs' has no significance itself. There is no *contra-dictio*, because there is no *dictio* for the *dictio* 'square' to oppose. You cannot contradict unresisting imbecility. Neither is there *confusio* even, since there is no form of bligs blags blugness. Medievals examined below of course rejected the (verbal) suggestion that God could make a square bligs blags blugs. But this was not on the grounds that no such thing could be, and hence no such thing could be brought about by God (as Aquinas would deal with suggestions of square circles). It was on the previous ground that no (scientifically usable) assertion to the effect that God could make there to be square bligs blags bluges could be made, since there was no possible truthmaker of the sort required for either kind of analysans. By contrast, 'Squareness is circular' is literally contra-dictory: not unintelligible (as it was to be for Hobbes), merely necessarily false; and hence usable scientifically, as in the antecedent of a true hypothetical.

If the general form of a composing-apt proposition may be represented on the lines of:

Someone composes/divides ⟨ . . . , . . . ; R⟩,

where what is to be represented between the angle brackets is some (necessarily) ordered object of judgement, then a 'predication' analogous to that expressible in a narrowly predicative proposition can be had. In the latter, the juxtaposition which symbolises predication joins objects of different logical types: the predicate-expression is being taken *formaliter*, the subject-expression *materialiter*, as Aquinas repeatedly insisted. In composing-apt propositions too what is representable between the angle brackets is a structured object of thought, in effect a form abstractly considered; while what is representable to the left of the angle brackets stands for some concrete activity of judging on someone's part.[13]

Cum modo propositions of one kind—propositions asserted *cum determinatione*—play a central part in the Power Distinction. Both the option-tied and the option-neutral arm are of this kind; either arm implying at least one composing-apt proposition.[14]

---

[13] This analogy between the ways in which propositions of the two types can express their respective forms of "predication" may not only make it easier to accommodate them in a calculus, but may provide a guard against certain kinds of paradox. See Prior, *Formal Logic* (1962), 290, 291, for a need to see that 'the juxtaposition that symbolises predication can only join objects of different logical types' (291).

[14] A systematic and comprehensive study of *cum determinatione* assertions in medieval dialectics is not yet known to me, though there is no shortage of detailed work to accommodate within the framework needed from such a study. Important work from G. Klima and A. Bäck has already been mentioned at Introd. above, n. 17. See also G. Sinkler, 'Roger Bacon on the Compounded and Divided Sense', in O. Lewry (ed.), *The Rise of British Logic: Acts of The Sixth European Symposium on Medieval Logic and Semantics, Balliol College, Oxford, 19–24 June 1983* [Toronto, 1983], xii + 421 pp., 145–71; M. Mugnai, 'La "expositio reduplicativarum" chez Walter Burleigh et Paulus Venetus', in A. Maierù (ed.), *English Logic in Italy in the 14th and 15th centuries* [Naples, 1982], 388 pp., 305–20, and 'Intensionale Kontexte und "termini reduplicativi" in der *grammatica rationis* von Leibniz', in *Die intensionale Logik bei Leibniz u. in der Gegenwart* (Studia Leibnitiana, Sonderheft 8; 1979), 82–92; I. Angelelli, 'On Identity and Interchangeability in Leibniz and Frege',

15. *Predicates, subjects, predicables*

A predicate, in the usage followed here, is the 'formal part of an
assertion (*enunciatio*), apt to make it complete' (Aquinas, *In Periherm.*
1, lect. 8, par. 9, Leon. edn. 1*, 1 (1989), 41). In this usage, in
line with what was said above about 'propositions', the predicate
is not just that which is signified by the expression in predicate-
position, it is

- (*a*) the expression in predicate-position,
- (*b*) taken *formaliter*, to signify what, out of context, it is apt to
  signify; but to signify that, not of whatever it may stand
  for, out of context, but of precisely what the expression in
  subject-position stands for.

In 'Some rose is red' the predicate is

- (*a*) the (verbal) expression 'is red',
- (*b*) taken *formaliter*, to signify the form of redness which may
  (or may not) be found individualised in things in the world
  of the categories.

By the predication, that which 'red', out of context, is apt to
stand for (some or other red thing, or someone's mental construct)
is determined to something of the rose kind. In 'Some rose is
red', it is being said of some x of the rose kind, that it is red. As
was noted above, it may not be being understood—as we
nowadays might be inclined to take it—as saying of some
individual x (unrestricted as to kind), that it is a rose and is red.
(The difference between the two analyses comes out in a square
of opposition.)

The subject likewise is not to be understood as just that which
the expression in subject-position is taken to stand for, but as

- (*a*) that which the (nominal) expression in subject-position
  stands for,
- (*b*) taken as an individual of the kind specified in the subject-

---

Notre Dame Journal of Formal Logic, 8 (1967), 94–100, and '*Analytica Priora I*, 38 and
Reduplication', *ND Journ. Form. Log* 19 (1978), 295–6; and A. de Libera, 'De la logique à
la grammaire: Remarques sur la théorie de la détermination chez Roger Bacon et
Lambert d'Auxerre (Lambert de Lagny)', in G. L. Bursill-Hall *et al.* (eds.), *De ortu
grammaticae: Studies in Medieval Grammar and Linguistic Theory in Memory of Jan Pinborg*
(Amsterdam, 1990), x + 372 pp., 209–26. In medieval texts the matter is to be found
chiefly in commentaries on *De sophisticis elenchis* and in treatments of the Incarnation.

expression which expression is being said to be taken *materialiter*, to stand for that individual).

In 'Some rose is red', 'rose' is being taken *materialiter*, to stand for some individual of the rose kind.

A practical difficulty sometimes faces the reader of medieval texts from the fact that the writers often use 'proposition', 'subject', and 'predicate' indifferently concerning "predications" in the looser sense appropriate to the discourse of dining and backgammon, and concerning predications in the stricter, analysed sense, which concern only narrowly predicative propositions, and not composing-apt ones. Writers will thus readily speak of 'predicating' a genus of a species, though at the analysed level that can be done only within a composing-apt proposition; in the analysis of which the 'predication' in question is not necessarily to be expressed by a verbal (as against a nominal or participial) form.[15]

Predicables, in line with predicates and the rest, are likewise to be understood as

(*a*) structurally appropriate expressions,

(*b*) signifying, even out of context, some kind of thing.

What counts as structurally appropriate—to bear significance, even out of context, and to serve in the proper context to stand for something of some kind—is normally a matter for schoolroom grammar, and perhaps ultimately for speakers' arbitrary decisions.[16]

[15] Broader uses of 'predicate' are noted in L.-M. De Rijk, 'On Boethius's Notion of Being: A Chapter of Boethian Semantics', in N. Kretzmann (ed.), *Meaning and Inference in Medieval Philosophy: Studies in memory of Jan Pinborg* (Dordrecht, 1988), xii + 400 pp., 1–29, 8: 'The Greek *katêgorein ti kata tinos*, the Latin formula: *praedicare aliquid de aliquo* primarily stands for "to say something of something else". As is quite obvious, the two expressions are most frequently used to mean "to predicate something of something else by means of a sentence". However, the verbs *praedicare* and *katêgorein* are used, time and again, for just "using a name" or "designating something through a name", regardless of the systematic role performed by that name in a sentence.' When, as sometimes happens, a medieval speaks of predicating, when in fact the assertion is one which must be analysed as composing-apt, what should be understood will very often be that one of the broader ways of 'predicating', such as those indicated by De Rijk, is in question.

[16] Kilwardby, one of the users of the Distinction examined below, would insist that 'the true supposes the congruous, and not inversely'; and William of Conches in the 12th cent. had already said: 'Before signifying the true or the false and entering into reasonings, [a] sentence must (in order to have a sense) be constructed according to certain rules, which are the concern of the grammarian'. For these see Rosier, *La Grammaire* (1983), 44, citing K.-M. Fredborg *et al.*, in *Cahiers de l'institut du Moyen Âge grec et latin*, 15 (1975),

Not simply red—what 'red' signifies—but 'red', taken as in (*b*), is the predicable in this usage. Out of context, it might be understood to stand for either some or other red thing in extra-mental reality, or someone's mental construct (or, in a platonist reading, a Platonic Idea, presumably). Within this approach, missing shades of blue (shades of blue not found exemplified in extra-mental reality) offer no great problems, even on non-platonist readings. Compare Peter of Spain's remark that 'a predicable is what is naturally suited *to be said of* more than one' whereas 'a universal is naturally suited *to be in* more than one' (*Summulae*, tr. E. Stump and N. Kretzmann, *Logic and the Philosophy of Language* (Cambridge, 1958), 81, emphasis added). There is no reason of course why some expression's being 'naturally suited' (structurally appropriate) or not should not be decided arbitrarily, i.e. by someone's arbitrium, in accordance with the rules of grammar.

16. *Sorting for analysis into composing-apt and narrowly predicative propositions*

What is the principle in accordance with which unanalysed assertions are selected for either analysis rather than the other? It seems to me to be as follows:

(1) Those assertions which are understood to imply something ineliminably modal, something which cannot be made to collapse into a purely extensional analysis, are to be analysed into composing-apt propositions.

(2) All others, including those which, like *de re* modals, may initially seem to be modal, are to be analysed into narrowly predicative propositions.[17]

1–143, 24 (Kilwardby), and J. Jolivet, *Arts du langage et Théologie chez Abélard* (Paris, 1969), 390 pp., 28 (William of Conches).

[17] Aquinas, for example, after listing types of proposition "modal" in a broader sense says: 'quidam [modus] qui determinat compositionem ipsam praedicati ad subiectum, ut cum dicitur "Sortem currere est possibile": et ab hoc solo modo dicitur propositio modalis. Aliae vero propositiones, quae modales non sunt, dicuntur propositiones de inesse.' Cf. Abélard's remarks at the *In De. int.* of the *Logica 'Ingredientibus'*, ed. Geyer in *Beiträge*, 21 (1919–33), 367, where there may be an omission in the manuscript between *concedimus duplicem esse propositionum* and the editor's ⟨*secundum*⟩ *intellectus scilicet compositos*.

The following genres of assertion are thus to be analysed in the composing-apt manner:

1. Assertions purported to be about concepts, or anything else signified by words of second intention generally.
2. Assertions purported to be about privations. 'Blindness is damnable' is not to be analysed like 'Socrates is damnable', even by a descriptivist. (The latter sentiment is one I recall seeing expressed on a wall in the rue Socrate in Rouen, around the time of the bac.) For that matter, 'Socrates is blind' cannot be analysed either in the atomic *Fa*, or in the truth-functional $\sim Ga$ ('Socrates is not possessed of sight'). This is doubtless because a stone can be said with truth not to be possessed of sight, but cannot necessarily be apt for calling either blind or not blind, properly speaking. Blindness is typically treated by medievals examined below, as a privation of something due specifically to things of a certain nature. Both the 'due to' and the 'nature' there call for a treatment which is not purely extensional.[18]
3. Assertions purported to be about fictions:[19] Pegasus, or unicorns, or Shakespeare's Macbeth (as against the Macbeth of history, a rather decent king by the standards of the time). Aquinas calls all of these *fabulosa*, reserving *fictiones* for fictions of a more dubious sort.[20]
4. Assertions involving *de dicto* modalities generally. As was noted earlier, *de re* modal assertions were regularly treated as disguised propositions *de inesse*, and thus narrowly predicative.[21]

---

[18] In the early 14th cent. this was still how privations were being treated: 'Licet privationes non sint entia positiva extra animam, sunt tamen entia positiva in anima, ut patet IV Met Text 9 et sunt entia secundum animam' (Thomas of Erfurt, 140, cit. I. Rosier, *La grammaire spéculative des Modistes* (Lille [1983], 226 pp., 58).

[19] If a fiction is described in precisely this way and not that, its being (understood to be) this way and not that is something necessary: 'just as a fictional character can have only those properties he is described as having, and an object of perception (sense-datum) can have only those properties it is perceived as having, so a mental construction can have only those properties which we understand it as having, i.e. which we have either stipulated or proved it to have . . .' (M. Dummett, *Elements of Intuitionism*, with the assistance of Roberto Minio (Oxford, 1977), XII + 467 pp., 386).

[20] Some might think of the Donation of Constantine, perhaps, or the Thatcher ministry's unemployment figures.

[21] From Thomas of Erfurt again: 'Et quia privationes et negationes et figmenta sunt entia secundum animam, ideo cadunt sub proprietate entis, quae est proprietatas habitus et permanentis . . .' (Thomas of Erfurt, 154, cit. Rosier, *La grammaire spéculative* (1983), 59).

17. *The emphasis on speech*

The caveats on anticipating and avoiding possible confusions arising from medieval ways of approaching things which may be different from those we may find natural, might have seemed excessive to some. In particular, the caveats on medieval emphases on speech might still seem excessive. If it is to prove possible to analyse assertions of the form 'God can in option-tied/option-neutral power___', will the utterances into which they are analysed not have to be propositional? If they are, and if none of their terms should have to be thought to introduce special problems (of indeterminateness, for example), then are they not in principle susceptible of a formal treatment of a general kind already familiar? If they are going to prove susceptible of such a treatment, would it not then be permissible and even preferable to transpose the medievals' positions into sentential expressions straight away?

To anticipate, it may be said that the analysantia of the arms of the Distinction, to the extent that they are distinguished from each other, do prove to be of a kind which lends itself to a more formal treatment, and perhaps one which does not need any formalism not already tested and available. But if in both cases it is God's option-tied/option-neutral power which is in question, and if by 'God' is meant the God of a rigorously negative theology on the divine nature, then constraints appear on what sorts of terms can be used in the distinguishing components of the analysantia. It is at this point that recourse to utterances— rather than to sentences used within a formalised language— becomes needful, in a way which will appear. It is also at this point that the properties of a certain range of purposefully usable utterances makes resource of the kind needed, to be possible in reliable argument. All that, however, is to anticipate. What is being said to be needful, is needful if the medievals now to be considered are indeed to be seen as understanding the Distinction in certain ways, and not in others; and using it in certain ways, and not in others. To discover how they were understanding and using it, with the assistance of the key now provided in the working notions outlined, is the task of the next few chapters.

2

Early Use of the Distinction: By the Pupils of the Masters

In the present chapter I examine the earliest available passages in which the Power Distinction itself is being recognisably used. Even where the terminology is not always precisely the same as that which imposed itself later—*de potentia ordinata dei*, and *de potentia absoluta dei*—these passages arguably show the Distinction itself, and not merely anticipations of it. My concern here is in isolating the Distinction from the texts and seeing how it was being used. I do not think that any of the passages so far found exhibits the first conscious adoption of the Distinction. They must, however, take us towards it, if it can be identified, so I note in passing what scholars have said about the sources or the entourage of the authors whose texts are examined. Perhaps others will find clues there, to lead them further towards historical origins—though a word of caution is in order. If, as appears below, the Distinction itself is to be seen as a dialectical device, and one refined in dialectical debate, it may be well to mark that some of the characteristic features of such debate tend to make it harder to identify historical origins. In the words of a skilful modern dialectician:

A given thesis is commonly debated again and again; and sometimes the same person acts as a defender of it or else as attacker time after time. Written minutes or abstracts of the argument-sequences deployed are kept and consulted. Consequently the arguments for and against a given thesis undergo a progressive development and crystallization. I, in attacking the thesis, say, that Virtue is teachable, redeploy question-chains that I and others have deployed before, as well as try progressively to fortify them against past or present rebuttals, misinterpretations and exceptions. Like chess-players' 'combinations', lines of argument are public property, and a tactical improvement made by myself becomes henceforth a part of anyone else's stock of arguments for or against the same thesis. (Ryle at Owen 1968: 75, as at Ch. 9, n. 1 below.)

It could be too dogmatic to apply generally to concepts or procedures refined in dialectics the judgement that 'To ask whether the finally crystallized refutation of the thesis that pleasure is not a good is the handiwork of Aristotle or of someone else is an unanswerable question. It has passed between all the millstones' (same ref. 76). Yet the thought is one which could usefully dampen expectations, without necessarily extinguishing them.

Before examining the early uses—up to and including those of Philip the Chancellor—I recall a phenomenon of the times, against which the introduction of the Distinction into theologians' discussions should be seen. This is the remarkable efflorescence of the *magistri*, and the proliferation of both instruments and institutions in which their teachings and technical innovations might be transmitted. When they were, the transmission went pari passu with the transmission of doctrines and techniques of earlier or contemporary authors admired by them. It is not always easy, in reading even non-dialectical texts from such a milieu, to be sure that this innovation or that should be attributed to this author rather than that. When texts in addition reflect dialectical development, it can well seem, as from a hasty reading of Ryle, as though the theses themselves were in development in such a milieu, with the contributions of the human participants—expressing, asserting, modifying, rebutting the theses—as something subservient. This is of course not strictly so. The relation between a 'dialectical development' and the actors in the related discussions is by no means the same as that between an unfolding drama, composed by a playwright, and the actors playing roles within it. To the extent that information is available on the actors in the discussions involving the texts examined below, I try to bear that in mind.

MASTERS AND TRANSMITTERS

Towards the twelfth century appears a new class, of *magistri*: in the feudal world but not quite of it, tonsured as a rule but not to be regarded as clerics first and foremost. Some of them would move to developing centres from regions with better established traditions of instruction in grammar or rhetoric. In the earlier days the most typical movement was from Italy to the north, to settle in established teaching positions of a traditional kind. Anselm moved in this way to both Bec and Canterbury, Peter Lombard moved, becoming Bishop of Paris. In the mass, however, they must have appeared far from settled to many contemporaries. They plied a craft, like the burgesses from whom (or to whom) they rented their houses. They marketed a product, and were prepared to travel to concentrations of likely customers, or to environments where the burgesses or the ecclesiastical authorities were likelier to smile on them. They had something in common, therefore, not only with the poets of the time (who also tended to travel, before settling into positions as advisers or ministers of church or state), but with the travelling merchants or bankers, who themselves were viewed as something of a threat to feudal stability and good order. Through this movement of the Masters, however, rigorously argued philosophy came back to the market-place where the midwife's son had brought it to vigorous life, and where Hypatia had sold it to the passers-by. It came back from the groves and colonnades and cloisters where it had so long been kept among a consenting few, often sharing values and positions of substance (and the limited horizons which that can entail). The pupils of the Masters were no longer *claustrales* but *scholastici*, who compared products and were themselves prepared to move, either singly or en masse, not only to other Masters but to other market-places, in order to find what they thought they wanted.

There is a robust vulgarity about the Masters, and perhaps the "craft" elements of academic philosophy—the teachable, marketable skills—did at times predominate in their teaching, to the detriment of studious contemplation of respected, even venerated texts, or genial discovery. No doubt not all was gain, and no doubt not all the resistance to the Masters should be put down to threatened interest or "envy", the bête noire of generations reared on the *Timaeus*. At the same time there is hardly room to doubt but that the emphasis on craft elements—not least on a body of shared dialectical devices, distinctions, received moves in analysis—was in general benign. Such elements, and the vehicles in which they were to be transmitted economically (the teaching institutions, the *instruments de travail*...), gave students of mediocre intellect or a little less, the possibility of mastering in a few years complex bodies of skills and knowledge alike (*scientiae*, and *usus scientiarum*) which in former times only a few might have hoped to have managed. That sort of thing, admittedly, has concomitant disadvantages. Körner noted an example from nearer our own day, in the argument against "metaphysical propositions" as being neither empirical and verifiable, nor analytic:

The anti-metaphysical argument is easily learned and applied. In the thirties of the present century it gave much pleasure to undergraduates; and, among philosophers, whose views were more complex, less streamlined, and less adapted to concise formulation, it probably caused equally great annoyance. (S. Körner, *Kant* [Harmondsworth, 1955], 17.)

At least some of the opposition to the dialectical devices given currency by the Masters and their pupils almost certainly arose from a rather similar source; not least because the devices—the Power Distinction among them—were in many cases 'easily learned and applied'. Peter Damian's violent irritation at the application of dialectics to theological questions by the inexpert had already been provoked by much less.

As the twelfth century edged into the thirteenth and the movement of the Masters became less agitated, emphasis shifted to some extent from the Masters themselves to the vehicles in which their craft was to be continued: institutions like the embryonic universities; *instruments de travail* like the translations of admired sources (Greek and Arabic above all), or textbooks offering codifications of the mystery of the Masters, or the core of a teachable syllabus, or concordances, indexes, and handy techniques of reference.[1]

---

[1] A noteworthy proportion of the identifiable, leading poets of the times—Walter of Châtillon, Peter of Blois, Peter the Chancellor, for example—were 'wandering scholars' only for a time, before settling into "establishment" positions in princely courts and the like. See J. de Ghellinck, *L'Essor de la littérature latine au XIIe siècle*, 1 (Paris, 1946), 270–99. For this section generally see M.-D. Chenu, *La théologie au douzième siècle* (Paris, 1957), 413 pp., 323–50; and J. de Ghellinck, *Le mouvement théologique du XIIe siècle* (Brussels, 1948), XII + 594 pp. For the medieval writers mentioned see A. M. Landgraf, *Introduction à l'histoire de la littérature théologique de la scolastique naissante* (Montreal, 1973), 209 pp. More generally still see É. Gilson, *History of Christian Philosophy in the Middle Ages* (London [1955]), xvii + 829 pp.; J. Marenbon, *Later Medieval Philosophy (1150–1350): An Introduction* (London [1987]), xii + 230 pp. (clearly set out bibliogr. 194–224); F. Van Steenberghen, *La philosophie*

Only a few of the Masters and transmitters can be mentioned here. In transmitting both puzzles and means for their solution Hugh of St Victor plays a part, as one of the transmitters of the crucial Abelardian questions on divine power, which were to crystallise the more general issues behind the puzzles to which the Distinction was (as would appear) first addressed. Pre-eminent as a transmitter, in this as in theology generally, was Peter Lombard and his book of Sentences: through which, even more than through Hugh, the relevant questions of the Abelardian treatise on divine power were in effect plucked from the flames to which Bernard and those of his persuasion had consigned the works. Through the Sentences above all, the Abelardian questions—Could God do anything other than he is doing? Could he leave off what he is doing? Could he do better than he is doing?—retained prominence on the agenda of the schools of theology until long after Luther. Gratian's *Decretum* too played its part, and not only through what Lombard would borrow. The *Decretum* provided not a few convenient can-and-cannot puzzles of an earlier genre, canvassed in patristic times. It was through the *Decretum* that Aquinas, for example, came to treat Peter Damian's puzzle (and Jerome's) about the undoing of the undone. Translators are often undervalued in histories of intellectual movements. In the present matter they seem to have been important more for providing terminology of interest, and for related distinctions, than for transmitting any ready-made solutions. The translation of Aristotle's *De sophisticis elenchis*, which made a great impact on the early theology faculties, almost certainly played a part of importance in winning currency for the Power Distinction. The Distinction itself can be seen as a way of avoiding the 'fallacy' (not a strictly logical fallacy) of Secundum Quid.[2]

au XIII⁴ siècle (Louvain-la-Neuve, 1991), 551 pp. (chronological table covering the period, 540–6).

[2] For Gratian: Ae. Friedberg (ed.), *Decretum Magistri Gratiani* (Leipzig, 1979). For Lombard: *Magistri Petri Lombardi, Parisiensis Episcopi Sententiae in IV Libros distinctae*, 3rd Quaracchi edn., 2 vols. (1971). On Lombard see I. Brady. 'Peter Lombard: Canon of Notre Dame', *Recherches de Théologie Ancienne et Médiévale* 32 (1965), 277–95, and in Introd. to the 1971 Quaracchi edn. of the Sentences, 8*–45*; J. de Ghellinck, *Le Mouvement théologique* (1948), 214–21; and the references in Landgraf, *Introduction ... scolastique naissante* (1973), 130–36. On the importance of translators see remarks by L. Minio-Paluello in various articles repr. in *Opuscula. The Latin Aristotle* (Amsterdam, 1972), esp. 405–24, 'La tradition aristotélicienne dans l'histoire des idées'.

The bones of the modal logic needed in an understanding of the Distinction had already been available, along with at least suggestions of the metaphysical notions needed, in the older translations of the *De interpretatione* and the *Categories*. But the key notions of a two-type analysis of scientifically important assertions into 'absolute' (narrowly predicative) or 'necessary' (composing-apt) propositions, and of the Avicennian essence susceptible of two-way possibility, were to come rather from Avicenna: as will appear from a number of places below.[3]

The versatility and practicality of the Masters themselves are well instanced in the work of Stephen Langton, which has endured in a wide range of contexts. It would have been grounds enough for praise to have drafted England's Magna Carta, some of whose provisions have been dismantled only in very recent years; or to have composed the beautiful sequence *Veni, Sancte Spiritus* which endures in the Pentecost liturgy. Langton is credited with both. He also left his mark as an indexer, by providing the Scriptures with the divisions into numbered chapters which, in turn divided into numbered verses by Dominicans of a generation later, have come to be endowed with an odd kind of canonicity: both by Protestant fundamentalists who would think themselves far from medievalism of any stripe, and in the liturgical readings of Protestant or Reformed churches which made much of possessing a narrower canon than medieval churches had come to recognise. One of his innovations was soon to be deplored by some who, like Roger Bacon, were neither fundamentalist nor Protestant: the choice of a non-Scriptural text for the object-text of the initial instructions in serious theology. For it was Langton who was first to provide a commentary on Lombard's Sentences. It is, incidentally, a good commentary on the text, with a conciseness and a clarity in which he was by no means always followed. Like Anselm and Lombard, he did not grow old as a Master or an outsider, but settled in a key position in the older teaching establishment, as Archbishop of Canterbury. It is as though, through the acceptance of such Masters as Lombard at Paris and Langton at Canterbury, a patriarch's blessing was being passed from the older to the newer forms of theological

---

[3] For Avicenna's treatment of necessity and possibility see e.g. the influential medieval translation of the *Shifa*, ed. S. Van Riet in *Avicenna Latinus* (Louvain, 1977), 43–55.

instruction. Langton played as Archbishop a part in secular and ecclesiastical politics alike. A measure of his skill is that although he was engaged for a time in vigorous (independent) disputes with both the papacy and the English monarchy, he was able to survive not only with his head but with his cardinal's hat.[4]

It is for an analytical contribution that I cite Langton here: a distinction which serves to dissolve some of the older puzzles on divine power, and will also serve to show the sort of thing provided by the Masters to those who followed them. At what we, following Alexander of Hales and his colleagues, call distinction 42 of Book I of the Sentences, Langton takes up the question of whether God can do everything. His *Responsio* begins as follows. 'God is able' (*Deus potest*) and the like can be understood in either of two ways: as a complete proposition ([*propositio*] *perfecta*) or an incomplete proposition ([*propositio*] *imperfecta*). The distinction is evidently that between a proposition (a closed propositional expression) and a propositional function (an open propositional expression), provided that we take 'proposition' to mean, not a bare propositional content, but such a content expressed linguistically, and normally asserted. Langton notes that if we take 'God is able ___' or *Deus omnia potest* ___ as an incomplete proposition, to be completed no doubt by an infinitive, diverse completions (*diversae . . . suppletiones*) can be supplied, and the truth-value of the whole will depend on what we fill the blank with. If we supply 'act' or *agere*, the proposition so completed will be false: the case he has been considering is where some base deed is in question. If on the other hand we supply 'bring about' or *facere* for the deed in question, the proposition then completed may be true. Langton is thus allowing that God can bring it about that base deeds are done, but not allowing that God can be said to be the actor of base deeds, the one to whose quasi-moral responsibility they are to be ascribed. 'God is able' or *Deus potest*, unrestricted, can also be understood as complete propositions. In English this usage survives only in such contexts as 'Jones is able, but must pay more attention to detail' in school reports. When *Deus omnia potest* is being used in this way, as a

---

[4] See the I. Brady items at n. 2 above.

complete proposition, then it is false (says Langton) unless the universe of application is restricted in some way (*nisi restringatur universitas*).[5]

It is worth noting that what Langton is saying here does not necessarily conflict with what Albert, Aquinas, and others will be seen to say, to the effect that 'God can do things', taken unrestrictedly, should be thought true. Langton here is concerned with verbal completions. The later writers, no less than Langton, did not imagine that just any grammatically correct completion of 'God can bring it about that____' could be read as a true proposition. (Consider the completion 'green dreams sleep furiously'.) They were in effect restricting the universe in the way envisaged by Langton, to verbal completions apt to signify 'things' (Aquinas) or 'works' (Albert), actual or possible. And of course neither Langton nor any of the later writers mentioned is to be thought of as being concerned with merely ad hoc restrictions, brought in to block unwelcome cases. Ad hoc restrictions of that sort at least seem to have been used in some patristic discussions of what God can or cannot be said with truth to be able to do.

If I am right in seeing Langton's distinction here as being between proposition and propositional function (open propositional expression), it would seem worth a footnote in a revision of Bochenski or the Kneales. Bochenski's own earliest examples of an appreciation of propositional functions are from quite modern times, and his earliest examples of a concept/function distinction of any kind are from Frege, Peirce, and Russell. The concept of function, Bochenski insisted, does not effect anything radically new. (He said the same of the concepts of variable and of truth-value.) Its adoption, however, like theirs 'yet produced so marked a development of the old concept of logical form' (Bochenski–Thomas, *History* (1961; repr. 1970), 319). I mention Langton's anticipation of it as an example of the clarifications provided by the Masters for discussions at a 'dialectical' level. There were many other clarifications for discussions on the same level, being introduced and codified and passed into currency. It is in part because they were, that a philosophically sophisticated

---

[5] Ed. A. M. Landgraf, 'Der Sentenzenkommentar des Kardinals Stephan Langton', in *Beiträge*, 37/1 (Münster, 1952), 58. On Langton, Landgraf, *Introduction* (1973), 167–72.

understanding of the Power Distinction, on the part of theologians of the early Theology faculties, need not be thought at all surprising. I now turn to the earliest uses of the Power Distinction which have either surfaced in the literature, or have appeared in manuscripts seen by me.

EARLY USERS

Geoffrey of Poitiers (fl. 1215)

1. Geoffrey (Galfridus, though sometimes listed as Godfrey or Godefridus) was a pupil of Stephen Langton's and compiled a *Summa theologiae* between 1212 and 1219; perhaps between 1213 and 1215 (*Dictionnaire d'histoire et de géographie ecclésiastiques*, s.v. 'Godefroy de Poitiers'). In 1231 he was still active, in Rome, playing a part—with William of Auxerre, to be examined presently—of importance to the University of Paris. Book 4 of Geoffrey's *Summa* was extracted from the *Summa* of Robert de Courson, and whole questions in other books were taken over from the *Summa* of Praepositinus of Cremona. There are also close affinities between passages in Geoffrey's *Summa*, on the one hand, and passages in the *Summa Fratris Alexandri* and in William of Auxerre's *Summa aurea*, on the other. Since, in addition, Geoffrey's *Summa* 'depends in very large measure on Stephen Langton' (Landgraf, *Introduction* (1973), 172), it can be seen that no great originality is intended in the work, but that it is something of a paradigm of the vehicles in which the dialectical teachings of the Masters might be registered, modified, and transmitted.[6]

All the more interesting, then, that in this professedly unoriginal work should be found one of the earliest undeniably recognisable uses of the Power Distinction. It may even be the earliest in a surviving text, though I deliberately drew attention to some sources which have been identified, in case students of those Masters' ideas may be able to trace earlier examples. (I would not expect any uses to be found in either Langton or Praepositinus, though the latter does use the narrowly cognate *de*

---

[6] On Geoffrey, *DHGE*, s.v. 'Godefroy de Poitiers' (Aubert) and refs.

potentia/iustitia distinction which goes back to Augustine at least).[7] Geoffrey's *Summa* reveals an author or compiler not unworthy of his master Langton, with a care for analytical clarity in the service of theology. His treatment of reduplication, for example, which becomes important in handling certain puzzles raised by the theologians' doctrine of the Incarnation, shows a sure enough hand:

Of proper [predications], some are consequent (*consequentes*), others inconsequent (*inconsequentes*). I call them consequent inasmuch as the predicate is kin (*familiaris*) to the subject; inconsequent, as in a certain [predication] *per accidens*, that is, by something *per extraneum*. (*Summa*, G 102vb, o 96ra, cit. W. Principe, *William of Auxerre's Theology of the Hypostatic Union* (Toronto, 1963), 322 pp., 99.)

In the case of a bishop who is also a duke (or military commander), Geoffrey continues by way of expounding what he has said, 'A bishop is singing mass' and 'A duke is singing mass' might equally be true; but the latter predication is 'inconsequent', as the duke is singing mass not *secundum quod dux* but *secundum quod episcopus*. Note that Geoffrey here is using the reduplicative phrases—*sec. quod dux, sec. quod episcopus*—as determinations of the predicate. He is not indulging in the fantasy of imagining two distinct subjects. *Familiaris* suggests Boethius in the background, and *consequens/inconsequens* may be related to Anselm's terminology in opposing *necessitas consequentis* and *necessitas consequentiae*. Principe notes that in his treatment of reduplication Geoffrey was followed by William of Auxerre. Aquinas and others would speak rather of *per se* predication where Geoffrey had used *consequens*, but were agreed in speaking indifferently of *per se* (consequent) predication, of *per se* (consequent) propositions,

---

[7] At what came to be called d. 43 of *1 Sent.*, Langton considers the Augustinian remark '*poterat per potentiam, sed non poterat per iustitiam*', and seems unaware (or affects to be unaware?) of the quasi-technical use of *per iustitiam* which anticipated the *de potentia ordinata* of the Power Distinction. He notes (correctly) that it is Lot's justice, not God's, which is concerned in the Genesis passage referred to. If, he adds, you understand God's own justness (the justness held identical with the divine nature) to be in question in *poterat per iustitiam*—and this, he also adds, is the proper sense of *iustitia dei*—then it is false that there is anything God can do *per potentiam* and not *per iustitiam*. (The *sic* in the MS is correct, and pace Landgraf ought not to be 'corrected' to *set*.) Langton is not against the substance of the (later) Distinction, and praises Lombard for an implicit recognition of that substance: 'Dicit [Magister] quod potestas non est maior voluntate dei quam econverso, et tamen plura sunt subiecta potestati quam voluntati dei; et hoc verum est.' (After Landgraf, 1952 edn. 62.)

and of the related predicative propositions' being true, when true, *per se.*

Geoffrey, or the source he may be retailing, is also concerned to sort out diverse surface-uses of *potest* or *potentia*. He makes it clear that a different response is to be made, on the one hand, to the *potest* which is in effect the sign of modality in a modal function, where the modality is of the austere, logical sort, and, on the other, to the *potest* which—whether we might wish to represent it by a modal operator or otherwise—carries more narrowly semantic content:

Sometimes this performs only the task of a copula, as in *potest credere*; but sometimes (signifies) a possibility (*possibilitatem*), as when *Antichristus potest esse* is being said. (Geoffrey of Poitiers, *Summae*, MS Bruges Stadb. Cod. lat. 220, fo. 35, cit. A. Landgraf, *Dogmengeschichte*, I/1 (1952), 245.)

The *possibilitas* there is to be understood as the 'capacity' captured in Aristotle's two-way possibility. *Possibilitas* is sometimes found in that sense in translations of Avicenna, in whom two-way possibility applies only to the abstract Avicennian essences of things, which are to play such a crucial part in a satisfactory understanding of the Power Distinction. The 'task of a copula' here is to indicate the "tropic" or mood in which the content of the proposition is to be asserted or "nodded", when it is to be.

In general, though, the sorting of surface-uses is not systematic. It is enough to obviate superficial misunderstandings, so that more substantial issues can be tackled. The noun *potentia* can be taken in any of the following ways, he says:

(1) A *potentia* may be a capacity (*habilitas*) which may dispose a man to perform some act. An attribution of this sort of thing is being made when 'This man cannot walk' is said, pointing to one who is bound.

(2) It can be a resource (*facultas*), as in 'I cannot give you...'.

(3) It can be an endowment by pure favour (*facultas gratiae*), as in 'He gave them power to become sons of God', or 'No man can come to me [unless the Father draw him]'.

(4) It can be a dignity of pre-eminence, as in 'Let every soul be subject to higher powers'.

(5) It can be a quality tied to an office, as in 'Any priest has the power of binding and loosing'.

(6) It can be what is due, as in *Potuit quidem de potentia, sed non de iustitia.*

(7) It can be the will to do something, as in 'They could not believe Isaias', or in 'God is faithful, who will not suffer you to be tempted above what you are able for'.

It is the believing which is being viewed as voluntary in the first example. The *potest*, he adds, is the sign of the mood of assertion (*habet officium copulae*).

The diversity of uses indicated, and the Scriptural quotations in the examples, are evidence enough of the pre-eminently practical aim of the list, and may in addition suggest that the audience envisaged is not a narrowly academic one.

Landgraf, *Dogmengeschichte*, I/1 (1952), 245 n., quotes a further passage from Geoffrey which might have something to tell us about his treatment of divine power, but without more of a context than is available, it must remain obscure.

Where the Power Distinction appears, is in a discussion of whether God could give to Christ power of just any kind, and in particular the power of justifying and saving. The passage runs:

I say that he was able *de potestate absoluta* to give him such power. For who would dare to dispute his power and his immensity (*de potestate eius et immensitate disputare*). But he was not able *de potentia conditionali*, to wit, while the decrees remained in force, which he has established (*manentibus decretis, constituit*). For if he were to give [to Christ] the power of justifying and saving, hope would in this way be put in a man, whereas 'Cursed be the man that trusteth in man...' [Jer. 17: 5]. And in this way the rivers would not be returning to the place whence they had gone out; that is, that men would not be returning towards the first cause (*primam causam*) from which they have come out (*processerunt*).[8]

The background of the puzzle considered is narrowly theological, the *inconveniens* envisaged is arising from a 'decree of God'

---

[8] Item quaeritur Utrum potuerit dare omnium potentiam. Si dicit, non; quare non? Quid impedivit potestatem illius, quare hoc non potuit? Si dicit, ita—sed 'Dedit quicquid potuit, ergo dedit'. Dico, quod de potestate absoluta potuit ei dare: quis enim auderet de potestate eius et immensitate disputare. Sed non potuit de potentia conditionali, scilicet, manentibus decretis quae ipse constituit. Si enim ei daret potestatem iustificandi et salvandi, sic spes poneretur in homine, cum 'Maledictus sit qui confidit in homine'. Sic non revertentur flumina ad locum unde exierunt, idest, homines ad primam causam a qua processerunt. (Cit. A. Landgraf, *Dogmengeschichte*, II/2 (Ratisbon, 1954), 103 n. from MS Avranches, Bibl. de la ville, Cod. lat. 121, fo. 137.)

extracted by theologically forced (and at best dubious) interpretation from a Scriptural text. And the puzzler's own intellectual
background is no doubt revealed in the neoplatonist elements: the
rivers of creation flowing back to their source, the identification of
this with the first cause.

In content, however, this is the Power Distinction. The *de
potestate absoluta* is modifying the *potuit*, and the *potestas* is one
which can be called in question by calling in question either
God's having power, or God's having immense power. Where
the passage—whose context I have not yet seen—remains
ambiguous, is on whether the immense power referred to is to
be identified with:

(1) That power of God held identical with the divine nature,
   or
(2) Some power of God's to do things ad extra, immense in
   its extension, in the way in which the *potentia absoluta
   dei* was to be understood by Albert and Aquinas, and other
   later users of the Distinction.

The *de potentia conditionali* is being used precisely as *de potentia
ordinata* will be used by others; the *manentibus decretis* and *constituit*
indicate as much. In the *Summa* of Geoffrey of Poitiers, from not
later than 1219, is thus to be seen an unambiguous use of the
Power Distinction.

An Earlier Use?

2. It has been suggested (W. J. Courtenay, 'The Dialectic...'
(1985), 247 and note, and again at Ritter, *Wörterbuch*, 7 (1989),
1157) that an earlier use can be found, in an anonymous commentary on Romans, from 'around 1200' (Courtenay) or even
'towards 1160' (Glorieux, in *Pour revaloriser Migne*).

The passage is indeed interestingly close in some features to
the Power Distinction, but cannot be said with truth to be an
example of it. The question is the one to which the Distinction
came to be most typically addressed: *an Deus potuit facere con-
venientiorem modum redemptionis*. If it may be said that he could not,
says the author, the power of God is going to seem to have a
limit (*terminum*), and not be immense. If it may be said that he
could, how could the present [mode of redemption] be the

most convenient? The solution, or rather a brace of alternative solutions, runs:

Although in this [present mode of redemption], it [God's power] does have a limit, yet it is not to be conceded *simpliciter* that it may have a limit; or, although this mode [of redemption] is most convenient to our wretchedness, yet it is not necessary that it should be the most convenient *absolute*.

The author's solutions are neat, and they involve distinguishing assertions made *cum determinatione* from the same base-assertions made *absque determinatione*, or *simpliciter*, or *absolute*. (In the Power Distinction, two contrasting *cum determinatione* assertions, involving contrasting determinants, are in question.) The first solution is that:

(1) 'God's power has a limit in the actual order of things' is true, but

(2) 'God's power has a limit in the actual order of things' must not be conceded *simpliciter*.

(1), taken as an unanalysed utterance can be thought of as true, because at least one interpretation (analysis) is true. But that interpretation, under which the utterance comes out true, is one which contains a determinant. (The determinant *de potentia ordinata* would serve admirably: but the anonymous writer does not say so.) That is why (2) is also true. We might wish he had gone on to expand on what he said, but like many another medieval disputant, he says no more than he is obliged to, in order to answer the objection.

The second solution is that

(a) 'This mode of redemption is the most convenient to our wretchedness' is true, but

(b) 'This mode of redemption is the most convenient *absolute*', is not necessarily true.

In (a), the 'to our wretchedness' determines 'convenient', in (b) 'convenient' is *absque determinatione*. Compare:

The Duchess of Plaza Toro could pass for forty-four, *absolute*; and

The Duchess of Plaza Toro could very well pass for forty-four, in the dusk with the sun behind her.

As for the writer on Romans, he has once more said no more than he had been obliged to say, in order to answer the question. Of course, had he known about the Power Distinction, and had he wished to use it, he could indeed have used it aptly at that place. But he is silent on the matter, and nothing is called for under the conventions of medieval debate. We can therefore neither infer that he did know of the Power Distinction, nor infer that he did not. We do not have a use of the Distinction here, and what might or might not have been known to the anonymous author is not to the point.

'Quidam' (a. 1229) reported by William of Auxerre

3. I do not yet know who these were, though their use of *pura potentia* might suggest some acquaintance on their part with translations of Avicenna. In the passage reported by William they concede Augustine's formula to the effect 'Another manner of our redemption was possible to God' (cf. *De Trin.*, PL 42: 1024), but with the proviso:

as though he were saying 'If we are referring to the unconditioned power of God (*ad puram potentiam dei*), then 'Another manner was possible to God' is true, to wit, another manner was possible *quantum ad puram potentiam dei* to God; but it was necessary by the terms of the promise which had already been made [when Christ's passion etc. was occurring], that the Son of God should suffer, and that the human race should thus be redeemed.'[9]

Both predicates refer to active powers, and both are modified. *Quidam* are contrasting:

(1) possible to God, *quantum ad puram potentiam dei*, and
(2) possible to God, by the terms of the promise which had already been made (when Christ's passion etc. was occurring).

What is being envisaged as possible to God in either of these

---

[9] The text runs: 'quasi diceret Augustinus: si respiciamus ad puram potentiam dei, alius modus possibilis fuit deo, scilicet quantum ad puram potentiam dei; sed propter promissionem quae iam facta erat, necessarium erat Filium Dei passurum, et sic redimendum genus humanum' (in J. Ribailler (ed.), *William of Auxerre's Summa Aurea*, 3 (1986), 96). In Augustine there are already semantic links between *iustitia* and *ordinatio*: God is *iustissimus ordinator* (*De civ.* 11. 17; *De lib. arb.* 1. 5. 11).

two ways is a manner of our redemption: something extrinsic to
the divine nature. Both related *cum determinatione* predications are
thus to be taken as systematically misleading, to be understood
as true, if true, not of the divine nature, but of a manner of our
redemption, actual or envisaged. So far, we seem to have from
Quidam the groundwork for a straightforward use of the Power
Distinction, and the assertion of both

(1) God could, *quantum ad puram potentiam dei*, deploy another
   manner for our redemption than the one actually chosen,
   but

(2) God could not, by the terms of the promise etc., deploy
   another manner.

(2) is readily inferred from *Quidam*'s assertion that 'it was
necessary by the terms of the promise... that the Son of God
should suffer, and that the human race should thus be redeemed'.

But *Quidam* (are reported to) go on to say

(3) *Simpliciter*, no other manner of our redemption was possible
   to God.

There are at least two diverse kinds of reason for which that
might be asserted, by someone willing to assert both (1) and (2).
The first is from an importantly different understanding of what
is involved in option-neutral assertions such as (1) appears in its
context to be. This would involve understanding such expressions
as 'a manner of redemption other than the actual one' as
purporting to name some actual state of affairs; and necessarily
failing to do so. Given the Immutable Decree rider, whatever is,
necessarily is, and whatever is not, is impossible to be. On such
an understanding of the option-neutral arm of the Distinction,
option-neutral assertions are trifling. Whenever 'God can do A
in option-neutral power (*quantum ad puram potentiam dei*), but cannot
do A in option-tied power (by the terms of the promise)' is true,
it is going to be necessarily false that God can do A. A
'determination' of 'can do A' which cannot necessarily exclude
'cannot do A' is no better than a determination of 'pound note'
which cannot necessarily exclude the note's being of no value as
a pound note. An attribution of divine power which is no more
than a verbal cloak for something in sober truth impossible to
God, and nothing else, is not the theological currency in which
honest theologians should be trading.

A fear that the option-neutral arm may sometimes have been understood in such a way, or even a (misplaced) fear that it has to be so understood, has no doubt been behind some of the more sophisticated objections to the Power Distinction. But I would doubt whether any such fears are motivating *Quidam* here, in saying that (3) *Simpliciter*, no other manner of our redemption was possible to God.

For there is another kind of reason for which someone willing to assert both (1) and (2), might wish in addition to assert (3), and it does not make (1) to be such a dubious coinage. Unfortunately, it tends to make (2) dubious instead. It involves in some way distinguishing 'real' from 'empty' possibilities, and in identifying real possibilities with (timelessly) realised ones. An abstract possibility which is not actualised on some occasion, is not a 'real' possibility. This kind of view can be put forward with considerable plausibility, but tends to come down eventually to tying 'reality' to what we or others in some way continuous with us can run across or be damaged by. It is not hard to allow some kind of privileged status for things of that sort, and it is attractive to all who wish to take human experiences, hopes, or fears as the origin of their metaphysics. In the hands of a Hume, the parochialism of this sort of metaphysics is honestly spelled out; the limitations made as obvious as the appealing features. In the hands of a Kant it is lost in the breathtaking sweep of the project. The parochialism is still there at the origin, though, and with patience can be spelled out. To impose such a metaphysics on the formulas of the Power Distinction would be to nullify it. What the Distinction permits is precisely the deployment of a metaphysics which is not parochial in the ways in which a Humean or a Kantian scheme has to be; and which yet can be deployed by users who are situated every bit as parochially (whose assertions are indexed) as either Hume or Kant. These points are spelled out later (Ch. 9). I am not suggesting that they are at the surface of William of Auxerre's dispute with *Quidam* at this place.

What I would note is the unease which surfaces when someone who asserts both (1) and (2), in line with the Power Distinction, wishes additionally to assert (3). I doubt whether the additional assertion can with truth be made, without trivialising either (1) or (2). Yet it is an assertion attractive to all those who are inclined to put the heart of man at the heart of things. And such are not uncommon in the Augustinian ways of seeing things which have so often coloured the vision of theologians. My suggestion is that *Quidam* here have been using the Power Distinction, asserting both (1) and (2), but additionally asserting (3), not through subscribing to any alternative understanding of the Distinction, but rather out of an anthropocentric concern. *Quidam* are not being reported as being the inventors of the Distinction. They are being recognised (by William) as users of a distinction already in currency, and as asserting in addition something only uneasily if at all to be reconciled with it. If this is so, it is noteworthy that that source of unease should have appeared so early, and to William's credit that it should have been recognised as a source of unease. In this brief report of William of Auxerre's, from not later than the third decade of the thirteenth century, can be seen not only a use of the Distinction, but the germ of much of the unease of the more sophisticated critics of later times; often articulated no better.[10]

William of Auxerre (d. 1231)

4.   William is not to be confounded, as he was in former times, with a namesake who was bishop successively of Auxerre and of Paris, and died in 1223. The William whose contribution is examined here, was a master active in the schools of Paris, and praised by his contemporaries for his skill in disputation. After the *événements* of 1229 (see below) he was sent to Rome as one of the delegates of the French king, in a matter in which he did not succeed. While in Rome, however, he had more success on other matters touching the University, and it was he who was to procure on the University's behalf the bull *Parens scientiarum* of 13 December 1231, which became the charter of the University of Paris. Around the same time he was appointed by Pope Gregory IX to the three-man commission charged with examining the works of Aristotle, with a view to bowdlerising them for "safe" use in the University. (Works of Aristotle had been under ban in

---

[10] William's objections to *Quidam's* argument (at *Summa aurea*, ed. Ribailler, 3: 96, 97) are not without interest, but do not particularly contribute to the story of the Distinction, and are omitted here.

Paris, from the decision of a provincial council in 1210.) In the event William died in Rome in the autumn of 1231, before he could return to Paris. The University's regard for him, not least for his part in procuring the charter, one may suppose, is shown in the choice of 3 November for his annual service of commemoration: the first day free after the Commemoration of All Souls and the Feast of All Saints.

An almost contemporary witness credits William's *Summa* with having been the first commentary on the Sentences into which disputed questions had been integrated. Whether or not the witness is correct about William's priority, the innovation is a significant one, calculated to integrate teaching-vehicles from the two complementary traditions of university teaching. The commentary as such is a form of *lectio*, itself a teaching-vehicle calculated to transmit organised units of received knowledge (*scientiae*) with economy and a minimum of distortion; no negligible aim to achieve in the days before printing made possible relatively cheap printed copies of object-texts. The disputed questions of the masters were the paradigm of the *exercitium* or scholastic exercise, providing discussions which not only provided a vehicle for deepening and testing the masters' own grasp of their subject, but were important pedagogically as models for the students' *exercitia*, in which the primary aim was the perfectioning of the students' own practice in applying what they had learned, practice in their *usus scientiarum*. In the dialectical thrust and parry of the scholastic *exercitium* the students' own active grasp of their subject was calculated to be developed; and there too was their first institutional opportunity to contribute creatively to it.

Viewed as *an* innovative teaching-vehicle, William's *Summa* looks back to the period of the Masters; it consolidates and takes forward something already available, though not in such a readily assimilable form. Viewed for the content of its innovation, the partial integration of *lectio* and *exercitium*, William's *Summa* sets something of a pattern long to be followed in the schools. From William's references to 'the Master', and to authorities and arguments retailed by him, it is plain enough that William looked on his *Summa* as a commentary on the Sentences, not as an independent work. The *Summa* survives in two versions, of which it is the longer one which we are apparently to regard as something of an *ordinatio* put by its author into the public domain.

The shorter one—which shows significantly greater textual variations—presumably represents actual teaching at various stages, more closely than the longer version does. The longer version especially was much copied, and a number of *abbreviationes* also survive. It was printed at Paris in 1500, and at various places thereafter. A critically established edition (= *Summa*, ed. Ribailler (1980–7)) using work already done by R.-M. Martineau, OP, was prepared by Jean Ribailler, and on his death was brought to completion by Jean Châtillon, Goulven Madec, A. H. Gondras, Mme Hudry, and members of both the Quaracchi and the Leonine editorial teams.[11]

At the very beginning of the *Summa aurea* William declares his policy: to deal with 'divine things' not through reasons grounded on the things of nature as such, but from theological ones.[12] His reason for adopting the policy is not declared, but surely appears from the text from the Pseudo-Denis which he places here like an admiral shaking out a battle-flag: 'Universally, not to dare to say or to understand anything of the superessential and hidden divinity, save for those things expressed to us in the sacred utterances' (*De div. nom.*, ch. 1 PG 3: 587, PL 122; 1113, cit. Ribailler). William, in other words, is plainly declaring his adherence to a Negative Theology programme on the nature of God.

Tractate 11 of Book 1 deals ex professo with divine power. One argument will reappear in some later discussions:

Some effects can be brought about by God, although not in virtue of the inherent natures of things. We do not concede that God can bring it about that the same thing should simultaneously be a man and an ass, or (*aut*) simultaneously be black and white, because [God] cannot deny himself, or do anything against himself. And he would be doing something against his wisdom and ordering and goodness by which he

---

[11] For William's life and work see J. Ribailler in the Introduction Générale (1987), 3–24, of the Ribailler edn. of the *Summa aurea* of William of Auxerre; and the works referred to there, esp. Ribailler's own art. in *Dict de Spiritualité*. C. Ottaviano, *Guglielmo d'Auxerre († 1231): La vita, le opere, il pensiero* [Rome, 1930], 151 pp., and W. Principe, *William of Auxerre's Theology of the Hypostatic Union* (Toronto, 1963), 322 pp., provide background. For bibliography see all of these, and Jules A. de St Pierre in *RTAM* 33 (1966), 147–55. The Ribailler edn. appeared between 1982 and 1987 from Quaracchi, in 5 volumes.

[12] Nos ergo propriis rationibus rerum naturalium non innitemur, sed ex theologicis rationibus et consonis rebus de quibus loquimur circa res negotiabimur. (*Summa aurea*, ed. Ribailler, 1 (1980), 20.)

has best disposed all things, if he were to bring it about that the same thing should be a man and an ass. (Ed. Ribailler, 1 (1980), 205.)

Note that it is the wisdom etc. *qua optime omnia disposuit* which is in question in the contrariety envisaged: not the divine nature. Given William's declared intent for maintaining a Negative Theology, we should hardly look for anything else anyway.

In ch. 5 of the same Tractate 11 he addresses the question whether God could damn Peter and save Judas, and in particular an objection mounted on Augustine's gloss on Gen. 19: 22, where the angel is saying to Lot: 'I cannot do any thing till thou go in thither'. Augustine had added the gloss: 'I can *de potentia*, but I cannot *de iustitia*'. The objection then runs: 'Therefore God can do many things *de potentia* which he cannot do *de iustitia*; therefore although *de iustitia* he cannot damn Peter and save Judas, he can do so *de potentia*; therefore he can *simpliciter*' (p. 211). To this William replies:

we say that God *de potentia pure considerata* can damn Peter, with respect to the power of God and the natural power of Peter by which he was able to sin and not sin. But 'Therefore he can damn Peter' does not follow, because this verb *potest* in the conclusion has reference to merits.[13]

To appreciate William's rather dense reply, we may consider a related objection and reply, which omit some complications referred to in the reply just quoted. The related objection had run:

God could not have punished the Sodomites eternally, save in goodness; therefore he could not have done so, save justly; therefore whatever he could have done there *de potentia*, he could have done there *de iustitia*. (*Summa aurea* ed. Ribailler, 1: 213.)

William rejects the consequence 'whatever he could have done there *de potentia*, he could have done there *de iustitia*', because when 'whatever God can do' is being said in the conclusion of the objection, the 'can do' is being understood to express both that the thing envisaged is, abstractly speaking, of a content such as to be instantiated by God, and that it is ordered to be

---

[13] Ad primo obiectum dicimus quod deus de potentia pure considerata potest damnare Petrum habito respectu ad potentiam dei et potentiam Petri naturalem qua potuit peccare et non peccare. Sed non sequitur: ergo potuit damnare Petrum; quia hoc verbum 'potest' in conclusione respicit merita. (*Summa*, ed. Ribailler, 1 (1980), 212.)

instantiated in extra-mental reality, whereas when 'whatever God can do *de potentia*' is being said in the premiss, the 'can do *de potentia*' is being understood to express only that the thing envisaged is, abstractly speaking, of a content such as to be instantiated by God; prescinding from whether or not it is ordered for instantiation in extra-mental reality. The notion of divine power relied on in the premiss is not the one the conclusion demands, and the argument (as William notes, in the terminology of the *De sophisticis elenchis*) exhibits the 'fallacy' of *Secundum quid et simpliciter*.

That account omits some interpretative steps, and in particular speaks of existence in extra-mental reality where William speaks of *bonitas*. It is, however, the *bonitas* of Avicennian usage which is in question, the *bonitas* of actual existence: even though the objector is playing on the susceptibility of *bonitas* to other senses, in his step 'God could not have punished the Sodomites eternally, save in goodness'.

In William's reply to the objection quoted above, about damning Peter, a similar fallacy is being detected. The objection had run: God can *de potentia* damn Peter, therefore he can damn Peter *simpliciter*. William spells out just how he is prepared to allow the premiss:

we say that God *de potentia pure considerata* can damn Peter, with respect to the power of God and the natural power of Peter by which he was able to sin and not sin.

The adverbial phrase 'with respect to the power of God . . . and not sin' should be seen to be modifying 'we say': indicating that the assertion used in the premiss is being made *cum determinatione*, and spelling out the determination. As in the objection about the Sodomites, the 'power of God' in question is none other than God's option-neutral power, whose object is some or other abstract content. In the present case, there is nothing in the notion of the damnation of someone with Peter's descriptive characteristics to imply that it cannot be done by God; and there is no difficulty about those characteristics including 'the natural power of Peter by which he was able to sin and not to sin'. Pelagianism-watchers may like to note that there is nothing sinister in that: actual sinning cannot be done without actually choosing to do or not do something or other. To make the premiss true in the sense in which William is prepared to accept it, no more than the weaker, abstract notion of divine power (and, for that matter, of the creaturely power referred to) is required. What this amounts to is that 'damn Peter' in the premiss is being taken in an etiolated, merely descriptive sense: equivalent to maintaining someone of Peter's description at an infernal temperature in perpetuity.

In the conclusion, however, 'the verb *potest* has reference to merits'. In 'God can damn Peter', asserted *absque determinatione*, 'damn Peter' has its full force, which William is apparently taking to imply a reference to merits which is not part of its descriptive content. Intrinsic contents of envisaged performances may well be adjudged meritorious, but only on the strength of being descriptively such as to be pronounced actually meritorious (on the criteria used) if executed. Intrinsic contents of performances are thus meritorious only by some kind of analogy. Actual merit is attached or refused to actual performances. 'Damn Peter', therefore, in the conclusion, is to be taken as implying a reference to actual performances, items of the actual order of things. There is no damnation, sans phrase, without a reference to merit, and no merit sans phrase other than in relation to items of the actual order of things (which, as William and other schoolmen supposed, is the only order of things).

If Peter's performances in the actual order of things are in fact meritorious—stand in a particular relation to the merits of Christ[14]—as William evidently takes them to be, then Peter's being actually damned is not possible to be true, and 'God can damn Peter' (asserted *absque determinatione*) is false. Once more, though in a different manner, there is a fallacious process from a premiss using a weak notion of 'can damn Peter' to a conclusion using a stronger one.

If this is even broadly correct, we already have from William of Auxerre, before 1230 and perhaps considerably before, re-cognisable use of the Power Distinction, and an appreciation of how it worked dialectically.

1. Both arms were seen as having the form of *cum determinatione* assertions.
2. The determination in the option-neutral arm—whether

---

[14] Cf. *Summa aurea*, Bk. 3, tr. 7, ch. 3, ed. Ribailler, 3/1, (1986), 102.

expressed as *de potentia pure considerata*, or as *de potentia* (in the terminology owed to Augustine)—was a weakening (*diminuens*) determination: so that from 'God can *de potentia pura considerata* ___', a conclusion of the form 'God can ___', *absque determinatione*, could not safely be drawn.

3. The nature of the 'weakening' was that when the determinant *de potentia*, or *de potentia pure considerata*, understood as intended by William, was used to make an assertion of the form 'God can *de potentia* ___', that assertion might be made true so long as the expression to be put in the slot stood for something intrinsically capable of being brought about by God, whether or not it ever would be: and from such an assertion, made true in such a way, 'God can ___' *absque determinatione* could not safely be drawn.

4. In the option-tied arm William used the determinant *de iustitia* and implied a determinant *habito respectu ad merita*, in just the way in which *de potentia ordinata dei* came to be used, i.e. so as to permit 'God can ___' sans phrase to be drawn from 'God can in option-tied power ___'.

I would add a remark of more general bearing. Both in the Middle Ages and in more modern times it has often been suggested—taken for granted, at times—that the Power Distinction is not essentially different from the distinction made in the contrasting determinants *de potentia/iustitia*, which goes back at least as far as Augustine. I have yet to see an entirely convincing argument for identification, and continue throughout the present book to treat it as an open question. Yet the passage from William's *Summa aurea* which has just been seen, does seem to confirm that at least by William's day the distinction using the determinants *de potentia/iustitia dei* was being used essentially as the Power Distinction, however expressed, was to be used in the period covered by this book.

William uses the Power Distinction (again), in a question in Book 4 of the *Summa aurea* in which it is the power seen as ordered in the sacraments of the Church which is under discussion. This is more readily recognisable as a use of the Distinction, and concerns a power which is manifestly to be seen as a sub-system of *potentia ordinata dei*. Yet William's use is less clearly and, it seems to me, less knowingly made than Geoffrey of Poitiers's had been.

Specifically, what is at issue is the identity of the power in virtue of which humans are baptised. St Augustine had asserted that Christ, had he wished, could have given power (*potestatem*) to some servant of his, transferring to that servant as much power to baptise as Christ had received from God. Christ could have given such power to his servants, Augustine continued, but had not wished to do so: *Et potuit hanc potestatem dare, et noluit* (*In Ioann.*, PL 35; 1417). Since the option-neutral arm of the Power Distinction concerns precisely something which God could provide, but may not wish to, the issue would seem an inviting one for users of the Distinction.

William of Auxerre's problem here is to identify this power which, as Augustine had maintained, Christ could have given to others, but had not wished to give. He eliminates a number of candidates, whose names I list, but whose content or import does not need to be known, for present purposes. The power could not have been the *potestas primae auctoritatis*, since that cannot but belong to God alone. It was not the *potestas invocationis*, such that, had he given it to (say) Peter, baptisers would have been saying 'I baptise you in the name of Peter', which God had not given to anyone. It was not the *potestas ministerii*, given not only to priests but to anyone to use in a case of necessity. (Since it had been so widely bestowed, it was manifestly not a power which Christ had been unwilling to give to people.) This left two possibilities entertained by William. The first was the *potestas excellentiae*, in virtue of which—according to the supposition of some—a holier baptiser could give a greater grace. The second was the *potestas cooperationis*, by which a man might co-operate with God in baptising, in something of the way in which people in utilitarians' puzzles co-operate with their fellows in pushing cars over the brows of hills (or in calculating agonisingly about not doing so). These last two powers had been the favoured candidates of Peter Lombard and the *Glossa ordinaria* respectively. William argues that, despite appearances, *potestas cooperationis* is a worthy candidate; and it is precisely in order to explain just how this *potestas cooperationis* can indeed be a power which Christ could have given to his servants, but was unwilling to, that William arguably appeals to the Power Distinction:

To this we say that God could out of his own power (*potuit de potentia sua*) have given this kind of power [*p. cooperationis*], but was not able to do so out of option-tied power (*sed non potuit de potentia ordinata*). Just as he can out of power (*potest de potentia*) save Judas, but cannot out of the just power (*de iusta potentia*); and [just as] he could have (*posset*) punished someone to the extent to which he merited punishment—he could have, insofar as [the 'could have' is restricted by] 'out of power', but could not have done so out of the merciful power (*non posset de misericordi potentia*); so likewise he could have given this kind of power [*p. cooperationis*] out of power (*potuit . . . de potentia*), but could not have given it out of option-tied power (*non potuit de potentia ordinata*). (*Summa aurea*, Bk. 4 [= *Spicilegium Bonaventurianum*, 19] tr. 5, ch. 2 qu. 2, ed. Ribailler (1985), 90–1.)[15]

'The just power' and 'the merciful power' alike are to be understood there as definite descriptions, and holding of the same thing: the actual order of things or *ordinatio dei*, which was also the referent for 'God's option-tied power' (*potentia ordinata dei*). The phrases mean (signify) very different things out of context, of course, but are to be understood as standing for the same thing, having the same *suppositio*, in the contexts in question; presenting the actual order of things to us in different lights.

Of course it is likely to sound odd to us, to hear someone say (*a*) 'God has damned *x* out of the merciful power', or (*b*) 'God has given *y* more than his deserts out of the just power'. The oddness arises because 'just' and 'merciful' have their familiar senses, the ones which are less likely to sound odd to us, from application to the doings of humans. It would be reason for concern if such words did not sound odd, when transferred to contentions about God's doings. For to the extent that they did not, they would be liable to mislead us, when transferred to God's doings, by encouraging dangerous fancies on our part.

We might reasonably wish to resist *saying* such things as (*a*) or (*b*); but our reasonable grounds are linguistic, stylistic, concerning the manner of expression. Neither (*a*) nor (*b*), with 'just power' and 'merciful power' understood in the manner explained, can reasonably be resisted on grounds of truth and falsehood, by one

[15] Ad hoc dicimus quod deus potuit de potentia sua dare huiusmodi potentiam, sed non potuit de potentia ordinata. Sicut potest de potentia salvare Iudam, sed non potest de iusta potentia. Et posset aliquem punire quantumcumque meruit: posset inquantum de potentia, sed non posset de misericordi potentia. Similiter potuit dare de potentia huiusmodi potentiam, sed non potuit de potentia ordinata. (*Summa aurea*, Bk. 4, tr. 5, ch. 2, qu. 2, ed. Ribailler (1985), 90–1.)

accepting the (fairly standard) doctrine involved. Whether we view someone's damnation, or his being favoured gratuitously, as the sort of thing we might be inclined to call merciful, just, or whatever, is beside that point. If it is part of the *ordinatio dei* then, however we may or may not be inclined to view it, (*a*), (*b*), or like assertions, will hold true on the meanings given.

Of course this calls into question excessive reliance on even Scriptural ways of describing God's doings, understood in ways which, placed as we are, we can hardly avoid having, from our experience of the doings of the humans around us. But any prudent and honest theologians will be disposed to welcome this, just as they might be led by Negative Theology considerations into avoiding excessive reliance on even Scriptural ways of speaking about God, understood likewise in the light of our experience. (We may think of the various figures applied to God in which he is spoken of as a forest fire, as a cuckolded husband, as an expanse of dry rot...) William of Auxerre's own uneasiness over the free use of 'just' and 'merciful' in connection with God's doings has already been noted.[16]

That uneasiness is not the least of William's contributions to retain. Others are his clear declaration of a Negative Theology policy—which to some extent makes the uneasiness understandable—and his terminology. William's uses of the Distinction, as I take both the passages mentioned to represent, are the first to be encountered here to show the phrase *de potentia ordinata (dei)*. Geoffrey of Poitiers had used *de potentia conditionali* for the same purpose. (*Conditio*, from *condere*, had long been widely used as a synonym for *ordinatio (dei)*, and play had sometimes been made on the accident that *conditio* served as the noun both from *condere* and from *condicere*, and in turn permitted two related

---

[16] William's wish to take 'omnipotence', or its Latin equivalents, non-relationally may also have to do with his Negative Theology policy. Unlike knowledge of all things, he said, which the (human) soul as such is open to, and could therefore be given to Christ, omnipotence is proper to God: 'omnipotentia proprium est dei'. (*Summa aurea*, Bk. 4, ed. Ribailler, 4, 89.) William's definition of omnipotence, amending Augustine's, is worth noting: 'Sed melius dicendum est quod deus est omnipotens, quia potest facere ex se et per se quicquid vult facere. Et per hoc quod dicitur "quicquid" intelligitur ampliatio potentiae quae non est determinata ad aliquem effectum, sicut potestas calefaciendi determinata est ad calefacere. Per hoc quod dicitur "ex se et per se" removentur tria, scil. indigentia auxilii extrinseci, et coactio, et impedimentum extrinsecum. Si enim posset impediri vel cogi, vel indigeret auxilio, non esset omnipotens.' (*Summa aurea*, ed. Ribailler, 4, 215.)

senses for *conditionalis.*) On the other hand, William retains *de potentia* for the option-neutral arm: his real unease appears to have been with *de iustitia*, or *de iusta potentia*, or *de misericordi potentia*, for the option-tied arm. He does not follow Geoffrey in the latter's *de potestate absoluta* for the option-neutral arm.

Philip the Chancellor (d. 1236)

5.   Philip was respected among theologians in his own day, and is being respected increasingly by theologians in ours. In the Renaissance, however, his fame was in decline, and between 1523 and 1927 his very identity was confounded with that of Philip de Grève (d. around 1222). The Philip whose views are examined here was very much alive for years after that.[17] He was the son of a priest, an archdeacon of Paris, and became Chancellor in 1217. The role of chancellor which Philip exercised was an ecclesiastical, not an academic one, and was a working role. It is not to be confused with that of the figure of eminence whose office is not so much to do as to be in certain modern universities: where he is expected to move in mysterious ways for the university's good, to epiphanise on important occasions in the university's life, but not as a rule to take a hand in its internal polity. The ecclesiastical chancellor, Philip's sort, is a dignitary of the cathedral chapter, which is the custodian of the traditions and the material property of the diocese.[18] It is because

[17] For Philip's life and works see the Introd. to N. Wicki (ed.), *Philippi Cancellarii parisiensis Summa de bono*, ad fidem codicum primum edita (2 vols.; Berne, 1985).

[18] Strictly speaking, two ecclesiastical roles should be distinguished: that of the bishop's chancellor, and that of the chancellor of the chapter (who was also nominated by the bishop). The older authorities indicate that Philip was the chapter's chancellor, but the conferring of the *licentia docendi* (which Philip was at times involved in) was the prerogative of the bishop, the *doctor ecclesiae*; until the universities surrogated it for themselves. The granting of the *licentia docendi* was regularly delegated by the bishop to his own (the bishop's) chancellor, and it became thought of as part of the role of (bishop's) chancellor. The role of capitular chancellor, not in evidence before the 12th cent., gained in importance pari passu with the development of academic responsibilities, and with bureaucracy generally. See J. Gaudemet, *Le gouvernement de l'Église à l'époque classique* (Paris [1978]), 126. Did William of Auvergne make a point of appointing Philip to fill both roles? Others may be able to clarify the question. In the text, I evade it, calling him 'diocesan chancellor'. The point of mentioning the possibly conflicting roles, is to help to make sense of Philip's shifts of alignment in the power struggles mentioned below; during which the University of Paris was able to consolidate its position, and the friars were able to gain access to its chairs with greater ease than might otherwise have been expected.

the chapter was also in many cases (as in Paris) the body which provided for formal instruction, in cathedral schools for example, that Philip was able to play a crucial part in the consolidation of the University, vis-à-vis other institutions of church or state; and of the Theology Faculty in which the Power Distinction was to flourish, largely in step with the Faculty itself.

In Philip's day the University of Paris was still in something of a minority as a moral person, and the (diocesan) Chancellor of Paris still had a certain oversight of the young University's teaching. It was as diocesan Chancellor, for example, that Philip came to confer the *licentia docendi* on Roland of Cremona, OP, in 1229. This sort of thing would not normally call for mention in a chapter of intellectual history, but in Roland's case it marked the entry of the friars into the establishment of the University. That entry was to prove of consequence not only to the University generally, but to the transmission of the Power Distinction within it, and beyond.

The times favoured the entrepreneurial spirit. When the bishop of a diocese is strongly entrenched, and times are tranquil, the chancellor's role is routine. The chancellor may even come to be thought of as an administrative functionary of the bishop, rather than an officer of the chapter. The prominence which Philip showed in some of the early troubles of the University no doubt came in part from his personal qualities. But we ought not to overlook the rapid succession of short-lived bishops in the period, and the repeated contests in which the Bishop, the Chapter, the Pope, the King and the populace all took a part, in varying alignments.

In the disputes over (in effect) the institutional autonomy of the University vis-à-vis the Diocese, Philip not surprisingly opposed the masters and scholars in 1219. After a fairly general strike in the University, Pope Honorius III intervened against him. Disputes of the sort continued, and in 1229 the Parisian police—the 'savage police of a savage city', commented Hastings Rashdall, in an untypically energetic aside—killed a student, after a brawl involving townspeople. The latter may have had some justice on their side, and it could be a mistake to carry Rashdall's view too far, and imagine the deed as CRS thuggery *avant la lettre*. Philip intervened this time on the side of the University: but since it was also, this time, the side of clerical

privilege vis-à-vis the powers of the secular police, no great
change of heart need be ascribed to him. It meant, however,
that he was also opposing the Pope and, more particularly,
William of Auvergne, Bishop of Paris. Since the Pope had just
appointed William bishop against the wishes of the Chapter,
including Philip, that is not surprising either.

At the same time he was one of those who remained in Paris,
after the massive withdrawal of students and masters in protest
against what had been going on. And he was among those who
made efforts to persuade those who had left Paris for Orleans,
to return. This was in line with an apparent desire on his part,
which was also in the Chapter's interest, to preserve Paris as the
important centre of studies it had become. The same desire can
be seen in his contemporary moves to introduce the friars into
the establishment of the University. Whether that was altogether
in the Chapter's interest can be argued in more than one way.

Yet the moves to ease the way for the friars may also have
gone some way to easing the friction between the Chancellor
and the new Bishop. The latter, William of Auvergne, was eager
to bring the instruction of the clergy within structures which he
was doubtless more confident of being able to control, than the
creation of the Masters which had grown so robustly within his
cathedral city—and with a stronger tradition of independent
academic standards than many bishops (and secular governors)
seem to find welcome. Gilson drew attention to one source and
precedent for the kind of independent standards in question:
'Abelard's influence was momentous. . . . Abelard imposed, so to
speak, an intellectual standard which no one thenceforth cared
to lower.' Gilson is surely correct there, and perhaps also in what
he added: 'The history of mediaeval theology would show this
much better than the history of mediaeval philosophy, for if he
himself was somewhat unfortunate in this domain, the illustrious
disciples who took up and continued his work witness to the
fecundity of the new spirit he had brought to it' (É. Gilson,
History (1955), 163). From William of Auvergne's point of view
the friars could well have looked like an instrument for smuggling
the supposedly more meditative and controllable studies of the
cloisters into the schools. There were times when some of them
claimed as much—most notably around the time of Bonaventure's campaigns against the independent, philosophical spirit

of admirers of Averroes, towards the end of the period considered in this book. But in general they proved rather to institutionalise the exploratory, stravaguing spirit of the Masters; often settling, like the Masters, into key positions in the older structures. Out of the handful of friars mentioned below, a remarkable proportion became bishops or cardinals.

In the content of their instruction, as against the environments in which they thought it ought or ought not to be carried out, Philip and William (of Auvergne) were both among the adventurers anyway. William played an important part in introducing the metaphysics and philosophical logic of Avicenna, which makes at least one coherent account of the Power Distinction possible. Philip was a considerable innovator in his own right. In the opinion of Landgraf, he is one of the greatest theologians of any period (*Introduction* (1973), 179). He has been said to have been influential in his own day: 'Perhaps no other work of the first half of the thirteenth century exercised such a wide influence upon the theologians of the time as the *Summa de bono* of Philip the Chancellor'.[19] In the matter of the Power Distinction, which after all was one of the most striking contributions from theologians of that period to their posterity, that is simply not borne out. Despite Philip's rather impressive treatment of the Distinction, and a terminology of merit, his *Summa de bono* could have fallen dead-born from the scribe, for any trace that has survived of Philip's 'influence' in this matter of such prominence in theology from the second half of the century on. What Callus offers in support of that judgement, at the same place, may make things clear: 'The Franciscans John de la Rochelle, Alexander of Hales, the Cistercian John of Limoges ... and not a few anonymous writers borrowed from it question after question, transcribing many passages almost verbatim and faithfully following its conclusions'. What Callus is describing is literary currency: a form of influence no doubt, but not one on the strength of which 'influential' sans phrase can necessarily be said with justification. If it were, the calendar would be more influential on philosophers than the works of Plato. Incorporation of earlier literary texts was in any case part

---

[19] D. Callus, 'Philip the Chancellor and the *De anima* ascribed to Robert Grosseteste', *Med. Ren. Stud.* 1 (1941–3), 105–27, 125.

of the recognised way of doing things. This has been seen in earlier writers examined, and appears also in Philip. He copied extensively from the *Glossa* of Alexander of Hales,[20] and from the *Summa Duacensis*.[21] His own *Summa*, composed between 1225 and 1228 (Wicki 1985, Introd. 66*), depends also on William of Auxerre and on Hugh of St Cher's *De anima*, though not, it has been noted, on the latter's Sentence Commentary.[22]

It is all the more intriguing, then, that this pivotal Parisian theologian should have chosen not to follow William of Auxerre and others in precisely their ways of putting the Power Distinction; and that he himself should have been followed by few if any thirteenth-century successors in either his way of putting it, or his helpful points in explanation of it. What he had to say on it will now appear.

In Question 8 of the *Summa de bono*'s treatise on faith, ed. Wicki (1985), 2: 613–14, Philip asks whether the propositional objects of faith have to be necessary, or may be contingent. He considers, among other things, the propositional content (*dictum propositionis*) that Christ is to be made incarnate. A well-known authority from St Augustine, to the effect that 'another manner for our salvation was possible', might seem to suggest that it is not necessary but contingent that Christ was to be made incarnate. (This was part of the propositional faith supposed to have been had by Abraham.) The authority had long been commonplace in the discussions of the "necessity" of the means of redemption in which Anselm's *Cur Deus homo* had been so prominent. It has already been seen in contexts where the Power Distinction has been used.

---

[20] W. Principe, *Philip the Chancellor's Theology of the Hypostatic Union* (Toronto, 1975), 21. This is vol. 4 of *The Theology of the Hypostatic Union in the Early Thirteenth Century* (Toronto, 1963–).

[21] J.-P. Torrell, *Théorie de la prophétie et philosophie de la connaissance aux envers de 1230: La contribution d'Hughes de Saint-Cher (Ms Douai 434, Question 481). Édition critique avec introd. et commentaire* (Louvain, 1977), XL + 304 pp. (1977), pp. XIV–XV; N. Wicki, Introd. to 1985 edn. of *Summa de bono*, 64*.

[22] A. Landgraf, *Introduction* (1973), 179. W. Principe, *Philip the Chancellor* (1975), 19: 'Neither the *Summa de bono* nor the Scriptum of Hugh of St Cher show evidence of knowledge of one another: they may well have been written at the same time'. (For an alternative explanation see below, under Hugh.) Before the Wicki edn. appeared, and at a time when Victorius a Cena, *De fide, ex Summa Philippi Cancellarii (d. 1236)* (Rome, 1961), (containing a relevant passage) was otherwise not available to me, Prof. Principe kindly made his own copy available, together with valuable bibliographical commentaries.

In reply Philip distinguishes the case where 'that Christ is to be made incarnate' is taken to be the content or *dictum propositionis* of the prescriptive ordinance,

(1) It is ordained that Christ will be made incarnate,

expressible as a non-collapsably modal proposition; and the case where it is to be taken as the content of the prediction:

(2) Christ will be made incarnate,

expressible as a narrowly predicative proposition *de inesse*, and not strongly modal.

The first of the two propositions is, he says, "necessary". By that he means: non-collapsably modal, no matter whether the specific modality is necessity, possibility, impossibility, or anything else. For by 'necessary' here he is referring to the logical status of the proposition, not necessarily to its specific modality. This had been Avicenna's way too.

Avicenna had distinguished propositions into "absolute" and "necessary" ones. Absolute propositions are those which, when analysed for use in scientific demonstrations or inquiries, take the form of narrowly predicative propositions of a kind true, when true, in virtue of something which is the case in extramental reality. (Avicenna's 'absolute' propositions are thus in substance the "narrowly predicative propositions" introduced in Ch. 1 above.) Necessary propositions, which apparently cover all the other cases, are those which, when analysed, prove to be ineliminably modal. (These are in substance the "composing-apt" propositions introduced in Ch. 1.)

It becomes apparent that Philip is following Avicenna here; as in a number of other matters of philosophical logic, and of metaphysics. The prescriptive ordinance 'It is ordained that Christ is to be made incarnate' is to be understood and treated as a "necessary" proposition; the prediction that Christ will be made incarnate, as an "absolute" one in Avicennian terms. What the two have in common is (specifically) the same *dictum propositionis*, expressing the basic (descriptive or quasi-descriptive) content asserted or at least entertained in the proposition, and (correspondingly) the same *res propositionis*, 'Christ's being to be made incarnate', in virtue of which either proposition will be true, if it is true. (In the case of the modal or "necessary" proposition, it is not in virtue of this alone that it will be true, if it is true.)[23]

Now if (1) is to be understood as a "necessary" proposition, what are we to say to (2), 'Christ will be made incarnate'? We might expect this to be straightforwardly "absolute", nothing more; taking the things of extra-mental reality to be at bottom contingent, as is widely done in modern times. But this is not Philip's answer. What he says is that (2) is both contingent *secundum quid* and necessary *secundum quid*. (From neither does '(2) is necessary/contingent, sans phrase' necessarily follow.) 'Necessary' here, as he makes clear, refers directly not to the logical status of the proposition, but to the species of modality; but of course a necessary proposition in this sense is "necessary" in its logical status too.

The necessary, as a species of modality opposed to the impossible, is diversified according as the impossible is diversified. And the impossible and the possible, he continues, alike have a reference to power; either to *potentia prima sive [potentia] simpliciter*, or (*vel*) to *potentia ordinata*. This at least sounds as though Philip is bringing in semantical considerations where, from Aristotle on, the oppositions in question have usually been thought of as holding, antecedently to the choice of specific interpretations. Yet before commenting on his use of the terms just introduced, it is useful to continue with his line of argument.

In no matter which of those two ways of taking *potentia*, it goes on, 'It is necessary that Christ is going to be made incarnate' is going to be true; in so far as the original propositional content (that Christ is to be made incarnate) is taken as the one required for 'It is ordained that Christ will be made incarnate' to be true. Philip does not expatiate, which could suggest that what he has in mind is no more complicated than the following. 'That Christ is to be made incarnate' is ambiguous. Is it merely Christ's going

[23] This way of spelling out, at a "dialectical" and incompletely analysed level, differences between the logical status of "absolute" and "necessary" propositions was not uncommon in medieval times, under one set of names or another. It is worth comparing with the way deployed in more recent times for displaying—also at a "dialectical" and incompletely analysed level—how, despite logical differences between descriptive propositions and strongly evaluative ones, both types share a certain descriptive content (displayed in the "phrastic"). The medieval *res propositionis* is, I think, a notion of wider application than the Harian phrastic, but may include it. See R. M. Hare, *The Language of Morals* (1952; repr. 1964), 17 ff.

to be made incarnate, or his having to be made incarnate which is in question? If it is the latter, then it substantiates not just 'Christ will be made incarnate' (as the former does), but 'It is ordained that Christ will be made incarnate'.

In the case where 'that Christ is to be made incarnate' is being taken to represent the propositional content of 'Christ will be made incarnate' it can be considered in either of two further ways. In the first it is considered only in relation 'to the *res*': its intrinsic content or Avicennian essence, that is, is being considered in itself, prescinding from any relationships to anything extrinsic to that essence (not least, prescinding from whether it is instantiated or not in extra-mental reality). With 'Christ's going to be made incarnate' considered in that way, it is contingent that Christ will be incarnate.

In the second way of considering 'that Christ is to be made incarnate', it is considered (the intrinsic content is considered) in relation to its instantiation or non-instantiation; or in relation, as Philip puts it, to some power such that (if it is present) the "thing" (Avicennian essence in question) will be instantiated, and that (if it is not present) the "thing" will not be instantiated. This too is a way of speaking which Avicenna had used. Given the cause (the instantiating "power"), the effect (the instantiated Avicennian essence) necessarily took its place in extra-mental reality. No such cause (instantiating "power") being given, the effect (any related instantiated Avicennian essence) was impossible to be in extra-mental reality. Considered in this way, then, things which are instantiated are necessary (necessary *ab alio*, in the terminology of Avicenna's translators), things which are not are impossible (impossible *ab alio*). So of course it follows that, with 'Christ's going to be made incarnate' considered in this way, it is necessary that Christ is to be made incarnate.[24]

---

[24] The necessity there is logical necessity, as defined: Not possible not to be. The *ab alio* does not weaken the necessity, but signifies the ground on which the necessity arises: a ground which is in itself contingent on there being a *potentia ordinata*, on there being a cause given. Necessity *ab alio* is opposed to necessity *per se*, which in Avicennian usage applies only to the divine nature. There is no way in which God's Avicennian essence— if he could be imagined to have one—could be considered, prescinding from its actually being in extra-mental reality. For anything other than God, whether necessary or not (and in Avicenna's view, nothing existent was not necessary, as has been noted), such an abstract way of considering it, in its own intrinsic content only, is possible. But to purport to conceive something which might be what God is, and which might not exist, is not to conceive anything. The difficulty is at bottom one about what can be asserted without

This shows, he says, that the following argument is not valid:

The opposite of something is possible to God,
Therefore that something itself is contingent.

The premiss is not sufficient. We would need, he says, to conjoin (*a*) 'and is contingent *in subiecto sive in materia*', or (*b*) 'and is not contrary to *potentiae ordinatae*'. A case which shows (*a*) to be needed is that of the prophecy 'Ezechias is to die': 'For although its opposite was possible to God, it was not contingent, for it was necessary *in subiecto vel in materia* in the course of nature'. Ezechias was by nature mortal, so Ezechias's going to die was a natural necessity, not a contingency. It is unnecessary to add that Philip has extracted the point he needs from the Scriptural text by a deadpan exegesis whose inadequacies scarcely need elaboration. A case which shows (*b*) to be needed is precisely that of 'Christ will be made incarnate'. He emphasises that this is something whose opposite is not impossible to God, but not when it is understood as 'It is ordained that Christ will be made incarnate', and taking it that the content of that is instantiated in extra-mental reality. It is something whose opposite is not impossible to God, when we attend only to the intrinsic *exigentiam rei*: what is necessarily implied in 'Christ's going to be made incarnate', prescinding from relations to anything beyond the intrinsic *exigentiam rei*, and in particular from whether or not it is to be instantiated in extra-mental reality. Having said this, he applies it not to the earlier 'authority' from St Augustine, but to a conceptually parallel one from St Leo, which had not appeared in the question before.

Philip's argument here should be looked at a little more closely. 'Christ's going to be made incarnate', *Christum esse incarnandum*, can serve as the *res propositionis* or formal truthmaker for either of two logically diverse propositions:

self-contradiction. 'There is some F, and it is possible that there is no F' can be asserted with truth, provided that 'there being some F' can be considered in its Avicennian essence, its intrinsic content, only; and prescinding from whether or not that essence is instantiated. This can be done for anything other than God, even Aristotle's eternal spheres, which in Avicenna's view were actually perpetual, and necessary (*ab alio*). In 'there is some God', if it is to be true properly of the divine nature, there can be no *significatio* to be considered by us, only a *suppositio*. In 'It is possible that there is no God', what is being contradicted is that 'God' has any *suppositio*. When 'God' stands for a being necessary *per se*, as in Avicenna, 'There is some God, and it is possible that there is no God', can never be asserted properly, and with truth.

(1) It is ordained that Christ will be made incarnate, *and*
(2) Christ will be made incarnate.

If understood in the sense in which it serves for (1), which is to be analysed as expressing a proposition 'necessary' or 'composing-apt' in type, then 'It is necessary that Christ will be made incarnate' will be true; and 'God can bring it about that Christ will not be made incarnate' will then not come out true, no matter which sense of 'can' you may wish to use. This is unmysterious. By understanding (the English translation of) *Christum esse incarnandum* as the formal truthmaker for 'It is ordained that Christ will be made incarnate', the speaker or hearer has made it impossible from the outset for 'Christ will be made incarnate' to be made to be false, by no matter what power you may wish to mention; because, though Philip does not spell it out at this point, what is ordered by God to be, cannot not be.

There remains the second way of understanding 'Christ's going to be made incarnate', *Christum esse incarnandum*, as the truthmaker for (2), an 'absolute' or 'narrowly predicative' proposition. In this way, impossibility has not been built in from the outset by the understanding of the hearer or the speaker. It is in this second way that room appears for 'Christ will not be made incarnate' to be said to be possible to be true.

For within the second way of taking *Christum esse incarnandum*, there are two further ways, in which 'Christ's going to be made incarnate' (some event future to the speaker) can be considered. In the first of these we consider Christ's going to be made incarnate in relation only to its intrinsic content or (*seu*) *res* or (*seu*) Avicennian essence. The question then arising is: Is Christ's going to be made incarnate, taking into account only its intrinsic content, something of a sort which is possible to be brought about by some sort of power which it is not false (or worse) to ascribe to God? The answer here will be, Yes; just as it would be, No, on the criteria to be understood, to the question, Is this circle's going to be squared, taking into account only its intrinsic content, something of a sort which is possible to be brought about by some sort of power which it is not false (or worse) to ascribe to God?

It is fairly clear that Philip's first way of taking 'Christ's going to be made incarnate' is in effect as a name, which cannot be successfully applied, unless the event of that description is going to occur. The logical impasse ensuing is only to be expected.

Philip's second way of taking 'Christ's going to be incarnate' is in effect as a description of a certain kind of event, a *res* with a determinate intrinsic content. Something of such a kind can be said to be possible to be, provided its intrinsic description does not necessarily involve self-contradiction, and whether or not any event of the kind is going to occur. This abstract way of understanding phrases like 'Christ's going to be made incarnate' is precisely the way needed, if a distinction of the general kind of the Power Distinction is to be had, and is ever to be usable without logical absurdity.

Philip's further two ways of considering Christ's going to be made incarnate, within the abstract way of taking the phrase, are precisely the ways distinguished in the Power Distinction.

In Philip the Chancellor's Tractate on Faith, from between 1225 and 1228, is thus to be found a clearly expressed use of the Power Distinction. Of interest is his terminology. The "determinations" of *potest* in *Deus potest___* would seem to have been expressed in more than one way. One is: [*secundum*] *quod habet comparationem ... ad res*, for the determination in the option-neutral arm, contrasting with [*secundum quod habet comparationem*] *ad potentiam ordinatam*. Another is *de ordinatione quae est secundum exigentiam rei*, in the option-neutral arm, contrasting with *de ordinatione divina* in the option-tied arm.

William of Auvergne (d. 1249)?

6.　William long outlived the users of the Distinction examined already. But the text examined now is from a work said by its editor to have been composed around 1223: before Philip's contribution, therefore, and perhaps before that of William of Auxerre. William of Auvergne's contribution is not beyond cavil a use rather than an anticipation of the Distinction. It is plainly addressed to the same problématique, however, and is at the very least providing the material for a distinction of the same genre. For both those reasons it is already worth marking.

Born at Aurillac around 1180, William of Auvergne was a canon of Paris by 1223, master of theology there in 1225, and ordained priest in 1228. In the same year he was consecrated bishop and appointed to Paris, against the wishes of the Chapter. After the *événements* of 1229 William supported the Regent and the police against the University and the Pope. Both he and Philip the Chancellor were compeared at Rome over the affair, for discussions in which the University and the new King were also represented: the latter by William of Auxerre, whose use of the Power Distinction has been seen. As was noted above, one result of the Roman discussions was the bull which became in effect the charter of the University. As a bishop, William is remembered for a number of condemnations, most notably of the Talmud, which was condemned in both 1240 and 1248.[25]

William is disconcerting to read. His technical language owes much to translations from Islamic sources, not least from Avicenna, whom he evidently admired. Much of that language was not taken up by those who came after him, even if they were taking up essentially the same notions. This makes him difficult to follow, even by readers familiar with the more common parts of the logical and dialectical terminology of the twelfth century, and the more enduring metaphysical terminology of the later thirteenth century. His florid and exuberant style, with an abundance of vivid (not to say rococo) imagery, aggravates the difficulties for many readers. Yet he expounds his thought systematically, with a particularly praiseworthy exposition of some of his philosophical logic, and metaphysics, at the very beginning of the first tractate of his main work, the *Magisterium divinale* ('theological instruction'). With much of his work, this is still only beginning to receive the serious attention it merits.

The passage germane to present purposes is from that first tractate, *De Trinitate*, of the *Magisterium Divinale* (ed. B. Switalski (Toronto, 1976)). Perhaps significantly, it appears only in the Vatican Borghese manuscript, which in the judgement of its editor is the "best" manuscript, though incomplete, and is independent of the others. The discrepancy between this manu-

---

[25] On William's life see A. Masnovo, 'Guglielmo d'Auvergne e l'Università di Parigi dal 1229 al 1231', *Mandonnet Festschrift*, 2, (1930), 191–232, and *Da Guglielmo d'Auvergne a san Tomaso d'Aquino* (3 vols., Milan; vol. 1, 1945), ad init.; *Dict de Spiritualité* and *DHGE* (s.v. 'Guillaume d'Auvergne'). For the MSS of William's works see B. Allard, 'Nouvelles additions et corrections au "Répertoire" de Glorieux: à propos de Guillaume d'Auvergne', *Bull. de Philosophie Médiévale*, 10–12 (1968–70), 212–24. For the *De Trinitate* see B. Switalski (ed.), *William of Auvergne De Trinitate: An Edition of the Latin Text with an Introduction* (Toronto, 1976), xii + 269 pp.

script Vb and all the others in this passage is not due simply to
a homoteleuton (as many of the differences appear to be). Does
Vb perhaps represent (the copy of) a revision of the (lost) original?
It may not quite use the Power Distinction, yet it provides a
basis for understanding it in the way in which it was already
being understood. When considering God's power (on things
extrinsic to the divine nature), William distinguishes two ways of
considering this *posse primi potentis*. It is not enough, he says, to
say that it is *posse in mundum* or *posse in universum*.[26] It is needful to
distinguish:

(1) posse ... in universum quod est, *and*
(2) posse ... in universum simpliciter.

In (1) we understand 'everything' (*universum*) as *universum hoc*,
everything there actually is. In (2) we understand 'everything'
simpliciter et in universali. In the latter case our understanding
concerns 'everything which is intrinsically possible', *de universo
quod est possibile in se*; and in that case the *primus potens* is going to
have power over all that is intrinsically possible, is going to be
potens super omne quod est possibile in se. In consequence, it will in
that case 'have power to create something new, which may not
depend on any of those things which are' (*De Trinitate*, ed.
Switalski 1976: 69).

By contrast, 'if someone should say that the power of the first
power-bearer is over everything which is only, then [the first
power-bearer] does not have the power to make anything new.
But that is false, because this man can generate progeny, and yet
will not generate; and there can be men from his generation,
and yet there will not be; and their souls [can] be created, and
yet they will not be created' (*De Trin.*, ed. Switalski 1976; 70).
This gives William what he needs to reply to the (Abelardian)
questions from which, on p. 69, he started this particular discussion:

a power of a certain and determinate end is tied to some [or other]
mode: either to an instrument, or to a subject by which it is drawn to
that end, just as the power of walking is in the feet, and in the other
things by which walking is accomplished, things which by their form
and nature are adapted to walking. And generally, that restriction to

[26] William appears to treat *posse in mundum, posse super mundum, posse in universum, posse
super universum*, as intersubstitutional.

any one end makes a power to have in it not to be free and unrestricted in all modes, in that beyond the end prescribed it can do nothing. Either an obstacle does that, or a lack of power. (*De Trin.*, ed. Switalski 1976; 70.)

The car climbs the hill in virtue of the power of its engine. Anything beyond that—stopping, say—is to be attributed either to a prohibens (the brakes, the steepness of the hill) or to a defect (the weakness of the engine). 'That wells of water [*fortes aquae* is presumably a happy misprint] both bubble over in plenty, and are various and many, is to be ascribed to the strength and abundance of the well; that they are rare, or few and weak, is thus to be ascribed to a defect' (same ref.).

Does William use the Power Distinction? He shows himself aware of a distinction of that general kind, perhaps the *de iustitia/potentia* distinction. This is where, at the beginning of the *De Trinitate*'s chapter 8, he has been listing the questions he intends to take up, including the one raised notoriously by Abelard, on whether God's goodness compels him to do whatever he has it in him to do, 'as men of enfeebled thought (*debilis cogitationis*) opined'. One response to this is of those who 'argue among themselves (*argumentantur*) that unless God brings about the whole of what he might be able to do or might know, it would prove him to be greedy or envious'. Some 'argue: either one thing in respect of power, or (*aut*) another thing in respect of will' (*aut aliud potentiam, aut aliud voluntatem arguunt*). It is not clear to me whether these latter are included among the former, but *aliud potentiam, aliud voluntatem* is certainly apt for expressing, if not the Distinction itself, then a distinction of the same genre. And if some of the Augustinian contributions seen already are kept in mind—*potuit, non voluit*, and *de potentia/iustitia*, notably— there is no reason why a use of the Distinction itself on the part of those referred to, should not be seen as alluded to here. Who are they, those men of 'enfeebled thought'? The position that God's goodness compels him to do whatever he has it in him to do was already widely taken to be the view of Plato in the *Timaeus* (29d–30ab), even before the passage had been given further emphasis in the later Theologies of Abelard. The word *cogitatio* suggests an allusion to the pagans of Romans 1 who 'although they knew God they did not honour him as God or give thanks to him, but they became futile in their thinking (*Vg:*

in cogitationibus suis) and their senseless minds were darkened. Claiming to be wise, they became fools...' (Rom. 1: 21–2). In view of the weight of Augustinian allusion in the context, however, and St Bernard's notorious accommodation of the verse against Abelard, to whom the view was also (albeit dubiously) ascribed, a further and unkindlier allusion is not excluded. In Augustine *cogitatio* was successfully exercised intellectual power, putting *nosse* into actual exercise. Abelard's mutilation had left him with carnal *nosse*, but no more than a *debilis cogitatio* in the relevant genre of knowledge.

In (1) and (2) above, in any case, William would at least seem to have the concepts needed for the Distinction: *posse in universum quod est* is the core of what *potest de potentia ordinata* commonly signifies; *posse in universum simpliciter*, which concerns 'everything which is possible in itself', is the core of what *potest de potentia absoluta* commonly signifies. So if he were to use these concepts in order to say something like,

(1*a*) Primum potens non est potens de posse in universum quod est creare/facere novum aliquid, quod non pendeat ex aliquo corum quae sunt, *and*

(2*a*) Primum potens est potens de posse in universum simpliciter creare/facere novum aliquid...

meaning respectively,

The first power-bearer is not capable within a power over everything actual, to create/bring about something new and such as not perhaps to depend on any one of the things which actually are, and
The first power-bearer is capable within a power over everything *simpliciter*, to create/bring about something new...

he would obtain the answers which in substance he gives on pp. 69 and 70, and would be obtaining them from materials which he had been providing at the same place. Normally there should be no hesitation in arguing that what is in question is a use of the Power Distinction, albeit in a terminology which was not generally taken up.

Moreover, what is said in the Responsio, in another terminology which hardly became current, might seem to confirm that it is the Distinction which is in question.[27] The terminology is of particular importance here, if William's points are not to be missed. Corresponding to his earlier 'power over everything actual' (*posse in universum hoc*) and for that matter to God's option-tied power, is the power he mentions here which is directed to a discernible and determinate end (*potentia certi et determinati finis*), which is tied to a determinate mode. Corresponding to his earlier 'power over everything, sans phrase' (*posse in universum simpliciter*) and to God's option-neutral power, is the 'power free and neutral vis-á-vis all determinate modes' (*potentiam ... liberam et absolutam omnibus modis*).

But anything which can be said with truth to be possible in itself, is said to be so *simpliciter*, not *cum determinatione* (William: *et non alicui, nec ad aliquem determinate*). So what is powerful in virtue of itself, and not of anything outside itself (the *potens per semetipsum*), which was earlier said by William to be correlative to the possible in itself, 'is not powerful over something in a cut-off and determinate manner, but will be powerful over the possible sans phrase (*possibile absolutum*)'. He develops his argument here, still on p. 70, and then says: Therefore absolute, primary power (*potentia absoluta prima*) is necessarily [power] over what is possible sans phrase (*possibile absolutum*), and hence is [power] over what is possible sans phrase (*possibile absolutum*).[28] 'And it is certain that this sort of thing—[the 'something new' under discussion] which does not depend in any way on the things which actually are— is possible in itself. So the first power-bearer (*primus ... potens*) has power over it', can bring it about, that is.

'The first power-bearer' (*primum potens*), like *primum ens*, is used throughout *De Trinitate*, chapter 9 to designate the divine nature. But what of the *prima potentia*, declared topic of the inquiry in chapter 9: is it that power of God to be identified with the divine nature; or is it something else?

On the one hand, William insists that the first power-bearer has to be power-bearing (*potens*) through its own self and by its own being (*per se ipsum* and *per essentiam suam*). Anything powerful otherwise than *per essentiam suam* derives its power from something

---

[27] Here, and in other places in the *De Trin.*, ought not *Redeamus et dicamus* to be read *Respondeamus ...* ?

[28] Reading '*possibile absolutum*' in both occurrences, with MSS CDTMOV, preserves William's argument.

extrinsic to itself. From this William moves to assert that the power (*posse*) of the first power-bearer is nothing other than the first power-bearer itself; and that its power (*potentia* here) is nothing other than its being (*essentia*) (p. 55). He repeats as much a little later: the *potentia* of the first power-bearer is nothing save himself (*ipse*, referred to God), and his being (*essentia*) (p. 57). Not only God's *sapientia* and *bonitas*, but whatever attributes of his there ultimately are (*quaecunque alia illius in ultimo sunt*), are to be treated likewise. This is worth noting, as it means that the three classical attributes of power, wisdom, and goodness are not being given a privileged status; and that indefinitely many other "attributes" can in principle be treated under the same strategy. What he goes on immediately to say, that unless all such attributes were something *essentialiter*, they could be neither *primae* nor *maximae*, might otherwise suggest that something positive and significant was being intended: which cannot with consistency be done within a Negative Theology approach, or indeed within any approach which is not immediately vulnerable to destructive arguments of the kind made (in my opinion, successfully) by Hume and Kant. If no set of attributes *in ultimo* is to be privileged, a merely negative understanding of William's assertion is sustainable, and could well be what needs to be understood as being in the background here.

So far, then, *prima potentia* may look as though it too (like *primum potens*) ought to be understood either as at least (*a*) a designation of the divine nature, and perhaps (*b*) nothing besides. At p. 57 it looks as though William wishes to hold not only (*a*) but (*b*), for from the position that God's power (*potentia ipsius*) is nothing other than his being (*essentia*), William goes on to argue: Nothing can get worse in virtue of its being, or bigger or smaller, so neither can [God's] power in itself (*potentia in se ipsa*). There is still nothing there (p. 57) to indicate that *potentia [dei] in se ipsa* is anything other than other designation of the divine nature.

What he then tells us is that the careful build-up has been so that we might 'know that his power to do things is over all things (*posse, super omnia*) and that he himself is the widest and strongest power to do things (*posse amplissimum et fortissimum*)' (p. 57). Since he immediately adds the gloss 'widest, towards either of the opposites, to wit bringing about or not bringing about' (*amplissimum ad utrumque oppositorum, ad facere scil. et non facere*), the suspicion already invited by *super omnia* is confirmed: William is concerned here with power to do things ad extra. Moreover the *ad utrumque oppositorum*, read with William's familiarity with Avicenna's doctrines in mind, can give a further clue. In Avicenna, only the abstract contents of things are susceptible of either being something, or not, i.e. of being instantiated, or not. The *omnia* therefore over which God's active power to do things may be understood to be, is the potential infinity of all abstract contents of intrinsically possible things: in sum, the "things" possible in God's option-neutral power, in later medievals. It should be emphasised, however, that this inference can be drawn only from conjoining the required Avicennian premisses, and although William certainly admired Avicenna he did not conjoin any such premisses here.

By p. 62, however, he is certainly talking about power to do things:

These three are one quality in the artisan, and every praiseworthy operation is out of them: power (*potestate*), wisdom (*sapientia*), and good will (*voluntate*). Of these, good will does the duty of a commander (*imperantis*), power (*potentia*) that of a servant offering an abundance of schemes susceptible of implementation (lit. 'things such as to be done', *ministrantis affluentiam operandorum*), wisdom that of the one fabricating and forming (*fabricantis et formantis*). Whence wisdom is legitimately called the artisan of all things: 'all things were made by him' (Jn. 1: 3).

At p. 64 he takes matters further:

all things lie under the primary power or mastery (*primae potestati sive dominationi*), since not anything derived from it is derived save through his good will, and not anything holds in being, save because he wills and when he wills and how he wills, and since it altogether cannot be held in check or be compelled (p. 64).

Both the language there and the emphasis on things existing by God's good will have something to tell us. In a list of senses of *potentia*, earlier in the *De Trinitate*, William drew attention to one in which 'by *potentia* is expressed a certain superiority and as it were lordly mastery' (*superioritas et velut dominatio*), which, however, is nothing save the obedience or consent of a will other [than the one professedly concerned], and is called by the widely used name *potestas*'. By this kind of power, 'what kings and others who preside can do (*possunt*), the will or obedience of subjects does (*facit*)' (pp. 49–50). William is in effect treating *potentia regis*, in the sense of *dominatio* or *potestas*, as systematically misleading. 'King Blogg has the power (*potestas*) to take the well-defended enemy citadel', a proposition in which we might express William's point, is true if and only if some obedient or consenting subject does it for him. Now in the text quoted above William alludes to this sense of power, saying that all things lie under the primary power or mastery (*primae potestati sive dominationi*). So if we again rearrange William's materials grammatically, to obtain a proposition (whether in English or in Latin), what we obtain (whether in 'The first power-bearer has power over all this actual order of things', or in 'Primum potens est potens in universum hoc') is equivalent to the option-tied arm of the Distinction; and may be true, so long as what we are to understand as "really" being true is some proposition not about the *primum potens*, but about everything there actually is in the world of the categories being willed by him to be something or other in the world of the categories. In this way it is open for what William said also about *posse in universum simpliciter* to be treated correspondingly; and for William himself to be judged able to use what is recognisably the Power Distinction, and without being committed to conflating God's option-neutral power with that power of God to be identified with the divine nature. It may be worth noting that in chapter 9 of the *De Trinitate* he uses *potentia, sapientia, bonitas* for the classical attributes, but substitutes *potestas* for *potentia* and *voluntas* for *bonitas* when speaking of God as the *artifex* of things (p. 62).

From the account just given William has not strictly been shown to be a user of the Distinction; but he has been shown to have provided elements useful to an understanding of it. Is it in substance the same understanding of it which is implied in pretty well all the uses identified and examined in this book? The reason for raising the question is not from what he says on Power Distinction matters. On that basis the identification could hardly be refused. I raise the question on account of some doubt as yet unresolved as to the nature of his views on philosophical theology generally, and on certain points of his philosophical logic. Unlike many and perhaps most of the medieval academics examined in this book he shows no predilection for a Negative Theology approach, and some indications of a view incompatible with it.

He at least seems to be taking attributes generally to be what predicates (are supposed or stipulated to) designate, much in the way regularly followed today. He sometimes seems to wish to take divine attributes in this way too, almost like a modern academic theist: speaking of God's attributes (*ea quae eius sunt*) and those of others (*ea quae aliorum sunt*), as being quite narrowly proportional to each other (*proportionalia, ut sicut est ipsum ad alia* [!]). He at least *seems* to draw inferences from the supposed content of his divine attributes: though in at least one place he explained after doing something of the sort that he had merely been providing a 'suasion' (unnecessary, he added, for the 'intelligent') in favour of what could have been said by one committed to a Negative Theology approach. He rides freely on imagery. In short his philosophical theology sounds like a rather florid version of the familiar post-deistical genre practised by most of the more analytically careful philosophical theologians today: a genre within which the Power Distinction is liable to be either superfluous or incoherent. And this is where William can be seen to part company with modern academic theism.

According to William it is needful to distinguish power over everything there actually is, and power over everything sans phrase; to distinguish

(1) posse ... in universum quod est, *and*
(2) posse ... in universum simpliciter,

and it is not incoherent to do so in the way he indicates. If something of this sort—in effect, the core of the Power Distinction—is needful, as William says, in explaining attributions to divine power, as is in question, then God does not have attributes (in the sense of what significant predicates designate). If he had, nothing of the sort outlined by William would be needful. So while I do not find an identifiable use of the Distinction in William of Auvergne, I do find the recognition of a need for something of the sort, and the logical core needed. But William's language does offer special difficulties, and what used to be called particular inquiries into certain parts of William's work will be needed before more definite judgements can be made. The 'suasion' passage in chapter 9 shows the difficulties presented to the particular inquirers, whose monographs I am prepared to await.

EARLY USE

Before 1230 the Power Distinction was already established within a circle of masters—seculars, all those who are known by name—in the Theology Faculty of the University of Paris: Geoffrey of Poitiers, William of Auxerre, some otherwise unidentified users recorded by William, and Philip the Chancellor. (The case of William of Auvergne stands a little apart.) The uses examined include the earliest uses of the Distinction to be cited so far in the literature, and all are from before 1230. Geoffrey's is from a work assigned to between 1212 and 1219 but is not itself presented as needing special introduction, and can hardly have been the earliest use. Earlier ones can still be hoped for, perhaps in Geoffrey's own commentary, whose manuscripts I have not yet been able to see. On the other hand, one text quoted more than once as containing an earlier use has been seen above not to contain a use of the Distinction.[29] Geoffrey's and Philip's uses especially reveal a more knowing understanding, in a diversity of expressions, than has hitherto been commonly expected for writers at their dates.[30] It seems now beyond cavil that the Distinction as understood by the masters examined above—in some cases not just figuratively but literally pupils of the Masters from the generations who preceded the formally organized University—is specifically the same as the one which becomes current and remains dominant for the period covered by this book. Even the 'seems' is called for only by a relative lack of contextual materials, which are more abundant for writers examined in later chapters.

Despite the intrinsic interest of some of the uses of the Distinction seen above, despite the historical interest they have today, and despite the prominence of the users in the academic

[29] The identification is argued against in Sect. 2 above.

[30] One writer who will not be surprised, but may find some independent support for his own bold thesis, has written with emphasis: 'if by "philosophy" you mean the practice of argumentation, the medieval theologians ended up by philosophising as much if not more than the "professional" philosophers. It is now an evidential truth: *analytical philosophy was born in the Middle Ages and among theologians*. The fact is that that logico-linguistic treatment of questions, that formal and critical manner of thinking was not directly the outcome of "specialised" texts: it is not to be found, first and foremost at any rate, in university lecturing on Aristotle, but is to be found in the quintessence of institutionalised theological practice—in the commentaries on the Sentences of Peter Lombard.' (A. de Libera, *Penser au Moyen Âge* (Paris [1991]), 413 pp., 152 n.)

affairs of their time, they seem to have fallen into neglect remarkably quickly. At least, the early users examined were not themselves the transmitters to whom the later currency of the Distinction is arguably due. It was not their uses, so far as would at present appear, which were the ones taken up by the later medieval writers who in turn caught the attention of historians in our century. There are reasons for all that. Some will appear in the chapter which now follows.

3

The Distinction Wins Acceptance

An essentially coherent understanding of the Power Distinction was already received within the Faculty of Theology, before the University of Paris had the support of its charter in 1231. The texts examined in the last chapter revealed that. They also revealed a pattern of use, in connection with narrowly theological puzzles of the 'But might not man's redemption have been otherwise?' variety. Yet the very earliest texts are as yet available to me only in fragments, and even those of William of Auxerre, Philip the Chancellor, and William of Auvergne appeared in a context which has become opaque. The very success of the work of those now to be examined has contributed to that.

CONTINUITIES AND BREAKS

1. As it happens, however, the texts examined in the present chapter reveal continuity with the earlier users, both in the understanding and in the use of the Distinction. These later texts have come to us with more of a context within which they can be read. It is a context to which we can have access through something of a settled tradition of use which the medievals of the present chapter were themselves establishing. The core, of their understanding and their use, was not their own. It was the one they had received from the pupils of the Masters. But it was their transmissions of the core which was to catch the attention of later generations, who were to re-evaluate the Distinction, sometimes seeing in it something of wider significance. This was in great part by giving the Distinction currency within the traditions of those powerful institutions for the transmission of cultural possessions, the orders of friars.

This was a (further) mark of continuity with their predecessors. Nearly all of those named in the last chapter had been active in creating institutions favouring consolidation of cultural innovations: the University, its Theology Faculty. The friars in the present chapter go further, more particularly, in this line. In general outlook too there is great continuity. It is true that, to a man, the early users of the Distinction were secular clerics engaged in academic work in urban centres, and that those to be examined now were just as uniformly friars, whether Dominican or Franciscan. But at this early period in the history of the friars, no great discontinuity of outlook or even of interest should be read into that. The friars were still finding and consolidating their missionary policies, and were still something of a novelty. (Dominicans attracted papal regulation from Honorius III in 1216 and 1217, Franciscans attracted the like in 1223.) The men who were becoming friars were still, often as not, men whose cultural formation had been as secular clerics. Hugh of St Cher, Roland of Cremona, and Alexander of Hales are all thought of nowadays as friars. But each one of them had already been making his way as a secular cleric. Each had been working through the Sentences, for example, under a secular master, before ever becoming a friar. In the present chapter we are thus dealing with essentially the same population as we were dealing with in the last. Socially and culturally speaking, the friars of the present chapter are practically indistinguishable from the urban seculars. The labels OP and OFM are new, but the men involved are still in important ways the pupils of the Masters.

They differed, though, in possessing an enduring institution (or so it proved to be) in which a good many of the ideals of the Masters, for good or ill, can be perpetuated more successfully than in anything else the urban seculars could then have seen, within the universities or elsewhere. They differed too, in having machinery apt for amassing cultural goods and conserving them for posterity. A religious order needs an "identity", and must "market" itself, if it is to survive long. Its interest is in giving its remarkable men their head, whether as scholars (if the order's "identity" is to be scholarly) or as goliards, if that is what is wanted. It has the means to do this: what parish priest could have afforded Aquinas's three amanuenses, for example, or a retainer for the services of one of history's great translators? What bishop has time to amass the library of even a modestly enduring convent of academic friars? Even more importantly, perhaps, a religious order has the rationale to "authorise" its members to engage wholeheartedly in such work. Even provided with the infrastructure (and the talents) available to Aquinas, it would be hard for a secular priest to overcome the feeling that his real job was to minister the Word and Sacrament as a Chaucerian Poore Persoun. A Dominican, by contrast, and a post-Bonaventure Franciscan presumably, could tell himself that a scholarly life was not a deformation of his ordained mission, but a specification of it, carried out in pious obedience, as a kind of division of ecclesiastical labour. Whether this sort of thinking is anything more than a rationalisation, and whether in the long run this sort of division of labour—or even the kind presupposed in the role of the Poore Persoun—is not just a deformation of a priestly or preaching mission anyway, is not a question for this book. More to the point, it was not a question which divided the friars of the present chapter from the urban seculars of the last. The secular masters and the friars who were at odds over the manner in which the friars were appropriating teaching posts in the University and closing them to seculars were at odds over the legitimacy of means and the desirability of detailed goals. They were at one on broader aims and on values; or where they were not, the divisions were not necessarily drawn with the friars on the one side and the seculars on the other. In the latter part of the thirteenth century, it is true, there were deeper quarrels, ostensibly on the legitimacy of alienating all property to an institution such as an order of friars. (Strictly speaking, this issue directly concerned Franciscans but not Dominicans, since the latter do not have a vow of "poverty".) Around 1230 the friars—at Paris—must often have looked like associations of urban seculars, only better supplied than their non-friarly peers with means, and protection from episcopal whimsy, to achieve precisely the kinds of thing which the urban seculars had already been trying to achieve in the University. I have rather laboured this point, not just because the differences between friars and seculars at this time have so often been exaggerated, and misrepresented in rather facile ways. (Pious, forward-looking friars; grasping, reactionary seculars.) I have laboured it because it is quite possible that the very homogeneity, in cultural terms, of the population of friars and old-style secular masters played its part in the precise way in which the Distinction won acceptance in the schools.[1]

INFLUENTIAL ADOPTERS

Roland of Cremona, OP (d. 1259, apparently)

The chronology and doings of both Roland of Cremona and Hugh of St Cher at Paris between, say, 1225 and 1232 are far from transparent, even from normally helpful Dominican sources. It is possible that that was how they were intended to be, since both Roland and Hugh played arguably crucial parts in two remarkable actions of the time in which the interests of the Dominican Order and the moral principles of its members did not seem quite to coincide: the appropriation by the order of a teaching chair in the Faculty of Theology, and the *événements* of 1229.

2. First, the *événements*. I retain the convenient word which, by its associations with the *événements* of 1968, permits non-committal reference to an untidy entanglement of cultural, political, and physical conflicts in Paris, involving students, police, citizens, authorities in church and state, ... susceptible of passionately conflicting judgements by historians. If I sometimes imply contentious judgements where space does not permit substantiation, it is usually where I have no dispute with the historians (e.g. Grabmann) on the facts they describe, but where I think that their own contentious evaluations need some rebuttal or serious questioning, and at least need to be recognised as contentious.

Both in the original tavern brawl and in the arbitrary attacks on townspeople the next day, as described by the English Chronicler Matthew of Paris, the students would appear to have been more at fault than the townspeople involved. (Matthew himself does not say as much.) An ill-considered and poorly specified order to the police to act against the students then led

---

[1] See the considerations raised (largely to purposes complementary to those of the present section) in M.-D. Chenu, 'Moines, clercs, laïcs au carrefour de la vie évangelique (XIIe siècle)', *Revue d'histoire ecclésiastique* 49 (1954), 59–89; and in Y. Congar, 'Aspects ecclésiologiques de la querelle entre mendiants et séculiers dans la seconde moitié du XIIIe siècle et le début du XIVe', *AHDLMA* 36 (1962), 35–151.

to a massacre of students by the police. Matthew castigates both the hot-headed Regent for giving the order (*muliebri praecacitate simul et impetu mentis agitata*) and the police for their eagerness to get at the students without the normal restraints. He puts this down not to frustration at the increasing numbers of students who, as clerics, were in most things protected from the ordinary police of the town, but to a CRS-type personal character: *proni erant ad omnem crudelitatem exsequendam.*[2] The Parisian authorities, civil and diocesan, rather signally failed to apply the law against the police involved, and some of the University's functionaries rather shamefully colluded in the matter. Failure to apply the law where there are prima-facie serious violations of it by those whose task is to execute the law is a serious matter in any society with pretensions to being a society abiding by the rule of law. Not surprisingly, the University of students and masters reacted strongly. They agreed to withdraw the schools from Paris, originally declaring a suspension of six years. Unwisely, the police had included among their dead victims two rich students—from Normandy and Flanders—who were subjects neither of France nor of the diocese of Paris, and opposition to the Parisian authorities was by no means purely academic. Moreover, other cities could see the advantages of having what Paris was losing.

The University's functionaries risked being held responsible for the considerable economic damage threatened by such moves, and interest lay in their seeking by any means to keep the institutional University functioning, or at least to seem to be functioning. Not just their own interest either: at least some longer-term interests of the University itself were no doubt seen to be served in the same way. There was, in other words, a large enough morally grey area to be exploited, and the Parisian authorities moved in connivance with the rump of University functionaries to exploit it, and find masters to replace those who had gone.

This is where Roland comes in. Already a master of arts of Bologna, and a Dominican, before studying at Paris, Roland had been lecturing on the Sentences under John of St Giles, and was evidently far enough advanced for Philip the Chancellor—who

---

[2] Matthew of Paris, cit. A. Masnovo, 'Guglielmo d'Auvergne e l'Università di Parigi dal 1229 al 1231', in the *Mandonnet Festschrift* (2 vols.; Paris, 1930), 2: 191–232, 192 n.

as chancellor of the chapter of Paris still had technical jurisdiction over the issuing of a licentia docendi—to authorise a licentiate for Roland in the May of 1229. In 1229–30 he was teaching as a master, the first Dominican to do so in Theology at Paris. The Dominicans may well have been preparing to appropriate a chair anyway, and the ease with which they were soon able to appropriate a second chair suggests that they need not have been without considerable support in so doing, from within the University of students and masters. But whether the Dominicans themselves saw the circumstance as a boon or a complication, it remains true that they gained their first chair by providing "scab" labour to undermine an arguably just strike over a matter of great seriousness.[3]

It is said that Roland far exceeds any of his contemporaries in the use of Aristotle and is apparently the first to use what was by then practically the whole range of Aristotle's works; that he is an early user of Alfarabi and Abumacer, drawing also on Algazel and Avicenna, but not on Averroes. It is also said that he was the first of his peers to make frequent use of the *Liber de causis* (he gave it that name, and attributed it to Aristotle); but recognised that the *Liber sex principiis* was not Aristotle's. He follows the plan and sometimes the substance of William of Auxerre's *Summa aurea*. Juridical, canonical sources were important to him: he was after all a Bologna man. He cites Stephen Langton, Peter Comestor, Hugh of St Victor, and Gilbert de la Porrée, but gives more space to Gratian, to four of the first five *Compilationes*, and to Praepositinus of Cremona. His most famous pupil was Hugh of St Cher, but it has long been known (thanks

[3] On the dates and doings in these paragraphs, some good scholars are positively evasive, and it may be wiser to follow them. O. Lottin, in *RTAM* 12 (1940), 136–43, says: 'Nous avons laissé aux dates l'imprécision résultant des divergences qui séparent les biographies récentes' [Glorep I, 1933, notices 1 and 2; E. Filthaut 1936; H. C. Scheeben 1938, ch. 4]. M. Grabmann, *I divieti* (1941), 88, refers us to A. Masnovo, *Gug. d'Auvergne* I (1930), 1–27 for an account of the *événements*. For this see now F. Van Steenberghen, *La phil. au* XIIIe s., (1991), 93–101 and refs. For Roland see also the treatments referred to in Kaeppeli, s.v. 'Rolandus', incl. H. Weisweiler, 'Théologiens de l'entourage d'Hugues de Saint-Cher', *RTAM* 8 (1936), 389–407. When Roland, after teaching just long enough at Paris to count as having been a regent master in Theology, went off to Toulouse (in the Dominicans' heartland), it may have been to put a firm Dominican hold on the new Faculty there, as much as for any other reason. (Thus M.-H. Vicaire, who also emphasises that Roland's part there should be distinguished from that of the first wave of students and masters: who had gone there in active withdrawal from Paris, after the *événements* of 1229. See ch. 5 passim of *Dominique et ses Prêcheurs* (Fribourg [1977]), vii + 444 pp.)

to Dom Odo Lottin) that in not a few places it is Hugh's
Commentary on the Sentences which is the literary source of
Roland's *Summa*, and not the other way round.[4] Neither Roland
nor Hugh appears to have used Philip the Chancellor's work (O.
Lottin in *RTAM* 11 (1930), 311 n.).

If, as Mangenot says (*Dictionnaire de Théologie catholique*, 7: 222),
Hugh was Roland's pupil in the biblical phase of the course,
there need be no mystery. Hugh, for whatever reason, had
interrupted his earlier theological studies while still a bachelor.
Even had he done so while a 'sentential bachelor' and before
qualifying to become a 'biblical bachelor', he could still have
had at least some if not all of a Sentence commentary completed,
and at least some related *exercitia*. These could be of the same
general form as the disputed questions of the master, and like
them could contain material apt for integrating into the published
version or *ordinatio* of a commentary. Might not Roland even
have interrupted his course—studying law and becoming a
Dominican—with a view to resuming it later, when an opportunity should arise for being able to complete it under a Dominican, so assuring a plausible candidate in place to retain a
Dominican succession in the chair?

Whatever may be said to that last point, there is no problem
about the literary dependencies noted as going from Hugh's
Sentence Commentary to Roland's *Summa*, and not conversely.
Hugh was Roland's bachelor in biblical study. He was not
Roland's bachelor but his senior as a lecturer on the Sentences.
Why might Hugh not have encouraged Roland to make use of
his (Hugh's) Commentary, if he wished, in order to undertake
master's classes on the Sentences without delay, even though he
might not have been planning to start doing so quite so soon? It
is known that Roland was either unable or unwilling to draw up
any *ordinatio* of his commentary before leaving Paris. If it had
contained liberal borrowings from Hugh, who was returning to
teach in Theology at Paris, Roland's decision not to produce
an *ordinatio* of his (Roland's) commentary would be entirely
understandable. The later surfacing of some of the borrowings

[4] For Roland's literary sources see C. R. Hess, 'Roland of Cremona's Place in the
Current of Thought', *Angelicum*, 45 (1968), 429–77, 429–35, and more especially G.
Cremascoli, 'La "Summa" di Rolando da Cremona: Il testo del prologo', *Studi medievali*,
ser. 3, 16 (1975), 825–76, 825–41.

in Roland's *Summa,* completed as would appear in Italy, would likewise be entirely in order by the customs of the time.

For whatever reason, Roland was not left any great time as a teacher in his Parisian chair. After barely a year, succeeded by Hugh of St Cher, he left for Toulouse and thence for Italy, where he also served as an inquisitor under both Gregory IX and Innocent IV.

3. *Roland on a question of prophecy*

Despite the master–pupil relationship of Roland and Hugh, then, which may have been little more than a tactical arrangement to safeguard a Dominican succession to Roland's chair, the use of the Distinction in Roland's *Summa* ought probably to be thought of as posterior to the ones to be considered from Hugh's Sentence Commentary. Since a probability is no more than that, I nevertheless examine Roland's use here, in its place in the conventional priority of Roland to Hugh as a master in Theology.

The difficulty Roland is considering, where he uses the Power Distinction, elegantly compounds a theological difficulty long canvassed in Christian writings, and a philosophical difficulty which held particular significance for Muslims. The first is the question whether the human race could have been redeemed otherwise than in the manner believed by Christians: a difficulty already raised in Augustine, much discussed in Anselm's day, and seen behind some of the earliest uses of the Power Distinction in Chapter 2 above. The other concerns the nature of the connection between the (veridical) revelation of a future event, and that event's being able to be said to be in itself contingent. The core of this difficulty is essentially the one to be seen in the Sea Battle (on at least one common interpretation of the passage in *De interp.*, ch. 9). Imposed on the core are human anxieties, as well as questions about the nature and trustworthiness of prophecy. Roland's statement of the difficulty opens as follows:

Some have said that the human race could not have been redeemed otherwise than it has been redeemed, because [God] showed the means of redemption to Adam when he was in an ecstasy, and he made a similar showing to the prophets... (Roland of Cremona, *Summae*, Bk. 3, par. 50, ed. Cortesi 1962: 133.)[5]

If certain events are revealed by God as going to come about, they are unavoidably going to come about, much as it may be true of events which have occurred, that they unavoidably have been.

Roland sees an equivocation in the use of 'can' in the objection. In 'God could not have redeemed the human race otherwise', the objectors could be understanding it to mean that God could not have done so *de potestate conditionata rebus*: that is, he continues, while the effect of the prophecy which he showed to the prophets remained in being, he could not have redeemed the human race otherwise. That was not, he adds, how Augustine had been taking the *potuit* in the text on which the objection had been constructed. In the place where Augustine had been saying that God could have redeemed the human race otherwise, 'he understood that the word *potuit* was to be signifying *potentiam absolutam*. And in so far as [the *potuit*] was [*potuit*] *de illa potentia absoluta*, God could indeed have redeemed the human race otherwise than he did. And if it is said that he could not, in that signification, then that negative assertion is false.'

'According to this distinction', he continues, 'we will reply to the objections. We shall therefore say that God could *de potentia* have redeemed the human race otherwise than he redeemed it.'

He accepts the point from a further objection that God is indeed *summe benignus*, but insists that the effect of his benignity (*effectum suae benignitatis*), which is what is in question in the

---

[5] Si autem ita distinguerent equivocationem in hoc verbo *potest*, aliquid viderentur dicere, ut dicerent quod Deus non potuit aliter redimere genus humanum de potestate conditionata rebus (hoc est, existente effectu prophetiae quam ostendit prophetis, non poterat aliter redimere genus humanum), ita quod li *potuit* significet huiusmodi potentiam, sive potestatem, conditionatam rebus. Et non sic accepit Augustinus hoc verbum *potuit* quando dixit quod *Deus potuit aliter redimere genus* humanum, sed intellexit quod hoc verbum *potuit* significaret potentiam absolutam. Et quantum erat de illa potentia absoluta, Deus poterat aliter redimere genus humanum; et si dicitur quod non potuit illa significatione, falsa est et illa negativa. Secundum hanc distinctionem respondebimus ad obiecta. Dicimus ergo quod Deus potuit aliter redimere genus humanum—de potentia—quam redemerit... At this point Roland turns to further matters: not so much as though forgetting to make a corresponding option-tied assertion, as though taking it that it had been covered by what he had been saying. The edition is A. Cortesi (ed.), *Summae Magistri Rolandi Cremonensis O.P. Liber Tercius*, editio princeps (Bergamo, 1962), 1401 pp.

redemption of the human race, could well have shown forth God's goodness differently: equally *convenienter*, considered in itself, even if not so *quantum ad nos*, 'for the Lord can show his benignity as he wishes'. It was false, therefore, to say, as the objector had been saying, that God could not have shown his benignity in any other way (ed. Cortesi 1962, par. 137–8). The rejection of this objection shows that Roland gives short shrift to the anxieties behind objections characteristic of deistical traditions, and would suggest a sympathy at least on Roland's part with a Negative Theology approach. When more of his *Summa* is published, it should be possible to be more apodictic.

Roland is plainly using the Power Distinction here, and is using it plainly enough. The tie between that which God can do *de potentia ordinata sua*—or *de potestate conditionata rebus*, as he puts it—and God's volitum, is expressly made. So is the fact that, in option-tied assertions, and in issues raised by such things as the manner of our redemption, it is an effect of God's which is in question. So too is that, when we contrast what can be done in God's option-tied and option-neutral power, we are talking in the option-neutral arm of 'thing' considered in abstraction from how it might appear *quantum ad nos*, no matter how crucial that might be to us.

Roland presents the Distinction as a matter of semantics, a distinction between two significations of *posse*.

1. The speaker who was saying that God could not have redeemed the human race otherwise than as he had revealed in the prophecy in question, was to be understood as taking the 'could' in such a way that 'the word "could" will be signifying... power conditioned to the things (*potestatem conditionatam rebus*)'.

It is clear enough that God's option-tied power is being referred to here; but less clear just how it is. William of Auvergne had used *potestas* or *dominatio* for a power some ruler may be said to have in relation to some effects, on condition that his subjects are prepared to produce those effects in obedience to his will. In the passage quoted Roland says:

ita quod li potuit significet huiusmodi potentiam—sive potestatem—conditionatam rebus.

His point is that this kind of *potentia*, or of *potestas* rather, is subject to the will of the ruler of all. The *rebus* in question are thus to be understood not as the ordinary things of the world around us, but their conceivable intrinsic contents or Avicennian essences. A *potestas conditionata rebus* is one which is logically posterior to the (set of) *res* in question; as indeed instantiations are to the "essences" they instantiate. A related *potentia absoluta* will not be logically posterior in that way. Just how the *potentia absoluta* mentioned here is to be thought related to (the set of) such *res*, is not pursued by Roland at this point. But the slight oddity in 'a power conditioned to the things' can, when considered with the rest of Roland's remarks, even without the prompt from William of Auvergne, point us in a useful direction.

2. The speaker who was saying with Augustine that God could have redeemed the human race otherwise, was to be understood as taking Augustine's *potuit* in such a way as to be signifying option-neutral power.

It seems to me that this way of presenting the Distinction, as being between two possible significations of *posse*, is not necessarily objectionable. It is correct as far as it needs to go in the present passage, and indeed for pretty well any occasion when no more than an initial account is called for. It arguably conceals some of what can be spelled out even on a still informal level, by presenting the Distinction as though it were a matter of semantics, as between two senses of *potuit*. This could conceal that the Distinction is better understood as a matter of pragmatics, as being between two ways of using *posse* or *posse F-ere* (in essentially the same sense, but) in contrasting *cum determinatione* assertions. Yet it does not misrepresent the Distinction completely, or exclude more explicit or more illuminating presentations. (More illuminating to the appropriate audience.) In its favour, a semantic presentation is often going to be a better way of presenting the Distinction initially to audiences who may not be au fait with the medieval rules for inferring from *cum determinatione* "predications" (in the broader, unanalysed use of the word); in other words, to most audiences, even in the thirteenth century. That Roland's own understanding of the Distinction was clear enough for practical purposes, and was standard enough for the period of this book, is confirmed by what he adds at one point: *quantum erat de potentia absoluta, Deus poterat aliter redimere genus humanum.* The outcome is exactly what is to be expected from a medieval Christian academic making a *cum determinatione* assertion with a determination referring to God's option-neutral power in that way.

4. *Further on the question of prophecy*

As though emboldened by success, Roland goes on in something of the manner of the later users of the Distinction, who so shocked some historians of the present century. He says: Even if God had done otherwise than he showed to the prophets, he would not have deceived them. He could have brought it about that the significatum in their prophecy was not that significatum which was signified (to them) in the utterance in question at the time God inspired them to make the prophecy.

The terseness of Roland's answer could make it sound more hollow than it needs to sound. In at least some cases, as medieval commentators fairly generally seem to have held, a prophecy might be not (merely) for the instruction of the prophet or the prophet's contemporaries, but for the edification of a later audience. In such cases the later audience could well have been intended ("intended" by God, as author of the message to be conveyed in the prophecy) to take from the formula in which the utterance was recorded, a signification which was not (so far as we can know) available to the prophet and his contemporaries, and which they might not have been psychologically able even to imagine. What could a seventh-century BC prophet have made of the kind of content encouraged by scenes from a medieval passion play? Yet such was doubtless often the sort of signification a medieval commentator could be expected to have. For that matter, what did Balaam's ass make of his prophecy?

Let us suppose that in such cases as Roland needs, at least one 'intention' of God's, in showing the scene to the prophet, is to lead the prophet to make an utterance permitting the later audience to understand the formula in which the utterance is recorded, as expressing *p*: some truth about the actual means of man's redemption, as understood by medieval theologians.[6] In order to do so it is at least conceivable that God could present some scene to the prophet's fancy, knowing that the prophet could not but think the scene to support that *q*, some proposition implying not-*p*, and of course false if taken as a report of the actual means of redemption, as these were later to appear. The question then arising is this. Is God in such a case

(1) deceiving the prophet,
(2) giving him a coded message for others to decode, or
(3) doing (1) by (2), or vice versa?

Roland's contention in the passage was that God is to be understood as doing (2), and not (1) or (3). It is a contention which can be disputed, and the question of whether this sort of thing ought to count as deception, like the question whether deception ought to be counted among the things God cannot do, will surface more than once in later Power Distinction discussions.

5. *A platonist understanding of option-neutral power?*

In Book 3, qu. 42 Roland addresses a question from unspecified *Philosophi*, who say that God could not have done better than he did. He has already proved this false in Book 2, he adds (p. 144). In his final reply at Book 3, qu. 42, there is an instructive contrast:

(1) manente primo proposito et prima bona voluntate, idest primo volito, de re quae primo proponebatur, *and*
(2) manente primo proposito et prima voluntate quod et quae deus est.

In (1) what is in question is the instantiation by a volitum of God's, of the instantiable *res* or Avicennian essence of something. While that volitum stands, no better thing and indeed no other thing can be done in its place, since whatever is willed by

---

[6] The supposition is one permitted by views on the "inspiration" or "divine author-ship" of the Scriptures which were widely held in medieval times. It is not necessarily one which a liberal academic exegete, prescinding from doctrinal considerations, might feel entitled to make. But Roland was quite obviously not engaged in that sort of exegesis here. The pictorial language (on divine "intentions") in this paragraph is from me, but need do no harm if it is understood as no more than pictorial. I would not impute to Roland the absurdity of ascribing intentions properly to God. Within Roland's genre of theology, God can no more have intentions than he can tell the time.

God is ineluctably and punctiliously carried through. (1) thus corresponds to *de potentia ordinata dei*, as used in the Distinction, and is in some ways more explicit.

The more intriguing phrases are in (2). Within the Augustinian tradition *voluntas dei* had long been taken as susceptible of being taken in either of two diverse ways: to designate the divine nature, or to designate some volitum of God's. Both of these ways are found in texts seen elsewhere in the present book, for example, and neither was thought to raise any special difficulties. The *voluntas quae deus est* will thus be nothing other than the divine nature. But why *propositum quod deus est?* My suggestion here is more hesitant.

A first possibility is that no more than superficial telescoping need be seen here, and that the sense of the phrase can be captured by expanding to read something like

"manente proposito quod deus est, et manente prima voluntate quae dei est, ... ",

where the scare-quotes are to indicate that the expansion is factitious, is not from Roland, and is being no more than entertained here. In the expansion, the *propositum quod deus est* can be understood as some creature's *propositum* to the effect that God exists, and the *prima voluntas* as the *primum volitum*. Against this possibility, however, is that Roland's text does not contain *dei* but only *deus*.

Another possibility is that Roland is envisaging divine activity on the model of human artifice. The *propositum* is in the first instance that which is envisaged as some set of instantiable *res* being entertained by God with a view to their instantiation or non-instantiation. The *propositum* is thus envisaged on the analogy of the *proposita* which human agents entertain and sometimes try to execute.

A complication arises when someone tries to get behind the pictorial features of the analogy. Where are the *res* or Avicennian essences supposed to be located, and what sort of existence are they supposed to have? In a number of other medievals examined in this book, the *res* in question have intentional existence merely, in the understanding of some creature.

Within a platonist view of things, however, the question of locating the *propositum* envisaged as being entertained by God, can be seen as part of a wider question, about locating Platonic Ideas generally. Within the usage of Christian theologians given to platonist ways of thinking, it had long been customary to locate the Ideas in the (eternal) knowledge of God. The *propositum* here, understood on platonist lines, will likewise be located in the (eternal) knowledge of God.

But in virtue of what was also received, quite uniformly, about divine simplicity, it will follow that the *propositum*, and the Ideas generally, will have to be identified with the divine nature. Hence, of course, the *propositum quod deus est*.

The difficulty then arising is that, since they are to be identified with the divine nature, the *res* which supposedly make up the content of the *propositum*, and the Ideas generally, are going to have to be unintelligible to us in their "real" natures precisely as the divine nature is unintelligible to us.

This permits a specification of the working notion of the Power Distinction as presented in Chapter 1 above. At that place I presented the notion of a distinction considered on a dialectical level, of regimented but not fully analysed discourse. I wish to continue thinking of the Distinction as taking its place on that level of discourse. But I left open the possibility of competing interpretations of the Distinction ('the sense(s) established in the medieval schools'), and in particular of competing interpretations of its option-neutral arm. The working notion was accordingly left with the deliberately ambiguous and incompletely specified member which ran:

(2) in abstraction from whether any such thing is to be instantiated or not in extra-mental reality, provided that such a thing is susceptible of instantiation by an unrestrictedly active power (such as was, in one way or another, attributed to God).

What Roland of Cremona can be seen to be providing, if I have not misunderstood his *propositum quod deus est*, is one way of specifying that member, to express a platonist understanding of the Distinction, using a platonist way of attributing an unrestrictedly active power to God. It is not the only understanding of the Distinction put forward in the period, and may have drawbacks to the would-be user which some non-platonist understandings of it do not have. But it can be put forward coherently, and any difficulties against its use are best left—like further analysis of the interpretation itself—to a later chapter, when comparisons can be made more instructively. It is enough here to note the hints towards a platonist interpretation provided by Roland in addition to an essentially straightforward use of the Power Distinction.

6. *Roland and the Distinction*

That he used it, is no longer in doubt. That he wished to understand it in a platonist manner, is something for scholars to test further. Even if his words should turn out not to be expressive of such a wish, they have at least the merit of alerting the reader to such a possibility.

Before leaving Roland, a word may not be out of place about his retention of the Augustinian *de potentia* for the *de potentia absoluta* which was to become standard. Whether he does so merely because others had been doing so, or as an insinuation of continuity with the *de iustitia/potentia* distinction, is not evident from his texts.

Medieval theologians were rather given to insinuating continuities between their own contributions and those of their honoured predecessors, the *sancti*. Roland and his contemporaries could have found additional reason for insinuating continuities (with patristic terminology) in one reading of Gregory IX's letter to the theologians of Paris. When Gregory intervened after the *événements*, on the side of the students and masters, he intervened in more than one direction. In one, he was in effect giving the theologians more security in academic freedom. In another, he imposed restrictions. Among these was a command to teach a theology free from 'the leaven of worldly science (*mundanae scientiae*)'. They were to avoid the 'fictions of the philosophers (*philosophorum figmentis*)' and were to be *contenti terminis a Patribus institutis* (Denzinger–Bannwart, D443). What Gregory seems to mean by that last phrase is that theologians ought to keep their speculations 'contained within the bounds established by the Fathers'. The horizon of their theology, that is, should be one within which puzzles can be resolved by appeal to Councils, to Scriptures, to opinions of the *sancti*. Theologians, in other words, were not to engage in the external questions—external to that horizon—encouraged by Abelard and by those who had been taking up his approach to theology. But word-play was not unpleasing to medieval academics, and there could well have been some satisfaction in being "content with a patristically inspired terminology", as against the new terms becoming current from Aristotelian and Muslim works.

Gregory's restrictions on the theologians of Paris appear in emphasis in his even more famous letter of 1231. They ought not to pass themselves off as philosophers, *nec philosophos se ostentent*, and only questions which can be determined by appeal to the opinions and indeed the ostensible written texts of the *sancti* are to be aired in the public disputations in the schools: *de illis tantum quaestionibus disputent quae per libros theologicos et sanctorum Patrum tractatus valeant terminari.* (Cit. Grabmann, *I divieti* (1941), 97.)

This has significant implications for the history of subsequent medieval theology. If the external questions of the new *theologia* are not to be treated openly in the Theology Faculty, they are going to have to be treated in Arts. For even if they did not arise—as they do—from any thorough enough inquiries into the already traditional questions of positive theology, they could hardly have been left unasked by the sophisticated non-Christians envisaged in, say, Aquinas's *Summa contra Gentiles*, who were very much a part of the culture within which the medieval academics worked. That such questions ought to have been left to the Arts men had an older precedent in its favour. In the earlier twelfth century, as has been thought worth remarking, there is almost no trace of treatises *De deo* of the kind so prominent in post-Reformation treatises, and indeed in the thirteenth century. The *opus conditionis* was for study in secular science, the theologians' proper concern was the *opus redemptionis*.[7] It is easy to miss the novelty of the whole genre of theology in which the Power Distinction played a central part, and its expansionism into traditional Arts areas. In warning theologians off "worldly science", Gregory was in effect calling on them to abandon the very genre of theology in which the Theology Faculty of Paris had so much excelled (and was for a time to continue to excel) in the period of its greatest flowering.

Gregory's letter of 1231, therefore, counts not only as a charter

[7] See H. Cloes, 'La Systématisation théologique pendant la première moitié du XIIe siècle', *Ephemerides theologicae lovanienses*, 34 (1958), 277–329. On the *opus conditionis* as the preserve of the secular inquirer, see esp. pp. 318–19.

for the University, and as a protection for its theologians. It ought to be seen as something of a charter to the Arts Faculty, inviting it to reclaim the study of the *opus conditionis*, which the theologians—stimulated not least by Abelard and by the influx of muslim theology—had so exuberated in from the earliest years of their Faculty's existence. It in effect charged the Arts men with the fundamental questions of "philosophical" as against positively "doctrinal" theology. It is only fair to add that it was not perceived in that way at the time; and even Grabmann, who missed little, did not advert to these consequences in the place in *I divieti* where he treated Gregory's letter. It may have encouraged people to remain teaching in Arts well into their maturity, though this was still thought unusual enough when Ockham did it. It was a well-established practice by Buridan's day, but by then there were motives for it, independent of any narrow connection with Gregory's letter.

Hugh of St Cher, OP (d. 18 Mar 1263)

7. Born at St Chief, near Vienne, Hugh was already a doctor of laws of Paris and a bachelor in theology there when he became a Dominican in 1226. He succeeded Roland of Cremona in the first Dominican-held chair of theology at Paris; like him, he was to continue lecturing on the Sentences after becoming a master. In due course, moved out of teaching and into ecclesiastical management, he became the first Dominican to be created cardinal, and served for a time as papal legate in Germany. This did not lead to total neglect of either academic or Dominican interests. It was in his time as legate that he played a crucial part in persuading the order to send Aquinas to Paris, as Albert the Great had been urging; and in persuading the University to accept both Aquinas and Bonaventure in a politic "double ticket", in dubious circumstances and a frankly irregular manner.[8]

As a philosophical theologian Hugh produced work worth

[8] For works by and on Hugh see Kaeppeli, *Scriptores Ordinis Praedicatorum Medii Aevi* (3 vols.; Rome, 1970–80); vol. 2 (1975), 269–81, and the bibliographies in W. H. Principe, *The Theology of the Hypostatic Union in the Early Thirteenth Century*, III. *Hugh of St Cher's Theology of Hypostatic Union* (Toronto, 1970); and J.-P. Torrell, *Théorie de la prophétie et philosophie de la connaissance aux envers de 1230: La contribution d'Hugues de Saint-Cher (Ms Douai 434, Question 481): Édition critique avec introd. et commentaire* (Louvain, 1977), XL + 304 pp.

attention in its own right, not just for its historical interest. In systematic theology the main works are his Commentary on the Sentences (1231–2, says Kaeppeli); an abbreviation of the same which once passed for an early draft; and some *Quaestiones disputatae*. Hugh's integration of disputed questions into the body of the Commentary was still unusual enough to attract remarks from historians. Largely for this reason it has been thought to mark a new phase in the development of the Sentence commentary as a genre,[9] but as was noted apropos of William of Auxerre, it is the latter who was credited with the innovation by a contemporary or near contemporary. In Hugh's case the development was attractive because, unlike most of his predecessors, he had come to lecturing on the Sentences not merely as a stage in his formation as a recognised teacher, but after earlier studies as a secular cleric in both theology and law. With some quantities of material in readiness, and the occasion to use it (as was seen above, apropos of Roland of Cremona), Hugh would have been remiss not to have taken the step, whether or not he had the model of William of Auxerre in view. That the developed, question-integrating style of Sentence commentary became the norm (after a gap of some years) is not hard to understand. The standards of teaching in Theology were by then already beginning to be set by friars, as they appropriated more and more teaching chairs. Friars were regularly provided with a trial run of teaching in their own schools before teaching within the Faculty, so they too were being provided with opportunities to develop discussions on theological topics before lecturing on the Sentences within the Faculty. It seems to me that this is one of the genuine benefits to be ascribed to the "friarisation" of teaching in the Theology Faculty.

8. *Damning Peter, saving Judas*

Hugh introduces the Distinction in *In 1 Sent.*, d. 42, the first of three 'distinctions' on divine power which in Lombard contain the Abelardian treatise on divine power. It is not in connection with any of the Abelardian questions, however, that he introduces

---

[9] Thus J. Fisher, 'Hugh of St Cher and the Development of the Sentence Commentary as a Genre', *Spec.* 31 (1956), 57–69.

it. It is in reply to an objection raised from a comment in the
Glossa on 2 Tim. 2: 13, which had seemed to imply that 'God
can damn Peter and save Judas' was to be held false. The passage
is worth quoting in full, and I translate fairly literally to begin
with, to draw attention to some expressions which might not at
first suggest that it is the Power Distinction which is in question:

> To the third [objection] we say that the power of God is twofold, that
> is, is asserted (*dicitur*) in two ways, as absolute (*absoluta*), and conditioned
> (*conditionata*). Absolute power (*potentia absoluta*) is that very power con-
> sidered in itself. By this power, [God] has in himself power over all
> things, even to damn Peter and save Judas, and so on. 'Conditioned
> power' of this sort is asserted in so far as it refers to the condition or
> law which God in his goodness has laid upon things. While this
> condition or law remains in force, God cannot do the contrary [of
> what he is doing by the 'conditioned power']. And he would be doing
> that if he were to damn Peter and save Judas, because the truth and
> justice of God demands that Peter should have eternal life, and Judas
> eternal punishment. For this is the law laid down (*lex data*) by God,
> that he should reward the good and punish the wicked. This 'con-
> ditioned power' the *Glossa* on Gen. 19, where it concerns Lot, calls
> 'justice'. (*In 1 Sent.*, d. 42, qu. 1, ed. Randi 1984: 534.)[10]

1. There are two ways in which God may be asserted to be
   able to do things. Hugh spells this out in *idest dupliciter dicitur*,
   obviating any 'two powers in God' nonsense.
2. Asserting God's power as absolute, is asserting that God
   can do so and so, in so far as doing so and so is being
   considered in itself, and prescinding from whether so and
   so is or is not to be done in the actual order of things.

It is thus an assertion made *cum determinatione*, with a deter-

---

[10] E. Randi, 'Potentia dei conditionata: Una questione di Ugo di Saint Cher sull'onnipotenza divina (*Sent. 1*, d. 42, q. 1)', *Rivista di storia della filosofia*, 39 (1984), 521–36, 534.
Besides an edition of this important text, the article contains valuable commentaries.
Wider historical background is provided in the same author's *Il sovrano e l'orologiaio*
(Florence, 1987), mentioned already. The passage quoted runs: 'Ad tertium dicimus quod
duplex est potentia dei, idest dupliciter dicitur, absoluta et conditionata. Absoluta potentia
est ipsa in se considerata: hac potest in se omnia, et Petrum damnare et Iudam salvare
etc. Huiusmodi potentia conditionata dicitur inquantum respicit conditionem vel legem
quam deus sua bonitate rebus indidit: qua manente, non potest deus facere contrarium;
quod faceret si damnaret Petrum et salvaret Iudam, quia veritas et iustitia dei exigit ut
Petrus habeat vitam aeternam et Iudam poenam aeternam. Haec enim est lex data a
deo ut bonos remunerat et malos puniat. Hanc potentiam conditionatam vocat *Glossa*
super *Gen* XIX 'iustitiam', ubi agitur de Loth.'

minant expressing the envisaged instantiable content of doing so and so.

3. Asserting God's power as conditioned, is asserting that God can do so and so, in respect of 'the condition or law which God in his goodness has laid upon things'.

This is likewise a *cum determinatione* assertion, but with a determinant implying a reference to execution in the actual order of things. What God is in this way being said to be able to do, he is being able to do within the order he has imposed on things.

4. In *conditionem vel legem quem deus sua bonitate rebus indidit*, we might think of a law or order imposed on things there already; as in the *Timaeus*, where the Artisan imposes an order on the chaotic elements. But we might equally think of a law or order imposed on things (instantiable contents) when actually instantiated in a volitum of God's.

It seems to me that the latter interpretation is appropriate here, and the former might not be. We have already seen that *sua bonitate* may allude to such a volitum: *bonitas* and *voluntas* could be used interchangeably in such contexts. And in both Avicenna and his early thirteenth-century readers *bonitas* has connotations of existence in extra-mental reality, viewed as an overflowing goodness of God. (See various *Summae de bono* of the time.) Sometimes, as has also been seen, they used *benignitas* for this, reserving *bonitas* for the goodness identified with the divine nature. In addition, the latter of the two interpretations is in line with how Roland of Cremona was seen to use *potentia conditionata rebus*.

The juridical overtones may suggest the model of the legislator, which will be alluded to in passing by Aquinas, and brought to the fore in Scotus. *Conditio* had long been taken as the noun from *condere*, signifying the created order as something of a city founded by God, as well as being the noun from *condicere*, with its logical and juridical sigifications. The *lex data*, in an expression suggesting a sort of positive statute of God's, and standing in a contrast unexpressed here with the *lex aeterna*, is identified with the law *quam deus... rebus indidit*. The *lex aeterna* was identified rather with the divine nature.

5. *Veritas et iustitia dei exigit*... needs attention. We are not to imagine that Hugh (as though anticipating Deistical propensities) was arguing like this:

Veritas here is the eternal *veritas* which God is, and the *iustitia* likewise is the *iustitia qua ipse iustus est*;

If anything is true and just by nature, it cannot do what is untrue or unjust;

Damning Peter and saving Judas would be untrue or unjust;

So God cannot damn Peter and save Judas.

There is no need to consider the worse than dubious merits of the argument, since Hugh is presenting nothing of the sort. It is not the morality of damning Peter or saving Judas which is in question, pace the second premiss. And the first premiss travesties what Hugh should be seen to be saying.

The *veritas dei* here is to be understood as the providential order which God faithfully executes; as it is in Psalm 116/117's *veritas Domini manet in aeternum*, where *veritas* translates a word with the sense rather of faithfulness to the execution of a declared policy, much as in the phrase 'true to his principles'. (The same psalm's *in aeternum*, translating *le 'olam*, likewise does not have to be read as though implying the notion of eternity, as against perpetuity; a distinction given currency by Boethius, after a hint from the *Timaeus*.) Had we any doubt, Hugh gave us the means to resolve it, by his reference to Augustine's *per iustitiam/per potentiam* distinction.

9. An important ambiguity of reference was left under points 2 and 3 of Section 8 above. Just what "power of God" is being asserted: as absolute, in the one case; as conditioned, in the other? We may begin with Hugh's *Absoluta potentia est ipsa [potentia dei quae dupliciter dicitur] in se considerata*. The expression supplied within the square brackets is taken from the clauses immediately preceding, but does not of itself resolve the puzzle. The expression, in the context, is indeed functioning as a referring-expression. But which "power of God" is its referent? Is it the power with which God can be held identified, so that the expression *potentia dei* is on a par grammatically with 'Caesar's forces' in 'Caesar's forces began to fail him, as blood poured from his wounds'? Or is it some power which God orders, or can be envisaged to order, so that the expression *potentia dei* is on a par grammatically with 'Caesar's forces crossed the river, while he remained in the camp'? Out of further context, the *ipsa* could well lead us to think (mistakenly) the former.

But the expression is not given to us out of context. There is already a hint, if we wish to take it, in *duplex est potentia dei, idest dupliciter dicitur, absoluta et conditionata*. The *dicitur* is carrying weight. It is not a matter of the expression 'the/a power of God' being understood in two ways. It is some power of God which is being asserted (*dicitur*) in two [*cum determinatione*] ways.

It cannot be that power of God which God was held quasi-definitionally to be. That power logically cannot be said to be itself conditioned. If it is to be anything at all, it can therefore only be some power ordered by God, some "power of God's" other than the divine nature. So if *potentia [dei] ... in se considerata* is indeed to be taken as a referring expression, it can in the context refer successfully only if it is being understood to refer to some power envisaged as able to be ordered by God. And it is then an expression on a par grammatically with 'Caesar's forces' in 'Caesar's forces crossed the river while he remained in the camp'.

This interpretation is confirmed if we take the originally problematical expression not only in its immediate context (the reply) but in the whole context of objection-and-reply, in which it is to the objection we should look, for any setting of scope or reference which might be needed. In the objection it is the *veritas et iustitia dei* which is in question: not the truth or justice which God was sometimes said quasi-definitionally to be, but that *veritas et iustitia dei* which has been encountered in more than one medieval text already, and which is identical with the *ordinatio dei*. It is, as Hugh says here, that order of truth and justice 'through which God has promised eternal life to those who persevere'.

That "power of God" which the actual *ordinatio dei* is held to be, is indeed a 'power of God' which can be asserted to operate with reference to 'the condition or law which God in his goodness has impressed upon things'. It thus cannot be identified with that "power of God" which is to be identified with the divine nature, the "thing" which God is. If we assert God to be powerful, and mean to refer in that to the power which God is, we logically cannot assert it with reference to any imposed condition or law. God would still be powerful, in that sense, even if no condition or law were ever imposed on anything. So what sort of "thing" can it be, which can be asserted either as *conditionata*, with reference to 'the condition or law which God has imposed upon things', or as *absoluta*, prescinding from any such reference? It cannot be any actual thing: as Hugh has no call to deny, all actual things, if they can be asserted to be powerful at all, are to be asserted to be powerful only in so far as their power is subject to the 'condition or law which God in his goodness has imposed upon things'. Hence it can only be something like the schema of an *ordinatio* which God could in principle execute, but which (in an option-neutral assertion) we are considering in abstraction from whether or not it is executed, or ever to be executed.

This is recognisably the set of Avicennian essences, met above in related contexts. And the use of *bonitas* in 'the condition or law which God in his goodness has imposed upon things', likewise suggests that some further Avicennian notions could be lurking in the background. Now three features of the Avicennian essence, abstractly considered, are narrowly germane in a discussion of Hugh's meaning here. (This is an improper way of speaking. What is meant are three characteristics of the kind of abstraction which is in play.) One has already been seen: an Avicennian essence, abstractly considered, is being considered in abstraction from whether it is ever executed, or to be executed. Following on this, is the relational feature that Aristotle's two-way possibility applies to essences abstractly considered. It does not apply, in his view, to any essences concretely considered. These either necessarily exist (either *a se* or *ab alio*) or are impossible to exist, in his view. The medieval Christian academics of the Western schools had an interestingly analogous view. What actually exists, it ran, either is God, or is all or part of the *ordinatio dei*, the actual order of things viewed as ordered by God, and willed by God to be the only actual order of things. That which is God, the view continued, exists absolutely, exists sans phrase, and for that reason cannot in any way be said with truth to be able not to exist. That which is ordered by God cannot, if it is being viewed as ordered by God, and willed by God to be part of the only actual order of things, be said to be able not to exist, or indeed to be able to be in any respect other than it actually is. Nothing actually exists, save what exists either as God, or as some or all of God's ordering; and nothing actually being ordered by God can, while being considered as actually so ordered, be said with truth to be able not to exist, or not to exist in precisely the way in which it does exist.

But what does exist as some or all of God's ordering— and this is what users of the Power Distinction were in effect emphasising—can none the less be considered not as something actual, instantiated by God's ordering will, but in its intrinsic content merely, abstracting from whether it actually exists or is ever to exist, or not. Only by abstracting from whether a thing actually exists, or not, or from precisely how it actually exists, as ordered under God's will, can a Western theologian following this view have any room for applying Aristotle's two-way possibility. In other words, only for those "things" which he can say to be able to be done in God's option-neutral power, can he have any room for applying such a notion. Only such "things", so considered, can be allowed contingency sans phrase (as against possible contingencies relative to creaturely willing, if allowed for within God's ordering) by such a theologian.[11]

Avicenna's essences abstractly considered had a third relational characteristic. They were considered in isolation not only from whether or not they were (to be) actually instantiated. They were considered in isolation too from any necessary relationships with any comparable essences. The essence of being red, for example, could thus be considered in isolation from being green. Are the Western analogates, the *ordinationes dei*, abstractly considered, to be considered likewise in abstraction from any necessary relationships between the given schematic *ordinatio* under con- sideration, and any comparable schematic *ordinationes*? More particularly, does Hugh of St Cher think that they are? Hugh does not explicitly provide an answer to that at this place.

Yet we are now in a position, through reconsidering what he does provide, to answer the question, What sort of thing is this unique *potentia dei* which, asserted in one manner, is *in se considerata*, and, asserted in another manner, *respicit conditione vel lege quam deus sua bonitate rebus indidit*? The answer, on what Hugh provides, is that what is being considered, sometimes in itself, and sometimes as coming under the condition or law which God has in his goodness imposed on the things, is some schematic content of something: either something actually willed by God to exist in

---

[11] On Avicennian essences see the places referred to at n. 3 to Ch. 2 above.

the actual order of things, but considered in abstraction from being so ordered; or something envisaged by us as in principle susceptible of being instantiated in some order of things able to be willed by God.

'The power of God, considered in itself', will then stand not for that power of God which was to be identified with the divine nature, but for some schema of an envisaged, ordered creature of God (seen as being itself actively powerful, to at least some extent), considered by us in isolation from whether or not it is ever actually ordered under God's will. 'The power of God, considered as subject to the condition and law which God in his goodness has imposed on the things' will likewise not stand for that power of God to be identified with the divine nature, but with any or all of the intrinsic contents or Avicennian essences of things such as to be instantiable in some order willed by God, precisely as actually instantiated by God's will. In this place in Hugh's commentary, therefore, the power of God to which he is referring is some set of things envisaged either as willed by God to exist, as some or all of the actual order of things, or as in principle susceptible of being instantiated in an order willed by God, but prescinding from whether they will or will not be so instantiated. *Potentia dei* here is thus being understood by Hugh as systematically misleading, standing not for God or for any non-relational attribute of power such as a Deist or for that matter a modern academic theist might imagine God to have, but for something other than God, but considered in one way or another in relation to execution by God. In this way Hugh can treat attributions to divine power consistently with maintaining a rigorously negative theology on the divine nature; such as he has long been acknowledged to wish to maintain.[12]

---

[12] That Hugh was among those who wished to remain within Negative Theology assumptions is hardly to be doubted. Some have thought him excessive in this direction, for maintaining as he does that 'contemplating the *substantia* of God is impossible to any creature' (H.-F. Dondaine, 'Hugues de S. Cher et la condamnation de 1241', *Revue des Sciences Philosophiques et Théologiques* 33 (1949), 170–4, 171. The question *Quid sit videre in speculo?* and discussion can be found at J.-P. Torrell, *Théorie de la prophétie* (1977), 20–31 and 205–7 respectively. The article condemned—in a University regulation—is *Quod divina essentia in se nec ab homine nec ab angelo videbitur* (cit. from Paris *Chart.* I, n. 128, 1889, at H.-F. Dondaine, 'L'objet et le "medium" de la vision béatifique chez les théologiens du XIIIᵉ siècle', *RTAM* 19 (1952), 60–130, 60–1); pp. 119–21 of the same article give relevant text from Hugh's Postilla on Jn. 1; 16. In the same year, 1241, some papal condemnations concerned less academic matters. One bull of Gregory IX to the Archbishop of

When, on these principles extracted from Hugh, we say that God can in option-neutral power F, we are not to be understood as saying anything directly about God, about the divine nature. For example, if we say that God can in his option-neutral power make there to be humans with their feet situated typically above their heads, we are not to be understood as saying anything about the divine nature. We are to be understood as saying of our schematic content of 'there being made to be humans with their feet situated typically above their heads' that, considered purely as a schematic content, and in isolation from whether any such thing is ever (to be) found in extra-mental reality, and from any necessary connections with any comparable schematic contents, it is the sort of thing which can satisfy 'God can do x', or indeed, 'x is something that can be done in extra-mental reality'.

When, on the same principles, we say that God can F in option-tied power, we are to be understood once more as saying something not about God but about F-ing. If we were to say, for example, that God can in option-tied power make there to be humans with their feet situated typically above their heads, we would be saying of the schematic content of 'there being made to be humans with their feet situated typically above their heads', that, considered as a referring-expression, it referred successfully, and that the related proposition 'There are humans with their feet situated typically above their heads' is among those which are (ordered by God to be) true of extra-mental reality; and that the more narrowly related proposition 'It is made to be true that there are humans with their feet situated typically above their heads' is likewise true. (Hugh himself might well have considered the option-tied assertion, and the related propositions, to be false, while allowing the corresponding option-neutral assertion to be true.)

Because of what they are to be understood to be "really about", when analysed on the principles extractable from Hugh, both option-tied and option-neutral assertions turn out to be less dramatically informative than they may at first appear to some. Option-tied assertions, if true, may inform us about the world

Trondheim, whose province then included Orkney and Shetland, condemned the use of beer for baptising. (Denzinger–Bannwart, D447.)

around us, implying a contentious relationship between it, as it is, and God's will (in the sense here of *volitum*, that which is willed by God: the end or 'final cause' of the created order). Option-neutral assertions, if true, may inform us about a range of our fictions: our schematic conceptions of things, considered in isolation not only from whether they are ever (to be) found instantiated in extra-mental reality, but in isolation also from whatever necessary relationships external to themselves they may be seen to stand, when considered in comparison with comparable schematic conceptions of things.[13] What option-neutral assertions, if true, can tell us about that range of fictions, is whether they are or are not to be understood to be in the range of divine infinite power; the active power unrestricted as to kind, extent, or anything else, with which the divine nature was held to be identical. No matter how many true assertions of the sort we can list, and no matter what sort of thing they are about, they are incapable of informing us in any positive way whatever, about divine infinite power itself.

It follows that from 'God can in option-neutral power F' and 'God can in option-neutral power G', we are not necessarily entitled to conclude 'God can in option-neutral power F-and-G'. In a couple of further objections in the same question, Hugh appears to exploit this. But some textual obscurities would call for kinds of discussion which, if carried on to the extent needed, would be out of proportion here. None of the most likely ways of resolving the obscurities, as it happens, create particular obstacles for the interpretation of Hugh's handling of the Distinction, as already outlined. The conceptual and theological

[13] Cf. Hugh's remarks on the (created) schematic content of that which is revealed by God to a prophet: 'res nonciata, ut res potest dupliciter considerari, scil. secundum modum existendi in causis inferioribus quae sunt merita hominum vel physica res, vel secundum modum existendi in causa superiori quae est divina dispositio ordinata ad inferiores ut imperans ad necessario oboediens'. (Disputed question, *Quid sit videre in speculo?* in Torrell, *Théorie de la prophétie* (1977), 26, emphasis added.) The relation of "subjection" to a divine ordinance, analogous to the obedience of a feudal subject to his lord, was one of the notes caught in the use of *potestas* or *dominatio* which appeared above in William of Auvergne's use of *potentia*. It is one of the relationships from which we prescind, if we assert of some *res* that God can in option-neutral power make it to be. See also, from the *In Sent.* d. 42 passage, ed. Randi 1984; 534, Hugh's explanation that in *Deus potest omnia, ergo potest currere*, the term *omnia* is one which *supponit absolute* (*idest sine comparatione ad aliquod subiectum*) *omnia subiecta divinae potentiae*. By contrast, the term *currere* in the same argument is to be taken as one which *supponit rem subiectam divinae potentiae, retorquendo ad deum tamquam ad subiectum*.

issues which appear to be concerned, are raised by Albert the Great in a more explicit manner, in passages to be seen presently. They will be taken up at that place.[14]

10. A further use of the Distinction, in reply to objection 5 of the same question, opens wider horizons:

> we say that God might (*possit*) in option-neutral power (*de potentia absoluta*) dissolve angels and souls out of existence, so that they would not exist at all; but that perhaps he might not be able (*forte... non posset*) to do so in option-tied power (*de potentia conditionata*). (*In 1 Sent.*, d. 42, qu. 1, ed. Randi 1984: 535.)[15]

Hugh's application here is of interest for being in appearance at least an application not to a narrowly theological puzzle, but to one raised by the natural philosophy of the previous century; a 'science' dependent on the *Timaeus* and its fellow-travellers, and already long out of fashion in scientifical circles. It is a point made in the *Timaeus* that the souls of creatures, and even the Soul of the World, are not by nature indissoluble, but are so purely by the will of the Artisan.[16] In Jowett's neo-Jacobean:

> my creations are indissoluble, if so I will. All that is bound may be undone, but only an evil being would wish to undo that which is harmonious and happy. Wherefore since ye are but creatures, ye are not altogether immortal and invisible, but ye shall certainly not be dissolved... having in my will a greater and mightier bond than those with which ye were bound at the time of your birth (41ab).

This passage may have been seminal in more than one later philosophy. It adumbrates the *malin génie* who threatens the

---

[14] The two passages run: (1) Ad vii dicimus quod de potentia absoluta posset facere hominem asinum et in una persona. Sed de potentia conditionata, manente natura utriusque et lege, non posset; quia sic faceret contra legem suam; *and* (2) Ad viii dicimus similiter quod manente natura contradictionis non posset facere ut duo sic opposita essent vera simul, nec est hoc ex impotentia aliqua, sed ex lege quem indidit rebus. Sed de potentia absoluta posset deus removere oppositionem, et ita simul essent vera; sed tunc non essent opposita. Quomodo hoc sit, solus deus intelligit, qui solus intelligit suam potentiam. (Both after Randi 1984; 535.)

[15] Ad v dicimus quod deus possit angelos et animas corrumpere, ita ut omnino non essent, de potentia absoluta. Forte de potentia conditionata non posset. (Ed. Randi 1984; 535.)

[16] Abelard had used three verbatim quotations from the same passage, and had alluded to it in various places. But he had not used the quotations in his seminal treatise on divine power. See L. Moonan, 'Abelard's use of the *Timaeus*', *AHDLMA* 56 (1989), 7–90, 39–42.

reliability of the only order with which science may be concerned, in Descartes: 'only an evil being would wish to undo that which is harmonious and happy'. It adumbrates one famous riposte to the sceptical difficulty raised by the *malin génie*: Berkeley's riposte, in which science is reliable not because of a created causal order of material substances, but because a Berkleian God provides us with reliably connected arrays of "ideas", on which our true scientifical assertions will depend. This was in the future, in the after-history of the Power Distinction.

In Hugh's application here, what should be marked is that it was perhaps not the departure it might at first seem, from a practice of using the Distinction for narrowly theological puzzles. The *Timaeus* and its genre had been largely abandoned for whatever science it could provide, and could well have begun to look to at least some in the Theology Faculty as the good old-fashioned, Christianity-favouring view of the world which the natural philosophy of the Muslims and of Aristotle looked like threatening to overturn. If things did look like that, then Hugh's application, so far from being seen as innovative, might have appeared rather as piously reactionary.

In *In 4 Sent.* he uses and to some extent expounds the Distinction again, in connection with a theological problem which Geoffrey of Poitiers and William of Auxerre have been seen to treat, in texts examined in Chapter 2 above. The problem is that of a particular kind of power which God might or might not be said to be able to bestow on human beings charged with baptising others: the power called co-operative power (*potestas cooperationis*). What Hugh says is:

It must however be distinguished that the power of God is twofold, *absoluta* and *ordinata*. In option-neutral power (*de potentia absoluta*) God could and still can give to a mere man (*puro homini*) [the power known as] co-operative power (*potestatem cooperationis*). In option-tied power (*de potestate ordinata*), that is, with the order of things not having been changed, he cannot. For *potentia absoluta dei* and [*potentia*] *ordinata* [*dei*] is altogether the same thing. But *potentia ordinata* has reference to the order built into things by God.

Perhaps those who say that God could not give [co-operative] power (*potentiam*) to a mere man are understanding the aforesaid power (*potestatem*) [to be being asserted under the determinant] 'in option-tied power' (*de potentia dei ordinata*), and the Master understood it [to be being asserted under the determinant] 'in option-neutral [power]' (*de* [*potentia dei*] *absoluta*), and thus there is no contrariety. (*In 4 Sent.*, MS Leipzig Univ. Cod. lat. 573, fo. 223, cit. A. Landgraf, *Dogmengeschichte*, III/1 (1954), 184; and cf. p. 207.)[17]

The first part of the quotation shows essentially the understanding of the Distinction seen above in the passages from *In 1 Sent*. The second part shows how "dated" some of Peter Lombard's ways of speaking were already appearing to Parisian theologians. They already called for "charitable" interpretations and historical annotations. Both parts show that Hugh, like others, was prepared to use *potentia* and *potestas* indifferently in Power Distinction contexts. In general, however, Hugh's use of the Distinction leads his readers forward towards later uses, and not least towards those of his more famous brother Dominicans examined in Chapters 4, 6, and 7 below.

Alexander of Hales, OFM (d. 1245) and his Corpus

11. Alexander, an Englishman, was an MA of Paris by 1210, and teaching in Theology there before the *événements* of 1229. If Roger Bacon is to be believed, it was Alexander who first took Lombard's Sentences for the object-text of his systematic teaching in theology. In the aftermath of the *événements* Alexander was among the masters who left Paris. He spent some time in England, whose king was in any case one of those who favoured the masters and students against the Parisian police and their

[17] Distingui tamen debet quod duplex est potentia dei, absoluta et ordinata. De absoluta potentia potuit deus et potest adhuc dare puro homini potestatem cooperationis. De potestate ordinata non potest, id est non mutato ordine rerum. Idem enim omnino est potentia absoluta dei et ordinata. Sed potentia ordinata respicit ordinem rebus a deo inditum. Forte illi qui dicunt quod deus non potuit dare potentiam puro homini, praedictam potestatem intelligunt de potentia dei ordinata, et Magister intelligit de absoluta, et sic nulla est contrarietas. (*In 4 Sent.*, MS Leipzig, Universitätsbibl. Cod. lat. 573, fo. 223, cit. Landgraf, *Dogmengeschichte*, III/1 (1954), 184.) Landgraf also refers here to the passage from William of Auxerre's *Summa aurea*, Bk. 4, tr. 3, ch. 3, seen in Ch. 2 above. It is where Landgraf quotes the St Cher passage again at p. 207 of the same vol. III/1 of *Dogmengeschichte* that he draws attention to a use of the Distinction on the part of Guerric of St Quentin, OP: 'Potestate absoluta potuit dare, sed non potestate ordinata, quae respicit ordinem rerum.' (On 1 Cor., cit. from MS Paris BN lat. 15 603, fo. 11.) I am unable to comment on Guerric's use of the Distinction; lacking contextual information beyond that given incidentally by Landgraf at pp. 169–209 of the same volume.

protectors. He was a canon of Lichfield and archdeacon in Coventry by the time he returned to Paris, in the general return. He was re-established in his chair, and when he became a Franciscan around the beginning of the academic year of 1236–7 he succeeded in retaining it as a Franciscan, and permitting the Franciscans to appropriate it. It was their first chair in Theology at Paris. He is thought of now as the great founder of a Franciscan tradition in academic teaching. But he was not only formed as a secular cleric, he had pursued a distinguished career as one before ever joining the Franciscan order. He had served, for example, as a negotiator: on the University's behalf, in negotiations with the papacy; and for the English king, in negotiations with the French court. Becoming a Franciscan did not end his public career. Under William of Auvergne he played a part in one or two ecclesiastical condemnations. With Hugh of St Cher and two other cardinals he was deputed, at the Council of Lyons, to examine the case for canonisation of Edmund Rich, who duly became St Edmund of Abingdon. Alexander survived the Council, but died in an epidemic, on his return to Paris, in 1245.

Besides a glossary, the *Exoticon* (MS Gonville and Caius, Cambridge, 136), Alexander is credited with *Glosae in 4 libb. Sent.*, from before 1234–5, and perhaps well before; *Quaestiones disputatae 'Antequam esset frater'*, written between 1220 and 1236; *Quaestiones quodlibetales* (four of these, with a total of 30 questions, are listed in Glorep 1933, No. 301); and the great *Summa theologica*.[18]

The Franciscans appropriated the *Summa* as completely as the teaching chair. It is because of the uncertainty which still lies over the authenticity of specific parts of this influential book that 'and his corpus' was added in the subheading above. John of la Rochelle, OFM, for example, is credited with major parts of Alexander's *Summa*, Books 1 and 3, as they now stand; but is not treated separately here. (See I. Brady in *Dict. Sp.*, s.v. 'Jean de la Rochelle'.) The notorious problems of authenticity are most fully treated by V. Doucet in the long Prolegomena to Tomus IV, 1957, of the Quaracchi edition. Further guidance on using the different parts of that uneven edition is given by Doucet in

---

[18] The evidence on Alexander's life is collected and annotated comprehensively in the Introduction to the 1951 Quaracchi edn. of the Sentence Commentary, vol. 1, 7*–75*.

Archivum franciscanum historicum, 43 (1950), 196–200, and in I. Brady, 'The *Summa Theologica* of Alexander of Hales (1924–1948)', in *AFH* 70 (1977), 437–47, which explains how much of the edition was carried through. The published extracts from the *Exoticon* do not show anything to present purpose, and I have not yet seen the unpublished parts. Much the same holds for the *Quaestiones quodlibetales*. The *Quaestiones 'Antequam esset frater'* are published in a Quaracchi edition, but show little to present purpose. We could note that the expression *potentia ordinata* is used, but in reference to human psychology, for what had been called a *virtus ordinata* in some translations of Avicenna. (See Qu. 18, Quaracchi edn. 304.) Damascene's *voluntas antecedens/consequens* is used, and that is arguably part of the prehistory of the Power Distinction. (Qu. 10, Quaracchi edn. 110. See *De fide orthodoxa*, II, ch. 29, and especially the twelfth-century translation, at PG 94; 970A.) In general, Alexander is still working here within older traditions.

Glosae in 4 libb. Sent.

12.   This is a thoroughgoing commentary on the Sentences, not to be thought of as a series of glosses; though I have found no more than a couple of uses of the Distinction in it. One is at the very end of the treatise on divine power (*In 1 Sent.*, dd. 42–4):

let it be noted that God can do all things which, to be able to do, does not come down to either not being able (*non posse*) or not being seemly (*non decere*). So although [God] could (*posset*) take flesh, in so far as his option-neutral power is concerned (*quoad potentiam absolutam*), he could not in so far as his seemly power is concerned (*quoad potentiam decentem*). (*In 1 Sent.*, d. 44, Quaracchi edn. (1951), 448.)

The terms contrasted are not explained, and are apparently expected to be already familiar to the intended audience. The determinant *quoad potentiam decentem*, with its connotation (out of context) of a power conformed to an approved standard, is plainly to be understood as an expression of the option-tied arm of the Distinction; balancing *quoad potentiam absolutam*. *Decens*, however, also brings connotations (out of context) of decency or seemliness by some independent standards, whether aesthetic or moral. *Decens* would continue to be used from time to time, perhaps especially in Franciscan writers, and would continue to cause some unease to at least some of its hearers. In one of its famous occurrences, in the tag *Potuit, decuit, ergo fecit*, it is only the relative prominence of the "seemliness" connotations to modern hearers which may cause puzzlement. By the primary sense of conformity to an arbitrarily determined standard, *Potuit, decuit, ergo fecit* expresses a valid argument; merely one in need of some decoding.

The next passage (*In 3 Sent.*, d. 25 (AE), pp. 301–2) is from the version transmitted in the manuscripts of Assisi and Erfurt. It does not appear in the earlier version, transmitted in the Lambeth manuscript. The question under discussion is whether only the necessary can be an object of faith, and Alexander distinguishes diverse ways in which something may be said to be necessary:

(1) necessary *secundum potentiam dei*, like God's not being able to create an equal to himself, *and*

(2) necessary, *ut ordinatum est secundum sapientiam dei et non dependens ex singulari arbitrio alicuius*, in which way it was 'necessary that Christ should be incarnate'.

Alexander does not expatiate on this either, but these two diverse routes to (a logical) impossibility have been seen in other writers above, and will be seen again. No comment is called for here, beyond that the determinants *secundum potentiam dei* and *ut ordinatum secundum sapientiam dei et non dependens ex singulari arbitrio alicuius*, would seem to be doing essentially the same work as those in which the Power Distinction came to be more usually expressed. The *et non dependens ex singulari arbitrio alicuius* is merely spelling out a point.

SUMMA THEOLOGICA

Theology, in Alexander's usage is *scientia de deo, qui est causa causarum*, dependent on God's grace. It differs from 'the theology of the philosophers' in having an affective as well as a cognitive character. The theology of the philosophers—metaphysics at its most general—shares and specifies the cognitive element. Since it is Aristotle whom he quotes here, Alexander's views on the differences between theologians' theology and philosophical theology are worth examining further.[19]

13. On the knowability of God's nature he expresses his essentially Negative position so suavely as to require readers to look twice: as though suavity of the sort were demanded out of concern for our *affectionem ad bonitatem*. Yet the *cognitio secundum veritatem* is there if we look for it. 'In forms and things separated from material location, such as the very Godhead and the Trinity of Persons, is another mode of knowing; to the effect that by [awareness of] the operation we may come to know the power [applied in the operation], and by the power, the very substance of the Godhead.' Alexander then quotes Rom. 1: 20: 'For the invisible things of him, from the creation of the world, are clearly seen, being understood by the things that are made. His eternal power also and divinity;... '. He thus distinguishes three levels of possible or putative knowledge, and insinuates that Romans does the like. Alexander's lowest level is that of the *operatio*. By awareness of the operation we come to know the *virtus* behind the operation. Having done that, we come to know the *ipsam divinitatis substantiam*. If I understand him, the *operatio* is any or all of God's option-tied power, the actual order of things; the 'virtuality for operation' (the *virtus*) behind this corresponds to God's option-neutral power; 'the very substance of divinity' (*ipsam divinitatis substantiam*) is the divine nature.[20] What Alexander does

---

[19] 'Theologia... est scientia de deo, qui est causa causarum... est scientia perficiens cognitionem secundum veritatem; est etiam movens affectionem ad bonitatem.' By contrast, 'Prima philosophia, quae est theologia philosophorum,... est de causa causarum, sed ut perficiens cognitionem secundum viam artis et ratiocinationis...' (*Summa Hales*, tr. introd., qu. 1, ch. 1, Quaracchi edn. (1924), 1: 2). On theology vs. philosophy in Alexander, see E. Gössmann, *Metaphysik u. Heilsgeschichte: Eine theologische Untersuchung der Summa Halensis (Alexander von Hales)* (Munich, 1964), 22 f. and refs. On the knowability of God, see Gössmann 1964: 38–48; I. Gorlani, *La conoscenza naturale di Dio secondo la Somma Teologica di Alessandro d'Hales* (Milan, 1933), XVI + 221 pp., esp. 1–46, 177–221; also E. Bettoni, *Il problema della cognoscibilità di Dio nella Scuola Francescana (Alessandro d'Hales, S. Bonaventura, Duns Scoto)* (Padua, 1950), esp. 67–92.

[20] We can have knowledge of what sort of thing a created *operatio* is—knowledge *quid sit*—and of what sort of thing the abstract content of some particular *operatio* is. (Alexander speaks here of the latter as a *virtus* made actual in the *operatio*.) But in the case of *ipsam divinitatis substantiam*, no knowledge *quid sit* can be had by us; or so at any rate is the view Alexander maintains in the question examining 'the knowability of God in his immensity' (*Summa Hales*, tr. introd., qu. 2, ch. 2, ed. Quaracchi (1924), 1: 17.) H.-F. Dondaine draws attention to a passage in which Alexander might seem to deviate from a strict Negative Theology view, only to note that the passage is 'probably not authentic', and to add that

not spell out until a couple of questions later is that he is equivocating on 'come to know', used of coming to know the operation and the virtuality on the one hand, and coming to know the divine nature on the other. We can know something of what divine operation or even the virtuality for operation is, we can know no more than that the divine nature is.

When explicitly treating 'the knowability of God in his immensity' (*Summa Hales*, tr. introd., qu. 2, ch. 2, Quaracchi edn. (1924), vol. 1, par. 9), Alexander declares his hand on 'coming to know the very substance of divinity through the virtuality for operation'. For he makes the familiar distinction between the way of affirmation (*per modum positionis*) and the way of negation, and concludes: 'The divine substance in its immensity is not knowable by a rational soul, in positive knowledge': a knowledge by which, if we could have it, we could come to know what God is. This is what he means by *per modum positionis cognoscimus quid est*: to be understood as a quasi-definitional point about the *modus positionis*, not as a substantive flat contradiction of what he is preparing to assert as his conclusion in the very next sentence; which is, as has already been noted, that 'The divine substance in its immensity is not knowable by a rational soul, in positive knowledge'. Coming to know the substance of divinity through the virtuality is thus nothing more than being able to assert with truth that so and so is not true of the substance of divinity, on the grounds that we know something about the virtuality; perhaps that so and so is not true of it, and that nothing of the so and so's kind can be lacking in it.

In the three-element understanding of the Power Distinction spelled out in Chapter 9 below, this is essentially how the Distinction is applicable in this matter. The set of things which God can in option-neutral power (Alexander's virtuality for operation) do is, in that understanding, held to be (potentially) infinite, and to be lacking in nothing that can be made to be, by any unrestricted power whatsoever. So of any "thing" which falls outside of that set, it can safely be said and indeed must be said that God cannot do that "thing"—say, making a successfully squared circle. (By knowing that the thing cannot be done in

Doucet had been able to find no parallel to the supposed deviation in the parallel question in Alexander's authentic work. (H.-F. Dondaine, 'Cognoscere de Deo "quid est" ', *RTAM* 22 (1955), 72–8.)

God's option-neutral power, we may come to know (1) that God exists, since that is held implied in an assertion of God's option-neutral power, and (2) something of what God is not, i.e. not such as to be capable of the "thing" in question.) This passage from early in the *Summa* would thus seem to tell us already about how Alexander's understanding of the Distinction can be expected to lie: in line with the understanding which is to be found in the period of this book generally, and in the service of a theology (or, in the present case, an apologetics perhaps) which respects a rigorously negative theology on the divine nature.

14. In the opening question of the treatise on divine power, Alexander's reply distinguishes two ways in which some agent can be said (*cum determinatione*) to be able to do this or that: in respect of the extent to which the ability is being understood as something complete in itself, in which case the ability is being predicated *secundum perfectionem*; and in respect of the extent to which the ability is being understood as something in need of (further) completion, in which case the ability is being predicated *secundum imperfectionem*. (*Summa Hales*, vol. 1, par. 131.) Any *potentia* attributed to God must be attributed *secundum perfectionem*, not *secundum imperfectionem*. Alexander's point here concerns 'is able' or *potentia* whether understood as signifying an active capacity or a passive potentiality. Either of these can be thought of as somehow open to completion: a capacity, when it is yet to be exercised, a potentiality, to be actualised. 'I can ride a bicycle' can be true on the strength of a capacity attributed *secundum imperfectionem*, a capacity open to completion by its exercise. 'A city can be built here' can be true on the strength of a potentiality, not yet realised and perhaps never realised.

Any *potentia* putatively attributed to God, however, any values for 'God can___', if the "attribution" (even broadly understood) is to be true, must be understood as being attributed *secundum perfectionem*, not *secundum imperfectionem*. Behind this is not merely the (pious) point that God does not botch things, but the metaphysical point that whatever is God, cannot be determinate in any way. For a capacity to be open to completion in exercise implies determinateness of some kind in it, and potentialities of their nature are determinate, limiting. No potentiality, therefore, and no capacity thought of as open to completion by exercise, is attributable with truth to God.

It follows from this rather neatly stated view of Alexander's that the Power Distinction, which involves two *cum determinatione* ways of attributing to God power to do things, ought not to be understood on the model of a creaturely capacity and its exercise. More precisely, it ought not to be so understood, if assertions attributing a capacity are to be understood as true, if true, in virtue of some kind of "quality" inhering in an agent.

But can such assertions be analysed otherwise? If three diverse elements and their relationships are kept in mind, anticipating the understanding of the Power Distinction to be spelled out below, they can. The first element is in effect God's option-tied power, or a set of Avicennian essences of things viewed as instantiated in extra-mental reality under God's will. The second is God's option-neutral power, or a set of Avicennian essences of things, considered in their intrinsic content merely, and prescinding from whether they are or are not ever to be so instantiated. The third is the divine nature itself, referred to obliquely but crucially in the standard descriptions of the other two. Assertions in which a capacity is purportedly attributed to God will then be analysed as being systematically misleading: to be understood not as being about the divine nature, but as being about the "thing" for which there might be imagined to be the capacity in question; and to be true, if true, in virtue of the aptness or otherwise of the "thing" in question to take its place in the set of the things of God's option-neutral power. Assertions in which the exercise of such a supposed capacity is likewise attributed to God will also be analysed as being systematically misleading: not about any exercise of the capacity imagined, but about the relevant Avicennian essence's instantiation or non-instantiation within the set of things of God's option-tied power; and true if true if the 'thing' in question is so instantiated. There is no need, therefore, to interpret Alexander's talk about capacity and exercise as anything more than an expository device eliminable if challenged in favour of an understanding of the Power Distinction beginning to be discernible as standard for the period of this book.

Of course the capacity-and-exercise model has a certain appeal to someone engaged in a rough, initial exposition of attributions to divine power, including attributions made in what became the terminology of the Power Distinction. And the appeal could well rest precisely on treating a capacity as some kind of quality inhering in an agent, and then imagining such a quality to inhere in God. But the capacity-and-exercise model will not necessarily bear any strictly explanatory weight, and it need not be imagined that Alexander intended to put any such weight on it. On Alexander's plausible rule excluding *secundum imperfectionem* attributions of power to the divine nature, and indeed on widely held views on divine simplicity, there can be no such quality to be seen as inhering in the divine nature. And if that is so there would seem nothing to be gained—for honest exposition and worthwhile refutation alike—by transferring such models to treatments of divine activity, or reading them into texts such as those just considered from Alexander, where they are not necessarily to be found.

15.   At ch. 3 of the same question Alexander distinguishes determinations *per temporale* and *per aeternum*. When we say that God is capable of understanding, the word(s) signifying the capability—say, the *potentia* in *potentia intelligendi*—is being determined *per aeternum*, and nothing created is necessarily connoted in such a determination. 'God is capable of understanding', or indeed 'God can understand A', will thus be true, if it is, whether or not there is any creation, any created A. In 'God is capable of creating', or 'God can create A', something created is necessarily connoted in the corresponding determination—say, *creandi* in *potentia creandi*. Alexander is not disputing that, in general, a power to F is to be specified by reference to F-ing; or that a power to understand is to be specified by something intelligible. But in the sense in which God may be said to be capable of understanding, he is also to be said to be intelligible to himself, whether or not there ever is anything other than God to be understood. By contrast, God is not capable of creating, without creating something other than himself. (See *Summa Hales*, vol. 1, par. 133.)

What is not spelled out in par. 133 is what is involved in connoting something created. From what he says a couple of paragraphs later, it appears that this is done not only when something actually created is mentioned, but also when its possibility is. If the possibilities envisaged are the possibilities which some creature is thinking about, when (as in a composing-apt proposition) he entertains or asserts them as possibilities, this is what can be expected. To a platonist, by contrast, possibilities of things are to be understood as things analogous to Platonic Ideas. To Christian Platonists, the Ideas had long been located in God, as objects of God's (eternal) knowledge. Because of beliefs about divine simplicity, the Ideas were thus not to be distinguished, in their "real" existence, from the divine nature. And they were thus to be held opaque, in their "real" existence, to our understanding. Moreover, determinants connoting possible creations, in this platonist view of things, would surely have to be understood as being made *per aeternum* anyway, not *per temporale*. A platonist understanding of possibilities, and therefore of the option-neutral arm of the Power Distinction, is for this reason additionally unlikely to appeal to Alexander: despite the tone of some of his rhetoric.[21]

16. At par. 135 he compares concepts of power and will both as to logical priority and in extension. To determine the logical priorities he first distinguishes

(1) potentia potens, *or* potentia in habitu, *and*
(2) potentia exsequens, *or* potentia in effectu.

The concept of power mentioned in (1) is logically prior to that of will, which in turn is prior to the concept of power mentioned in (2). The *potens* in (1) doubtless alludes to Augustine's *per potentiam/iustitiam* distinction, and there is scarcely doubt but that

[21] Some expressions, out of context, may be taken to have something of a bias in favour of being read one way rather than the other. Alexander accepts the related view that some expressions are to be applied to God *quoad se* ('wise', 'good', 'omnipotent', he says), others *quoad nos* ('merciful', 'just', and the like). (He takes this view from a work of unknown authorship which can be seen at PL 62; 212–13 and is now often attributed to Gregory of Elvira, late 4th cent.) The latter, when they are taken without determination, are to be understood as connoting an effect in some creature. 'God is just', sans phrase, may thus be (defeasibly?) presumed to mean 'is just towards some creature or other'. In 'God is wise', by contrast, the 'wise' is not to be taken to connote anything created, save with a determination added, as in 'wise in his works', or 'good towards us'. (*Summa Hales*, 1: 204 ad fin.) In line with what he says here, Alexander regularly uses *omnipotens* sans phrase to signify divine infinite power, and not the relational 'almightiness' which Hobbes purports to commend. It is noteworthy that when the fathers of Trent use *iustitia dei* in the decree on justification, they spell out the determination both in the case where the expression is apparently being used to refer to the divine nature (... *qua ipse iustus est*) and in that where a created effect is connoted (*qua nos iustos facit*) (Sess. 7).

God's option-neutral power is to be understood as a *potentia potens*, an abstract capacity for operation, and his option-tied power as a *potentia exsequens*, the operation in actual execution.

It is in reply to an objection about the comparative extensions that Alexander uses the Distinction, particularly in the text,

Option-neutral power (*potentia absoluta*)... is distinguished from option-tied power (*potentia ordinata*). For option-neutral power extends to those things concerning which there is no divine pre-ordinance; but option-tied power extends to those things concerning which there is a divine pre-ordinance, that is, to those things which are pre-ordained or disposed by God. (*Summa Hales*, vol. i, par. 135.)

Alexander is plainly speaking of the Power Distinction here. By speaking of concepts (*intentiones*) with extensions to be compared, he is at least giving grounds to confirm the suggestion already made, that he wishes to understand the Distinction in the way now discernible as becoming standard for the period covered in the present book. In that understanding, both arms of the Distinction express concepts in principle intelligible to us.

If the option-neutral arm is taken—as in principle it can be taken, and for a time was taken by me—to express the unique truth about God, if there is one, it can still be held properly and absolutely true, but at the cost of being literally unintelligible, lacking all signification (despite appearances). Moreover, the usual formulas of the Distinction can still, on such a way of taking them, be used for saying something true. But they can then no longer be used to make a genuine distinction, in which comparable concepts are contrasted to some clarifying purpose. In Alexander's understanding of the Distinction, so far as it has appeared up to now, a genuine distinction, with comparable concepts to be contrasted, would seem to be safeguarded.

17.   At par. 140, where he alludes in passing to the Distinction, Alexander introduces the prima-facie intriguing expression *potentia creabilis dei*. Replying to an objection about creating everything creatable in the first moment of creation, he distinguishes two senses of 'creatable'. The first is that of being creatable within the actual order of things or, as he puts it, 'in the disposition or pre-ordinance of the cause which is creating' (*in dispositione creantis causae, sive praeordinatione*). The second is that of being within the power of the cause which is creating (*in potentia creantis causae*).

With *potentia* left unrestricted, and with God as the creating cause in question, this comes down to being in the set of things which God can do in option-neutral power. (See Alexander's remarks above, apropos of *potentia potens*.) Many things creatable in the latter sense, are not creatable in the former.

By *potentia creabilis*, he adds, he does not understand a potentiality of any material, but a power to bring things about (*potentia agentis*). The power to bring things about, in its turn, can be understood either absolute or else *cum dispositione seu praeordinatione*. In the light of what has preceded it is not hard to interpret this as follows. The *potentia agentis* in question is (God's) power to do things external to his nature, if he wishes to do so. It is thus to be identified with what Albert will refer to as God's 'operant power'. That power considered *absolute*, prescinding from any such will to do so, is God's option-neutral power, and the same power considered *cum dispositione seu praeordinatione* is (God's) option-tied power. 'Creatable' may accordingly be said either in the sense of creatable by that power considered *absolute*, or creatable by that power considered *cum dispositione* etc. The expression *potentia creabilis* [*dei*] thus adds nothing to what is already available from the Power Distinction; save perhaps a distracting suggestion.

Since a suggestion rather like it might seem to have been found in a later writer, Hugo de Novocastro, it might be useful to bring it more plainly into the open. The suggestion—which could perhaps be taken from the expression, out of context—is that out of the set of things which God can do in option-neutral power, say,

{a, b, ⟨a,b⟩, ⟨c,d,e⟩, f, ... }
only the subset (say, {b, ⟨ab⟩}) corresponding to the set of things which God can do in option-tied power, say,
⟨b, ⟨a,b⟩⟩,

might be imagined to be *potentia creabilis*. In context it is clear that it is not Alexander's view. In addition, it would not be a suggestion open to anyone who wished to maintain a rigorously Negative Theology on the nature of God.[22]

---

[22] Hugh de Novocastro (fl. 1321) was to take further suggestions invited by such expressions as *potentia creabilis dei*. He speaks of *potentia ordinabilis dei*, which is *eadem secundum rem* as *potentia absoluta dei*, but is called *ordinabilis* on account of the dictum 'Quod

18. For much of par. 141, where he is considering some of the Abelardian questions on divine power, he does not use the Distinction in his answers, preferring a formula of Hugh of St Victor's. But he does make a comparison with a distinction between power de facto and power de iure, remarking on the crucial difference between its application to human agents and its application to God's agency. In God '*posse de facto* is the same thing as *posse de iure*, according as the *ius* implies the seemly arrangements of divine goodness (*condecentiam bonitatis divinae*)'. This is doubtless because everything God does, he does *iuste*; because his *posse de facto* is what he does; and because his *posse de iure* is what he does *iuste*. Later writers, including Scotus, Ockham, and Bradwardine, noted comparisons between distinctions between power *de iure* and *de facto*, on the one hand, and the Power Distinction, on the other. But they do not always have the same aspects of comparison in mind as Alexander, or each other.[23]

19. In the same par. 141, where the possibility of damning Peter and saving Judas is being entertained, Alexander uses the Distinction:

potentia dei is understood in two ways. In one [it is understood as]

contradictionem non includit, habet rationem sapientialem in deo, secundum quam si fieret, bene fieret'. Again, he says 'illud enim potest deus de potentia ordinabili quod contradictionem non includit et habet aliquam rationem sapientialem secundum quam, si poneretur in esse, bonum fieret ... '. (Hugh, *In 1 Sent.*, d. 42, qu. 2, ed. E. Randi, *Il sovrano* (1987), 135–6.) Hugh's usage adds nothing conceptually to what can be achieved by using only *absoluta/ordinata*, and what it adds rhetorically is an invitation to psychologising speculations which can scarcely be reconciled with a Negative Theology, and are only dubiously desirable in any kind of honest theology. Hugh appears to recognise as much, on the same page: 'God can do this *de potentia ordinabili* too ... For the world not to be, includes no contradiction, ... and this has in God some sufficient sapiential reason— say, on account of [obviating] the sins of intellectual creatures—or on account of some other reason which to us is unknown, but to God is known.' Hugh's 'sufficient sapiential reason' is a long way from Candide, or even from the historical Leibniz. But it marks some kind of turning from a rigorously negative theology, and at least opens the door to Deism and its concomitant absurdities. The expressions themselves—*potentia creabilis/ordinabilis dei*—do not necessarily open this door, and I am not (yet) aware of anything in Alexander comparable to Hugh's emphasis on 'sufficient sapiential reasons'. Perhaps it is no bad thing that neither way of speaking seems to have caught on in its time.

[23] For Scotus and Ockham see Randi, *Il sovrano* (1987), 51–83. I am by no means convinced of all Dr Randi's interpretations of the comparisons between Scotus's and Ockham's appeals to *de facto/de iure* contrasts. Some of these are among the very few points of real importance in that admirable book which do not convince me.

absoluta, in the other [it is understood as] *ordinata* according to the plan of divine justice of pre-ordination of the one who renders to each according to his merits. In option-neutral power (*de potentia... absoluta*), therefore, [God] could damn Peter and save Judas. In option-tied power according to pre-ordination and retribution according to merits (*de potentia vero ordinata secundum praeordinationem et retributionem secundum merita*), he could not. And in this there is no derogation from his power, but the immutability of the ordering of power according to pre-ordination and justice, is being shown.

It is to be said likewise that he could recall Peter to life, and Judas, and so on. (*Summa Hales*, 1: 220–1.)[24]

The specification of *potentia dei ordinata* recalls the wording of the allusion noted above from p. 204, where Alexander had spoken of *potentia determinata per dispositionem praeordinatam*.

20.   At par. 155, p. 236, Alexander tackles the question of whether opposites' being the same thing is something possible to God. This was a question to which Alan ab Insulis had given currency, and which would be taken up (with Alan's puzzles) by Albert the Great and others. In Alexander's reply is no more than a passing reference to the Distinction. Yet it comes with further confirmation of his understanding of it:

If the power of God is conceived by the soul *absolute*, the soul will not be able to determine the question, or to take in the boundless ocean of his power. But when the soul considers (*speculatur*) divine power as ordered in accordance with the condition of power, of truth, of goodness, I say: What is possible to God is that sort of 'capability' which is a power to do things (*posse potentiae*); and he is not 'capable' in that sort of 'capability' which is a potentiality for having things done to its possessor (*posse impotentiae*).[25]

---

[24] On the same p. 220 he distinguishes between *congruentia in habitu* (in which God *non potest facere nisi quod iustitiae eius congrueret, si faceret*) and *congruentia in actu* (according to which *non potest facere nisi quod iustitiae eius congruit modo*). In both cases *iustitia eius* has the sense not of the 'justness by which God is just' (cf. n. 21) and which may be identified with the divine nature; but of some just disposition of things. In one case, the disposition is envisaged as now obtaining. In the other, it is one envisaged as able to obtain, if brought about by God. The *habitus* in relation to which the actual order of things is being viewed as the act, is thus not the divine nature, but the by now increasingly familiar set of Avicennian essences of God's option-neutral power (understood non-platonistically).

[25] In this question he starts the hare, apparently, of attributing to Anselm, *De conceptu virginali*, the puzzle of whether God can make a living steer out of a joint of meat. The Quaracchi editors note that the reference should be to Alan ab Insulis, *Theol. Reg.*, reg. 58 (PL 210; 648), loosely paraphrased. At the same reg. 58 is treated the puzzle of making

Alexander is not to be understood as saying here merely that we cannot grasp the divine nature (which he also held), and that for just that reason we are unable to determine an answer to the question. There is weight, which should not be missed, on 'conceived': 'if the power of God is conceived by the soul *absolute*'. For the adverb *absolute* here indicates not a way of taking expressions like 'power of God' (as in 'if "the power of God" were to be taken out of context (*absolute*)...') but a way in which we may conceive the power of God in our understanding. The "boundless ocean of God's power" referred to in this context is not the one to be identified with the divine nature as such, for that cannot be conceived in our understanding. It is that "power of God" to do things conceived by us *absolute*, and characterised more properly as the infinity of instantiable "things" or Avicennian essences. It is, in other words, God's option-neutral power.

The reason for which we are unable to settle the question one way or the other, is not that the nature of God (referred to obliquely in what is said) is something which escapes our understanding. (It does, of course, and Alexander is not one to deny that it does.) It is rather that even the power of God as conceived in our understanding in the manner indicated, is infinite. (Not necessarily in the same manner.) It is for that reason that we cannot settle the question. There is an infinity of "things" susceptible of being considered abstractly by us, as instantiable by an infinite, unrestricted power; for that reason we can never safely draw a line, saying, 'And those are all the instantiable possibilities that there are'. Even the "ocean" of "things" which we can conceive in our understanding as being not impossible to God, is in that manner a "boundless ocean" (*pelagus*).

The distinction crucially in play here is thus not that between the divine nature (which indeed we cannot understand) and some or all of creation (which may or may not be understandable by us). It is between two ways in which we may conceive of divine power in our understanding:

(1) divine power conceived in our understanding as being 'ordered according to the condition of power, of truth, of goodness', and

something black to be white. The two puzzles, which raise diverse but contrasting issues, appear from time to time in tandem; as here, and in Albert the Great (as will appear).

(2) divine power as conceived in our understanding *absolute*, in abstraction from whether or not it is actually ordered according to the condition of power etc.

On both sides of the distinction Alexander intends here, it is not divine power in itself which is imagined to be in play, but one or other manner in which we may conceive of it in our understanding. Alexander's choice of *speculatur* is apt, since we are not pretending to consider divine power directly, but in some reflection of it in our understanding; as in a glass, darkly. Since the distinction Alexander intends here is none other than the Power Distinction, the passage further informs us on his understanding of it.[26]

ALEXANDER AND THE POWER DISTINCTION

21. In later books of the *Summa*, even on topics where his predecessors had been using the Distinction, I have not (as yet) found any plain uses of it. This could suggest that the Power Distinction passages in Book 1, as we have it in the Quaracchi edition, are from a reviser who did not think it worth while to make similar revisions in later books. The passages in the *Summa* where the Distinction is used are very much of a piece with Book 1's treatment of divine power as a whole: if there is a reviser to credit with these, I would be inclined to identify him with Alexander himself.

This might seem to leave Alexander as a user of the Distinction, but not a particularly enthusiastic one. That may be so, but it is

[26] From what has been said, it should also be clear that the passage in no way substantiates the impression that Alexander 'understood absolute power to refer to everything that comes to mind—whether contradictory or not—while ordained power refers to the logically morally, or physically nonrepugnant'. Only if weight is put on 'comes to mind', so that only what is not self-contradictory can be said to come to mind, and thus be an element of the set of things God can do in option-neutral power, can the remark hold of the option-neutral arm. Intrinsically non-contradictory elements of the (inconsistent) set can indeed be viewed as contradictory with other elements of the set. The interpretation 'ordained power ... nonrepugnant' appears to rest on a failure to appreciate that *secundum conditionem potestatis, veritatis, bonitatis* refers here not to the classical attributes, but to the power or faithfulness (*veritas*) manifested in the *conditio* or *ordinatio rerum*. It is in any case not a true report of Alexander's view. The interpretation quoted is given in A. Funkenstein, *Theology and the Scientific Imagination* (1986), 129, despite a quotation from the passage at 129–30 n.

worth noting that the undramatic uses of the Distinction are of a piece with Alexander's almost sotto voce profession of a Negative Theology position on the nature of God. We could easily miss it. He gives just enough for us to appreciate the *cognitionem secundum veritatem* of his theology on the point. It is not impossible that no more is given, not because he does not think it important, but rather in order not to disturb whatever *affectionem ad bonitatem* he can suppose in his hearers.

What does appear from Alexander is that his own understanding of the Distinction was a non-platonist one. God's option-tied power is distinguished significantly from the comparable concept of God's option-neutral power. Neither is to be identified with God, who is referred to obliquely in expressions of both, and whose existence is required if either is to have justified application in the contexts in which the Distinction is used. It is not just any voluntary agent's option-tied or option-neutral power which is in question. Ideally, the whole of Alexander's treatises on divine power and divine knowledge ought to be taken more explicitly into account; for the contextual information they provide, and for the way they allow a clear picture of his sometimes understated views to emerge. For the present, however, it is time to take stock of what can be taken as established so far.

WINNING ACCEPTANCE

Roland and Hugh and Alexander all accepted the Power Distinction as identifiable by the working notion from Chapter 1 above. Can more now be said, towards specifying that notion? And ought we to note differences of significance in the manner of their acceptance, with a view to appreciating better the subsequent development of the Distinction?

As to what they accepted, the following can be said:

1. They all accepted a distinction 'between two ways in which we may consider God's power (to do things extrinsic to his nature): (1) in its supposed actual effect (or manifestation), the actual created order... and (2) in abstraction from whether any such thing is to be instantiated or not in extra-mental reality, provided such a thing is susceptible of

instantiation by an unrestrictedly active power (such as was, in one way or another, attributed to God)'. (Working notion, from Ch. 1 above.)

2. Except perhaps for Roland of Cremona, they all seem to have held a three-element, non-platonist understanding of the Distinction: in which God's option-neutral power is not to be identified with the divine nature. On the strength of one passage I left open the question of whether Roland of Cremona might not have held a platonist understanding, in which the option-neutral arm may be thought of as collapsing into the (true but literally insignificant) assertion of God's existence. I doubt in fact whether Roland could really be happy with a platonist interpretation of the option-neutral arm, because it would seem to evacuate *potentia conditionata rebus* (in his expression of the option-tied arm) of significance too. It may be that Roland, like Alexander of Hales in a couple of places, is platonist only in tone. In any case a more definite answer needs access to more of Roland's work than has yet been available to me, and I am prepared to take the matter to avizandum.

On the way they expressed the Distinction, this is to be said:

3. Not one of the three accepted and held rigidly to the canonical notation: *Deus (non) potest de potentia ordinata/absoluta sua F-ere.* One good reason for this is that in their time there was no canonical notation to accept. It has sometimes been said, for example, that it is in Alexander (whose use of the Distinction was apparently later in time than those of Hugh and of Roland) that the contrast *de potentia ordinata/absoluta dei* is first to be found.

They not only used expressions readily identifiable as variants for the canonical notation—*potentia regulata*, say, or *potentia conditionata rebus*, for *potentia ordinata*. They also used quite diverse ways of speaking, which may well conceal from modern readers that it is the Power Distinction which is being used in those ways of speaking. Yet when modern readers make the effort of comprehension which is needed, if we are to understand what is going on in those texts, the rewards can be considerable. Precisely by providing complementary information, in the alternative ways of speaking, such texts can reveal to us features of the Distinction which the canonical notation, by its very familiarity, may leave unaccented.

In what concerns the way the Distinction was used, this may be said:

4. All of the three men whose work was scrutinised in the present chapter, continue to exhibit the pattern of use already noted in the work of the pupils of the Masters, in Chapter 2. The Distinction, that is, is used knowingly, but in a limited range of narrowly theological puzzles, concerned in one way or another with whether the human race could have been redeemed otherwise than it was understood to have been redeemed.

More precisely, that holds for the texts seen above. Since for both Roland and Hugh further texts could come to light, the conclusion is provisional.

On the significance of the acceptance of the Distinction on the part of these men, this may be said:

5. Beyond a crucial threshold, passed by catching enough attention in their own time, the significance does not really depend on their merits as theologians. (And they were theologians of merit.) It depends on the part they played in their respective orders, and in the institutional involvement of their orders in academic theology. As was said above, it was these orders which at that time had easily the best adapted machinery for amassing cultural goods and conserving them selectively for posterity. Roland, Hugh, and Alexander were the men who set the machinery in motion at the crucial time.

It was apparently Hugh who introduced the Distinction into the theological discussions of the Dominicans; into those, at any rate, conducted where it mattered in those days, in the Theology Faculty at Paris. Roland, who seems to have followed Hugh in his use of the Distinction, was important not so much as a transmitter of particular ideas—not in Paris, at any rate, which he had left long before completing his *Summa*—as an instigator of institutional arrangements within which ideas could be examined or transmitted. Both at Paris and at Toulouse it was Roland who appropriated and handed on to the Dominicans their first chairs in Theology. Alexander was, as a user of the Power Distinction, later than the other two. But his teaching in the first Franciscan chair at Paris, and his *Summa*, were to be of extraordinary importance within the Franciscans and beyond. The *Summa*, revised on many points by John of la Rochelle and others, provided the model of a co-operatively produced Franciscan intellectual work. (The co-operative model was not taken up to any great extent, but the *Summa* itself was extensively used.) And Alexander's teaching in effect provided the model of a bourgeois academic career within declared Franciscan ideals, within little more than a dozen years of the death of Francis. Whether Francis himself would have thought much of the bourgeois academic model of Franciscan living, is unclear. The results, for philosophical and academically theological studies at any rate, were certainly benign. The model was taken up and institutionalised by Bonaventure, giving us the achievements of Duns Scotus and William of Ockham, and a number of others whose work is not all that far behind in intellectual interest.

No doubt the Distinction might have caught on, without having been taken into the staple of the teaching of the new orders, and into the enduringly influential *Summa* of Alexander. It might have survived through independent recourse by later scholastics to William of Auxerre, for example, whose work retained a certain currency.[27] As it happened, however, it was through Hugh and Alexander, and through the chairs established by Roland and Alexander, that it was transmitted.[28] To users who, in some important cases, were prepared to use it to rather more radical purpose.

[27] For the "fortune" of William of Auxerre's work in later times see the Introductory volume of the Ribailler edn., as at n. 11 to Ch. 2 above, esp. 6–24; also *Dict. Sp.*, s.v. 'Guillaume d'Auxerre'.

[28] A more detailed historical treatment would have to examine further examples from the present stage in the career of the Distinction. An example from Guerric of St Quentin, OP, successor of Hugh of St Cher in the chair appropriated for the Dominicans by Roland, was given in n. 17 above. A further example, kindly communicated to me by Dr Randi, from MS Vienna ONB 1532, 18rb, is from Odo Rigaud, OFM, teacher of St Bonaventure and 'an important witness to the influence of Alexander of Hales' (Gilson, *History* (1955), 683). An *abbreviatio* of his Sentence commentary contains a number of references to the Power Distinction, including: 'Potentia dei intelligitur dupliciter. Sicut esse dupliciter, esse absolutum et esse ordinatum, similiter potentia absoluta vel potentia ordinata.' (*In 1 Sent.*, d. 42, a. 1; text from Dr Randi, punctuation from me.)

4

St Albert the Great, OP

Albert's contribution to an understanding of the Distinction is considerable. He makes it plain in more than one place that it is God's power to do things extrinsic to his nature, which is in question when the Power Distinction is applicable. He uses the helpful name of God's 'operant power' (*potentia operans*) for it. And he has some particularly helpful ways of describing God's option-neutral power. He is also determinedly adherent to a Negative Theology.

ALBERT THE GREAT (a. 1196–15/NOV. 1280)

1. Albert, said to be from Lauingen on the Danube, not far from Ulm, was a big man physically and a prodigy of learning over a vast range of matters. He seemed to get everywhere and look into everything. He was known even in his own day, and only in part in deference to his physique, as Albertus Magnus. He was also known as *Doctor universalis* and *Doctor expertus*. He imposed a strongly personal mark on pretty well everything he touched.[1] Unlike most of the prominent schoolmen, he gave

---

[1] On Albert's life see J. Weisheipl, 'The Life and Works of St Albert the Great', in *Albertus Magnus and the Sciences: Commemorative Essays 1980* (Toronto, 1980), 13–51; and s.v. 'Albert' in *New Cath. Enc.* Still basic: H. C. Scheeben, *Albert der Grosse: Zur Chronologie seines Lebens* (Vechta, 1931), XIV + 167 pp.; and P. de Loë, 'De vita et scriptis B. Alberti Magni', *Anal. Boll.* 19 (1900), 257–84; 20 (1901), 273–316; 21 (1902), 361–71. More recent discussions of biographical matters are reviewed in pp. 70–6 of C. Wagner, 'Alberts Naturphilosophie im Licht der neueren Forschung (1979–83)', *Freiburger Zeitschrift für Philosophie und Theologie* 32 (1985), 65–104. On byways of Albert's life and cult, especially in Germany, see *Albert von Lauingen... Festschrift 1980* (Historischer Verein Dillingen an der Donau, 1980), including the bibliogr. by A. Layer, esp. for publications reflecting German interest in the post-1930 period. The critical Cologne edn. of Albert's *Opera*, in progress from the Albertus Magnus Institute, is published in Munster; a score of volumes have appeared since 1951. Two earlier 'complete editions' were by P. Jammy, OP (Lyons, 1651), and by A. Borgnet (Paris, 1890–9). The introductions to the Cologne edn., where available, are to be consulted on all matters of authenticity and chronology. For Albert's thought see

explicit attention to concerns, real or supposed, of women. Almost alone of leading schoolmen, he gives the impression of actually knowing some.

He imposed his mark on his reading. If some respected authority was contradicted by his experience, or by that of personal acquaintances whose testimony he thought worth reporting, he would say so. If he thought certain matters unsuitable for treatment in a certain genre of work, he would act accordingly. So he kept strictly theological issues and devices (the Power Distinction among these, it would appear) out of works he intended to be non-theological. Even when expounding the *De interpretatione*, for example, he refused to treat 'the necessity of the order of causes, fate, fortune, design, chance, the certitude of divine providence in singular and voluntary contingents' as *quidam* had been doing (*In Periherm.*, Bk. 1, tr. 5, ed. Borgnet, 1: 423). Never mind that Aristotle himself had shown the way. Despite his consuming curiosity both in science and in matters of common life, Albert is quick to scorn *curiosi* whose inquiries he judges unprofitable. In what was perhaps his last reference to the Power Distinction he was addressing one of the 43 questions put to him (as to Kilwardby and Aquinas) for a verdict by the Master-General of the Dominicans. Albert answered the question, continuing not to dispute the legitimacy of the Distinction, which he had been using for many years. But he began his answer by noting that the argument in question depended on a fatuously imaginary supposition: *de fantasia fatuitatis procedit*. He also concluded the series of answers by informing the Master-General that he had complied out of friendship and respect for his office, but that at well over 80 he (Albert) had better to do with his remaining time and failing sight than answering silly questions. A number of these, it may be worth noting, are of the 'what if' sort whose proliferation some historians have thought the Distinction to encourage.[2]

now A. de Libera, *Albert le Grand et la philosophie* (Paris, 1990), rev. *Tijdschrift voor filosofie*, 53 (1991), 544–5, which unfortunately appeared too late to be of assistance in the present book. For bibliography 1960–80, J. Schöpfer in G. Meyer, A. Zimmermann, P.-B. Lüttringhaus (eds.), *Albertus Magnus: Doctor universalis 1280–1980* (Mainz, 1980), 495–508, also refers to the main earlier bibliographies. For current bibliography the *Rassegna di letteratura tomistica* nearly always has a section on Albert.

[2] Cologne edn. 17/1: 45–64. The question is treated below.

2. The breath of fresh intolerance which comes through in his writings was not necessarily so welcome to his contemporaries, when it impinged on those around him. His own practice was to travel everywhere on foot. This was common enough in those times for people not of the equestrian classes or higher clergy, or their emulators. But Albert's itineraries, into his 80s, were rather more far-ranging than those of most of his contemporaries. They included areas of what are now France, Latvia, Italy, some Balkan countries, and countless places between. As a Dominican provincial, however, he erected his practice into an inflexible norm for his subjects, ignoring the pleas of weaker brethren who had sought to travel by coach or on horseback. It may well have been intolerance in other practical matters which led to an episcopal career—as Prince Bishop of Ratisbon—of only two years, ending in separation by mutual consent. Albert, incidentally, was allowed to continue drawing some of the episcopal income.

From a reader's point of view the countervailing gain from what may have seemed to acquaintances something of a disregard for others' points of view, is a determination pervasive in Albert's writings to understand things in his own words, to make himself understood to others, and to sift things thoroughly for himself to begin with. Comparisons with Ryle, who likewise remained athletic into a fair age, are not entirely out of place.

3. Albert's theological work is largely concentrated into two periods, separated by the twenty years during which he was compiling the expositions of Aristotle and the encyclopaedic treatments for which he long enjoyed a great reputation. In the later period the chief work is the *Summa theologiae* from *c*.1270. In the earlier period, from before 1240 to around 1250 (when his protégé Aquinas was becoming the Dominicans' leading light in Theology at Paris) three works are prominent. The earliest, the *De natura boni*, is not a work of systematic theology, properly speaking, and has practically nothing to present purpose. The second is the Commentary on the Sentences, begun in the early 1240s if not before, and revised for the public domain by 1249. This will be used below. The third work is a kind of Summa, whose treatments of matters of divine power would suggest that

it was not a work addressed to academic theologians.[3] Difficulties which Albert treats frankly and carefully in the roughly contemporary Sentence Commentary, are rather glossed over or skated round in this "Summa": by means, at times, of devices provided by Anselm, and used with acknowledgement. At the same time the incidental treatments of philosophical *communia* are presented as though to a knowing audience. This early "Summa", then, not to be confounded with the later *Summa theologiae*, could represent an encyclopaedic and relatively elementary course of christian doctrine, addressed to an audience who have already completed important parts of their Arts courses. One such audience could be of Dominican students who had completed at least part of the Arts course, but were not (yet) due to study academic theology. Another could be of students for the priesthood, whether Dominicans or not, who were not necessarily intended for the study of academic theology, but had been studying in Arts. For that matter, it might even have been thought appropriate to students who, after Arts, were studying medicine or law. In twentieth-century Scottish universities, undergraduates in secular subjects who might wish to teach later in Catholic schools, used to attend lectures in christian doctrine: at a level supposedly higher than that taught in the schools, but without pretensions to being academic. I mention the non-academic allure of the early "Summa", because in it is no apparent trace of the Power Distinction. If the work is not intended as a contribution to academic theology, that will not be surprising. The evidence for Albert's use of the Power Distinction comes chiefly from the Commentary on the Sentences and from the *Summa theologiae*, his chief works of systematic theology. Before reviewing it, it is worth noting the backcloth of rigorously Negative Theology against which it should be appreciated.

---

[3] Weisheipl, citing Glorieux, says that the work 'originated in Albert's public disputations in the University of Paris', and calls it the *Summa parisiensis* (at *Albertus* (Toronto, 1980), 22). From the passages in which divine power is touched on, it would seem rather to be a work of *vulgarisation*, and not particularly *haute*. On the less academic Dominicans referred to: 'These "Fratres Communes", no matter what their age, are the "iuniores", "incipientes" and "simplices" who are addressed in so many Dominican prefaces. They are, on the whole, those who had not had the chance of a higher education in the manner of Albert or Thomas... or other intellectual lights of the "docibiles" or Lector class.' (L. Boyle, *The Setting of the* Summa theologiae *of Saint Thomas* (Toronto, 1982), 30 pp., 2–3.)

ALBERT AND NEGATIVE THEOLOGY

4. That Albert held a Negative Theology view on the divine nature is not usually doubted, even by interpreters who are reluctant to see such views in other well-known medievals. His forthrightness leaves no room for the doubts which some of his contemporaries can leave in the minds of even careful interpreters. Then too he put more weight on the view than many others, by permitting its constraints to direct or constrain his method in theology quite generally.[4]

Even in the case of the blessed, Albert will not allow essentially more than a knowledge that some God exists—what he calls a *quia est* knowledge of God:

> We say that all the blessed will see that God exists (*substantiam dei*)—the *quia est* of it. But no created understanding (*intellectus*) can see what it may be (*quid autem sit*). (*In De div. nom.*, cit. from a Paris and a Vatican MS in H.-F. Dondaine, 'Cognoscere de Deo "quid est"', *RTAM* 22 (1955), 72–8, 74.)

H.-F. Dondaine saw this as *une audacieuse distinction* between *quia est* and *quid est*, but it is surely the one already long in use. A comparable treatment by Alexander of Hales, and a comparable misleading use of the expression *substantia dei* (misleading to us twentieth-century, post-Deistical readers, that is) was seen above. No doubt, Albert concedes, the understanding of the blessed is less imperfect than that of the same people while alive (*in via*),

---

[4] Albert, 'à la différence de presque tous ses contemporains férus d'augustinisme traditionnel, lui [scil. à la négativité méthodique] témoigne grande estime' (É.-H. Wéber, 'L'Interprétation par Albert le Grand de la Théologie Mystique de Denys le Ps.-Areopagite', in Meyer, Zimmermann, Lüttringhaus 1980: 409–39, 409–10). Albert summarises his understanding of negative theologies near the beginning of one of his commentaries on the Pseudo-Denis: 'negativae theologiae, sicut in Tertio Capitulo dicitur, incipiunt a manifestis nobis sensibilibus, negando ea a deo, et sic procedentes removendo omnia ab ipso relinquunt intellectum nostrum in quodam confuso, a quo negantur omnia quae novit, et de quo non potest affirmare quid sit. Affirmativae autem theologiae producunt nobis occultum divinitatis in manifestum, secundum quod significantur ab eminentiae causa procedere ea quae sunt manifesta nobis, sicut cum dicitur deus bonus, significatur, a quo omnis bonitas in creaturis; et cum dicitur pater, significatur "ex quo omnis paternitas in caelo et in terra nominatur". Et ideo, quia ista doctrina considerat huiusmodi remotionem quae est per negationes, aliae autem considerat affirmationes de deo, ista magis debet dici mystica quam aliae, ex hoc quod in occulto nos relinquit, aliae autem ex occulta nos trahunt in manifesta.' (*Sup. Myst. theol.*, ch. 1, Cologne edn. 37/2: 454–5.)

for it is freed from many kinds of inhibition. But it remains a created understanding, with all the imperfections and short-comings which that entails. I translate the rather dense passage more freely and more tendentiously than I normally consider permissible, as a literal translation, without expansions, could be downright misleading:

We concede that a created understanding cannot attain perfectly to God, so as to bring it about that nothing of what may count as knowledge about God (*cognitionis eius*) on some creature's part, should remain outside that created understanding; but God is yoked to the understanding as something exceeding understanding; in that the "what" of knowledge—where God is concerned—cannot be taken in by that understanding, because what God is has no determinate bound (*non habet terminationem*). Neither can the "on account of" element in knowledge be taken in, because there is no "because of" in the case of God's existence (*non habet causam*). Neither can a determinate 'that____' be had, because God's existence has neither a remote cause nor a proportionate effect; and for that reason neither *in via* nor *in patria* will there be seen anything of God, save the confused "that" of knowledge that God exists, although God himself may be seen more or less clearly in accordance with the diverse modes of vision involved, and the diverse modes of those doing the seeing. (*In Epist. V Dionysii*, dub. 1, Cologne edn. 37/2; 495, already cit. Dondaine, *RTAM* (1955), 75, from Borgnet, 14; 895b.)[5]

Albert is here eliminating, in the case of coming to know God, a succession of kinds of knowledge or elements of the knowledge which might initially be thought to be obtainable, and which may be had in other matters. He leaves only one possibility.

Albert eliminates from our putative knowledge of God all the modes of knowledge about things which we have of the things around us. He eliminates the knowledge of what God is (*quid sit*):

---

[5] Strictly speaking, *in via* is not necessarily what might be recognised by us as 'alive', but signifies the condition of everyone who is not yet either finally blessed (*in patria*), or finally reprobate. The text, now available in Cologne edn. 37/2: 495, runs: Solutio. Concedimus quod intellectus creatus non potest perfecte attingere ad deum, ita ut nihil de cognitione eius maneat extra eum, sed sub quadam confusione iungitur ei quasi excedenti, eo quod non potest de ipso accipi "quid", quia non habet terminationem; neque "propter quid", quia non habet causam; neque "quia" determinatum, quia non habet causam remotam nec effectum proportionatum; et ideo nec in via nec in patria videtur de ipso nisi "quia" confusum, quamvis ipse deus videatur clarius vel minus clare secundum diversos modos visionis et videntium.

in so far as knowing what [something] is implies that comprehension which is the matching (*contactus*) of an understanding over the bounds of the thing, [what God is] is not known by any creature, either angelic or human. (*Sum. theol.* qu. 89, ed. Borgnet, 33; 168b.)[6]

In God's case there are no *termini rei*. Even God, who presumably knows himself perfectly, therefore cannot for his own case know *quid sit*, in the technical sense of that, which is of its nature applicable to things of a determinate kind. God is not such a thing, on Albert's view.

Albert also eliminates any knowledge *propter quid*, since that is knowledge which is had, when it is had, *per causas*. To be God, is to be something not susceptible of having causes. Again, then, even God cannot have knowledge *propter quid* of himself.

Most surprisingly perhaps, to us who almost inevitably work to some extent in the shadow of the Deists, Albert rejects even *scientia quia*, strictly understood. What Hume willingly allows through the characters Demea and Philo alike—'surely, where reasonable Men treat these Subjects, the Question can never be concerning the Being, but only the Nature of the Deity' (Philo, at *Dials.* 2, ed. Price 1976; 160)—Albert considers too indulgent.[7] He rejects even *scientia quia*, strictly understood: which may be nothing more than knowing of something determinate, that it exists (knowing that it instantiates a determinate concept, perhaps). It is a kind of knowledge we can have, in the views regularly followed in medieval aristotelian thought, from knowledge either of a remote cause, or a proportionate effect. There cannot be causes of God, as was seen, so there cannot be remote causes. And there is no proportionate effect. Those attracted to "analogies" or "models" as a putative ground for knowledge of God, as against some concept of ours which we may imagine

[6] Sed prout 'quid est' dicit comprehensionem quae est contactus intellectūs super terminos rei, non cognoscitur ab aliqua creatura, nec angelica, nec humana. (*Sum. theol.* 2, qu. 89, ed. Borgnet, 33: 168b.)

[7] In this Albert may appear more severe than Hume's Demea, who affirms his doubt concerning the nature of God 'from the Infirmities of the human Understanding'; and more severe than Hume's Philo professes to be (if we ignore Hume's irony), when locating the difficulty in 'our limited View and Comprehension'. (Hume, *Dialogues*, 2, ed. Price (Oxford, 1976), 159 and 161.) Albert, however, is not questioning 'the Being of the Deity', i.e. that some God exists, but only the precision or scientifical exploitability of the expressions in which it may be asserted.

(for whatever reason) to represent in some way the being of God, can usefully note Albert's arguments here.

5. The most Albert allows—not only *in via*, but *in patria*, to the blessed—is a confused variety of *scientia quia*:

Neither *in via* nor *in patria* will there be seen anything of him save a confused *scientia quia*; although God himself may be seen more clearly or less clearly in accordance with the diverse modes of the seers seeing, or the object of the seeing. (Cit. H.-F. Dondaine, *RTAM* (1955), 74, from Albert, *In Epist. V Dionysii*, dub. 1, ed. Borgnet, 14; 895b.)

Elsewhere he says:

Where knowledge of God is concerned, are not to be found any of the ways of knowing which are native to us, in which we acquire items of knowledge.... *scientia quia*, because [God] does not have a proportionate effect; but our mind takes in some kind of divine light, something above what is native to us, which elevates [our mind] above all the ways of seeing native to it, and by which it comes to the seeing of God, *confuse tamen, et non determinate cognoscens*... (*De myst. theol.*, ch. 2, ed. Borgnet, 14; 840a; referred to at P. Ribes Montané, *Cognoscibilidad y demostración de Dios según San Alberto Magno* (Barcelona, 1968), 192 pp., 124 n.)[8]

The "confusion" here, is that involved in knowing that some God exists, without being able to be more determinate—as we might wish to, by quantifying more determinately for example. That, I think, is what Albert intends by speaking of it as something *confusum*, or as known by one *confuse et non determinate cognoscens*, or as *sub quadam confusione* (as here in the *In Epist. V Dionysii* from the sentence immediately preceding the one just quoted through Dondaine, and also at *De myst. theol.*, I. 6, ed. Borgnet, 14; 835a, referred to at Ribes Montané 1968; 125 n.). It must not be misunderstood. In particular it must not be mistaken for the *confusio* of incompatible forms, as in a putative *compositio* of square and circular; which sets a limit on what can be known to be true. (Albert's use of this point appears below.) Yet both

---

[8] Dicendum quod in deo vacant omnes modi cognoscendi naturales nobis, quibus scientias acquirimus; neque per se notus est sicut principia, neque "propter quid", quia non habet causam, neque "quia", quia non habet effectum proportionatum. Sed mens nostra suscipit quoddam lumen divinum quod est supra naturam suam, quod elevat eam super omnes modos visionis naturales, et per illud venit ad visionem dei, confuse tamen et non determinate cognoscens "quia". Et ideo dicitur quod per non-videre videtur deus, scil. per non-videre naturale. (Cologne edn. 37/2: 466.)

are *confusio,* and alike set limits on understanding: where there is *confusio* on either head, there is no possibility of *contactus intellectūs super terminos rei* (as at *Sum. theol.* 2, qu. 89, ed. Borgnet, 33; 168b). The knowledge that some God exists is knowledge, albeit possessed *confuse.* That some God exists may still be true: that we can assert it only *confuse* does not mean that it cannot be true, only that we cannot understand what we are asserting to be true, and cannot know which truth it is. As will appear, Aquinas makes much of this sort of point. It imposes no great restriction on his theology, as in his view there can be no more than one truth about God anyway. (For all of this, see Ch. 6 below.) It seems to me that this is the tenor of Albert's view too on the "confusion" of our knowledge that some God exists, even when such knowledge is had in the conditions obtaining *in patria.* The reason in any case, for there not strictly being so much as *scientia quia* of God, but only a "confused" analogate of it, is that God, if there is a God, is not the sort of thing that can come in determinate multitudes or quantities, or in any determinate mode.

I add a further passage:

God is not bounded by boundaries, because he is simple; neither is his being comprehended in any respect, but he is pure actuality, free of all potentiality, not the sort of thing which can be *receptus* in any way in respect of his being. And for that reason an understanding cannot comprehend him in respect of what he is, neither can a name signify in such a way by expressing the whole of what he is. And thus his quiddity is not proportionate to anything, but an intellect by attaining to his existing (*ad substantiam eius*) comes to know him, either in his likeness (*similitudine*), as *in via* in a glass darkly, or immediately as *in patria.* (*In Lib. Dion. De div. nom.,* ch. 13, § 3, ed. Dondaine at *RTAM* 22 (1955), 74.)[9]

What even Albert leaves unemphasised here is that what he is asserting to be known immediately *in patria* rather than *in*

---

[9] In the Cologne edn. 37/1: 448, the reference is rather to *In De div. nom.* ch. 13, par. 27: Deus autem neque terminis terminatum est, quia simplex est, neque esse suum est comprehensum in aliquo, sed est actus purus, absolutus ab omni potentia, non receptus in aliquo secundum esse suum; et ideo intellectus non potest comprehendere ipsum secundum "quid est", neque nomen potest eum sic significare exprimendo totum id quod est, et sic nulli proportionata est sua quiditas. Sed intellectus attingendo ad substantiam ipsius cognoscit ipsum vel in sua similitudine, sicut in via per speculum et in aenigmate, vel immediate, ut in patria.

similitudine (as *in via*), is that some God exists: not *quid sit*. That way of using *substantiam dei* has already been seen in another passage from Albert, and in one from Alexander of Hales. It is used elsewhere in the work from which the last quotation was taken:

We say that God's existing—*quia est*—all the blessed will see; but what he may be (*quid autem sit*), no created understanding can see. (From Dondaine, at *RTAM* (1955), 74.)

This, he explains, is because the *quid est* type of knowledge requires that 'the bounds of its essence and the whole of its being should be enclosed in a created understanding; and so the created understanding would be greater than God, since everything which encloses is greater than that which is enclosed in it, which is absurd'. (Same ref. in Dondaine 1955.)[10]

One further passage provides convenient bridging from Albert's distinction between *ut est* (referring to existence in extramental reality) and *quid est* (referring to the content of what something can be said to be, whether the content is instantiated of not), to Aquinas's distinction of two ways of taking *esse* in the *De ente et essentia*:

We will see God *in patria* as he is (*sicuti est*).... But... it is one thing to see God as something existent (*ut est*), another to see what God is (*quid est deus*); just as it is one thing to see something (*videre rem*), and another to see what the thing is (*quid est res*). For seeing a thing 'as an existent' (*ut est*) is to see the being or existence of the thing (*esse rei sive existentiam rei*), but to see what a thing is (*quid est res*) is to see the proper definition of the thing, including all the defining limits (*terminos*) of the thing. (Albert, *De resurrectione*, ed. Dondaine *RTAM* (1955), 75 n.)

Albert's insinuation that *sicuti est* in the Scriptures was intended, in its context, to be read as he intends *ut est* here, is almost certainly unjustified on principles of good exegesis of texts in context. He is not to be read as offering that kind of interpretation.

---

[10] Dondaine's text, which I have not found in ch. 1 of the Cologne edn., runs: Dicimus quod substantiam dei—quia est—omnes beati videbunt; quid autem sit, nullus intellectus videre potest. Cum enim cognitio "quid est" sit principalis causarum, oporteret (si cognosceretur "quid est") ut circumspicerentur termini essentiae eius et totum esse eius clauderetur in intellectu creato; et ita intellectus creatus esset maior deo. Quod absurdum est. (Dondaine in *RTAM* (1955), 74, from Paris Mazar., fo. 105^{r}b, and Vat. lat. 712, fo. 118^{r}a.)

If challenged, he could well reply that what he is offering is (on his views on the knowability of God) the only interpretation which can be literally true. What is to be marked here is not the very different ways in which medieval theologians and the more cautious modern exegetes approach texts, but the commitment Albert persists in showing to a rigorously negative view on alleged knowledge on our part of the divine nature.

6.   In his Commentary on the *De divinis nominibus* of the Pseudo-Denis Albert explains the point of the negations of the *via negativa*. A doubt had been raised:

A denial proves (*certificat*) nothing. What proves nothing, cannot be a way towards knowing something. Therefore we cannot ascend towards God by denying everything or taking away from everything.

Albert replies:

A denial which leaves nothing behind, proves nothing; but by denials which do leave something behind, the confusion of our understanding is narrowed down to something certain; and we use denials in the place of *differentiae* in connection with those things on account of whose simplicity we cannot take positive *differentiae*. Just as, if I were to say that the soul is not a corporeal substance, leaving untouched that it is a substance, I narrow down (*determino*) "soul" towards something or other; and so on until the proper being of the thing may be reached; so likewise, as Rabbi Moses says, the confusion of our understanding in regard to God is in some way narrowed down by denials, although we may never reach his proper being. (*In De div. nom.*, ch. 7, par. 29, Cologne edn. 37/1; 358–9.)[11]

In the case of God, what is left after the denials is God's subsisting. This is what *substantia dei* means here: that something exists, sans phrase. Since, if anything does exist without restriction, there cannot be more than one of it, we are assured of correct reference, if there is successful reference at all in our

---

[11] Dicendum quod negatio quae nihil relinquit, nihil certificat, sed per negationes quae aliquid relinquunt, determinatur confusio intellectus ad aliquid certum, et utimur eis loco differentiarum in his quorum propter sui simplicitatem differentias positivas accipere non possumus; sicut si dicam quod anima non est substantia corporea, relinquendo quod est substantia, determino animam ad aliquid, et sic deinceps, quousque deveniatur ad esse proprium rei. Et similiter, ut dicit Rabbi Moyses, per negationes determinatum aliquo modo confusio intellectus nostri circa deum, quamvis numquam deveniamus ad esse proprium ipsius. (Cologne edn: 37/1: 359.)

dictiones purporting to refer to God. The trouble to be feared in general where there is *confusio*, is either that there cannot be anything for our locutions to refer to (in the case where there is *confusio* of forms), or that they might refer to something other than that which we intended them to refer to (in the case where the *confusio* is from a lack of determinacy in the target). What the denials of the *via negativa* are to be seen as doing, is to narrow down the *confusio* of the latter type, to the point where, if there is successful reference at all in our purported references to God (in short, if there is some God to be referred to), there cannot be reference to anything other than God. We are thus left with something *certum*, something which can be referred to without fear of error concerning the target.

COMMENTARY ON THE SENTENCES (1245-9?)

If I understand the account in Weisheipl 1980, and the introduction to vol. xxxvii of the Cologne edition, the text in Borgnet vols. 25–30 is that of the *ordinatio* prepared for the public domain after Albert had become a Master of Theology at Paris. He taught there between 1245 and 1248, succeeding Guerric of St Quentin in the second of the two chairs by then appropriated by the Dominicans. In 1248 he was instructed to return to Cologne, to found a *studium generale* (which he might have been running in all but name some time earlier anyway). There, it is said, he completed the Commentary on the Sentences. Both at Paris and Cologne in these years Albert was working with intensity in theology. During the same years he was completing the commentaries on the Pseudo-Denis, culminating in that on the *De divinis nominibus* around 1250.[12]

7.   On the knowability of God, the doctrine of the *In Sent.* is unsurprisingly the same as that just seen: 'that God exists (*divina substantia*), is seen by all the blessed. As to how he is seen, we

---

[12] The commentaries on the Pseudo-Denis were already being taught by Albert (and studied by Aquinas) before the return to Cologne. It now appears from independently mounted arguments that it was in Paris that Aquinas began to study Albert's works, and that he did not rejoin him (at Cologne) until some time after Albert's return. See L.-J. Bataillon's comments at *Rev. sc. ph. th.* 56 (1972), 498–500.

thus say, without prejudice, that his being is seen immediately
by being conjoined, to the effect that God offers himself to our
understanding, through his existing (*per substantiam suam*), like the
understanding to itself' (*In 1 Sent.*, d. 1, art. 15, sol., ed. Borgnet,
25; 36). That is tortuous, and might encourage some unreflecting
hearers to think of *divina substantia* as "divine substance", some
imagined divine "stuff", whose content they might imagine to
have access to *in patria*. That Albert has not abandoned his way
of using *substantia dei* for "God's subsisting", appears more plainly
from his reply to an objection on the same page: 'it is to be said
that God simply is incomprehensible—is incomprehensible, that
is, as the infinite God he is; because something of the like [i.e.
something infinite] cannot be grasped, save in a particular
modality, to wit, by coming to know that it is infinite' (same qu.,
ad 5, ed. Borgnet, 25; 36b). In the same column, in reply to the
objection numbered 8 in Borgnet, he repeats: 'it is to be said
that the infinite can be reached out to (*attingi potest*), but something
of it always remains outwith the one reaching out to it; and for
that reason, in that precisely it is something infinite, it is said not
to be attained'. And again, in that same reply to objection 8: 'an
understanding reaching God (*attingens deum*) reaches him, but in
such wise that something much, even infinite, of God's might
(*virtutis*) is always outside that understanding; and because his
might is his being, for that reason also the immensity of his being
is outwith understanding'. The shortfall is due not only to the
limitation inherent in any created intellect, and none but created
intellects can reach out in this way, but to something which
cannot be had in the infinite God, and is a prerequisite in
anything to be grasped by a (created) understanding: 'there is no
bound closing off the whole thing which is God'.[13]

In discussion of a doubt raised he gives a severely Negative
Theology content to another formula soothing to the pious, when
allowing that 'comprehension' can be understood in either of

[13] The texts run: 'dicendum, quod deus simpliciter est incomprehensibilis, et hoc est
ut est infinitus: quia sic attingi non potest, nisi secundum quid, scil. cognoscendo infinitum
esse' (ad 5); 'dicendum quod infinitum attingi potest, sed aliquid eius semper manet extra
attingentem: et ideo in eo quod est infinitum dicitur non attingi (ad 8); 'intellectus
attingens deum attingit ipsum, ita quod multum et infinitum virtutis semper est extra
ipsum: et quia virtus sua est essentia sua, ideo etiam immensitas essentiae est extra
intellectum' (later in ad 8); and cf. 'licet non sit terminus claudens totum quod est deus'
(ad 9).

two ways. In the first, what is meant is matching between the understanding and the boundaries of the thing (*tactus intellectūs super terminos rei*), and in this manner God is not comprehended. Albert's description of "comprehension" here is weaker than that which was to be current, amounting to no more than minimal understanding of content. It was readily allowed that even the blessed do not comprehend the divine nature (in the stronger sense of knowing it in all its respects). What Albert was thus denying, when denying that God could be 'comprehended' even in the weaker sense by the blessed, was any understanding of the nature of God, and any knowledge *quid est*; just as in the passages seen earlier. Perhaps the blessed have progressed over those still unjudged, in knowing more of what God is not; but progress of that sort is little if anything better than the progress possible in the expansion of π.

Albert's remaining sense for 'comprehension' does nothing to take away from the severity of his Negative Theology here. This is the sense of completely taking hold of something, as of an end to be sought, so as not to let it slip. This kind of comprehension, he says, is had principally in an affective relationship (*in affectu*); and in this sense God is 'comprehended'. Albert here was using a more familiar sense, and expressing a doctrine both familiar and more palatable to the pious. The blessed, *in patria*, were often called *comprehensores*, as against those still *in via*, who were called *viatores*. The usage remained familiar enough to be alluded to by Shakespeare's Hamlet, in 'that undiscover'd country [*patria*] from whose bourne | No traveller [*viator*] returns'.

8. At *In 1 Sent.*, d. 35, Albert provides the outline of a strategy for treating not only divine power, but other attributions to God, consistent with a Negative Theology. He leaves this as an outline, however, and does not develop it here. Knowledge, power, and will, he says, can all be conceived in either of two ways: *in se*, or *in relatione ad opus*. Power, considered in itself, is (logically) prior to knowledge and will. But when knowledge and power are considered *in relatione ad opus*, knowledge is to be seen as directing, power as executing. Power considered as 'operant' (*operans*), as power to do things extrinsic to the nature of the agent, is to be thought of as something subsequent to knowledge and will. (*In 1 Sent.*, d. 35B, art. 3, ad 4 and 5, ed. Borgnet, 26: 183–4.)

At *In 1 Sent.*, d. 42 he is concerned throughout with God's power to do things, considered *in relatione ad opus*. That something more has to be said on the kind of *opus* in question is already hinted in a heading to d. 42, in which the topic is described as God's power 'in comparison to the possible things which he can bring about'.

Albert does not forget here that power can also be considered *in se*, expressly allowing this in art. 5, apropos of an "authority" quoted from Richard of St Victor. Richard—one of Scotland's few recognised mystics—had been giving something of a logical pedigree with a view to making Trinitarian expositions: describing knowledge as 'out of power' (logically presupposing power), and love as being 'out of knowledge and power'. Albert does not dispute Richard's remarks, appropriate to power considered *in se*, but is more concerned with two other and contrasting ways of considering power (and God's power in particular) *in relatione ad opus*.

In one of these it is called power (to do things) in comparison, indifferently, with any or all of the *opera* attributable to it: *dicitur potentia comparata ad opus indefinite*. It is in this way, he adds, that we say God can do many things *de potentia absoluta*, which he neither does nor will do. It is thus a power to do things, when the "things" in question are, indifferently, any of the "things" possible to be done by the power in question. The point of this manner of comparison, is that it permits a power to be specified, and thus mentioned in reasonings, without necessarily implying that it is exercised or ever will be exercised in any *opus* of the kind envisaged.

Except on rather doctrinaire kinds of empiricist grounds, there would seem nothing inherently objectionable in specifying a power by reference to some merely envisaged exercise. Few would be incapable, on a commonsensical level, of understanding 'the destructive power of the explosives placed to destroy the tunnels and bridges into Switzerland, in the event of invasion in 1940'; though that power was not put into execution. And few would not be capable of considering it a power specifically distinct from the (musical) power of the man who brought his alpenhorn to the party, and was not called upon to play. A Hobbist will have to deny any difference between the two powers; but the problem just could be with Hobbism, rather than with distinguishing the kinds of power. In general, independently of narrowly empiricist considerations, power to F can be distinguished specifically from power to G, by reference to the *opus* of F-ing, made indefinite to any *opus* of the kind specified; even if no *opus* of the kind specified should in fact be put into execution.

Specification of a power by reference in an indefinite manner to an *opus*—the intrinsic content of the *opus*—is an essential feature of the appeal to option-neutral powers quite generally.

The indefiniteness of the manner of reference must not be confounded with the generality of the range concerned. In God's option-neutral power, any specifiable *opus* will serve. In other agents, whose powers are restricted, and restricted in various ways, the range will vary from agent to agent. We may not always know what our own is, until we try. But even in our case, the crucial issue is a metaphysical and not an epistemological one. Unless there is at least one *opus* possible to me in (my) option-neutral power, then I cannot be accounted an agent with any option-neutral power at all. In the case of God's option-neutral power, where the power envisaged is envisaged as unrestricted in any way, there is no room for restricting ranges of possible things. (Of course 'possible things' is carrying weight. As will appear, not everything we might seem to imagine will be able to count as a "possible thing" within this kind of view.)

What Albert in this place (*In 1 Sent.*, d. 42, art. 5) is opposing to *potentia comparata ad opus indefinite*, is power to do things, considered as 'a power regulated by an operative skill, and executing something preconceived in wisdom, and something willed by a will'. Power considered in this latter way comes down to the power to do 'things which will be done, or have been done, or are'.

In these two ways of considering (God's) power *in relatione ad opus*, we thus have the ways distinguished in the Power Distinction:

(1) potentia comparata ad opus indefinite, *and*
(2) potentia regulata ab arte operativa, et exsequens praeconceptum a sapientia et volitum a voluntate. (*In 1 Sent.*, d. 42A, art. 5, sol., ed Borgnet, 26: 362a.)

Albert, as was seen above, himself identified the power in (1) with *potentia absoluta (dei)*; which (1) serves to explain. The kind of *opus* susceptible of being referred to *indefinite* is what Albert elsewhere calls the "nature" of the opus in question; and which has correctly been identified with the Avicennian essence of it.[14] Proust's capacity for writing novels is indeed specified by reference to the novels written, but not in the way Sartre wished. With Albert, the "nature" of the writing of a Proustian novel is logically prior, regardless of how we may come to learn the content of that nature (as, *post rem*, by studying the novels). The content is specifically the same, in whichever mode it may be expressed:

> the essence is one and the same in itself (*in se*) and in someone's thought (*in anima*) and in the singular entity (*in singulari*): but in thought as something thought (*secundum esse spirituale*), in the singular as something material and nature-formed (*materiale et naturale*), in itself as simply being something (*in esse simplici*). (*Lib. de praedicab.*, ed. Borgnet, 1; 35a–b, cit. A. de Libera in *Rev. sc. ph. th.* 65 (1981) 68.)[15]

The *in esse simplici* is not to be read as any commitment on Albert's part to a platonist view on existence. It is to be read only as expressing the *esse* in virtue of which a composing-apt proposition is true, when it is, prescinding from whether that in addition has to be thought of as something existing *secundum esse spirituale*, or as existing *secundum esse materiale et naturale*.[16] Further

---

[14] 'On peut donc dire que la "nature" simple et invariable du Colonais [Albert] n'est autre que l'essence d'Avicenne, cette essence qui, prise en elle-même, n'est sujette à aucune fin mais constitue plutôt un des multiples rayons de la lumière de l'Intelligence qui agit universellement en toutes choses, et est Dieu.' (A. de Libera, 'Théorie des universaux et réalisme logique chez Albert le Grand', *Rev. sc. ph. th.* 65 (1981), 55–77, 62, citing a passage from Albert's *Liber de praedicabilibus*, Bk. 1, tr. 2, ed. Borgnet, 1: 24.)

[15] Et ideo una et eadem est essentia in se et in anima et in singulari: sed in anima secundum esse spirituale, in singulari secundum esse materiale et naturale, in se autem in esse simplici. In *ST* 1/78/3c Aquinas would retain *spiritualis*, the word used here in the sense of 'intentional', for the same sense, when opposing intentional (*spiritualis*) and natural change. See the remarks at A. Kenny, *Aquinas on Mind* (London [1993]), viii + 182 pp., 33–4. The reference to Sartre is to J.-P. Sartre, *L'Existentialisme est un humanisme* (Paris [1962]), 141 pp., 56–7: 'pour l'existentialiste,... le génie de Proust c'est la totalité des œuvres de Proust; le génie de Racine c'est la série de ses tragédies, en dehors de cela il n'y a rien; pourquoi attribuer à Racine la possibilité d'écrire une nouvelle tragédie, puisque précisément il ne l'a pas écrite?'

[16] Cf.: 'Dicendum... quod universale unum numero et essentia est in anima et in seipso et in singulari, nec differt nisi secundum esse determinans ipsum ad hoc vel illud: secundum enim simplicitatem in se secundum seipsum est; ut principium autem artis et scientia est in anima, et ut communicatum ad esse naturae particularis est distinctum in particulari.' (*Lib. de praedicab.*, Bk. 2, ed. Borgnet, 1: 346.) Albert's *in se* here seems left deliberately neutral as between a platonist and a non-platonist metaphysics. If this is so, it is in line with what has been argued to be of wider application in Albert: 'La

consequences are best left until some further information is taken from Albert.

9. *In 1 Sent.*, d. 42A, art. 6, provides limiting conditions for the "things" which God can do in option-neutral power; and for our being able to say that God can do them.

What is something possible to be (*ens possibile*), says Albert, has to be understood both in proportion to (1) the making-to-be of that which is being thought of as able to make it to be (*ad facere facientis*), and (2) the being-made-to-be of the thing to be brought about (*ad fieri rei faciendae*). As the last phrase confirms, there is weight on the 'something' in 'something possible to be'. It is not Aristotelian logic which is directly in question here, in which God is 'possible to be'. It is Avicennian metaphysics, in which only the Avicennian essence is something possible to be. Every actual being is something necessary to be: either in itself (God) or *ab alio* (every existent other than God).

Because any bringing-about attributable to God has to be successful and without botching, only certain kinds of thing can satisfy 'God can ——', or 'God can bring about ——'. This is what *proportio ad facere facientis*, considering "things" (Avicennian essences) in the perspective of the kind of bringing-about envisaged for them, requires. For this reason 'sin', 'die', 'eat', or their appropriate nominal counterparts cannot be put in the slots above, if the resulting assertions are to come out true. Albert's *conditiones non infirmantes potentiam efficientis, et non ignobilitantes eam*, echoes older ways of speaking, which at least suggest adhockery or special pleading by reason of God's supposed respectability. In fact what is concerned is a consequence of God's being held to be something unrestricted in any way: and that is a matter independent of whether the being in question is to be worshipped or not, or is to be thought respectable or not.

The *proportio ad fieri* condition excludes any "opposition", whether in contrariety or privation, intrinsic to the "things" which God can be said to be able to do (in option-neutral power). The set of such "things" may include things red all over and things blue all over. It may include Rangers winning the Cup next year, and Celtic doing so. But it includes no such "things"

métaphysique de l'essence est... en dehors de la logique' (A. de Libera, 'Logique et existence selon Albert le Grand', *Arch. de philos.* 43 (1980), 529–58, 558).

as any which might be supposed to be simultaneously red all over and blue all over, or red all over and not red all over. It includes no such "thing" as Rangers and Celtic simultaneously winning the Cup next year. Quite generally, the set of things which God can do in option-neutral power is to be seen as a (non-ordered) set of (ordered) elements. More precisely, and going on no more than Albert is saying here, it is to be seen as a (non-ordered) set of elements not themselves to be supposed internally ordered in a relationship of opposition.

It is from those conditions on the elements of the set of God's option-neutral power, and from the set's infinity (which is not explicitly made in this passage), that Albert can say

God can do many things *de potentia* which, however, cannot be done *in creaturis*, from opposition and confusion's preventing this: opposition as in opposites; confusion, as in unions (*uniones*) of forms different in species, as in the same thing being a man and an ass, and the like. (*In 1 Sent.*, d. 42A, art. 6, sol., ed. Borgnet, 26: 364b.)

Albert is apparently using *uniones* here in a non-coded sense, closer to that of our 'intersections'. The contrasting determinants

(1) in creaturis, *and*
(2) de potentia

are surely expressing the contrasting determinations of the Power Distinction. His introduction of the concept of *confusio* is abrupt, but is not to be thought of as some afterthought. In the article his concern was directly with whether God can do the impossible; with the *fieri* of the thing being envisaged as possible to be done, not with the internal consistency of its content. But of course before it is sensible to ask whether the conditions for the thing's *fieri* can be met—the *factum* condition of the envisaged *ens factum*, as Aquinas was to put it—a previous condition has to be met. Only of "things" which in at least some way "are something" can it strictly be asked whether they can be brought about. Now the weakest way of "being something" is that feeblest way in which the truthmakers of true composing-apt propositions can be said to "be something". The limit to that is set by *confusio*, as in a putative intersection of incompatible forms. Where there is *confusio*, as was noted above, no distinct reference can be counted on, and in consequence nothing distinct can be said to "be something". So even in the wider ontology, including the now-adays more familiar Quinian one as a regional ontology; even there, where the slogan might be not 'No entity without identity' but 'No entity without distinctness of reference'; there is a sharp cut-off point, and it is provided by the avoidance of *confusio*.[17]

That confusion of this kind should be avoided, is what Aquinas will make his *ens* condition for the *ens factum*. Without such a condition being met, not even composing-apt propositions can be said to be true, in the way in which these are allowed to be (by Avicenna, Albert, and Aquinas, among others). 'Pegasus is a winged horse' and 'Unicorns are susceptible to virgins carrying daisy chains' may, understood as composing-apt propositions, be true. In 'Pegasus is a square circle' there is a purported *compositio* of incompatible forms, and thus an implied *confusio*; and no possibility for being said to be true.

That *oppositio* should be avoided (in matters whose contents satisfy the *ens* condition) is what can be called (after Aquinas) the *factum* condition. 'Something simultaneously all red and all blue' purports to describe "something" which doubtless fails to meet it. So, for that matter, does 'God's being brought about'.

The upshot of this for present purposes is that (1) any thing whose content does not imply *confusio*, is to be accounted among those things which God can in option-neutral power do, but (2) only things whose content in addition does not involve internal *oppositio* is to be found among those things which God can do in option-tied power.

The article contains other points of interest. I shall mention only the contrasting determinants

(1) de potentia exsequente, *and*
(2) de potentia absolute considerata.

The power mentioned in (2), adds Albert, is wider in extension (*generalior*) than that in any related *ars* or *scientia practica*. Both skills and bodies of practical knowledge have to be determinate in ways in which an option-neutral power does not have to be. It is plain enough that (1) and (2) express the same determinations respectively as are expressed in the arms of the Power Distinction.

10. In 1 Sent., d. 43 concerns the *immensitas* of what God can do, and it may be recalled that it was in an earlier question on God's *immensitas* that Albert showed his Negative Theology hand most plainly. The question addressed here is the Abelardian one of whether God can do only what he is doing, and Albert acknowledges this in his *expositio textus*. The initial reply (alluding to Abelard's use of Plato's "World Soul" as an *involucrum* or "enfolding image" for what would be called in the West 'the temporal mission of the Holy Ghost') had already been helpfully expressed:

We make reply to these things, opening out a twofold understanding of the words, unfolding in this way the things made involved by them (*et ab eis involuta evolventes sic*): 'God cannot do save what is good and just'—that is, cannot do save what, if he were to do it, would be good and just—is true. But he can do many things which are not good or just, because they neither are nor will be; nor are done well nor will be done well; because they never will be done (ed. Borgnet, 26; 376).

Sadly, in view of the way Abelard was hounded and vilified by St Bernard and his allies at Sens and afterwards—and rather invited it by his persistent unclarity of surface expression—there is no reason to believe that Abelard, consistent with what he did say, would have to deny any of that statement.[18]

In the *expositio textus* Albert notes that the (post-Abelardian) objections he had listed, had been tackled by *Quidam* by claiming an equivocation in the use of *potentia*, saying in effect,

that when 'God cannot do anything save what he is doing' is said, then if 'in option-tied power' (*de potentia coniuncta actui*) is understood, the locution is true; but if 'in option-neutral power' is understood, it is false.[19]

This does not dissolve the difficulty, says Albert, because the original objection is intended to go through *de potentia, simpliciter*.

---

[18] Albert and Lombard do not exaggerate the involved nature of Abelard's treatment of the *involucrum* of the World Soul of the *Timaeus*; or his convoluted treatment of questions on divine power. For the first see L. Moonan, 'Abelard's use of the *Timaeus*', *AHDLMA* 56 (1989), 7–90. For the second, *From Mystery to Puzzle?*, in progress.

[19] Notandum quod obiecta Quidam aliter solvunt per aequivocationem potentiae, dicentes quod cum dicitur 'Non potest deus facere nisi quod facit', si intelligatur 'de potentia coniuncta actui', vera est locutio, si autem 'de potentia absoluta', falsa est. Sed haec solutio non dissolvit, quia obiectio procedit de potentia simpliciter. (Ed. Borgnet, 26: 377b.)

I take it that *Quidam* here have been using the Power Distinction, in the contrasting determinants

(1) de potentia coniuncta actui, *and*
(2) de potentia absoluta.

But Albert is not here objecting to the Power Distinction, nor even to its being used in this sort of matter. His counter-objection is a more formal one (as replies or counter-objections often are in his period, even in narrowly theological disputations, where modern theologians might be inclined to reply on more substantive, more theological grounds). The original argument had seemed to conclude that God *non potest* do what he is not doing, and so on. The *non potest* was taken to be asserted *simpliciter*, or *absque determinatione*. On purely formal grounds, therefore, a "solution" which countered that God indeed *potest*, but which did not of itself argue to more than a *potest* asserted *cum determinatione*, did not without further argument (which, in the individual case, might or might not be able to be provided) genuinely "dissolve" the objection. Albert here is not even claiming that, in the present case, the further argument cannot be provided. His objection is on strictly formal grounds, and provides no case for seeing in Albert's reply here either dissatisfaction with the Power Distinction, or even dissatisfaction with its being used in that sort of matter.

In a passing reference in art. 2 Albert remarks that it is *potentia exsequens* (option-tied power) which is coextensive with the *arti faciendorum*, and not *potentia absoluta*; 'and that was explained above' (ed. Borgnet, 26; 380a). (This reference is to Borgnet, 26; 366b.)

11. In art. 3, where the theologians' puzzle about damning Peter and saving Judas is raised, he uses the Distinction without either emphasis or fuss:

It is to be said that he can [damn Peter and save Judas] in option-neutral power (*de potentia absoluta*), but not in the power related towards the order of his wisdom (*de potentia relata ad ordinem sapientiae*). (*In 1 Sent.*, d. 42c, art. 3, ed. Borgnet, 26; 381b.)

The terminology is almost the only thing to note, as it refers back to *in relatione ad opus*, as used in earlier questions. The *ordo sapientiae* or providential order was of course the *opus* par excellence: both as *opus conditionis* and (in the present matter) as *opus redemptionis*, the traditional concern of theologians. Albert does not dispute that the present matter concerns that *opus*, and a genre of question long established among theologians as to whether some part of it might have been otherwise. He yet insinuates that the choice of such a case rather suggests prurience among those who raise it, whom he dismisses as *Quidam curiosi* (ed. Borgnet, 26; 381a).

At *In 1 Sent.*, d. 44, art. 6, on whether God can still do what he formerly could do, Albert expressly prefers a solution involving appeal to the Power Distinction, to the one he reports from Lombard:

> But more truly and more probably what seems to me to have to be said is that there is power considered absolutely (and that is always the same), and there is power conjoined to actuality, and the latter is determined in its mode of signification to the thing which is being referred to it; and the argument is not the same when that is being done (*in relatione illa*), and in respect of that power of his which is determined in this latter way he cannot now do just anything he has been able to do, yet this makes for no change in him, but in the thing on which the power is being exercised. (Ed. Borgnet, 26; 399.)

The terminology he chooses here is none other than that of the *Quidam* whose solution he had rejected, on formal grounds, in the *expositio textus* of d. 42: contrasting *potentia coniuncta actui*, and *potentia absolute considerata*. This would seem to confirm what was argued above, that Albert's rejection of the solution in that place ought not to be misconstrued as a rejection either of the Distinction or of its appropriateness in principle to the kind of discussion in question.

12.   In both *In 2 Sent.* and *In 4 Sent.* I find nothing which calls for treatment here, even in topics on which predecessors or contemporaries of Albert had used the Power Distinction. At *In 3 Sent.*, d. 20B, art. 3, however, is a very explicit passage. The question under consideration is: What is that possibility from which it is said that another manner [of man's liberation] was possible to God?

It is to be said that God's power (*potentia*) is one and simple, but can be considered in either of two ways: to wit,
(1) as executing a wise foresight and ordinance (*exsequens sapientiae*

praevisionem et ordinationem)—and so considered, it seems that no other way was possible for our liberation, than the one in the foresight of the ordaining wisdom; yet another manner could have been foreseen, and then the power operating (*potentia operans*) would be executing that other manner; in another way [God's power] may be considered
(2) according as it stands antecedently to the [ordaining] wisdom: for God can do things which through the wisdom ordaining all things he has not ordained that he will do—and speaking with a determination mentioning that power (*et de hac potentia loquendo*), another manner [of man's liberation] was possible; and the Saints often spoke [with a tacit determination exploiting] that possibility. (*In 3 Sent.*, d. 20B, art. 3, ed. Borgnet, 28; 358–9.)

It is plain that not two powers but two ways of considering one power, of God's, are in question. It is only a little less plain that the power in question is God's power to do things extrinsic to his nature: *potentia operans*. This power may be considered either as the power executing the actual disposition of things ordained by God, or the power executing some other disposition which, considered in abstraction from what may or may not have been ordained, God could have foreseen and ordained, had he chosen to. That is, as an actual creature of God, or as the creature of God there could have been, had God chosen to execute some other possible order of "things"; of what Albert called natures, and Avicenna essences.

The *de hac potentia loquendo* indicates that contrasting *cum determinatione* assertions are in Albert's mind; though we need not imagine that he is attributing to the *Sancti* of former times the modes of expression of the thirteenth-century schools.

More importantly, perhaps, clues are provided for anyone seeking to analyse matters further. At least three diverse things are indicated:

(1) Abstract contents: Avicennian essences, Albert's 'natures';
(2) Possibilities;
(3) Relationship to being (wisely) ordered by God.

From (1) we may take it that any acceptable formulation of the Power Distinction will have to have (1*a*) expressions for the contents of things and (1*b*) some way, analogous to the "abstractors" used in careful expositions of predicate logic, of indicating that it is the contents of things which are being considered, and that the expressions of the content are not to be thought along the lines of naming-expressions. From (2) we will need modal operators. Because Avicennian essences stand in necessary relationships with comparable essences, these will have to include operators for the strict logical modalities, as obtainable from Aristotle, for example. Because of the relationship in which Avicennian essences stand to instantiation in extra-mental reality, these may also have to include operators for two-way possibility (also obtainable from Aristotle). (This, if we wish to be able to give an account of them, in addition to using expressions of them.)

Most crucially, perhaps, we have clues towards settling

(4) Matters of scope.

In the option-tied arm some "operating power" (of God's)—say, this rose's being red, that pig's grunting—is considered as 'executing a wise foresight and ordinance' (of God's). We need, therefore, something like: 'For some narrowly predicative proposition of content specifically identical with that of *Fa* (this rose is red, that pig is grunting), It is (wisely foreseen and) ordered by God that the proposition in question is true.'

In the option-neutral arm the abstract content of some specifiable "operating power" (possible to be ordered by God) is being considered as no more than that, and without being within the scope of any operator to the effect 'It is (wisely foreseen and) ordered by God that'. All of these clues provided by Albert here, and further ones provided elsewhere, will be pursued further at more appropriate places, including chapter 9 below.[20]

SUMMA THEOLOGIAE

This work cannot be assigned to a date earlier than 1266, and at least some final touches were still being added after the Council of Lyons in 1274. (See the Prolegomena to *Summa* i, Cologne edn. 34/1 (Munster, 1978).) Within the treatise on divine power (*Summa* i, tr. 19 [= Qq. 76–8]), he uses the Distinction not a few times, though it rarely appears in other parts. Both in that treatise and elsewhere, he provides material useful towards an understanding of it.

[20] See also 'Putative Attributions to Divine Power', forthcoming.

13. The doctrine on God's knowability is in substance that of the Sentence Commentary, but some points from the Nicomachean Ethics enable him to explain the doctrine more succinctly. (*Summa* 1, tr. 3, qu. 13, ch. 2, Cologne edn. 34/1; 42a.)

In the *solutio* of Qu. 76 he notes differences between God's power and natural active powers. Apropos of the dictum *Virtus est ultimum potentiae in re*, from the *De caelo*, he says:

Just as if Hercules is able for a hundred and more, his strength (*virtus*) and the full extent of his power (*ultimum potentiae*) is for a hundred; and from this it is inferred [that he is able for] whatever [opposition] is short of this. For if he is able for a hundred, he is able for fifty... ten... five... one. But the converse does not follow. (Borgnet, 31; 795ab.)[21]

Hume was to make use of a point like that last one, in a famous argument against attributing to God any more power than is needed to account for the effects in which the power is supposed to be evident. (*Enquiry... Understanding*, Sect. XI, EUN, p. 136.) Albert was rather less generous than Hume towards that line of argumentation; insisting elsewhere that wherever God acted, he acted with the whole of his power, not some supposed fraction of it; and that we can therefore infer nothing of the magnitude of the power itself from inspection of its effects.

Limitations in any attempt to attribute power to God are considered a little later. Athanasius had contrasted our calling God wise, good, etc., on the one hand, and our calling him merciful, faithful, and just towards us, on the other. To an objection exploiting this he replies:

When names which name God *secundum se* are not determined *ad temporale*, as when we say that God is powerful, wise, good, simple, nothing is connoted. But when these names are determined *per temporale*, as when I say 'He can make the world', then without doubt something is connoted *in creatura* in the manner aforesaid. (ad 4, ed. Borgnet, 31; 796b.)[22]

[21] 'Now if a thing is able to move, or to lift a certain weight, we always speak with reference to the most it can do, e.g. to lift a hundred talents or to walk a hundred stades.... "its power" means its greatest power.' (Arist., *De caelo* 1. 12. 281a10, tr. Guthrie, Loeb edn.)
[22] 'Athanasius' here names a character in a dialogue, as it had done at Alexander of Hales, *Summa*, Quaracchi edn. 1: 204 ad 5, where the general topic is the same. See ch. 3, n. 21 above. The texts in Albert, Alexander, and at PL 62: 212–13, are all different.

'Nothing is connoted' is to be taken as absolutely as it is put. This is a view shared by Aquinas, as will appear: to the effect that "names" attributed to the divine nature, as may be intended in 'God is wise', can permit something true to be asserted thereby, only on condition of being strictly unintelligible (lacking signification) to us. In Albert it is predications *per aeternum* which are to be true, if true, of the divine nature, only on a like condition. Predications *per temporale* he treats as being systematically misleading; to be understood as being true, if true, of something other than the divine nature (though viewed as dependent on or similarly related to the divine will). In other words this passage shows that Albert is to be understood as being, like Aquinas, favourable to a strategy in which putative attributions of things to God may be treated as systematically misleading; as in the Power Distinction itself, understood at the period covered in this book.

14. In the course of Qu. 77, on whether God can create all that is creatable (*creabile*), Albert insists that a distinction is to be made. The questioner might be intending the enquiry to be answered with either *de potentia absoluta* or *de potentia disposita et ordinata* modifying the *potest*. He then goes into the analogy he had already explored in the Sentence Commentary between active powers and passive potentialities, before using the Distinction:

So when the question is raised whether God can create in one instant everything creatable, then if *creabile* expresses [*creabile*] *potens creari de potentia absoluta*, it must be said that in one instant everything creatable cannot be created: because if every creature were to be created in one instant, [God's] power would be bounded (*finiretur*) towards the work of one instant, which is impossible. For this power is infinite, and the infinite cannot be bounded towards the infinite, as Aristotle says in *3 Phys.* (Ed. Borgnet, 31; 812a.)

In the light of what was said, this is straightforward enough. It is worth noting how readily and unfussily points made in Aristotle's natural philosophy—something of a scandal to the authorities barely a generation before—are being used in the exposition of theological arguments, in a work addressed to theologians.[23] The reply then continues:

But if *creabile* expressed [*creabile*] a *potentia disposita per providentiam et praeordinationem*, that power is bounded (*finita*) towards that which is foreseen and pre-ordained, and *de hac* it can be conceded that everything creatable-in-that-power can be created in an instant. (Same ref. 812a.)

The *de hac* indicates plainly that that last 'can' is understood as determined 'can in option-tied power'; so Albert would seem to be implying here that the actual order of things is created in an instant.

That this is his view, is confirmed from an explanation he had given earlier (Qu. 23, ed. Borgnet, 31; 186, ad 3). Creation is not in time. In so far as it is in the creator, *in creante*, it does not refer to time at all, not even to a "now": *omnino non refertur ad tempus, nec ad nunc temporis*. In so far as it is in the thing created, it is not in any passing time: *non est a primo in ultimum cum interceptione medii*. In so far as creation is in this thing created, it is in a "now" (at a "now", rather), and that "now" is to be understood as a "now" from which time begins *continue*, not a "now" which would itself be something temporal, something in which time would be *secundum esse*.[24] He compares this with the point from which a line is understood to begin. It is that from which the extension of the line begins *continue*. It is not something in which the line is the sort of thing a line is. Just as a point, or at any rate the point from which the extension of a line is to be measured, is not to be thought of as an arbitrarily short line, so the kind of

[23] Albert worked on the Commentary on the Nicomachean Ethics after lecturing on the Sentences at Paris, before undertaking his series of paraphrases of Aristotle, and around the time he was completing the commentaries on the Pseudo-Denis: around 1250 therefore. See the Prolegomena to Cologne vols. 14, 34, and 37.

[24] Dicendum quod genesis temporis sive creatio non est in tempore. Prout enim in creante est, omnino non refertur ad tempus, nec ad nunc temporis. Prout autem in creato est ipso, non est a primo in ultimum cum interceptione medii . . . . Et cum dicitur quod creatum vel creatio facit esse post non esse, hoc verbum facit non dicit nisi esse facti quod numquam fuit in fieri; et hoc propter infinitam potentiam facientis, quod de extremo venit in extremum sine transitu medii. Et praepositio post, non dicit nisi ordinem absque successione et transitu per medium ad extrema. Et ideo creatio est in nunc temporis secundum quod est in creato; et illud nunc temporis est a quo incipit tempus continue, non in quo tempus est secundum esse. Sicut punctum quod est principium lineae, est a quo incipit continue lineae extensio, non in quo linea est secundum esse lineae. Albert's remarks on creabilis may be compared with those of Alexander of Hales at *Summa*, Quaracchi edn. 1, par. 140, on *creabilis* and *potentia creabilis dei*.

"now" at which creation may be thought of as occurring in the thing created, is not to be thought of as an arbitrarily short temporal duration. *Non tempore, sed cum tempore, finxit deus mundum*; as Augustine had put it before him.

15. The analogy mentioned above, between active powers and passive potentialities, should perhaps be considered at least briefly: it throws light on the sorts of thing which God's option-neutral and option-tied power ought to be thought to be. What he says at this place (ad 1; Borgnet, 31; 812a) is as follows.

1. Material location which has not been dedicated (*disposita*) to this or that work stands in an infinite or (*sive*) indeterminate potentiality towards any form, and (when a form is instantiated in that material location), it never individualises so many forms, as not to be able to individualise any more. Neither is it disposed more towards individualising any one form rather than towards any other; or to any one mode of individualisation rather than any other. Its potentiality exceeds as many of these (individualisations) as may occur.
2. By contrast, material location which has been dedicated and ordered stands in such relationship to the form so individualised, as to ensure that its potentiality (for that individualisation) in no way extends beyond that form so individualised.
3. It is likewise, Albert's comparison continues, with the power of the first agent (*de potentia primi agentis*); God's operant power, or power to do things extrinsic to his nature, as I would understand it.

God's active option-neutral power exceeds everything which is something (*potentia sua absoluta activa excedit omne quod est*). My understanding of this is that 'everything which is something' here refers not only to all *res reales*, in virtue of which narrowly predicative propositions are true, if true, of extra-mental reality. It refers not only to their abstractable contents, but to any specified content in virtue of which a composing-apt proposition is true, if true. Of such contents—Albert's "natures", Avicennian essences—only those expressed or specified by some thinker are on Albert's view to be able to be said to "be something" (with merely intentional existence). Had no one been around to specify a triangle, or for as long as no one had got round to specifying one, no triangle could be said to "be something". (See *Summa* 1, tr. 6, qu. 25, ch. 3 passim, Cologne edn. 34/1; 160–2.)

4. But the power disposed by ordinance of providence towards this or that, is located (*stat*) in the effect or work which it produces, so that it neither exceeds (the effect or work) nor is exceeded by it.

The comparison brings out that neither God's option-neutral power nor his option-tied power is to be identified with any actual entity. Both are objects of our consideration, (sets of) intentional entities. The elements of the sets are specific; just as the individualised forms in which potentialities are actualised, and the forms by which alone they can be actualised, are specific (not vague). This confirms that what was indicated by Albert's *comparatio ad opus indefinite*, in the Sentence Commentary, was a comparison with specific contents of envisaged *opera*, indefinite only as regards their relationship with any eventual material location. We were not to imagine any vagueness in the specific contents in question. As will be made clear in a passage from the *Summa* to be examined presently, Albert thought the notion that objects of thought could be vague, as against being perhaps only vaguely describable by us, to be not properly intelligible.[25] The "things" even of God's option-neutral power are to "be something", and hence must be free from *confusio*. They are to be able to be made to be something in extra-mental reality, if God so disposes; so they must not contain internal *oppositio*. The individualised forms in which potentialities are actualised are free from internal *oppositio*; only by forms free from *confusio* can such actualisation take place.

16. The kind of consequence permitted from Albert's views of option-neutral power in particular, appears in the reply to the next objection, at 31; 812a in the Borgnet edn. In the Sentence Commentary he had already argued that there are some things which God can (in option-neutral power) do, but which cannot be done. This, as was seen above, is because the conjunction 'God can in option-neutral power do A' and 'God can... do B'

---

[25] It can still be maintained that 'the notion that things might actually be vague, as well as vaguely described, is not properly intelligible' (M. Dummett, 'Wang's Paradox', *Synthese*, 30 (1975), 301–24, 314), even while insisting that 'terms whose application is to be determined by mere observation... must necessarily be vague' (316).

is true, provided that A and B are of the set of things which God can in option-neutral power do. Since that set is inconsistent, it can well happen that A and B cannot simultaneously be brought about. If the putative "thing" A-and-B involves two things internally opposed—like Rangers winning the Cup next year, and Celtic doing so—then A-and-B (supposed internally opposed) cannot be among the things which God can be said to be able to do in option-neutral power.

In the present passage he generalises the point. If we ask about the whole set of things which God can do in option-neutral power—*quaecunque potest facere potentia absoluta*—then, because that is an inconsistent set, it cannot be itself accounted one of the things which God can do in option-neutral power. So not only can the whole set not be done simultaneously; it is not the sort of thing which God can be said to do in option-neutral power. Of course if we could list the set, and ask of any member of the set, at any stage of the listing, Can God in option-neutral power do it?, the answer Yes might be expected: no matter how long the list then was, and no matter how many elements inconsistent with each other it contained. But no such question can sensibly be asked of "the whole set". If listing is effective, and the set is a potential infinity, how could it be? The *quaecunque* in *quaecunque potest facere potentiā absolutā* refers to the individual (internally ordered) members of the (non-ordered) set of the things of God's option-neutral power. But that set itself is as such not ordered, and contains inconsistent sets; and thus cannot as such be viewed as an ordered set. It cannot, in consequence, be viewed as a member of itself, so as itself to be something able to be instantiated by God. God can do nothing *inordinate*.

Albert here makes clear what his earlier treatment may not have spelled out. From the earlier treatment, it indeed appeared that putative things ordered internally by logical opposition, whether of contrariety or of "privation" (improperly understood), could not be accounted "things" which God could be said to be able in option-neutral power to do. In the present passage, the way Albert treats *quaecunque potest facere potentia absoluta* makes it clear that the "things" of God's option-neutral power are in themselves to be viewed as ordered; although they are not to be viewed as ordered externally, whether towards comparable "things", or towards instantiation (or not) in extra-mental reality.

A couple of pages later he uses the Distinction in an almost routine manner. God could have brought Judas back to life

(1) de potentia absoluta; but could not have done so
(2) de potentia praeordinata et praedisposita. (Borgnet, 31; 314b.)

On the same page he states that Augustine's *de potentia*, in the "authority" quoted, must be understood as *de potentia absoluta*; and his *iustitia* when contrasted with it must be understood as standing for *potentiam dispositam per ordinem iustitiae*.[26] This sounds like a conscious interpretation, but is doubtless (also) intended to insinuate continuity between the Power Distinction and Augustine's *per potentiam/iustitiam* distinction. Albert suggests an even longer pedigree some pages later, when saying that Plato calls the *ordo iustitiae* by the name *iustitia divina* (Borgnet, 31; 832).[27]

17. One of the further questions raised within Qu. 77 was one which men of former times (who?) had been raising for discussion (*antiqui quaesierunt*): Can God *de potentia* save someone damned in hell, like Judas, and damn someone saved, like Peter? One of the arguments considered had made use of the contention that 'In hell there is no redemption' was sung in the Church's worship. Albert replies that the Church does not sing that in hell there can, in God's option-neutral power, be no redemption, but that there is no redemption in option-tied power, through the justice which is retribution according to merits. The contrast here is between

(1) de potentia absoluta dei, *and*
(2) de potentia ordinata per iustitiam quae est redditio secundum merita. (Borgnet, 31; 815a.)

Things done out of that justice which is retribution according to merits are thus to be viewed as a subset of that wider justice which is nothing other than the actual, providential order of

[26] 'Justice', he notes elsewhere, can be understood in either of two ways. In the first it stands for the *condecentia divinae bonitatis* (in effect for the *ordinatio dei*, or God's option-tied power). This is the way it should be taken here. In a second way 'justice' can be understood as *retributio pro meritis*; much as it is in the discussions of some moral thinkers.
[27] Cf. 'Igitur siquidem iuste et sobrie disponunt, iustitia et sobrietate disponunt?', from Plato's *Meno* 73ab, in the 12th-cent. translation, ed. V. Kordeater and C. Labowsky, in *Plato Latinus*, 1 (London, 1940).

things: the *condecentia divinae bonitatis* of the passage noted at n. 26 above, or for that matter *potentia ordinata dei*.

Before leaving Qu. 77 the treatment of two further subsets of God's option-tied power, the *bonitas et gratia Christi*, is considered in two ways,

(1) secundum esse quod habet in se, *and*
(2) secundum ordinem ad opus redemptionis.

Taken in the first way—in its Avicennian essence, that is to say—'it can be better, because grace is finite'. Taken in the second way 'it cannot be better'; not from anything to do with Christological doctrines specifically, but for exactly the same kind of reason for which no one's grace, considered concretely, *secundum ordinem ad opus redemptionis*, can be better than it is; just as no one's yacht, considered likewise, can be longer than it is. This is confirmed in a further treatment on the same page, of the grace of the Virgin Mary; considered

(1) in se, *and*
(2) in ordine ad conceptum et partum redemptoris. (Borgnet, 31; 822b.)

18.   Qu. 78 concerns 'the possible, according as it depends on the power of God'. It opens with an account of "the possible", recapitulating for a theological audience the straightforwardly analytical background which consideration of the question requires. Almost as though to compensate for the sustained digression into philosophy Albert ends his account with the rousing declaration:

to theology it does not pertain to inquire save concerning the possible which is possible to God *secundum causas superiores*. To it is subjected every other kind of possible, and of impossible even. Whence Mt. 17: 19, 'Nothing shall be impossible to you', to wit, to those who believe. The distributive sign distributed both for possibles and for impossibles. (Memb. 1 ad fin; Borgnet, 31; 830b.)

On Albert's views that is an expression of sober truth, but could be read by modern readers as rather more exciting than it is. It is not an invitation to theologians to imagine themselves privy to some amazing genre of "possibility" *secundum causas superiores* by which logic can be flouted. Albert is speaking of possible and impossible *things*, not of just any chimera his hearers might fancy to put in words and claim as an object of their belief. His account had opened with a cold, prophylactic douche, to put them on the alert against any such fancies: 'the possible is a species of the true ... '.

19. In the second member of the question he reports how people had been trying to solve or dissolve the original puzzle— 'Whether something *per se* and *simpliciter* impossible is possible to God, like opposites simultaneously obtaining?'—and advocates caution:

To this it has become customary to be said that God's power can be taken *absolute*, and can be taken *ut disposita secundum rationem scientiae et voluntatis*. If taken *absolute*, then as Damascene says, it is being taken as an ocean of infinite power (*potestatis*), and then there is nothing which [God] cannot do. But if taken as power disposed and ordered in accordance with providence and goodness, then it is said that he can do those things which are marks of power, and not those which are marks of impotency. Whence he cannot bring about someone greater than himself; neither can he do anything contrary to the order of his truth (*contra ordinem veritatis suae*): and thus he cannot make anything to hold and simultaneously not hold of the same thing, or make other opposites to be simultaneously, because he would be doing something against the order of his truth (*quia faceret contra ordinem veritatis suae*).

But it seems to me that in this question, great care should be taken in speaking, so that nothing is attributed to [God's] power, in such a way as to detract thereby from his truth and goodness. (Borgnet, 31; 832ab.)

The caution concerns the *modus loquendi*, the rhetoric of it rather than the substance. Albert does not dispute the substance of his predecessors' approach, which was to use a version of the Power Distinction in their solutions. He uses the Distinction repeatedly in his own reply, which comes not in a general *solutio*, but in particular replies to a series of puzzles. This enables him to follow his own caution—'it seems to me that in this question great care should be taken in speaking, so that nothing is attributed to God's power in such a way as to detract thereby from his truth and goodness'. The 'truth and goodness', as appears presently, refers to the actual order of things. Albert here is unusual for his time in warning—in effect—against the dangers of thinking that considerations of what is possible within God's option-neutral power might interfere with the ineluctable reliability of the actual *ordinatio dei*. In the period of this book, and even in the celebrated condemnations of the 1270s, the dangers more likely to be warned against were of speaking so as to seem to confine the scope of divine power.

The substance of his predecessors' solutions had been in the Power Distinction, but as expressed in the determinations (as I understand them),

(1) absolute ... ut pelagus potestatis infinitae, *and*
(2) ut potentia disposita et ordinata secundum providentiam et bonitatem. (Borgnet, 31: 832a.)

That he accepts the substance, appears from the repeated use he makes of it in treating the series of puzzles in solving which he clarifies his own position.

1. Making a living steer out of a joint of meat, and making something white to be black. He had dealt in the Sentence Commentary with whether God could do this, but in a relatively superficial manner.[28] Here he relates the puzzle to the deeper issues raised by whether God can, in effect, create a "First Principle of all Scientifical Knowledge and all Truth" different from the one which, as he understands, bounds our understanding.

---

[28] See *In 1 Sent.*, d. 42A, art. 6, in reply to an objection, ed. Borgnet, 26: 365b; also *In 3 Sent.*, d. 20B, art. 1, sol., ed. Borgnet, 28: 357a. See also L. Moonan, 'Albert the Great, and Some Limits of Scientifical Inquiry', in B. Mojsisch and O. Pluta (eds.), *K. Flasch Festschrift* (2 vols.; Amsterdam, 1990), 2; 695–710. Cf. S. Ebbesen on 'Album potest esse nigrum', in N. Kretzmann (ed.), *J. Pinborg Festschrift* (1988), xii + 400 pp.: 'Concrete accidental terms: late thirteenth-century debates relating to such terms as "album" ', 107–61; and edn. of Peter of Auvergne's question on the topic, 162–74. The black/white puzzle has a long pedigree. In the *Phaedo*, from 101b, Socrates is trying to assure Cebes that he is not trying to persuade him of something logically objectionable. In response to a challenge he distinguishes: 'Then we were saying that opposite *things* come from opposite *things*; now we are saying that the opposite *itself* can never become opposite to *itself*—neither the opposite which is in us nor that which is in the real world' (tr. H. Tredennick, *Plato, the Last Days of Socrates: The Apology, Crito, Phaedo* [Harmondsworth, 1954], at *Phaedo*, 103b). Note that Socrates' 'the opposite in us' and 'the opposite ... in the real world' might suggest that grounds for a two-type analysis were already available before Aristotle finished writing. Socrates makes no difficulty over the red Ferrari being resprayed green. The τέρας (101b) would be for 'being red and being green' (at the same time, in the same respect) to be imagined as some kind of instantiable form. For a link between Plato's τέρας and the medievals' *confusio*: 'ita confusa est oratio, ita perturbata, nihil ut sit primum, nihil ut secundum, tantaque insolentia ac turba verborum, ut oratio, quae lumen adhibere rebus debet, ea obscuritatem et tenebras adferat atque ut quodam modo ipsi sibi in dicendo obstrepere videantur.' (Cicero, *De orat.* 3. 50.)

His first answer is, Yes, making a living steer out of dead meat, and making something white to be black, are alike such both that God can do them, and that they can be done. For God 'can make the succession of forms (1) joint of meat, (2) living steer' individuated at the same material location, as 'by the transmutation of the one into the other'. In a parallel manner he can make something white to be black (Borgnet, 31: 832b). The two cases are respectively of "substantial forms" successively individualised at the same material location, and of "accidental forms" successively inhering in the same subject. This is hardly worth raising a puzzle from, and Albert unsurprisingly takes up the less readily accommodated point, as he continues (I paraphrase):

But he cannot in option-tied power make a joint and a steer simultaneously (to be at the same material location), and likewise cannot make an individual (of some appropriate kind) to be simultaneously white and black, 'because it would detract from the order of his truth (*detraheretur ordinationi veritatis eius*)'. (Ed. Borgnet, 31: 832b.)

How would this be? His argument shows how:

Let it be granted that something is both dead meat and living steer. Then, since the one form on account of opposition excludes the other, there follows 'If it is dead meat, it is not living steer',[29] and 'If it is living steer, it is not dead meat'; and 'If it is white, it is not black' and conversely 'If it is black, it is not white': and thus occurs simultaneously affirming and denying the same thing. (Borgnet, 31: 832b.)

He then takes the argument further:

But the first principle of all scientifical knowledge and all truth, as Aristotle says in the Fourth Book of the Metaphysics, is (1) that simultaneously affirming and denying apropos of the same thing does not occur, and (2) that concerning no matter what, either a true affirmation or a true denial obtains, and that concerning nothing [is affirmation and denial] simultaneously [true]. (Cf. *Metaph.*, Γ7, 1011^b23-7.)

This conjunction of the Law of Contradiction and the Law of Excluded Middle has often been known honorifically as the First Law of Thought, or something of the sort. (See the Kneales,

<hr/>

[29] Aristotle had taken living bodies and corpses to be 'bodies' only homonymously. See *De an.* 2.1 412b10.

Development (1962), 46 ff.) Albert himself continues:

And since this is the First Principle of our Understanding, by which it accepts everything true, and against which there is nothing it will concede to be true, it is required that it should be *exemplatum et regulatum . . . ad ordinem primae veritatis.* And just as God can do nothing against the *ordinem primae veritatis*, so likewise he can do nothing against this [principle: *istud*]. For to do this is a not a mark of power, but a mark of impotency. (Borgnet, 31: 832b.)

What Albert is in effect allowing here, is that God can, in option-neutral power, bring about an order of things intelligible (in some way unintelligible to us) to some creature within it, in which the First Principle of *our* Understanding does not condition acceptance or rejection of truths. This is instructive, but needs to be taken together with what he says on truth: in Qu. 75 of Book 1 of the *Summa*, most notably.

20. There are three levels at which we can speak of something true. There is (1) that of ordinary, low-level truths, whether of the 'This rose is red' or the 'Blue is a colour' variety; true, in virtue of their appropriate *res*. There is (2) that of the first principles, a kind of truth always in the understanding, and 'by which, as out of a habit, we judge concerning all true things . . . it is the habitual rule by which we judge of all true things'. Among these first principles is the one Albert calls the First Principle of our Understanding. At a third level is (3) the truth which is 'the exemplar and paradigm in the divine mind', of the truths at the two lower levels: 'and by this truth we judge of all things, not as out of a habit, but as [by measuring them against] an exemplar or paradigm. And this truth is incorruptible and immutable, though many variations may be in those things which are under it.' (Ed. Borgnet, 31: 211; cf. p. 158.)

We judge propositions entertained by us to be true, or not, by the principles built into our understanding, much (if I understand Albert) as we ride horses or bicycles by principles of balance built into our organism. It is a part of how we are built, and our understanding would not be the human understanding it is if it were otherwise. The ultimate paradigm against which we judge of truths (using the principles built into us), is one which is not parochially human, or even parochially creaturely.

Crudely speaking, the truths at levels (1) and (2) are the truths which can be thought of as willed by God to be true, by willing the *ordinatio dei*. But what of the truth(s) at level (3)? The 'exemplar and paradigm in the divine mind' sounds rather as though it ought to correspond to a subset of God's option-neutral power, the abstract contents (and only those) instantiated in the actual order of things. But there is a difficulty, and Albert, struggling ingeniously to accommodate in eirenical formulas, frankly diverse and probably irreconcilable usages from respected "authorities", for once is less helpful than he could be.

Exemplars of their nature are exemplars *of* something or other: that is Albert's view. Because of that, exemplars as such are not things of the sort known to God in the eternal knowledge whose objects are to be identified with the divine knowledge. Exemplars are thus not 'in God's mind' in that sense, and are not incorruptible and immutable on that ground. If the truth at the third level is to be considered by us as an exemplar and paradigm, it cannot be identified with the divine nature.

The exemplars of things are doubtless among the "things" which God can do in option-neutral power. Considered as known to God in his eternal knowledge, they are no doubt incorruptible and immutable, but cannot (so considered) be known in their content to us, as they are then to be identified with the divine nature. How then are they to be accessible to us for use as exemplars and paradigms in the way Albert mentions? If the truth at the third level is to be an exemplar and paradigm for us, it has to be something other than the divine nature.

This is a kind of problem which is practically impossible to avoid, if you insist on working with a platonist understanding of the option-neutral arm of the Power Distinction. (Crudely put: you may be able to preserve the truth of what you say when using the Distinction, but at the cost of stripping what you say of practically all explanatory force. The point is taken up in Ch. 9 below.) Albert shows no concern either to attend to the problem or even to emphasise that one is there. He has a non-platonist understanding, and is apparently willing not to draw any more attention than he has to, to his Church Fathers' nakedness on the point.

Instead, he quietly allows two ways of taking *prima veritas*, using either at level three, although not to the same purposes. In one way *prima veritas* is used to designate the divine nature. (See *In*

De div. nom., ch. 7, Cologne edn. 37: 363a; *Summa* 1, qu. 25, Col.
edn. 34: 163a; and other places.) Taken this way, the *prima
veritas*—God, in other words—is opaque to us, and 'the light of
the first cause extending through all things, as Denis says' (*Summa*
1, qu. 25, Cologne edn. 34: 158). It is also 'an eternal truth': the
only one, indeed. 'The eternal truths of the mathematicians
(*rationes mathematicorum aeternae*) are not eternal according to the
true definition of eternity, but are called eternal by philosophers,
just as perpetual unchangeable things are called eternal, because
they participate in the condition of eternity which unchange-
ableness is' (*Summa* 1, Cologne edn. 34: 161b, ad 1). That is, they
are immutable, albeit not by their nature.[30]

In another way, *prima veritas* is taken to be intelligible: 'and
according to Augustine and Anselm, it is the light and the
intelligible rightness . . . against which each thing is measured
. . .'. (Same ref.) This is 'the prototype and exemplar of every
kind of truth'. 'Every created true thing (*verum*) stands as an
approximation to the *primam veritatem*, because it does not fill and
come up to it totally, but is excelled by it; like every temporal
thing towards something eternal, and like every circumscribed
thing towards the uncircumscribed.' (*Summa* 1, qu. 25, Cologne
edn. 34: 158–9.) Once more, Albert does not comment, but leaves
his readers to puzzle for themselves whether the *prima veritas* of
the Pseudo-Denis, on the one hand, and of Augustine and
Anselm, on the other, really can stand for the same thing.

21.   The present passage, from Qu. 78 of *Summa* 1, provides
complementary information, and permits a schematic presentation along the lines of the Waterfall Schema of Chapter 1,
Section 5, in which ways of taking expressions such as 'God's
power' were displayed. In the present passage Albert may usefully
be seen to be concerned with ways of taking expressions such as
'God's truth'.

22.   The *ordinatio veritatis eius* which (in the passages quoted
above) would stand to be detracted from if there were sim-

---

[30] Cf.: 'since ye are but creatures, ye are not altogether mortal and indissoluble, but
ye shall certainly not be dissolved . . . having in my will a greater and mightier bond than
those with which ye were bound at the time of your birth' (*Timaeus* 41b). This was one
of the *Timaeus* passages given currency by Abelard.

veritas dei

(C) 1. Standing for the divine nature.
    2. Not intelligible to us, or usable as an exemplar or paradigm.

        (D) 1. Standing for something other than God,
           considered by us in some way.
           2. Signifying either of two distinct kinds of
            thing.

(B) 1. Standing for some set of abstract exemplars or paradigms of things;
    whether of actual things, or of things possible to be ordered by God
    to be.
    2. Signifying either that (1) as known to God, the set is nothing distinct
    from the divine nature, or that (2) the set is of things viewed as not
    possible to be instantiated save by God's will.

        (A) 1. Standing for some truth expressed by
           some (creaturely) thinker.
           2. Signifying that it is an approximation to
           the *divina veritas* at (B).

---

ultaneous opposites, is the actual order of things. This is in line
with what Albert and others have been seen to say already, in
passages where *veritas dei* refers to the faithfulness with which the
actual order of things was believed to be being carried through.
But the *ordo primae veritatis* at least appears to be something else,
for it is that against which even the First Principle of our
Understanding is to be *exemplatum et regulatum*. And that, as was
seen in the passages on truth (from *Summa* 1, qu. 25 chiefly), is
what it is essentially, independently of how we grasp it. Yet it is
usable as an exemplar and paradigm only to the extent to which
we can grasp it. Understood as an exemplar and paradigm,
therefore, can it be anything other than as much of God's option-
neutral power as is manifested in what has in fact been ordered
to be: the *ordinatio dei*, once more. What may be said to be in
God's option-neutral power, in excess of that, is either not
independent of our ways of thinking (this is the non-platonist
option), or is not usable as an exemplar or paradigm (this is the

platonist, and indeed the Platonist, option). In the former approach, which is apparently Albert's, a first principle of under-standing diverse from ours, is not impossible in God's option-neutral power; but we, built as we are, can never be in a position to draw any safe consequences from that. Albert's treatment of the question of simultaneous opposites is instructive. There is more to be said about it than is possible here: but the instruction not least worth taking, is that talk of exemplars is practically impossible to free from its Platonic associations, that a marriage between Augustinian and Pseudo-Dionysian approaches to divine truth appears impossible from the outset, and that platonist interpretations of the option-tied arm of the Distinction (and related expressions) may not be reconcilable with a rigorously Negative Theology.

23. "Distant things", and things. No things are so distant as creator and creature, an objection ran. But God was able to bring about 'that the creator is a creature, because God is man. Therefore much more can he bring about that something black should be white, and that something existent should be [sim-ultaneously] inexistent'. Albert does not dispute the Hypostatic Union, and accepts that something analogous could be envisaged in the case of black and white: *et sic bene possunt uniri album et nigrum.*

He draws the line short of a hypostatic union of something and its absence: whether of some thing and no thing (*ens et non ens in oppositione contradictionis*); or of the simultaneous having of some characteristic and the not having it on the part of some subject (*privatio et habitus in oppositione quae vocatur privatio et habitus*). 'Non-being and privation, since they are nothing, are not unitable with anything.' (*Summa* 1, qu. 78, ed. Borgnet, 31; 833a.) The weakest "being" is the truthmaker of the weakest composing-apt proposition: in other words, a *divisio*. If there can be a *divisio* only between integral "forms" (or their complements), then even the "things" which God can do in option-neutral power are to be understood as (ordered sets of) integral forms (or their complements), permitting a true *divisio* to be had about them. In the case of God and man, no problem arises on this head: *ens ab alio* and *ens non ab alio* are alike *ens*, are alike something.

But even "distant" things which, like God and man, can be

united hypostatically (*per unionem naturarum in una persona*), cannot necessarily be brought together in other "unions": say, by the presence of opposite or disparate forms in one and the same subject or material location (*per inesse formarum oppositarum vel disparatarum in uno et eodem subiecto sive materia*) (ed. Borgnet, 31; 833a).

While it is not intelligible that two opposite forms should be in one subject *per concretionem*—where even a *divisio* cannot be had, there is nothing to be understood—it is imaginable that a single composite should be composed out of diverse forms in respect of diverse parts. He cites Horace's painter who can join a human head to a horse's neck (*De arte poet.*, ad init.) and says that God does this in great numbers, in the case of monstrous formations.

As with painters' putative "unions", so with those of speakers. An objection ran from a *dictum* of Hilary's, to the effect that the mark of complete power is to be able to execute whatever a speaker's utterance signifies. God, the envisaged objector argued, can therefore do anything you can put in words; but you can say black is white, and being is nothing, and a sighted person is blind, and a father is a son; therefore God can do this. Albert replies:

Hilary means that if a speaker's utterance may be referred to a thing (*rem*), that whatever then can be said, God can do. Because an utterance referred to a thing signifies the thing's being; and that is in accordance with the ordering of the first truth (*secundum ordinationem primae veritatis*). Speech in itself (Albert refers to *4 Metaph.*) may signify indeterminates (*infinita*) or opposites.

Note how Albert has made good his initially striking declaration that to 'the possible which is possible to God *secundum causas superiores* ... is subjected every other kind of possible, and of impossible even' (*Summa* 1, Memb. 1 ad fin.; Borgnet, 31; 830b). He has done so by spelling out that it is possible and impossible things which are in question, not just any fancies we might paint or put in words. And in what concerns the *possibile in dicto*, that which is possible *ex cohaerentia terminorum praedicati et subiecti*, he has done so by putting weight on *dictum*. The possible is a species of the true, and—the divine nature apart—only what is expressed in some creature's thought can be actually true; and expression in some creature's thought is possible only if God wills there to be a creature of the kind needed. Students of academic politics may note in passing that Albert is thereby quietly planting the flag of the theologians on the domain of modal logic.

THE 43 QUESTIONS (1271)

24. When over 80, Albert continues to use the Distinction, without any apparent reluctance. The Master-General of the Dominicans, perhaps to forestall a witch-hunt within the Order from a faction of young fogies, put to Albert, Kilwardby, and Aquinas a list of 43 questions on which to deliver a theological opinion.[31]

Question 17 was: Can an angel move the stuff (*molem*) of the earth as far as the sphere of the moon, even though it never does or will move it? This raises more than one question, and Albert replies to no more than he thinks he has to. He had already expressed irritation, and serious reservations, about the whole subset of questions about angels moving masses around. It is at the end of his answer that he adds: 'But I flatly do not believe (*non credo*) that it can move the earth *de potentia ordinata* [*dei*], because this would result in confusion to the whole of nature.'

Titanic earthmoving of the sort would of course cause confusion in an everyday sense, confusion sensible to observers accustomed to the way our world runs. For example, the "heavy" elements of earth and water, seeking their "natural" place at the centre of the universe, would no longer show specious centripetality from no matter what point on the earth's surface. If they seemed to move "down" at Lords, they would seem to move "up" at Melbourne and sideways at Karachi. Cricket could still be played at Lords, but would be difficult to umpire in

---

[31] Albert's answers are in Cologne edn., vol. 17, and had earlier been published by the same editor J. Weisheipl in *Med. St.* 22 (1960), 303–54. Kilwardby's are in M.-D. Chenu, 'Les Réponses de S. Thomas et de Kilwardby à la consultation de Jean de Verceuil (1271)', in *Mandonnet Festschrift* (1930), 1: 191–222. Aquinas's are in 'Responsio ad Fr Ioannem Vercellensem Generalem Magistrum Ordinis Praedicatorum de articulis XLII', ed. R. A. Verardo, in the Marietti *Opuscula Theologica*, 1 (Turin, 1954), 209–22; and in Leon. edn. 42 (1979), 325–35.

Karachi, and practically impossible in Australia, where, on leaving the anchorage of the pavilion, players, umpires, heavy roller, and all would be seen to take to the skies. Albert, however, may have a deeper confusion in mind.

We have already seen him use *confusio* in a more technical sense, for what results when we purport to instantiate an intersection of incompatible forms. The *moles* of the earth is made of the four elements, is elemental. In the sphere of the moon the only "stuff" permitted is quintessential. Hence the *moles* of the earth, moved to the sphere of the moon, would have to be simultaneously quintessential and elemental. If, as may be supposed, these are incompatible, there will be *confusio*. The 'whole of nature' is an *universitas*, an ordered whole. *Confusio* cannot be instantiated, so if there had been *confusio*, the *universitas* of nature could not be.

ALBERT AND THE POWER DISTINCTION

25.   Albert uses the Distinction in works in which he is specifically engaged in systematic theology addressed to a knowing, academic audience. He uses it first, as would appear, in the Commentary on the Sentences: the work dependent on his first academic teaching within the Theology Faculty at Paris. He shows himself familiar with the canonical terminology, but uses a variety of expressions. Some of these are highly instructive, and are used below in an attempt to understand the Distinction more systematically (Ch. 9).

Albert's own favoured understanding of the option-neutral arm, and of assertions of scientifical importance generally, is non-platonist. In his treatment of mathematical truths in particular, he seems to be following in a line developed by Avicenna. Even the "First Principle of our Understanding", or the "First Principle of all Scientifical Knowledge and all Truth"—the traditional aristotelian conjunction of the Law of Contradiction and the Law of Excluded Middle (for propositions, understood as in Ch. 1)—is not seen by Albert to be above possible revision (in God's option-neutral power). It is rather, like the "eternal truths" of the mathematicians, to be in its actual truth to be of a piece with the actual order of things, the *ordinatio dei*. It is not "constructed" by us, but in us; since we too and all our "natural powers" are

part of the *ordinatio dei*, and thus of God's construction. It is built
into our understanding, so governing the constructions we can
make and understand.

Albert is aware of a platonist and indeed Platonist way of
understanding the *ordo divinae veritatis* which is the 'exemplar and
paradigm' of the actual order of things; and closely related to
God's option-neutral power. He seems aware of the tensions it
creates for one who wishes, as he plainly does, to maintain a
rigorously Negative Theology on the divine nature. He plays
down the tensions, at one place insinuating a (non-existent)
agreement between the Pseudo-Denis, on the one hand, and
Augustine and Anselm, on the other: so as to persuade even
readers as careful as the Cologne editor to punctuate in accordance with the insinuation. Albert seems to accommodate the
platonism, not as a philosophical view in competition with the
Negative Theology one, but as information provided *secundum
fidem catholicam*, on the authority of a revelation, presumably.

The tensions are raised by the issues anyway, and the con-
flations between Christian doctrines and Platonist ways of understanding run very deep in christian thought. They have often
been creative tensions, and by no means always to be deplored.
As for Albert's treatment of Power Distinction matters generally,
it remains one of the clearest and most helpful which I have seen
from any period.

5

St Bonaventure, OFM

More than Albert, more even than Aquinas, Bonaventure has sometimes suffered from ill-directed praise: obscuring his real qualities. Both in academic theology, in dialectics, and in matters of practical politics these were considerable. He was also respected by many in his day for his sermons, and continues to find an audience for works of pious exhortation. Like Albert and Aquinas, he is honoured as a saint.[1]

BONAVENTURE (d. 15 JULY 1274)

1. An able politician, he played no slight part in the refoundation of the Franciscan Order—perhaps the real foundation of the institution which endures to this day—and in the growing domination by the religious, and above all by the friars, in the University of Paris in the second half of the thirteenth century. He made a point of remaining on good terms with a succession

[1] J. G. Bougerol, *Introduction à Saint Bonaventure* (Paris, 1988), XIII + 289 pp., is a model of its genre. The authentic works are listed at pp. x–xi. The critical edn, from Quaracchi, 1882–1902, is cited as 'Quar.', the derived *editio minor* from 1924 as *Opera theologica selecta*. J. G. Bougerol, *Bibliographia Bonaventuriana* (Grottaferrata, 1974), provides retrospective bibliography, and *Bibliographia Franciscana*, Quaracchi, current bibliography. J. F. Quinn, *The Historical Constitution of St Bonaventure's Philosophy* (Toronto, 1973), provides a documented survey, and for the matter of the present chapter É. Gilson, *La philosophie de saint Bonaventure*, (Paris, 1978), 417 pp., ch. 5, 'La Puissance et la volonté de Dieu' is helpful. Connections between Bonaventure's theological work and his involvement in the "political" upheavals of the time within the Franciscan movements are often made. P. Vian, 'Bonaventura di Bagnioregio di fronti a Gioacchino da Fiore e al Gioacchimismo. Qualche riflessione su recenti valutazioni', *Antonianum*, 65 (1990), 133–60, helpfully surveys important discussions. A practical difficulty is that—to a greater extent than is found with, say, Aquinas or Ockham—important critical studies on Bonaventure's thought appear in house organs or journals of piety, alongside articles of no particularly scholarly or critical intent. Bonaventure would doubtless have approved, but it makes it harder to persuade even large academic libraries to stock the serials in question.

of popes, to whom he was a valuable ally: in building up centralised papal powers at the expense of the more traditional powers of diocesan bishops more generally; and in absorbing possible competition from the newer and practically universal normative authority in theology which the University (and bishops) of Paris came very near to tacitly assuming. Refoundation of the Franciscan Order was secured when, on the motion of Pope Alexander IV, not least behind the scenes, Bonaventure displaced John of Parma (1257) as head of the Order. Residual support for John and his (perhaps more primitively Franciscan) ideals was weakened when Bonaventure saw to John's being tried by the Inquisition (1263). In the University Bonaventure's own official status was not always above dubiety. Yet long after he ceased to teach there, he lived by predilection at Mantes, from which Paris was readily and comfortably reached by boat. His influence in this later period was enormous, not least through the three successive series of Lenten sermons which fomented the spirit which had its day in the condemnations of 1270.

Bonaventure was a bishop for a time, but his career as one was even shorter than Albert's. Bonaventure had been appointed to the Archbishopric of York in 1265, but was not consecrated bishop until 1273, in preparation for the Council of Lyons. He was created cardinal around the same time, but died while the Council was still in progress (15 July 1274). Since he was never able to show his bulls of appointment to the cathedral chapter, he never actually became Archbishop of York.

2. In theology his teachers were Alexander of Hales and John of la Rochelle, but he is said to have been influenced also by the Dominican Guerric of St Quentin. On the face of it, he is thus indebted to a slightly older generation within the Theology Faculty, than his contemporary Aquinas was. It is not known who Bonaventure's teachers in Arts were, but he had not wasted his time there: Grabmann, well placed to judge, thought him one of the best dialecticians of the Middle Ages.[2]

Bonaventure admired Augustine: 'the outstanding Latin doctor' of the Church, the 'outstanding expositor of the whole

---

[2] For his exploitation of Aristotle 'avec compétence et maîtrise', see J. G. Bougerol, 'Dossier pour l'étude des rapports entre saint Bonaventure et Aristote', *AHDLMA* 40 (1973), repr. in *Saint Bonaventure: Études sur les sources de sa pensée* (1989), 135–222, 221.

of Scripture' (*In 3 Sent.*, Quaracchi edn. 3: 86; Serm. 4, Quar. edn. 5: 572; cit. Bougerol, *Introd.* (1988), 54). But like others he exploited Augustine's reputation to defend scientific studies against their pious despisers; emphasising the famous contention of the *De doctrina christiana* that without expertise in other sciences, sacred Scripture cannot be understood. The authority of that contention had arguably played its part in winning for university studies the crucial support they regularly had from the institutional Church. On a number of matters it was the more intellectual elements in Augustine's work which appeared to attract Bonaventure. When praising the *Confessions*, for example, it was the treatments of time and of matter that he picked out. (Modern translations have been known to leave out the subtle treatment of time; which is integral to Augustine's programme in the work.) More surprising to some, perhaps, is the extent of Bonaventure's declared debts to the Pseudo-Denis (Bougerol, *Introd.* (1988), 63–77).

CREATURES' KNOWLEDGE OF GOD: *QUID SIT*, OR JUST *QUIA EST*?

3. On the knowability of God by creatures, Bonaventure pulls out all the rhetorical stops to convey the impression that God is knowable. On the other hand, he sedulously avoids saying whether he is speaking only of knowledge *quia est*—exactly as Albert had allowed—or something stronger. 'God in himself, in something of the manner of a supreme light, is supremely knowable; and like light, is what supremely satisfies (*complens*) our understanding.' (*In 1 Sent.* d. 3, art. un. qu. 1c, Quaracchi edn. 1: 69a.) Albert had been happy to use this 'light' imagery too, but precisely when making points about knowing *quia est*, but not *quid sit*. When, in answer to objections, Bonaventure drops the rhetoric, he concedes: 'it does not follow that, if all of him (*totus*) is known, that he should be being comprehended; because our understanding does not include his totality, just as no creature includes his immensity' (*In 1 Sent.* d. 3, art. un. qu. 1, Quar. edn. 1: 69b).

An objection in the same question had sought to exploit the point: 'for knowing (*cognitionem*) to be had, there has to be in the

one knowing, a judgement concerning the thing known... '.
Bonaventure replies:

It is to be said that judging concerning something is had in either of
two ways: In the first way by discerning whether it exists or not (*utrum
sit vel non sit*), and in this way judgement is appropriate to every knowing
understanding in respect of every object; in another way by approving,
or reprobating, whether it ought to be as it is, and in this way one
does not judge concerning the truth, but judges according to it,
concerning others. (Quaracchi edn. 1: 69b.)

Since it is God's knowability which is in question at that place,
and *utrum sit vel non sit* is as much as Bonaventure is claiming, it
would seem to be knowledge *quia est* and no more which is
involved. I add 'and no more', because if Bonaventure had any
substance to support his rhetoric, this is where it was needed.
No such substance is provided. Even where speaking of the
knowledge of God had by the blessed *in patria*, which he calls
cognitio... apertae cognitionis as opposed to cognition which comes
by argumentation, he implies no more. The cognition of God
which is had by the blessed excludes faith, in that it excludes the
same thing's being known and believed. But *scitum* and *creditum*
are not necessarily in competition where *quid sit*, the content of
what is known or believed, is in question. They might be
in competition where the same content were concerned: but
Bonaventure does not allege that any such same content is in
question. They are in competition, to the extent that the one
makes the other redundant, where *quia est* is concerned. Once
more, therefore, what indications there are do not point to God's
being knowable save to the extent *quia est*, in Bonaventure any
more than in Albert. (See *In 3 Sent.*, d. 24, art. 2, qu. 3c,
Quaracchi edn. 3: 522b; and cf. the obscure passage at *In 3 Sent.*,
d. 14, art. 1, qu. 3, ad 6, Quar. edn. 3: 305b.) This is confirmed
from his treatment of God's susceptibility to being "named" by
us: the topic under which those who maintained a Negative
Theology position (and the view of "names" mentioned in Ch.
1, Sect. 13) treated problems of attributing things to God, at their
most general. God, says Bonaventure, is nameable not *secundum
perfectam expressionem*, but *secundum semiplenam narrationem*; and 'just
as he is incomprehensible by us, so he is inexpressible by us, and
so unnameable' (*In 1 Sent.*, d. 22, art. un. qu. 1c). Although God

is infinite, he is known in a finite manner by us (*finite cognoscitur a nobis*).

Scholars have often found it difficult to address the question directly. An exception is Gilson:

> It goes without saying that Saint Bonaventure does not... attribute to us a clear concept of the divine essence. What is to be found to be inseparable from, and profoundly imprinted upon, our own thought is the affirmation of the existence of God, and not to the slightest degree the comprehension of his essence.... Hugh of St Victor had already said that God proportioned our knowledge to him in such a way that we could never either know what he is, or not know that he is. Such also is the formula that Saint Bonaventure adopts... (Gilson, *History* (1955), 335, referring to Bonaventure *In 1 Sent.* 8, Quar. edn. 1: 154, and *De myst. Trin.* 1, Quar. edn. 5: 15; and to Hugh's *De sacramentis*, I. 3. 1.)

The source of the trouble here is in Bonaventure, rather than in the scholars.[3] Even in that text from *In 1 Sent.*, d. 8, Bonaventure chooses to emphasise the shortcoming in our intellect: 'Our intellect fails in thinking of the divine truth in so far as knowledge *quid est* is concerned, but does not fail in so far as knowledge *si est* is concerned' (Quar. edn. 1: 154b). He does not deny that not even God—who "comprehends" himself—can know his own *quid est*, for the reason spelled out by Albert, that if you exist without restriction you can have no *quid est* to be known, even in "comprehension". But Bonaventure is silent on the matter, at that place at any rate; and fairly consistently—without strictly implying anything—makes it *sound* as though the "knowledge of God" to which his commended *Itinerarium* is meant to take us, is of the *quid est* variety rather than merely being knowledge *quia*

---

[3] Bonaventure's vigorous rhetoric and elusive declarations of content may be due in part to constraints felt from the condemned *articulus parisiensis* of 1241: *divina essentia in se nec ab homine nec ab angelo videbitur.* He listed all 10 articles at *In 2 Sent.*, d. 23, qu. 3, sol., Quar. edn. 2: 546–47, '*ut evitentur*'. But see É. H. Wéber, *Dialogue et dissensions entre saint Bonaventure et saint Thomas d'Aquin à Paris (1252–73)* (Paris, 1974), 519 pp., 98–100. What I do not find established there is that either that article or Bonaventure's own opinion requires more than *quia est* knowledge of God on the part of creatures. The correct emphasis is surely that of J. G. Bougerol, 'Saint Bonaventure et le Pseudo-Denys l'Aréopagite', repr. in *Saint Bonaventure: Études* (Northampton, 1989), 33–123, 117: 'Saint Bonaventure ne veut connaître l'essence divine que comme subsistence . . .'. The rhetoric, by contrast, is striking. Cf. Cayré's remark on Bonaventure: 'N'alla-t-on pas jusqu'à essayer de démontrer le mystère de la Trinité par des raisons qui semblent dépasser la convenance et l'analogie?' F. Cayré, *La contemplation augustinienne: principes de spiritualité et de théologie* (Bruges, 1954), 287 pp., 249.

est; as allowed by Albert and—if the face value of the words is
to be understood—conceded as at least a possibility by Hume.

It is not good enough to speak of the problem as a 'failure' in
our understanding, when the cause of the failure is that in us
understanding is had by matching concept and thing, and in the
case under consideration it cannot be had because God is not a
'thing' of the kind which is strictly speaking understandable. It
is less than ingenuous to reproach our understanding for "failure",
when the cause of the "failure" is the absence of a possible object
of understanding. Whatever God is, it is not a possible proper
object of our understanding.

Even Gilson's forthright statement is not totally helpful. What
is important in understanding Bonaventure is to know whether
he allows knowledge of the *quid est* of God, or just knowledge
that some God exists, knowledge *quia est*. To say that what is to
be found is 'not to the slightest degree the comprehension of his
essence' does not as yet exclude the possibility of the *quid sit*
variety of knowledge. We might know the *quid sit* of some creature
without strictly comprehending its essence; and God presumably
comprehends himself, without having a *quid sit*, strictly speaking,
to know.[4]

THE POWER DISTINCTION IN THE SENTENCE
COMMENTARY

It seems that Bonaventure lectured on the books of the Sentences
in the order 1, 4, 2, 3.[5] I shall take the passages according to that
order.

4. A passage worth noting comes at *In 1 Sent.* d. 43, qu. 4,
where he is considering the 'erroneous position' that divine
power—God's power *ut agente et producente aliquid*[6]—was capable

---

[4] On God's knowability by creatures: E. Bettoni, *S. Bonaventura da Bagnoregio: Gli aspetti
filosofici del suo pensiero* (Milan, 1975), 233 pp., chs. 4 and 5; A. Pegis, 'The Bonaventurean
Way to God', *Med. St.* 29 (1967), 206–42; J. Bougerol, 'Sur le sens de Dieu', *Études
Franciscaines*, NS 14 (1964), 23–30. See also the works on exemplarism noted at n. 12 below.
[5] I. Brady, 'The Edition of the *Opera Omnia* of St Bonaventure (1882–1902)', in *Il
Collegio S. Bonaventura di Quaracchi* (Grottaferrata, 1977), 133–4, cit. Bougerol, *Introd.* (1988), 189.
[6] The question *U. deus possit aliquid aliud a se* is that of *In 1 Sent.*, d. 42, art. un., qu. 1.
Potentia agens in aliud, in God's case, simply is his own actuality, *suus actus*; it is not to act
per actum a se differentem. A distinction close to this reappears in the Disputed Question *De
myst. Trin.*, qu. 6, art. 1, in which the Power Distinction is used.

of no more than it was doing. That Bonaventure, who was to play such a vigorous part in denouncing what he saw as dangerous views in the schools of Paris, judges the position to be 'erroneous' is itself worth noting. The censure 'erroneous' was a relatively mild one. It was used typically of views whose content was philosophical or scientifical, rather than theological or concerning "the deposit of faith". Unlike 'heretical' or 'savouring of heresy', the charge of error did not in itself leave the holder open to burning. And Bonaventure, like Albert and Aquinas, does not himself impute the position to Abelard; saying no more than *dicitur fuisse Magistri Petri Baalardi.*

At issue in this question is whether the very notion of something's being done by God external to his nature has to be a notion of something finite. In reply Bonaventure contrasts two ways of specifying the power: as a standing "habit" out of which orders of things of the same broad genre as the actual order of things can be done, if God chooses to do so; and as the exercise of that "habit" which the actual order of things can be seen to be. To the habit he refers the *posse* of *posse facere*, in assertions to the effect that God 'can do' this or that external to his nature; to the exercise, he refers the *facere*.

He is thus treating the standing *posse* of *posse facere* there on the analogy of the powers—including powers thought of as persisting in being, even while not being exercised—which Aristotle had assigned to the category of quality; and in the sub-category of habit as opposed to disposition.

Some allusion may also be intended to the jurists' distinction between some "faculty" viewed as possessed *per modum habitus*, and able to be exercised whenever the possessor sees fit to do so, as against one able to be exercised only *per modum actus*, on a particular range of occasions. A modern curate, for example, has a standing "faculty" of this sort, *per modum habitus*, to officiate validly at marriages. A visiting priest may have no such faculty, but the curate can sub-delegate the 'faculty' to him *per modum actus*, so that he can validly officiate.[7]

---

[7] Some years ago a pair of twins, eminent in the Roman Curia, made something of a speciality of flying to distant countries and officiating at society weddings. It transpired that possessors *per modum habitus* of the "faculty" required had not thought to (sub-) delegate; thinking (mistakenly) that peregrinating curial cardinals might have faculties of their own. Since marriages so conducted are invalid, the results were convenient for some, disconcerting for others.

In the case of God's power to do things external to his nature, understood as the *posse facere* attributed to him *per modum habitus*, the range of cases to which his *posse* extends, is infinite; and the notion extends *ad infinita*.

In a second sense of 'God's power to do things extrinsic to his nature' we understand the power by reference to the actual operation (*operari*); the *facere* of the *posse facere*.

5.   In the light of earlier chapters, this is familiar enough. Bonaventure has in mind here God's option-neutral power and his option-tied power, respectively. Two things may be less familiar. The first is the "habit and exercise" model on which the Distinction is being expounded; as opposed to the "schematic notion and instantiation" model on which it was expounded by Albert and some of the earlier users of the Distinction. It seems to me that this is not a small discrepancy. It brings into the open a question as to whether:

(1) Bonaventure is expounding the same (specifically the same) dialectical device—the same distinction—as Albert was expounding;

(2) recognisable as the same, by agreement in results in the whole range of cases to which it is applicable;

(3) understood in essentially the same way; but

(4) expounded by using a different model, chosen for pedagogical reasons merely.

Questions of this sort are considered explicitly in Chapter 9 below. Provisionally, I shall accept (1), taking sameness of dialectical device as sameness of result of application to similar cases. (If necessary, neutral ways of describing the cases may have to be found, before they can be said to be similar or not.) I think that (2) is probably true, but Bonaventure does not provide a wide enough range of examples to encourage a reader to be sure. Provisionally, I think that Bonaventure and Albert part company not only on (4) but on (3), understanding the option-neutral arm importantly differently; in a platonist and a non-platonist manner respectively.

The second point in which a discrepancy appears between Bonaventure and Albert, is in their ways of understanding *condecentia divinae bonitatis*, an expression which both apparently owed to Anselm. Bonaventure expresses the "habit" as

(1) divina scientia et divinae bonitatis condecentia, *and the "exercise" as*

(2) divina dispositio et meritorum exigentia (Quar. edn. 1: 775a).

In other words, he was using the phrase in (1) to express God's option-neutral power, and the phrase in (2) to express God's option-tied power. Albert had used a superficially similar contrast, between

(1) condecentia divinae bonitatis, *and*

(2) retributio pro meritis,

but to importantly diverse purpose. In Albert, *condecentia divinae bonitatis* is used to express that "justice" of God's which is to be identified with the *ordinatio dei*, with God's option-tied power. *Retributio pro meritis*, in Albert's usage, concerned a subset of the *ordinatio dei*, viewed in a certain way. The corresponding phrase, *meritorum exigentia*, in Bonaventure, is apparently being used to signal that the *divina dispositio* in question is the actual one, not just any envisaged *divinae bonitatis condecentia*. It is worth adding, however, that the precise interpretation of Bonaventure in this passage would need more explicit attention than is in place here.

By contrast, Bonaventure's main drift is plain. The notion of a "power of God's to do things external to his nature" can be taken either as the notion of the power God has so disposed (in the actual *ordinatio dei*), and is then a notion precisely coextensive with that, and finite; or the notion of a standing 'habit' out of which the *ordinatio dei* can be seen as having been done, and out of which indefinitely many like *ordinationes* can be envisaged as possible to come, if God chooses. This is to consider God's power to do things ad extra in the ways in which it is considered in the Power Distinction; in addition, it is to understand the Distinction on a "capacity and exercise" or rather "habit and exercise" model. (In Aristotle's usage, a habit is a more settled kind of capacity or disposition.)

6. The main difference between a "habit and exercise" model, as here, and a "schematic notion and instantiation" model, such as Albert and some earlier users of the Distinction showed, is that whereas the latter model is neutral as towards a platonist or a non-platonist interpretation, the former is not. It at least

seems to accord well with a platonist interpretation, locating the supposed "habit" in the (eternal) *scientia divina*, and thus in the divine nature. It is not surprising to find Bonaventure preferring this sort of model; it is in line with platonist preferences which appear repeatedly in his work, and which in some cases have been seen already.

In reply to a related objection he provides confirmation of his acceptance of the substance of the Distinction, in a terminology which had been used by Hugh of St Victor, and which was taken up by a number of users of the Distinction, both before and after Bonaventure. God's *potentia exsequens*, he says, is necessarily subject to his 'disposition or foreknowledge or justice'. But what is *de potentia ut potente* is not. (Quar. edn. 1: 775; *Op. theol. sel.* 1 (1924), 615, 616.) The *ut potente* there refers to the *posse* of the "habit", as against the *operari* or "exercise of the habit". Once more the Distinction is at least being alluded to.

7.   In dubium 7 ad fin. of the same *In 1 Sent.*, d. 43, he reports a use on the part of *Aliqui* which he judges inappropriate to the argument to which it was addressed. He also goes on to use the Distinction in his own reply. The dubium had begun from the question of whether God might have saved Judas and damned Peter, but had been crucially complicated by the juxtaposition of a Scriptural text ('he continueth faithful, he cannot deny himself', 2 Tim. 2: 13) which put the earlier question within a different context, raising a different logical issue. Bonaventure first reported:

Aliqui distinguish here the power of God in two ways, saying that God can [do something or other] either (*aut*) in option-neutral power (*de potentia absoluta*), and in this way he can save Judas and damn Peter; or (*aut*) in option-tied power (*de potentia ordinata*), and in this way he cannot. (Quar. edn. 1: 778a; *Op. theol. sel.* (1924), 618.)

He then gave his own judgement on what *Aliqui* had been doing:

This distinction does not seem appropriate, because God can do nothing that he cannot do *ordinate*. For to be able to do something *inordinate* is not-being-able (*non posse*), like being able to sin, and being able to lie.

The Quaracchi editors of 1882 note correctly that Bonaventure is not arguing here against the Distinction itself, but was rejecting the appropriateness of it to the argument to which it was addressed.

Since the case of saving Judas, considered in itself, does not involve any necessity of doing anything *inordinate*, some readers of Bonaventure might be led to think that he was disposed to treat this case differently from some of his predecessors, as already seen. This is not so. It is worth spelling out that the *inordinatio* arises not from the Judas/Peter case itself, but from such a case being viewed as a case of God's breaking faith with his own disposition. The logical necessity which is causing the trouble is not to be thought as arising from that involved in what holds of the divine nature; but is the logical necessity which arises from so much as the falling of a leaf, if taken to come within the scope of what is willed by God (for execution without fail).

This restriction of scope—itself arising from the case's having been brought within the scope set by the Scriptural text from 2 Tim.—must also be understood to govern Bonaventure's own unfussy use of the Distinction here, which follows immediately on the last text quoted:

Whence neither in option-neutral power (*potentiā absolutā*) nor in option-tied power (*potentiā ordinatā*) can he lie. (Quar. edn. 1: 778a; *Op. theol. sel.* 1 (1924), 618.)

The 'lie' in question here is the denying of his own ordinance, mentioned at 2 Tim. 2: 13. It is because the case of Judas was being considered within the scope of this, that Bonaventure had rejected the solution of *Aliqui*. Their fault in his eyes was their having nullified the option-neutral arm of the Distinction they were professing to use. He was not objecting to their having sought to use the Distinction in the first place. By the juxtaposition of 2 Tim. 2: 13 they were smuggling the case of Judas back within a scope from which the option-neutral arm of the Distinction was precisely calculated to reserve it. Bonaventure thus rejected what *Aliqui* had been doing, not because he objected to the Distinction, or because they had been seeking to use it, but because while purporting to use it, they had in fact been nullifying it.

8. In *In 4 Sent.* I find no uses of the Power Distinction, but what may be mentioned is a hint of complications to come. It

concerns the *potestates ordinatae* of creatures, and what these can or cannot do *de iure* or *de facto*. Later Franciscans, Scotus and Ockham especially, were to make much of comparisons between *posse de facto* and *posse de iure*, on the one hand, and expositions of the Power Distinction, on the other.[8] In the present passage, Quaracchi edn. 4: 302b, no particularly contentious points are made.

9. At *In 2 Sent.*, d. 7 he uses the Distinction. The general difficulty is whether the will of an angel confirmed in grace (or rebellion) can change. *Sancti* and other sources of authorities had said:

the will of a devil can in no way be rectified, in so far as 'can' is predicating a power understood with reference to something actual (*ordinationem ad actum*). For if the 'can' is being understood of the power of an agent considered in isolation [from its actual exercise] (*si intellegatur de potentia efficientis absolute*), then without doubt God is able to restore a good will to a devil. On the devil's part, however, there is no directedness towards this: its will indeed has become impotent (*impossibilis*), as the *Sancti* say and as the arguments show. (*In 2 Sent.*, d. 7, pars 1, art. 1, qu. 1c, Quar. edn. 2: 175a.)

The 'can' here, if understood to be signifying a power to F, and in particular a power to make wills to be right, may certainly signify a power to F which can be attributed to God. But potentialities for being made F are likewise specified by reference to actually being made F. In the present case, the potentiality in question is a devil's potentiality for having its will made right. But "a devil's will's being made right" is not something which is to be found within the actual order of things. Hence while 'God can make devils' wills to be right' may express a truth (expressed option-neutrally), 'This devil's will can be made right by God' is not something which can be true, because it is presumably being understood as indexed to the actual order of things. More would need to be said on this, to do justice to the case, and to Bonaventure's treatment of it. But Bonaventure does not pursue the point.

10. Shortly afterwards, he takes up instead the objection (ratio 1 post oppositum): Surely God could in mercy have condoned

---

[8] See E, Randi, *Il sovrano e l'orologiaio* (1987), 51–83.

the punishment due to the rebellious angels? It is in reply to this that Bonaventure makes a further use of the Distinction:

it is to be said that there can be condonation in God's option-neutral power (*de potentia absoluta*); but in option-tied power (*de potentia ordinata*) which operates according to his wise decree—and God will not destroy (*corrumpat*) this order, but inviolably conserves it—it is not called for and cannot be, because the counsel and disposition of God cannot be changed in any respect. (Quar. edn. 2: 177a.)

This is a straightforward use of the Distinction, noteworthy if at all, only because Bonaventure is rather plainly spelling out the import of considering things as being within the scope of God's ordering.

THE POWER DISTINCTION IN THE *BREVILOQUIUM*

In this work, from around the same period as the Sentence Commentary, he set out to summarise 'not everything, but some things that are more opportune to be held' in sacred doctrine; adding under each topic treated a rationale for the doctrine summarised. (See his admirably clear statement of intent in the Prologue.) Not surprisingly—since the work is ex professo not an inquiry or a sequence of inquiries—he does not use the Power Distinction. He does, however, provide material useful towards an understanding of it.

11. When explaining the *magis opportune tenendum* on the omnipotence of God, he writes (Quar. edn. 5: 216a) as follows:

The First Principle is powerful by reason of power which is power *simpliciter*; and for that reason any distribution added to it distributes for those things which, to be able to do, is to be able *simpliciter* to do (*pro his quae posse est posse simpliciter*).

Because divine power is power unrestrictedly, any quantification is over what can be done sans phrase—never mind what kind of power is supposed to be at work. Only integral, ordered "things", therefore, can satisfy 'For any *x*, God can bring about *x*', or perhaps rather 'For any *x* of the ___ kind, God can bring about *x* of the _____ kind'.[9] "Things" lacking order—such as (the set of things of) God's option-neutral power itself—can be understood, can be said to be *entia*, in the sense of being objects of a judgement. But they are not such as can be instantiated—by no matter what power—so as to be *entia facta*, things existing in any order of things possible to be be brought about. Bonaventure himself continues:

Those things are, which issue from a complete and ordered power (*quae egrediuntur a potentia completa et ordinata*).

The alternative reading,

Things are what issue complete and ordered from a power,

would provide essentially the same doctrine. What immediately follows, however, explains 'complete power' and 'ordered power' in turn, so the first reading would seem the one called for. He first explains 'complete power':

I call complete, power which cannot fail, or submit, or be in need. Power in sinning fails; power which undergoes anything submits; power in corporeal actions includes a lack.

But divine power, because it is supreme and most perfect, by that is neither *de nihilo*, nor *sub aliquo*, nor in need of anything else (*alio aliquo*); and hence can do neither culpable things, nor things exacted, nor material things; and this, because it is omnipotent in complete power.

The completeness or incompleteness of powers is apparently to be judged in relation to the completeness or incompleteness of the *opus* (Albert) or *complementum* (Bonaventure) by reference to which the powers in question are specified as the kinds of power they are. "Sinning" or "blindness" is not an integral *opus* or *complementum*, so any 'power to sin' or 'capacity for making to be blind' would not count as a complete power.

Divine power is 'omni-potent in complete power'. (We might say: For any *x*, if *x* is an ordered thing, God can do *x*.) It is as though Bonaventure wished to say "Divine power is omni-potent, putting weight on both elements, because 'For any complete

---

[9] On distribution cf. Albert, in reply to an objection: 'signum distributivum 'pro omnibus' distribuit quae facere posse est, et quae facere potentiae est, et non impotentiae... '. (Albert, *Summa*, i, qu. 77, ed. Borgnet, 31: 801b.) On treatments along the lines of 'For any *x* of the_____ kind', and their appropriateness to many medieval authors see G. Klima, *Ars artium* (1988), essay II.

power, God has that power' is true". This is not a mere ad hoc restriction, to block obvious prima-facie counter-instances to claims that God is omnipotent, on the grounds that he is supposed incapable of sinning, growing weary, or the like: though it indeed obviates such irritants to serious discussion, which are still resuscitated at quarterly intervals. It follows from Bonaventure's standard rules for distribution (he is referring to the work *omni* should be taken to be doing in *omnipotens*), and from the truth as he takes it to be, that divine power is something unrestricted in any way. Bonaventure thus does justice to both the *omni* and the *potens*, not by adhockery but on principles of general application.

12. God, then, on Bonaventure's view, is to be said to be omnipotent by being potent in respect of every (complete) power without exception. He takes it no further here, but there are surely more ways than one in which that may be spelled out, from what Bonaventure has provided elsewhere.

1. The divine nature itself is a "complete power", so presumably we may first call God omnipotent on the grounds that he is something unrestricted in any way, and thus a complete power unrestricted in any way.

2. God's option-tied power is a "complete power" in the way in which an individual may be said to be complete.[10] God may thus be called omnipotent on the grounds that in option-tied power he can bring about every (complete) individual-of-some-kind which can be brought about as a complete individual of some kind.

3. God's option-neutral power, as known to God, is to be identified with the divine nature, according to Bonaventure. (This appears below in the present chapter.) So God can be called omnipotent on a ground appropriate here, though this reduces to the way taken in 1.

4. The "things" of God's option-neutral power, as understandable by us, and usable by us in scientifically serious arguments, are complete in the way in which an individual form is complete. God may also be said to be omnipotent because he can bring about any of these, without exception.

---

[10] Both individuals and individual forms can be said to be complete, or less than complete (*In 2 Sent.*, d. 12, Quar. edn. 2: 306b). But cf. what is said on the form of an embryo, at p. 300b of the same volume.

He cannot bring them all about simultaneously. Apart from other considerations, the set of these exemplars or *similitudines* of things as understandable and able to be used in reasonings by us, is of a potential infinity of "things", which as such is incomplete, and thus not a possible value for what can be done by a power that is unrestricted in any way. (The exemplars or *similitudines* of things will also be treated later in the present chapter.)

13. Having explained what he means by power being 'complete', Bonaventure turns to what he may mean by power being 'ordered'. Since this too is narrowly germane to present purpose, it may be useful to begin with his own statement of the matter:

Power falls to being called ordered (*ordinatam*) in three ways: either in respect of an act, or in respect of an aptitude on the side of the creature, or in respect of an aptitude on the side of uncreated strength alone (*solius virtutis increatae*).

What is possible to a power when the word [*ordinata*] is used in the first way, is not merely possible but also actual. What is possible [to a power, when the word *ordinata* is used] in the second way and not the first, is possible *simpliciter*, though not actual. And what is possible [to a power, when the word *ordinata* is used] in the third way, and not in the first or the second, is possible to God, but impossible to a creature.

But what is not possible in any of those ways—like that which directly clashes with order as understood with reference to the primordial and eternal causes and reasons, is impossible *simpliciter*: as if God were to make something actually infinite, or should simultaneously make something to be and in no way to be; as if he were to make that which was, not to have been, and other things of that sort: to be able to do which, is contrary to the order (*ordinem*) and accomplishment (*complementum*) of divine power. (*Breviloquium* 1, ch. 7, Quar. edn. 5: 216a.)

Bonaventure is concerned here with diverse ways in which power can be said to be *ordinata*. In the first of these it is called *ordinata* in respect of being ordered—'dedicated', in a more recent usage—in something actual. An example doubtless is Proust's literary genius, as "ordered" in his actual writings and no further. As Bonaventure adds, power 'ordered' in this first way is an actual something or other. This, I would add, is the fundamental way in which the *potentia ordinata dei* referred to in the option-tied arm of the Power Distinction, is being thought of as "ordered". *Aptitudo*, used of a power described as *ordinata* in this way, carries its central connotations of being fixed in a position.

In a second way, power may be said to be *ordinata* in respect of there being a (created) aptitude for accomplishing that towards which it is being said to be ordered; or in respect of there going to be such an aptitude. When power is "ordered" in this second way, then that towards which it is being said to be ordered, is possible *simpliciter*. When 'It is possible for this man to run' is true on this kind of ground, "this man's running" is possible *simpliciter*, provided either (1) he now has an aptitude for doing so (though he is sitting), or (2) will have one (when his broken bones heal): even if he is not now running. The case envisaged in (2) is the one where *ordinata* may be used 'in the second way and not in the first'. That this is so may be seen by comparing the text now under consideration with what he had explained early in the Sentence Commentary, when expounding his preferred *modus dicendi* for *possibile simpliciter*. (*In 1 Sent.*, d. 42 art. un. qu. 4, Quar. edn. 1: 757a.) 'Aptitude', as mentioned in the present *Breviloquium* text in connection with this first way of speaking of a power as "ordered", is carrying rather the connotation of being in a state of preparedness for action, being set to go.

In the third way, power is said to be *ordinata*, in respect 'of an aptitude on the part of (an) uncreated force alone'. The "ordering" involved here appears to be the intrinsic ordering of the things which God can be said to be able (in option-neutral power) to do. The examples given confirm as much: making something actually infinite, making something simultaneously to be and in no way to be. The *ordinem* of divine power here is, if I understand him, the intrinsic orderedness or *aptitudo*—in an extended or improper sense—of the "things" which are simply possible to be done: their satisfying the *ens* condition for an *ens factum*, in Aquinas's usage. The *impossibile quod claudit intra se utramque partem contradictionis* (Bonaventure, *In 2 Sent.*, d. 25, Quar. edn. 2: 619b) fails to meet that condition, and for that reason 'is impossible not only to a creature, but even to the creator's nature (*creatrici essentiae*), because to be able to do that is not to be able to do anything at all' (same ref.). Even the intrinsic ordering of "forms" needed for a true *divisio* to be made, is not had in such a case. In yet another place Bonaventure spoke of 'that impossible which is (1) impossible on account of deprivation of all existence, and that [which is impossible] (2) on account of the *illustrationem veritatis aeternae*'. Of both, Bonaventure asserted 'God cannot do them at all' (*non potest omnino*). It is the reasons which are to be marked. 'The first is not anything (*non est*), because being capable of that is not to be capable of anything. He cannot do the second, because it is a capability for doing things *inordinate*.' (*In I Sent.*, d. 12 art. un. qu. 3c, Quar. edn. 1: 752b.)

Bonaventure is here distinguishing two diverse grounds on which 'God cannot ___' is to be said. The first is where the expression filling the slot does not express anything: neither an individualised form or nature such as may make a narrowly predicative proposition to be true, nor even an integral composition of forms such as may make a composing-apt proposition to be true. In this case it would not matter particularly that we were denying it of God. Where the expression in the second slot of '... cannot ___' does not stand for anything of either of the two fundamental kinds of thing, it does not matter what the expression in the first slot may stand for. There is no possible substitution for which '... cannot ___' is going to come out false. The second kind of ground is where what goes in the slot of 'God cannot ___' is something which can be done, but only *inordinate*. In that case 'God cannot ___' —say, 'God cannot grow weary'—is always going to be true, but there may be many substitutions for which '... cannot grow weary' may come out false.

14.   Where something, as in the passage quoted at length from the *Breviloquium, directe repugnat ordini secundum rationes et causas primordiales et aeternas*, there is nothing (*non est*) of which it can even be asked, can it be done by God? Where there is no such inherent repugnance, but where what there is is something to be accomplished only *inordinate*, it cannot be found within the integral accomplishment (*complementum*) of divine power.

Two expressions from the long passage quoted, left in Latin in the explanation of the passage given so far, need comment. First, *directe repugnat ordini secundum rationes et causas primordiales et aeternas*, mentioned at the beginning of the present section. A cause is a productive principle (*principium productivum*), like an etcher's acid viewed in relation to the prepared surface. A *ratio causalis* is a rule directing such a principle in its operation, and to isolate such a rule is doubtless part of the chemist's discipline.

In the case of an uncreated agent—which cannot be thought of as acting in subjection to anything outside itself—the *ratio* or rule is to be identified with the *forma exemplaris sive idealis*. The *rationes causales*, in God's case, are thus *formae ideales sive exemplares*, and are the same thing *in re* as the *rationes primordiales*. They are called primordial because none come before them, causal because something comes after them; primordial in so far as they have reference to God as to a first principle, causal in so far as they have reference to God as to an ultimate end.

All of that is from Bonaventure at *In 2 Sent.*, d. 18, art. 1 qu. 2c, Quar. edn. 2: 436b. What is thus in question in *directe repugnat ordini* etc. is incompatibility with an order of things, where that incompatibility is arising from there being no exemplar which could be instantiated in an order of that description, no *ratio aeterna* in accordance with which its being brought about could be had.

The second expression, left in Latin in Section 13 above, is from 'that kind of impossible which is *impossibile propter illustrationem veritatis aeternae*', and which God cannot do because it is *posse inordinate*, and *contra ordinem sapientiae posse*. *Posse inordinate* is the kind of *posse* involved in sinning, or botching, and is impossible to God because it is impossible to any power which is power without restriction. *Contra ordinem sapientiae posse* would be the "power" to bring about that what has been decreed to be done in the actual order of things, shall not be done there, and is impossible for that reason. But why: *propter illustrationem veritatis aeternae*? In Cicero *illustrare* has connotations of making something manifest (see *OLD*, s.v.), and *lustrare* itself had sacral overtones, as in the holy water (*aqua lustralis*) of both pagan and Christian rites. If *illustratio veritatis aeternae* is intended to express the idea of making something of God manifest to creatures (and cf. Section 3 of the present chapter), then it would appear that what is impossible on account of it is the sort of thing which may satisfy the condition for being an *ens rationis*, the *ens* condition of Aquinas's *Summa contra Gentiles*, but is not an integral form or an ordered class of integral forms, and hence is not instantiable in extra-mental reality (in any divinely ordered set-up), so as to be able to manifest something of God's truth. What is in Bonaventure impossible *propter illustrationem veritatis aeternae* would thus seem to correspond to what in Aquinas's *SCG* treatment is something

God cannot do because it is not the integral positive "form" of an integral *ens factum*.

THE DISTINCTION IN THE *DE MYSTERIO TRINITATIS*
(1253–4 OR LATER)

These are Disputed Questions. The year is that given in Bougerol, *Introd.* (1988), 206 ff., for the original disputations. The edited text (Quar. edn. 5: 45–115) shows every mark of being the published *ordinatio*, revised by the disputant for the public domain; which sometimes happened long after the actual disputations.

15.   Qu. 6, art. 1, in which the Distinction is used in reply to an objection, asks whether *esse divinum* is immutable. It contains other relevant material, and ideally the whole article should be read. It is a model of concise exposition: which is not necessarily the unmixed blessing to us which it might have been to its contemporaries. Immutability is the great mark of genuine existence in Augustine especially and his stream of Platonism more generally. Bonaventure is able to open his reply with the observation that the *Sancti* and the *philosophi* are agreed that 'without a doubt divine being (*esse*) is incommutable' (Quar. edn. 5: 99a; and cf. Hayes, *Mystery of the Trinity* (1979), 229).[11]

Before answering the objections he outlines his policy on certain ranges of attributions to God:

Those things which are said of God with respect to a creature, signify the divine essence and connote something in the creature: and this can be done in two ways, actually or habitually. (Quar. edn. 5: 99b.)

Bonaventure is concerned here with such assertions as 'God is conserving A in existence' or with such "names" as 'creator',

---

[11] See, for example, indications of what his preferred analysis of God's power to do things extrinsic to his nature ought to contain: 'when it is said that God can do something (*posse aliquid*), it is simultaneously being insinuated that something is possible to him; and by that, that it cannot be held repugnant to the divine power, wisdom, and goodness, but can be produced *in esse* without any lesion of divine *posse*' (Quar. edn. 5: 102a). See also the treatments of willing changeable things, as against being changeable in one's willing. The further reference is to Z. Hayes, *Saint Bonaventure's Disputed Questions on the Mystery of the Trinity*, trans. with intro. (St Bonaventure, NY, 1979). I owe access to the Hayes reference, and the comparison with the Advent sermon at n. 15 below, to Dr Gregory Shanahan, OFM.

'saviour', and the like. 'Creator', for example, (1) signifies the divine essence, and (2) connotes that some creature is to be seen in some relation to God.

16.   The difficulty arising is that because God is in no genus, no expression we can understand can signify the divine nature sans phrase. Expressions may purport to signify it, but may do so only in some or other respect: in accordance, for example, with some idea of goodness or wisdom which we may have elaborated on the basis of observing things other than God. Aquinas exploits a move of this sort, involving "signifying *secundum quid*", even in connection with such assertions as 'God is good', taken as concerning God. "Names" such as 'good' are then to be taken to be 'signifying God, according as our intellect knows him'; and our intellect, when it knows God through creatures, knows him according as his creatures represent him. (See Aquinas, *ST* 1/13/2c, and 1/13/7 an 1.) On the face of it, this is an idolater's charter.

The question is whether '___ signifies A in respect of B' licenses '___ signifies A' sans phrase. When A is something determinate, and perhaps when A is anything determinate, then it may. 'Unscrupulous and dishonourable' may signify some prominent politician in respect of some exhibited pattern of behaviour. If it does, then the *absque determinatione* assertion is licensed, and may be said with truth of her, no matter how inadequately the respect in question might be thought to represent her, in comparison with indefinitely many other respects which might come to mind to those who know her from closer acquaintance. But if what A is is not determinate in any respect, then since being anything in some respect is being that in some determinate mode, there is no value of '___ signifies A in respect of B' for which '___ signifies A' sans phrase is licensed. So a move of Aquinas's kind will not profit Bonaventure here. Either he is being inconsistent, then, or is using 'signifies' in an even broader way than in 'signifies *secundum quid*'. It may be significant—and favour the latter interpretation—that he does not claim that such expressions *dicunt* anything; whereas he does use *dicunt* when explaining what the expressions connote in the creature.

17.   Before using the Power Distinction he distinguishes two

ways of being an agent: by acting *se ipso*, and by acting *per aliquid aliud a se*. The first kind of agent, which God is (on account of his simplicity)—cannot be changed in acting, because his action is the same thing as himself (*cum sua actio sit idem quod ipsum*). An envisaged ensuing objection leads to distinguishing the intrinsic act, 'which is the same thing as himself', and the extrinsic effect, which holds on the side of the creature, and 'comes into being and is to be counted according to the variation to be found in creatures' (Quar. edn. 5: 100). The sort of thing he wants us to say is: 'How many divine actions are there? Not more than one, if you mean the intrinsic act; as many as there are (possible) varieties of creatures, if you mean the extrinsic effect.' (See below, under 'Exemplars and Things', for analogous possibilities in his treatment of the exemplars.) He uses this in order to continue:

That several incompossible actions are put forward as being in God, is not by reason of the intrinsic acts, but by reason of the plurality of effects and connotata. For the intrinsic act, since it is God, is one and incommutable and eternal. But the extrinsic effect, since it is created, is multiple and changeable and temporal, taking 'time' broadly. (Quar. edn. 5: 100–1.)

An 'action' is something actual, so it is not surprising that 'divine action' should designate either the divine nature or some created nature viewed as an effect of divine action. By speaking of compossible actions, he is not speaking of any kind of actions, but of action-contents, Avicennian essences of extrinsic effects. These are indefinitely many, and are what 'divine action', when it designates the divine nature, can be understood to connote. If this is so, Bonaventure seems to wish a third sense for 'divine action': actual, in respect of what it ontologically is (something identical with the divine nature), not actual but potentially infinite, in respect of what it connotes (the Avicennian essences of extrinsic effects).

If 'divine action' is being understood as at bottom an utterance, as would be expected from someone of the time, it has to be a rather odd one. If it is used for what it stands for, it cannot (since God is in no genus) be permitted then to have any signification, and hence not to be connoting anything. If it is used as might be wished in the affirmative premiss of an argument, for what it signifies (connotes), it cannot be used to stand for the divine nature if that premiss is to be true. So it cannot be used in predicate position in such a proposition, if the term in predicate position is understood to stand for the divine nature.

This is no great loss. There are independent reasons for not thinking 'God is divine action' (understood as predicative rather than an identity) to be even possible to be true. When 'God is divine action' is understood as an identity, it will be true, on Bonaventure's assumptions, on the strength of what Bonaventure calls the intrinsic act. When '___ is (a) divine action' is understood as a predication and not an identity, then it will be true, on Bonaventure's assumptions, for any values other than anything standing for the divine nature. What of 'It is possible that ___ is (a) divine action'? This will be true, if what goes in the slot designates an Avicennian essence. 'It is simultaneously possible that A is a divine action and that B is a divine action' can be true even where A and B are not compossible; as with Rangers winning the Cup next year and Celtic doing so. The reason, on Bonaventure's account, is that the only multiplicity involved is not real, but is thought of because 'It is possible that ___ is a divine action' has a multiplicity of values, a potential infinity of them, in which it comes out true.

18. It is in reply to objections 11 and 12 that Bonaventure distinguishes what God can do

(1) quantum est de se, *and*
(2) quantum est ex parte ipsorum [i.e. quaecunque ... potuit et nunc potest].

Divine power endures always the same, in so far as it is *de se.* But because many things which were true are now false, and many which were possible, are now impossible, divine power does not endure always the same, *quantum est ad partem ipsorum ...* (*De myst. Trin.*, Qu. 6, art. 1 ad 11 and 12). The determinations in (1) and (2) are those of the option-neutral and option-tied arms of the Distinction. The *semper uniformiter perseverat* alludes to Augustinian/Platonic characterisations of divine being, so insinuating Bonaventure's preferred understanding of the option-neutral arm. He is thus to be understood as using the Distinction here.

EXEMPLARS AND THINGS

19. Pythagoras, as understood by Aristotle, had already distinguished archetypes (*paradeigmata*) and their derived likenesses
(*homoiōmata*). In Plato a notion of this kind was specified and
given metaphysical significance in the full-blooded theory of
Forms, which I shall understand here as

the idea that what we call universals are not simply concepts in the
mind, but objective realities displaying their character to perfection and
eternally, invisible to the senses but grasped after intensive preparation
by a sort of intellectual vision, with an existence independent of their
mutable and imperfect instances or copies which are all that we
experience in this life. (W. K. C. Guthrie, *A History of Greek Philosophy*,
5; 378.)

Some biases built into Greek ways of speaking, or perhaps
viewing things, may favour this manner of viewing 'Forms' as
objective realities. Even in modern shop-signs, electrical goods
are advertised as electrical *eidē*, electrical "forms". Austin's
"middle-sized dry-goods" will in this usage be "forms", *eidē*. I
make this point because (thanks no doubt to Aristotle) many
people nowadays find it difficult to imagine how others should
have been able to think of Forms as real things. Given the biases
noted, it must have been Aristotle whose view of "forms" initially
seemed odd. Even those of us who may think the Platonists to
be wrong in the matter, have no right to trade on different and
modern biases in accordance with which Platonists can be made
to seem wrong-headed in their whole view of the matter.

When Christian writers took to a version of the theory of
Forms they were faced with the scandal of self-explanatory
objective realities which on the face of it were eternal and
immutable, neither coming to be nor liable to corruption, over
and against the divine nature. The favoured response in the
West, and in any case the one to be seen behind Bonaventure's
views on exemplars, was the one given currency by St Augustine:

We can therefore call the Ideas forms or species in Latin, so as to be
seen to be translating word for word. If we should call them reasons
(*rationes*), we shall have departed from the strict propriety of interpreting,
for reasons are called *logoi* in Greek, not Ideas. All the same, whoever
may wish to use this word ['reason'], will not be wandering away from

the thing itself. For Ideas are certain kinds of stable and incommutable originating forms of things, and are themselves not formed after anything, and by this fact are eternal and always maintaining themselves in the same manner, and are contained in the divine intelligence. And since they neither arise nor perish, everything which can arise and perish, and everything which does arise and perish, is said to be formed in accordance with them. (*83 Questions*, PL 40: 30.)

Locating the Ideas ontologically in God, may solve one problem presented to Christian Platonists, but surely raises more.

Exemplars are "exemplars of ___". Their exemplarity cannot be expressed without necessarily implying some kind of reference beyond themselves. If they are to be anything, they are surely to be instrumental. Yet in order to be 'contained in the divine intelligence' they have to be nothing distinct from the divine nature: nothing is "in God" without being God, as was uniformly accepted by medieval academics. The divine nature, however, is whatever it is, whether or not there ever is anything besides. The God of Abraham, of Isaac, of Jacob, if it is to be God, is the God it is whether or not Abraham, Isaac, and Jacob exist. So how can anything be both the sort of thing an exemplar is quasi-definitionally supposed to be, and yet be nothing *in re* other than what the divine nature is supposed to be?

Also, exemplars are determinate, the divine nature is not; they are many, and internally ordered, the divine nature is neither. How can anything be both? Before examining Bonaventure's answer, it is worth considering the approach of a Franciscan augustinian who was still widely used in Bonaventure's day, especially among Franciscans.

20. Alexander of Hales, pathfinder of Franciscan academics, had been aware of such problems. 'The Ideas or reasons are multiple on account of the reference of creatures to them; not on any ground of their being from creatures, or of their taking their unity or multiplicity from creatures' (Alex. Hales, *Summa* 1, par. 175, Quar. edn. 1: 258b). He does not spell out his argument here, but if we were to supply an argument along the following lines, we would be supplying one whose assumptions are at any rate consistent with if not entailed by positions of Alexander.

  1. We call the Ideas 'exemplars' of creatures, because we suppose creatures to be instantiations of them. But there

might not have been creatures, whereas the Ideas contained in the divine intelligence would even then have been whatever they are when we speak; if we speak truly when we say that creatures have exemplars in the Ideas.

2. Creatures are many. But creatures might not have been many, but unique; whereas the Ideas contained in the divine intelligence, would even then have been whatever they are, in either case (of one, or of many creatures). Just as we cannot necessarily tell from the world around us whether there is one God or more than one, so we cannot tell from it whether its exemplar(s), if it should have any, is more than one. But because God, if there is a God, cannot be of any determinate quantity, and cannot come in any determinate cardinality, we will have to say the same of any exemplar(s) identical with the divine nature.

That in practice people speak of the divine nature in the singular, and of the exemplars in the plural, need not be an objection to this, as it may be taken as no more than a feature of the *modus loquendi*. It does not necessarily make it false that neither the 'one God' nor the 'exemplars' of that way of speaking necessarily implies any determinate quantity or cardinality in what is being spoken of.

21. Alexander had given further assistance, when distinguishing God's knowing things *in actu* and *in habitu*. The expressions may recall our common distinction between actual and habitual knowledge in human thinkers: permitting us to claim habitual knowledge of a number of matters to which we are not adverting, perhaps have not adverted for many years, and may not ever advert unless prompted. We may discover, for example, that we have habitual knowledge of how to light a coal fire in a damp, open grate, and use it for cooking. We may, when questioned, correctly state historical facts on topics we have not thought about since early schooldays. There are important disanalogies between the human and the divine case, as Alexander understands the latter. God knows things existing *in actu* when he 'understands things existing *in actu*, or as they actually are (*in natura propria*), and not only *in causa*. He knows things existing *in habitu* when he understands the things in their exemplar, or in the art by which they are to be executed (Alex. Hales, *Summa* i, Quar. edn. i: 246a). The *in actu* and *in habitu* both modify 'existing': it is not strictly and directly the knowledge that is being said to be actual or habitual. The distinction permits Alexander to accommodate his "authorities", including one from Hugh of St Victor, to the effect that 'knowledge is of existents'. What he means by understanding 'the things in their exemplar' is clarified a little later: 'The divine nature itself *de sua potestate* contains a likeness (*similitudo*) [of things known]: not the kind of likeness which is taken from creatures, but rather a likeness of a sort for creatures [to resemble], even if no creature should exist' (same, Quar, edn. i: 246ab).

Likenesses for creatures to resemble, even should no creature exist, are exactly what the "things" God can do in option-neutral power can be seen to be. Alexander speaks of the divine nature as containing these *de sua potestate*, and knowing them as existing *in habitu*. Things which are known as existing *in actu*, *in natura propria*, are the things of God's option-tied power.

Things as known by God, when knowing them as existing *in habitu*, are identical with the divine nature, and thus opaque to us; on the assumptions of a Negative Theology view of whatever sort. We may fancy them to be specifically identical with the things which God can do in option-neutral power, but this can be no more than fancy. If the divine nature is in no genus, nothing identical with it (more precisely, nothing that is not distinct from it) can enter into a specific identity with anything.

22.   From Alexander's view it follows that exemplars are not to be counted, by counting kinds of *exemplata*. This is not unreasonable if, as might independently appear, we are not in a position to know that the kinds of *exemplata* we might think to be there to be counted, are not necessarily the kinds there actually are—the kinds ordered by God to be. But that is not the fundamental problem, which is not to be located merely in our inability to identify correctly the kinds of things in fact ordered by God to be. Even if we could correctly identify these, and could thus count the correct kinds of thing, it would avail us nothing towards being able to count the exemplars, as they are (supposed) to be found in reality, as known in the divine essence. Precisely by being known in that way they are, on the principles of Alexander

and other medieval academics fairly generally, no more countable than the divine nature itself is to be held to be.

23. So by seeking to domesticate Plato's exemplars within the divine nature, we may find ourselves succeeding only at the cost of evacuating them of the explanatory power which Plato surely intended them to have. The world of generation and corruption is as it seems to be, to the extent that it faithfully reflects the Ideas. Even the 'errant cause' detectable in the motions of the 'wandering stars', and especially in their retrograde motions, faithfully reflects the scandal of the surd among the mathematical Ideas. The phenomena, even the ones initially recalcitrant towards explanation, are to be explained by reference to the Ideas. This whole mode of explanation is excluded to the professing devotee of Platonic exemplars who locates them within the divine nature, and maintains a Negative Theology on that.

We could hardly expect anything else. *That there are exemplars,* existing as known within the divine nature, is a dictum which (if it is to be true) 'affords no Inference that affects human Life, or can be the source of any Action or Forbearance' (Hume, *Dials.* ad fin.); or any verification in particular, we might add.

If this is so, it is difficult to see why so many Western medieval academics used such ingenuity and tenacity as they often did use, to accommodate a doctrine of exemplars. To the extent that they succeeded, they could no doubt derive some satisfaction from having accommodated Plato's great vision within a vision acceptable to Christian orthodoxy. That might have been no slight reason for satisfaction. There is surely truth in the claim that that vision of Plato's had so much kept alive in an age of contempt for the world, 'the Hellenic appreciation of the rational beauty of the universe' (R. Klibansky, cit. Guthrie, *A History of Greek Philosophy,* 5: 241). But had Plato's vision been accommodated in such a treatment? Or was it not rather a neutralised, neutered relic of the vision, deprived of its explanatory power? Maintaining the rhetoric of the exemplars might be enough to honour the memory of the *Sancti* who, like Augustine, had led the way in christening the exemplars. It should not be mistaken for maintaining the exemplars; any more than maintaining a temple to Hermes as a church in honour of St John the Baptist is to maintain a temple to Hermes.

24. Bonaventure maintains the rhetoric. Over and above, he seems to make what has been called 'divine exemplarism' an important plank in his theology. Divine exemplarism is 'the doctrine which teaches how God is the prototype of everything which exists, and which teaches the way in which the things are in him' (J.-M. Bissen, *L'Exemplarisme divin selon Saint Bonaventure* (Paris, 1929), 304 pp., 4).[12] The topic is not easy to discuss, even at the superficial level of finding non-distorting and non-misleading expressions in which to discuss it. I shall use 'exemplar' for Bonaventure's *exemplar*, but leave it open to stand for either an abstract archetype (such as may be expressed in an engineer's blueprint) or a token chosen to exemplify a type, and used as an exemplar in the production of other tokens. The iron-moulder's pattern is an exemplar of the latter kind: an individual on the same level—so far as observation goes—as the castings taken from it. In particularly accurate castings, such as those produced by a 'lost wax' process, the unassisted eye may not always be able to tell pattern from casting. I shall in general use 'example' for Bonaventure's *exemplatum*, used nominally. The verbs are difficult. To minimise risks of ambiguity, I use periphrases.

25. Bonaventure's broad understanding of exemplars is a common one: an exemplar is something in whose imitation something is made or done.[13] "Exemplarity" is one kind of process of coming to be, and Bonaventure contrasts

(1) procedere per modum exemplaritatis, *with*
(2) procedere per modum voluntatis et liberalitatis.

These are not to be thought mutually exclusive. Coming to be through exemplarity can, in its turn, be in either of two ways. In the first, which is that of creatures proceeding from God, that which is being said to proceed is properly called an example

[12] Bissen is still fundamental. See also chs. 4 ('Les Idées et la science divine') and 7 ('L'Analogie universelle') of Gilson, *Bonaventure* (1978); and C. Bérubé, *De la philosophie à la sagesse chez saint Bonaventure et Roger Bacon*, (Rome, 1976), 40 ff. See also J. Owens, 'Faith, Ideas, Illumination and Experience', *LMP* (1982), 440–59, esp. 452 n. 42; and cf. I. Brady, 'St Bonaventure's Doctrine of Illumination: Reactions Medieval and Modern', in R. W. Shahan and F. J. Kovach (eds.), *Bonaventure and Aquinas: Enduring Philosophers* (Oklahoma, 1976), 57–67.

[13] At *In 1 Sent.*, d. 31. P. 2, art. 1, qu. 1c, Quar. edn. 1: 540a: 'exemplar secundum proprietatem vocabuli dicit expressionem per modum activi—unde et exemplar dicitur ad cuius imitationem fit aliquid'. He notes at the same place that *exemplar* was sometimes taken abusively for what I am calling the example: 'quod ad imitationem alterius fit'.

(*exemplatum*). This way is 'under the command of the will, to the effect that the producer and the product differ as cause and effect (*causatum*); and the one is not in literal truth (*secundum veritatem*) in the other'. For all this see the Responsio at Quar. edn. 1: 129–30, where the second mode of "exemplarity" (appropriate to Trinitarian discussions) is treated too. A little later he adds:

> The example, in so far as it is something produced as an example (*secundum quod exemplatum*), is not in literal truth in that which is providing the exemplar (*in exemplante*), but rather by a similitude; and that similitude, since it is the grounds for knowing and for being able to be the exemplar (*cum sit ratio congnoscendi et exemplandi*), is called the exemplar. (Quar. edn. 1: 130b.)

From this it would seem that neither the moulder's pattern nor the abstract idea expressed in the engineer's blueprint is itself the exemplar, strictly speaking. The real exemplar is a similitude (*similitudo*) to the example, located in the idea expressed in the blueprint, or in the type held to be represented in the moulder's pattern. It is thus the property of what is already something abstract.

26. There is a curious tension here between the rhetoric and the logical implications of what Bonaventure is saying. The rhetoric is strikingly down-to-earth, rudely mechanical: 'process', 'producer', 'product'. The notions implied are rarified abstractions.

There is also a deeper tension, between the way in which words like 'exemplar' are to be understood, and are to be used in (scientifically serious) assertions, and the way in which the reality they are to be taken to stand for, is to be taken to be. The tension shows up even when we ask: Are there many exemplars? or no more than one? If we are asking, How many ontological realities?, the answer is, Not more than one. If we are asking, How many exemplars are we to think of or speak of?, the answer is, As many as there are things to which they can stand as exemplars. Bonaventure puts it: 'all the Ideas are one thing in God *secundum rem*, but more than one *secundum rationem intelligendi sive dicendi*' (*In 1 Sent.*, Quar. edn. 1: 608ab). There is no reason why we should not think or speak of 'the eternal multitude of Ideas' (*pluralitas idearum aeterna*), so long as we are not implying any actual plurality in the Ideas themselves. No more should we be thought to imply that God's power to do things is a plurality, if we should say that he can do many things (same, 1: 609b).[14]

Our inferences must reflect this, because of the crucial part which *suppositio*—the "standing for" relation—plays in questions of truth and consequence. Just as 'Many things are possible to God, or, Many things are known (to God), therefore many things exist' is not valid, so likewise 'There are many Ideas, therefore there are many things (*res*)' is not valid. This is 'because Ideas are not more than one, by reason of being [more than one ontological reality], but by reason of the [multiplicity of the things in] relation to which [they are thought of as Ideas]'. And again:

'Idea' does not imply only what is, but a relation towards what will be, or even can be; and is counted by reason of that relationship. (*In 1 Sent.*, d. 35, art. un. qu. 3 ad 5, Quar. edn. 1: 609ab.)

27. Ideas are in fact not numerable: this he takes from Ps. 146: 5, *Et sapientiae eius non est numerus.*[15] Also, they are not to be understood as ordered:

there is no order among themselves in Ideas or schemas for knowledge (*rationibus cognoscendi*). Ideas have indeed an ordering towards the *ideata*, but not among themselves, since neither is any one prior to any other, or posterior, or more noble; and for that reason order is not put there.

[14] See the Disputed Questions *De scientia Christi*, qu. 3c, 'U. deus res cognoscat per similitudines realiter differentes', Quar. edn. 5: 13–14; on *expressio* and truth especially.
[15] *In 1 Sent.*, d. 35, art. un., qu. 5c, Quar. edn. 1: 612a: 'quoniam non habent [ideae] numerum, non sunt numerabiles: ideo non sunt in numero finito, sed infinito'. *Cf.*: 'multitudo idearum est a multitudo ideatorum: dicendum quod ... non venit a multitudine ideatorum in quantum creata, sed in quantum connotata. 'Idea' autem non connotat ideatum secundum actualem existentiam, sed solum secundum potentiam. Et quia deus potest facere infinita, quamvis numquam faciat nisi finita, ideo ideae vel rationes cognoscendi sunt in deo infinitae, quia non tantum sunt entium vel futurorum, sed omnium deo possibilium. Nihil enim potest deus, quod non actu cognoscat.' (Same, Quar. edn. 1: 612b.) In a sermon he accomodates the same Ps. 146: 5 to Christ: justifying the Psalm's *Magnus Dominus noster* on the grounds that Christ is (in his divine nature?) *intimus cuilibet rei in essendo*, the Psalm's *magna virtus eius* on the grounds that he is (likewise) *potentissimus in agendo*, and its *et sapientiae eius non est numerus* on the grounds that he is (again, as God) *praesentissimus in cognoscendo*. In the context it is the secret thoughts and acts of creatures which are the object of (Christ's divine) *cognoscere*; which is infinite (*non tantum ... entium vel futurorum, sed omnium deo possibilium* (*In 1 Sent.*, d. 35, just quoted)), even though in Bonaventure's view God *numquam faciat nisi finita* (same ref.).

(*In 1 Sent.*, d. 35, art. un., qu. 6c, Quar. edn. 1: 613b.)

Earlier he had said 'it is not meet that one Idea should be simpler than another or prior to it' (same, 1: 610b). 'Just as, although God may know white things, there are no white Ideas in God, so although he may know ordered things (*res . . . ordinatas*), it is not required that they should be ordered in God' (same, 1: 613b). He considers the objection here that where there is plurality without order, there is *confusio* and disorder (*inordinatio*). It is to be said, he replies, that that is false, because there can be simultaneity (*simultas*) there; and so it is in the Ideas. Or (*vel*) it is to be said that this has place where there is a real plurality. There is no such plurality in the Ideas, for they all are one thing, and for that reason there can be no disorder (same, 1: 613b). One further passage ought to be considered:

> Ideas, by reason of their very name, express (*dicunt*) a reference to things known . . . . But 'order' expresses a new reference and a new kind of relationship (*novum respectum et novam habitudinem*), when one Idea is being compared with another. And since, when that reference is removed which there is to the instantiations of the Ideas (*illo respectu circumscripto qui est ad ideata*), Ideas are in God simply one thing, and have no order among themselves. For that reason it is not to be conceded that Ideas may have a plurality together with an ordering towards each other. (Quar. edn. 1: 613b.)

The phrase *illo respectu circumscripto qui est ad ideata* neatly spells out the work done by *absoluta* in *de potentia absoluta*. In Bonaventure's view, God's option-neutral power—ontologically speaking—simply *is* the one divine nature; though we may be entitled to treat it in our assertions as though it were a non-ordered set of (an innumerable potential infinity of) ordered "Ideas" (schemata of objects of knowledge).[16] We can understand and treat the Ideas in something of the manner of Kantian Ideas, but are not to suppose that they have any real existence as things of the description then purportedly applicable. We are to suppose them to have a real existence, but "objectively", to use another

---

[16] Cf. Quod enim ponantur in deo plures actiones incompossibiles, hoc non est ratione pluralitatis actuum intrinsecorum, sed ratione pluralitatis effectuum et connotatorum. Nam actus intrinsecus, cum sit deus, est unus et incommutabilis et aeternus: effectus vero extrinsecus, cum sit creatus, est multiplex et mutabilis et temporalis, largo modo accipiendo tempus: et hoc nullam inducit mutationem circa esse divinum. (*De myst. Trin.* qu. 6, art. 1, Quar. edn. 5: 100–1).

Kantian term; a real existence, unknowable to us, save to the extent we may know that they are something.

BONAVENTURE AND THE POWER DISTINCTION

28. Bonaventure uses the Distinction only a couple of times, yet he does so without reluctance, and with the air of one who has no reason to expect his use of it to be thought contentious. That he does use it so little may in any case be less to do with any inclinations on the matter, than with the nature of his *œuvre.* Despite the theological and philosophical quality of his writing, much of it is in works not primarily addressed to a narrowly academic audience. It has been noted already, and will be evident once more in Aquinas, that users of the Distinction generally at this period avail themselves of it chiefly or solely in narrowly theological works addressed to a narrowly academic audience. From its very nature, as the shorthand encapsulation of a rather dense piece of dialectics from the jargon of an "in" group, that is how it could be expected to be used at this period anyway.

At one place he indeed objected to a use of the Distinction on the part of *Aliqui.* The objection was not to the Distinction itself, or even to its use in connection with the topic. As the Quaracchi editors of 1882 had already noted, his objection was on the formal appropriateness of the use of the Distinction by *Aliqui,* in reply to the argument as put. (An objection on a not too dissimilar kind of grounds was seen above at one place from Albert too.) On the very same topic, and within a few lines, Bonaventure went on to use the Distinction himself.

In his many treatments of Ideas, exemplars, *similitudines* and the like, he provides a mass of material for understanding the Distinction in a platonist manner. Before it can be exploited for that purpose, it needs to be pulled together under that formality, from its many locations in Bonaventure. It is not that good studies of his "exemplarism" or his doctrine of "illumination" are lacking: a number have been exploited above, and more could be, within the context of a monograph of the proper scope. It is rather that even the good studies have tended either to play down or leave unexplained the dialectical point of what he is so often doing. Even the narrowly theological content is often played down, in order to emphasise Bonaventure's perceived "spiritual" aims or supposedly unscholastic methods of exposition. His 'warmth in the cause of virtue', a quality Hutcheson faulted Hume for exposing too little, may sometimes have distracted interpreters from the sober and austere substance of what he is so often saying.

29. On the question of God's knowability by creatures, for example, Bonaventure allowed only knowledge *quia est*, the knowledge that some God exists; not any knowledge of what God in his own being might be, knowledge *quid sit*. On the question of God's not being in any genus—and therefore not having a *quid sit* to be known—he was as insistent as any medieval academic.[17]

30. What he says on the exemplars indeed implies that he identifies God's option-neutral power, *as known to God*, with the divine nature. But Albert and Aquinas, who do not agree with him in their understanding of the option-neutral arm of the Distinction, are not in disagreement with him there. The reason lies in the 'as known to God'. All those mentioned were agreed that, as known to God, the 'things' of option-neutral power were to be identified with God, and so to be unknowable in their content, to us or any creature.

The difference is over the exemplars as plural, as *similitudines* of a potential infinity of things: not only of things ordered by God, but of things possible to be ordered by God. Bonaventure wishes to take *similitudo* to be expressible in a two-place relation, with or without a condition of irreflexivity. There just are likenesses in this sense, or there are not, whether or not there is anyone to see that they are.

In order to have an explanatory use, however, not merely likenesses of that sort are needed, but likenesses appreciable by someone or other. This might be called, for convenience, 'apparent likeness'; expressible in a three-place relation, a likeness *between* terms of the same kind as in the previous version, but *apparent to* or *appreciated by* some subject capable of appreciations

---

[17] He recognises it as a prerequisite for his exemplarism: 'Potens est autem veritas, quamvis sit una, omnia exprimere per modum similitudinis exemplaris, quia ipsa est omnino extra genus et ad nihil coarctata.' (Disputed Question *De scientia Christi*, qu. 3c, Quar. edn. 5: 13b.)

of the sort: capable of 'contrasting and comparing', indeed, as in Humean "reason" as against "passion" or "sentiment". Contrasting and comparing, like stepwise argumentation, ratiocination strictly understood, telling the time and feeling the cold, are not to be said of the divine nature. They cannot be true of something existing unrestrictedly.

Apparent likenesses therefore, likenesses of the kind needed in explanations by appeal to exemplarity, are not likenesses as known to God. If they are to be anything in Bonaventure's opinion, they are likenesses of the only kind left in his enumeration: likenesses as we can understand and use them in our discourse. But these are fictions of fallible creatures, so on the face of it explanations made by appealing to "exemplars" so understood, are at best going to come down to explanations given in virtue of the fictions of fallible creatures.

31. Doubts were already expressed above, in connection with Alexander of Hales, whether a platonist analysis of divine option-neutral power could be both coherent and to any explanatory point.

The question of explanatory point is left until later (Ch. 9, Sect. 17 below). On coherence I have not found anything necessarily to imply incoherence in Bonaventure's position, and am inclined to think that Bonaventure was not being incoherent: yet not because I am sure, even now, that I have understood it well enough to be positive on the point.[18] What supports my inclination even now is rather that any incoherencies in such a central matter could not in those days have in practice escaped the attentions of the sharp dialecticians around him.[19] In the

---

[18] Gilson, *La philosophie... Bonaventure* (1978), 165, remarks not unfairly: 'Le point où s'effectue le passage de l'essence créatrice aux choses créées est aussi le point où beaucoup de ceux qui suivent la pensée de saint Bonaventure perdent courage et l'abandonnent'.

[19] What makes the absence of reproaches on this matter more striking still, is that some of those involved in the conflicts, notably Aquinas, are acknowledged to have had at least (1) a very different perspective on knowledge of God on the part of creatures, and perhaps even (2) a profoundly different ground on which to conceive of God heuristically. For (2): 'Ce que l'on pourrait appeler l'expressionisme de saint Bonaventure, suppose une conception de Dieu dont l'inspiration profonde est assez différente de celle de saint Thomas et radicalement incompatible avec celle d'Aristote.' (É. Gilson, *La philosophie... Bonaventure* (1978), 134.) For (1), which may stand even if (2) should prove too strong: 's'il y a illumination spéciale de Dieu dans toute activité intellectuelle tournée vers la connaissance des choses divines, si Dieu est présent à l'esprit *ex parte obiecti*, comme source de la lumière intelligible en laquelle nous percevons toute vérité supérieure, enfin

heated and far from academic disputes of the 1260s and 1270s, a number of these dialecticians had every reason to wish to be able to cut the inquisitorial ground from under Bonaventure's feet; and finding incoherencies in such a central matter would appear ideal for such a purpose. It is not credible that they would not have looked hard for such incoherencies, had they had any hope of finding them; or that, if such incoherencies had been there, no one would have found them. They were much better placed to understand him than we are.

Grabmann was surely right to praise Bonaventure's dialectics, but he did not say that it is particularly easy for us to grasp. Often, the precise usage has to be found by collating uses in widely diverse passages. The excellent indexes and notes of the Quaracchi edition have for many years made this less difficult than it otherwise would be. But to be quite sure of what Bonaventure is saying on many points important to him remains difficult.

His use of the Distinction, though slight enough when measured against the volume of his output, is significant. That he should have used it at all might not have been expected, and that his use of it was straightforward enough—came up with standard results in a standard case—is already worth noting. If just how he wished to understand it needs considerable further study, in the light of his exemplarist positions, and of his general views on universals, that would seem something for Bonaventure specialists to take further.

si cette divine présence est en quelque façon perceptible, le problème de la connaissance de Dieu se posera dans une perspective tout autre que dans l'aristotélisme'. (F. Van Steenberghen, *Le problème de l'existence de Dieu dans les écrits de S. Thomas d'Aquin* (Louvain-la-Neuve, 1980), 90.)

6

St Thomas Aquinas, OP:
Understanding the Distinction

In this chapter I examine Aquinas's most detailed and explicit exposition of the Distinction; which is also the most detailed and explicit given by any medieval examined in this book. It dates from the beginning of his career as a Master in the Theology Faculty of Paris, and appears in the first theological work in which he was entitled, as a master, to put forward his own theology in his own right. Essentially the same understanding is shown in later passages, even in theological works from the last years of his life. He provides the exposition in connection with a narrowly theological puzzle, on a matter of the *opus redemptionis*, the traditional preserve of the theologians. The puzzle is whether God the Father could have become incarnate: one of the puzzles on whether the mode of redemption might have different, from the genre which had so much concerned theologians of the age of Anselm. It had been raised, and answered affirmatively, in Lombard's Sentences. At the beginning of his career at least, therefore, Aquinas was using the Distinction in precisely the narrowly theological genre of puzzle in which it had (by then) traditionally been being used within the Theology Faculty at Paris.

An account of Aquinas's uses of the Distinction—some thirty or more from his earliest to his latest theological works—is provided elsewhere.[1] Two further kinds of context are provided

---

[1] In L. Moonan, 'St Thomas Aquinas on Divine Power', in the *Atti* of the congress *Tommaso d'Aquino nel suo VII centenario* (Rome and Naples, 1974), 3 (Naples, 1977), 366–407 (= *Atti* 1974). A thoughtful review of that in *Rassegna di letteratura tomistica*, 11 (1975), 186–8, led to further revision. Besides specific points which are simply corrected here, the mutanda required in *Atti* 1974, are more generally those implied by the thesis that (*a*) Aquinas's own understanding of the Distinction was of a non-platonist kind, like Albert's, but (*b*) he did not rule out the possibility that a platonist or frankly platonist interpretation

presently: a historical one, in a brief account of his early circumstances and those of his Commentary on the Sentences, in which the Distinction is expounded; and a conceptual one, in a reminder of his rigorously Negative Theology approach in philosophical theology.

THOMAS OF AQUINO (D. 7 MAR. 1274)

1. He was a younger son—the fourth or fifth child—to a cadet line of a family which had already ceased to provide the Counts of Aquino. Thomas was one of the family names. The family was Lombardic in origins but several members owned land in or around Aquino: a proud and hospitable town lying just off one of the main routes from Rome to Naples. The family house in which Aquinas was born, in 1226 or thereabouts, was the castle of Roccasecca, some four or five miles from Aquino. It had been stolen by the family from an abbot of Monte Cassino. Nevertheless young Thomas, aged 5 or so, was dispatched to the abbey, barely a dozen miles away, whose school had long had a name. One early chronicler assures us that this was 'to be formed to a holy life, and be prepared to receive divine enlightenment'. Another near-contemporary, a Neapolitan lawyer, told the officials of the process of canonisation that Aquinas's father had sent him there to become abbot in time, so that the family could lay their hands on more of the abbey's properties. Aquinas in the event was not to remain there: perhaps as well, since it was not long before the Aquino family's troops were sacking it.

Yet he had been there long enough to have some experience of the older, monastic manner of teaching, before going to university. And it may be worth noting that a feature of teaching at Monte Cassino in those days was the holding of regular

(incompatible with his own, and such perhaps as Bonaventure's may have been) could be coherent. So although (*c*) the disposition-and-exercise model, used in *Atti* 1974 for expository purposes, should not (I would now say) be used as a basis for systematically expounding Aquinas's specific understanding of the Power Distinction, (*d*) it need not be rejected (as other models may have to be) as a model for expounding the Distinction initially, in contexts where either a provisional account or—as in glossing a passing reference to the Distinction—an embryonic one will serve.

academic discussions carried out in the vernacular. In his last years, in Naples, he habitually used the same vernacular in his main preaching.

When Aquinas did go to a university, it was to Naples: a creation of Frederick II's, with an emphasis, almost from the outset, on secular studies and attention to the translation and study (in translation) of Greek and Muslim sources. In Frederick's university there was also a detectable air of anti-clericalism. Since papal armies were regularly plundering and looting in the region, the anti-clericalism is understandable.

While at Naples Aquinas moved to join the Dominicans, and was dispatched by them after some time, and after some struggles within the family, for studies in Paris and Cologne. He was to return to Naples as a teacher towards the end of his life; and to return to a Benedictine roof. En route to the Council of Lyons, in 1274, he became seriously ill and turned back to the abbey of Fossa Nova, itself in the same region as Aquino. There he died, at an age of not quite 50. Throughout his life he had remained much involved in his extended family's affairs: actively promoting their interests even in his last years.[2]

KNOWABILITY OF GOD BY CREATURES

Aquinas is less evasive (or reserved) than Bonaventure on this, but less forthright than Albert. He is at his most reserved in early works, of the period of the Sentence Commentary, less reserved

---

[2] For Aquinas's life see J. Weisheipl, *Friar Thomas d'Aquino* (Oxford [1975]); A. Walz, *Saint Thomas d'Aquin*, tr. P. Novarina (Louvain, 1962), 245 pp.; and S. Tugwell, Introd. pp. 201–34 to *Albert and Thomas: Selected Writings* (New York [1988]), xv + 650 pp. For general background M.-D. Chenu, *Toward Understanding Saint Thomas*, tr. with authorized corrections and bibliogrphical additions by A.-M. Landry and D. Hughes, (Chicago [1963]), viii + 386 pp. is invaluable, despite the defects of the translation. For texts the Leonine edn. is properly critical from around vol. iv, and some replacements for earlier parts have already been made. Introductions to recent parts permit corrections to some earlier chronologies etc. Manual editions and translations are listed at J. Marenbon, *Later Medieval Philosophy*, 201–3. Current bibliography is provided in the *Rassegna di letteratura thomistica*, which continues the task formerly done in the *Bulletin thomiste*. Retrospective bibliographies are listed in Chenu, Introd. (1963), just mentioned.

in the *Summa contra Gentiles*, and not at all reserved or evasive—
on most points—in the *Summa theologiae*.[3]

2.   In the central issue of whether our knowledge of God is of
the *quia est*, not the *quid est* variety, he is quite explicit in the
Summa:

[a] where God is concerned, we cannot know what he is (*quid est*), yet
do in this [*scientia* of theology, or sacred doctrine] make use of an effect
of his, either of nature or of grace, in place of a definition, in pursuit
of those things which are considered concerning God in this discipline.
(*ST* 1/1/7 ad 1.)

[b] in order to prove something to be, it is necessary [in this kind of
case] to take as a means ['as a middle term', rather?] what the name
signifies, not what the thing is; because the *quid est* question follows on
the *an est* question.

   Names of God are applied (*imponuntur*) on the strength of effects of
his,... whence in demonstrating God to be, by means of some effect,
we can take for a means [again, 'for a middle term'?], what this name
'God' may signify. (*ST* 1/2/2 ad 2.)

[c] Having come to know concerning something whether it exists, it
remains to be investigated how it exists, to the effect that what it is [its
quid est] may be known. But because, where God is concerned, we
cannot know what he is (*quid est*), we cannot consider (in his case) how
he may be, but rather how he is not. First therefore to be considered
is how he is not, secondly how he may be known by us (qu. 12), thirdly
how he may be named (qu. 13). (*ST* 1/3 in principio.)

[d] a (natural) reason cannot get through to a simple form, to the point
of knowing, in its regard, what it is (*quid est*); but can come to know
about it, to the extent of knowing whether it exists (*an est*). (*ST* 1/12/12
ad 1.)

---

[3] For Aquinas's doctrine, wide choice is available. For his doctrine generally, A.-D.
Sertillanges, *S. Thomas d'Aquin* (2 vols.; Paris, 1912), is still helpful. On his analytical tools
see P. Hoenen, *Reality and Judgment according to St Thomas*, tr. H. F. Tiblier (Chicago, 1952),
xv + 343 pp., with an appendix by C. Boyer; and R. W. Schmidt, *The Domain of Logic
according to Saint Thomas Aquinas* (The Hague, 1966), xviii + 352 pp. For his doctrine on
God: H. McCabe, 'The Involvement of God', in *God Matters* (London [1987]), vi + 249 pp.,
39–51; and F. Van Steenberghen, *Le Problème de l'existence de Dieu dans les écrits de S. Thomas
d'Aquin* (Louvain-la-Neuve, 1980), 375 pp. For situating Aquinas's view on God in current
discussion, J. Owens, 'God in Philosophy Today' and ' "Darkness of Ignorance" in the
Most Refined Notion of God', in *Towards a Christian Philosophy* (Washington, DC 1990),
177–88 and 207–24; and B. Davies, 'Classical Theism and the Doctrine of Divine
Simplicity', in B. Davies (ed.), *Language, Meaning and God: Essays in Honour of Herbert McCabe
OP* [= *H. McCabe Festschrift*] (London [1987]), xii + 243 pp., 51–74.

There is more in this vein in the *Summa theologiae*, but there had already been some in the *Summa contra Gentiles*:

[*e*] Sensible things... cannot lead our understanding towards this, that divine substance should be seen in them for what it is (*quid est*), since they are effects of a cause which do not add up to the power [of that cause]. For from sensible things our understanding is led up to a divine knowledge, to the point of coming to know concerning God that he is (*quia est*), and other things of this sort, which it is proper to the First Principle to have atributed to it. (*SCG* I, ch. 3, and cf. I, ch. 31.)

Nothing so explicit as these leaps to the eye in parallel passages in the Sentence Commentary. Even the passage in the *Summa contra Gentiles*, I, ch. 31, for example, is less heavily veiled than its parallel at *In 1 Sent.*, d. 2, qu. 1 ad 4, ed. Mandonnet, p. 70. Are we perhaps seeing in the Sentence Commentary Aquinas's concern—or, since this is from Book 1, the concern of his master, John of St Giles—to expose himself in no way to charges of favouring the proposition condemned in 1241: *divina essentia in se nec ab homine nec ab angelo videbitur* (see É.-H. Wéber, *Dialogue et dissensions* (1974), 501)?

3. Further indications come from his views on *impositio*, "putting names on" God, in the present instance, for use in theological discussions. "Names", in Aquinas as in other medievals seen above, are not mere labels. As Bonaventure would put it, a *no-men* was in general expected to convey some *no-titia* of the thing. *Impositio*, putting names on either extra-linguistic entities or other names, had been a concern since the days of Boethius; perhaps from before Porphyry even. (Kneales, *Development* (1962), 195.) It was an important concern within Aquinas's own semantics for terms.

On "imposing" names generally, he follows Aristotle, with the further specification that each name of a being, when its being something is to be brought out, refers to its actually being something.[4] The diversity of *rationes intelligendi* (possible reasons

---

[4] Idem enim est dictum homo, et unus homo. Et similiter est idem dictum ens homo, vel quod est homo: et non demonstratur aliquid alterum cum secundum dictionem replicamus dicendo est ens homo, et homo, et unus homo (Aquinas, *In Metaph.* 4, lect. 2, n. 550); Sciendum est enim quod hoc nomen 'homo' imponitur a quidditate sive a natura hominis; et hoc nomen 'res' imponitur a quidditate tantum; hoc vero nomen 'ens' imponitur ab actu essendi; et hoc nomen 'unum' ab ordine vel indivisione... unde ista tria, res, ens, unum significant omnino idem, sed secundum diversas rationes (same, n.

for understanding "names") means that Aquinas's semantics for terms cannot be reduced to an existence-theory: in which 'house' will have a meaning if there is a house for it to refer to. 'It is certainly the same reality which is signified [in the aristotelian examples referred to at n. 4 above] by '*homo*' and '*ens homo*'—the human reality in question. Yet *homo* and *ens* do not have the same imposition: the first refers to the quiddity of the man, the second to his actually being something. This distinction of reasons for understanding rejoins the fundamental thesis of the real composition of essence and existence, whose expression, from the point of view of the theory of signification, is given in the celebrated proposition of *De ente et essentia*, ch. 4, according to which *omnis autem essentia vel quidditas intelligi potest sine hoc quod aliquod intelligatur de esse suo*... The consequence of this "distinction" is that we can understand what a man or a phoenix is, while not knowing whether they exist in reality: which considerably nuances the import of the 'aristotelian' remarks of Thomas on the identity of *ens homo*, *homo*, and *unus homo*.' (A. de Libera, *Le Problème de l'être* (1980), 14.)

Where God is concerned, we cannot know what he is, but 'names of God are imposed on the strength of effects of his', as at [*b*] above in Section 2. These effects can be either of nature or of grace. The latter still do not permit any *quid est* knowledge of God (*ST* 1/12/13 ad 1), but do provide 'more effects and more excellent effects' on which we may work in the ways open to us: the *modus eminentiae*, the *modus causalitatis*, and the *modus remotionis* (*ST* 1/13/8 ad 2), which Aquinas himself pursues in *ST* 1. It is noticeable that he spends significantly more time on considering *de deo quomodo non sit* (*ST* 1, qq. 2–11), than on the other parts of his programme as described at *ST* 1/2 in principio: *quomodo a nobis cognoscatur* (qu. 12) and *quomodo nominetur* (qu. 13). Revelation gives us a reliable ground on which to attribute names to God which we could not have permitted ourselves, if confined to what could be reached by a 'natural reason': whether in the sense of a reasoning creature, or an argument appropriate to one left to

553); both cit. de Libera, *Le Problème de l'être chez Maître Eckhart: Logique et métaphysique de l'analogie* (Paris, 1980), 63 pp., 14, who adds: 'Il s'agit de la doctrine d'Aristote lui-même, avec cette connotation particulière que tout nom d'étant, en tant qu'étant, renvoie d'abord à l'acte de l'être' (ibid., n. 558: 'Hoc nomen "ens" quod imponitur ab ipso esse'), and in turn refers to É. Gilson, *L'être et l'essence* (Paris, 1962), 92–3.

his own devices. But it does not provide us with any understanding of God's *quid est*. The example given of revelation's contribution is *Deum esse trinum et unum* (*ST* 1/12/13 ad 1). But the real point of that, which will appear presently from his comments on Boethius, *De Trinitate*, is that *Deum esse trinum et unum* is true, or may be taken on the assurance of revelation to be true, but is literally insignificant to us. It permits a "name" whose *suppositio* may be the divine nature, and can be counted on—on the assurance of revelation—to be the divine nature; but without any *significatio* whatever.

4. Because propositions, in Aquinas's usage, are to be understood as utterances (*dictiones*) of a certain kind, the suggestion that there might be non-intelligible (literally insignificant) propositions is not necessarily incoherent. He takes one such suggestion seriously, in a matter which bears narrowly on present concerns:

> it is to be said that in two ways some proposition can be said to be non-intelligible.
>
> In one way, from the side of the one doing the understanding, who is falling short in his understanding: this proposition, 'in the three divine persons is one essence', is like that. And a proposition of this kind must not be such as to imply a contradiction. (*In Boet. de Trin.*, art. 15 ad 1, ed. Decker 1950: 151.)

The point of the last proviso, is that the non-intelligibility is to be put to the account of the one trying to understand it, only if the defect is not in the proposition itself; as may occur.

> In another way, from the side of the proposition itself. And this in two ways. (1) In one way it implies a contradiction, absolutely: as, 'Something rational is irrational', and the like. Things of this sort cannot be made true by any miracle. (2) But other things imply a contradiction only when taken in some particular way, like this one: 'A dead man is returning to life'. For it implies a contradiction, according as he is being understood to be returning to life by his own forces, while it is yet being postulated (by this, that he is being said to be dead) that he is destitute of life... (Same ref.)

The Trinitarian assertion, understood as expressing some truth holding in literal propriety (*proprie*) of God,[5] is unintelligible, in

---

[5] Cf. M. Grabmann, *Die theol. Erkenntnis-und Einleitungslehre des hl. Thomas von Aquin auf Grund seiner Schrift 'In Boethium de Trinitate': Im Zusammenhang der Scholastik des 13. und beginnenden 14. Jahrhunderts dargestellt* (Fribourg, 1948), XV + 392 pp., 96–100.

the sense of being literally insignificant. Revelation may assure us that it is true, but not which truth it is. 'In order to determine whether a sentence is true, it is enough to know the reference of the various constituent expressions; but in order to know what information it conveys, we must know their sense.' (M. Dummett, *Frege: Philosophy of Language* (London, 1973), XXV + 698 pp., 104.) Mutatis mutandis, a parallel point is to be made about propositions, including propositions purportedly predicating something *proprie* of God. Before considering how serious it might be not to have the 'sense' of the expressions as a guide to which truth might be in question, I wish to note that the approach taken to the Trinitarian assertion can be generalised to hold for whatever is said *proprie* of God: as in 'God is wise', for example.

In *ST* 1/13/10 ad 1 Aquinas considers a dispute between a pagan, asserting that his idol is God, and a catholic saying that the idol is not God. In the case envisaged there is genuine contradiction, and both the pagan and the catholic are using 'is God' to attempt to signify the true God. Neither the catholic nor the pagan, however, knows what the nature of the true God is. Each alike knows it *secundum aliquam rationem causalitatis vel excellentiae vel remotionis* (ad 5). This is almost verbatim what was noted in the last Section, from another passage in the *Summa*. Each alike is in a position to "name" the divine nature in a way he can understand, in accordance not with what it is (which is unknown to either), but with some schema. In each case the schema is derived not from God but from something other than God, supposed related to God in some particular way. The catholic is not essentially advantaged in this, from having revelation; and it is worth noting that Aquinas is insisting on as much.

Given what was noted at Section 2 above, it follows that the notions of God which serve us in theology, in lieu of a knowledge which we cannot have of the divine nature for what it is, are not essentially privileged by virtue of arising from 'effects of grace' rather than from 'effects of nature'. These are alike effects, something created. And of course any revelation which either pagan or catholic can understand in the actual state and situation of man must itself be expressed in something created.

Apropos of the same envisaged dispute between catholic and pagan, Aquinas adds:

if there were someone, however, who knew God according to no schematic notion (*ratio*), such a one could not so much as name him, save perhaps just as we may utter names whose signification we do not know. (*ST* 1/13/10 ad 5.)

Names whose signification we do not know, can be of more than one relevant kind. It depends on whether our ignorance comes from there being a signification known to others but not to us, or from there not being any signification for us to grasp. Aquinas's phrasing thus covers both the case of someone who does not know God under any schematic notion at all (and has no other knowledge of God), and the mystic who might be thought to have knowledge of God, but not under any schematic notion. (In the latter case, no more than knowledge *quia est* would seem to be a possibility within Aquinas's assumptions anyway.) Neither the one nor the other is in a position to do theology, and the reason has nothing essentially to do with either faith, or disposition to worship, or having access to God. It has to do essentially with having a schematic notion of God—no matter how pagan, no matter how bogus it might turn out to be. A great Christian mystic might be incapable of doing theology, if he became amnesiac towards all other sources of information on God. A great charlatan might be able to do it superbly. In between, many theological mansions can be accommodated; some good, some less so.

But none of them is indispensable. God, if there is a God, is an absolutely existing simple, in Aquinas's view. But cult is not indispensable: there might have been no creation, or a creation with no creatures capable of cult. Likewise, religion is not indispensable. Theology shares the dispensability of these, and in addition can be done only if theologians are prepared to construct fictions of the appropriate kind—for fictions are what the schematic notions are, in Aquinas's view—so that God can be "named" and so discussed. This is a very different way of looking at things from the ways common in our days. Theology faculties and departments of religion are funded sometimes by people who in private at least are quite sure there is no God, but can see that there is something which men call theology, or religious studies, for which their universities may well be renowned. Aquinas had no such respect for subjects with no objects.

5.   I labour this point because even critical readers of Aquinas
may still be tempted to read him in an anachronistic and arsy-
versy perspective. In an article, for example, which helpfully
focuses a number of issues, we may read that Aquinas saw a
Negative Theology 'merely as a stage on the way to a correct
interpretation of the divine names'.[6] The later stage is rather his
discussion of preferable kinds of grounds on which to impose
(interpreted) names on a God whose nature is unknown to us;
with a view to using those "names" in theological discussions.
But it is the 'merely' which inverts the priorities: as though the
doing of theology (and the preparatory imposition of names)
were the important aim, and the Negative Theology stage a
possibly regrettable means. In Aquinas's perspective it is the
Negative Theology which is of primary importance, and the
discussion of grounds on which to impose "names" which *then*
becomes of practical importance, *if* one wishes to be able to do
the theology of the theology faculties. In Aquinas's perspective it
is *because* a Negative Theology has to be taken seriously, as he
takes it seriously in questions 2 to 11 inclusive not least, that
would-be theologians *faute de mieux* have to be content with doing
the best they can with the problem of imposing "names" (as he
does in qu. 12) and working with the names so imposed.

To a modern theologian, getting the theology might well be
the great priority, and getting the theory for imposing the names
the great means to that priority. To Aquinas the matter of
importance is how things are or are not: and that is what
Negative Theology—not theology, no matter how correct we
may hope its fictions to be—is concerned with. In his view, the
theology of the theology faculties is *facultatif*, even for quite
seriously reflective human beings. The question of the truth or
falsehood of a Negative Theology opinion arises whenever
humans reflect seriously on how the world ultimately is, or is
not; regardless of whether they have the slightest interest in the
theology of the theology faculties. To see a Negative Theology
as merely a stage towards an activity essentially dependent on
fictions might be a perspective found natural today. It is not to
be taken as that of Aquinas in the matter.

---

[6] A. Broadie, 'Maimonides and Aquinas on the Names of God', *Rel. Studs.* 23 (1987),
157–70, 161.

Yet Aquinas manifestly wants to be able to do the theology of the theology faculties. Since he cannot do it to his satisfaction without being confident that he can render it consistent with a Negative Theology, being cognisant with a Negative Theology is doubtless a prerequisite. So taking cognisance of one, and taking it seriously, can certainly be seen as a stage towards theology, and towards the intermediate stage of finding suitable kinds of grounds on which to "impose" names on God. It is the 'merely' which tends to invert the order of importance.

NEGATIVE THEOLOGY, AND THEOLOGY

Such assertions as 'God is (not) good' are of use and may be of importance both in common life—in cult, or in prayer—and in theology. 'But is God good, if he permits my child to suffer?' is an entirely reasonable kind of objection in many far from fanciful circumstances. Yet one who would keep to Negative Theology alone, with the rest silence, could make no sensible answer; having no access to how God is.[7] (Compare this with the parallel problem about 'Can God save my child from the plague?', as in Ch. 1 above.) The objector is concerned, on the face of it, with what sort of being God might be, regardless of what he may

---

[7] I use capitals in 'Negative Theology' to indicate that it is a negative theology view on the divine nature which is in question. Some writers appear to use the phrase in connection with other topics, in addition to its use in connection with the divine nature. Whether or not there is cause to do so, I wish to make clear that my own application of the phrase is narrower than some may expect. The early pages of V. Lossky, *Théologie négative et connaissance de Dieu chez Maître Eckhart* (Paris, 1960), 451 pp., give background on Negative Theology. Scholars have often pursued comparisons between Maimonides and Aquinas on negative theology. A. Wohlman, *Thomas d'Aquin et Maïmonide: Un dialogue exemplaire*, pref. I. Leibowitz (Paris, 1988), 417 pp., is particularly valuable in the present matter. See also D. Burrell, *Knowing the Unknowable God: Ibn Sina, Maimonides, Aquinas* (Notre Dame, Ind. [1986]); A. Broadie, art. cit. (above, n. 6); and J. Buijs, 'The Negative Theology of Maimonides and Aquinas', *Rev. Met.* 41 (1987–8) 723–38 (discussing I. Franck in *Rev. Met.* 38 (1985), 591–616, F. Sommers in *Judaism*, 15 (1966), 61–73, A. Pegis in *Med. St* 27 (1965) 212–26 focus particular issues. See also J. Dienstag (ed.), *Studies in Maimonides and St Thomas Aquinas* [Hoboken, NJ, 1975], 350 pp. The even vaster literature on 'analogy' in Aquinas also bears on some present issues. I mention only B. Montagnes, *La Doctrine de l'analogie de l'être d'après saint Thomas d'Aquin* (Louvain, 1963), 212 pp., bibliogr. 190–7; G. Klubertanz, *Saint Thomas Aquinas on Analogy: A Textual Analysis and Systematic Synthesis* (Chicago, 1960); D. Burrell, *Aquinas: God and Action*, (1979), xiii + 194 pp., chs. 2–5.

have disposed for the child (which is no doubt also a concern of such an objector).

6. What may be possible, is to find some analysis of 'God is good' and the like, which is consistent with maintaining a Negative Theology view on the divine nature, yet which permits a sensible answer to such questions as 'Is God good, if... ', whether in academically theological or more sharply human focus.

Some kinds of analysis can quickly be rejected. Aquinas rejects two in *ST* 1/13/2c. The first takes its inspiration from Negative Theology itself. Crudely expressed, it runs: take 'God is good' to mean 'God is not ___', where the slot is filled with "names" whose signification we can grasp from our experience of the world: 'vindictive', 'bullying', 'deceitful', and so on. The second takes its inspiration from exemplarism. It runs: take 'God is good' to mean 'God is the cause of goodness in creatures'.

He brings three arguments against both of these.[8] The first is that neither gives a positive reason for preferring, say, 'good' to indefinitely many comparable "names". Even 'God is a body' can be licensed on such an analysis, as understood to mean something like 'God is not prime matter'. The third is that neither analysis really accommodates what people mean when they say 'God is (not) good' or whatever: both are *contra intentionem loquentium*.

The main argument, the second, is that both have the consequences that all "names" so understood and used in assertions about God would be being said only *per posterius* of God. Consider the case of 'good', as in 'God is good'. We learn to apply 'good' in applications to creatures, and may think of it as applicable primarily to creatures, much as we may think of "that which we call health in animals" as something found primarily in animals. In the 'health' case, says Aquinas, we apply 'healthy' to other things (diet, urine) only *secundum intentionem et non secundum esse*: that is, we apply it with the same meaning (*intentio*) it has when said of a healthy animal, but without any implication on our

---

[8] From Dr Broadie's concentration on only two of the arguments, readers might be led to think that only two of the arguments bear on the proposal of a negative analysis: but Aquinas is explicit that both it and the exemplarism-based analysis are intended to be vulnerable to all three arguments, *utrumque istorum videtur esse inconveniens, propter tria*.

part that health is to be found *secundum esse* in the other things, as it is in the animal. The concept of health which is exhibited *secundum esse* only in a healthy animal, is applied *per posterius*—in the light of our understanding of the health of a healthy animal, and what conduces to it, and what manifests it—to other things.

Curiously, it is this kind of *per posterius* application of concepts which some modern readers of Aquinas seem to imagine to be that commended by Aquinas in the case of attributing things to God. It is not. In *In 1 Sent.*, d. 19, qu. 5, art. 2 ad 1 he argues that it is one of two ways of asserting things *secundum analogiam* which are not the one in which, alone of the three considered there, that may be done in the case of attributing things to God. And it is because the negative analysis and the causal analysis alike would come down to a species of this rejected way of saying things *secundum analogiam* of God, that Aquinas rejects them at *ST* 1/13/2c. Like many other medieval academics, Aquinas is content to have an austere, little more than formal ground on which to reject the proposals: they imply *per posterius* attributions, those in turn presuppose saying things of God *secundum intentionem tantum, et non secundum esse,* and that is not how things are to be said of God *secundum analogiam.*[9] Something of how they may be said of God *secundum analogiam,* in Aquinas's view, will appear presently.

It is important, incidentally, that what Aquinas is here imputing (rightly or wrongly) to Maimonides, and arguing against, is not Negative Theology: it is a proposal to use the model of Negative Theology to provide an analysis (a positive *sensus* as he calls it in *ST* 1/13/2c ad fin) usable in the ways envisaged above, as in the theology of the theologians. On Aquinas's philosophical logic, the proposal would seem to be a non-starter anyway: there are no "forms", such as a positive *sensus* would need, of non-vindictiveness, non-deceitfulness, and the like. Whatever may be true of this last point, what is to be retained is that it is the proposal of an analysis inspired by Negative Theology which is being rejected by Aquinas here, not Negative Theology as such. Had he not thought it important to accept a Negative Theology,

---

[9] For this account see *In 1 Sent.*, d. 19, qu. 5, art. 2 ad 1. For a different interpretation see R. McInerny, 'The Analogy of Names is a Logical Doctrine', repr. in *Being and Predication: Thomistic Interpretations* (Washington, DC, 1986), xii + 323 pp., 279 ff.

what reason could he have had to look for an analysis of the kind sought?[10]

This leaves room for a proposal of Aquinas's own.

7. Aquinas states his own analysis (*sensus*) of 'God is good' as follows:

That which we call goodness in creatures, pre-exists in God, and that in accordance with a higher mode [than the one in which it exists, or, may be said to exist, in creatures]. (*ST* 1/13/2c ad fin.)

1. Unlike the two analyses rejected, it is explicit in not professing to be about God, about the divine nature. It is openly about *Id quod bonitatem dicimus in creaturis*, is treating the (intelligible) assertion of 'God is good' as systematically misleading, and is taking it as "really being" about, not God, but contents of our judgements.
2. The parallel with a Power Distinction treatment of 'God is powerful' (taken as intelligible) is striking. 'God is good' can be true, affirmative, intelligible, and not reducible to 'The order of things caused by God is good', on the strength of what may be called God's option-neutral goodness, any or all of the things which could be actually good, if God were to bring them about.

"What we call goodness in creatures" can indeed be referred to the actual order of things: which was often referred to as *bonitas dei*, in Augustinian and Avicennian treatments alike. When we refer it to the actual order of things, we have what may be called God's option-tied goodness.

But "what we call goodness in creatures" can be taken for a "goodness" dependent only on the intrinsic content of that which is in this way being called good. It is that kind of goodness, sometimes called 'metaphysical goodness', in which 'Whatever is, is good'. Cats are good in this way. So are the characteristic activities of plague-rats and female anopheles mosquitoes, and the occurrence of an earthquake. Blindness is not. From this we might say:

In God's option-neutral goodness cats, unicorns, Pegasus, the

---

[10] Equally, it is not exemplarism as such which is being argued against in the arguments against the proposal of a causal analysis.

explosion of an atomic bomb, and the Lisbon earthquake are alike good; blindness, defective arguments, sinning, and telling lies are not (as arguments) good;

In God's option-tied goodness cats, mosquitoes, atomic explosions, and the Lisbon earthquake are good, unicorns and Pegasus are not.

If we do, it will surely be with the suspicion that what we are then talking about is not goodness as used in the ordinary moral or aesthetic judgements of our contemporaries.

3. 'That which we call goodness in creatures' is indeed not spelled out in that passage from *ST* 1/13/2c. Aquinas may well have wished to be neutral on the point, so leaving to libertines, Moloch-worshippers, and moralists alike the possibility of a theology. It may be true that 'The more corrupt the moral concepts, the more corrupt are the theological concepts' (I. Kant, *Lectures on Ethics*, tr. L. Infeld with J. MacMurray (1930; repr. 1963)). But even "corrupt" concepts, in Kant's sense, can be concepts, and wicked theologies can still be theologies.

4. What Aquinas's analysis needs here, in any case, is not moral or aesthetic goodness, as our contemporaries would usually intend these. What it needs is a notion of goodness in creatures, according to which

(1) any integral, actual thing can be said to be good, and cannot be denied to be good, provided it is something integral and actual—in effect a possible truthmaker for a narrowly predicative true proposition;

and according to which

(2) any intrinsic content which could be actualised—in effect a possible truthmaker for a composing-apt proposition— can likewise be said to be good, and cannot be denied to be good.

This is fairly obviously not a notion which, of itself, could be of use in understanding important ranges of, say, moral or aesthetic judgements.

But it could serve as a bridging notion: to moral goodness, at least. Nothing could be morally good for us to intend, unless it was of the set of things making up God's option-neutral goodness; though not everything of the latter might be morally good for us to intend. A life-size replica of the Tower Bridge, made out of match-sticks, is in principle a good thing, and not inherently defective in any way. But to intend to make such a replica, at the cost of destroying our happiness or that of our friends, might not be a morally good thing. And nothing could be accounted actually good, save things of the set of God's option-tied goodness. The kindness we might have done, but did not do, logically cannot be a morally good thing done by us, and cannot in consequence be to our merit. But not everything that is in God's option-tied goodness, will be accounted morally good on all criteria: 'the very coolness of a scoundrel makes him, not merely more dangerous, but also immediately more abominable in our eyes than we should have taken him to be without it' (I. Kant, *Grundlegung*, tr. H. J. Paton, *The Moral Law* (1948), 60).

This negative control (on the sorts of thing which may be pronounced morally good) might make for a certain measure of "objectivity" in moral judgements: supporting the intuition in 'ought implies can' without necessarily supporting any logical "is–ought" process. If it did, then it could be wise not to dismiss the sense of (ontological) goodness which Aquinas is offering in his analysis of 'God is good', as entirely useless to moral philosophers or others engaged in inquiries involving goodness of one kind or another as expressible in practical judgements of one kind or another. But it is true that of itself it 'affords no Inference that affects human Life, or can be the Source of any Action or Forbearance' (Hume, *Dials.* ad fin.). No doubt this would have been seen by the old Deists as a defect in the analysis: by one who would maintain a rigorously negative theology on the nature of God, it is positively required.

A final point is worth making on Aquinas's analysis of 'God is good'. "That which we call goodness in creatures" is, *as actually to be found or manifested in creatures*, to be identified with any or all of the created order of things: a created entity, dependent ontologically on God's will. "That which we call goodness in creatures" is, *as it is in itself*, an intentional entity merely: a construct or fiction of some creature's judging thought. "That which we call goodness in creatures" is, *as it pre-exists in God*— which is to say, as it is known to God's eternal knowledge—to be identified with the divine nature. It thus exists in God in 'a more excellent manner' than it exists either in the things of extra-mental reality, or in the minds of thinking creatures. On the important question of whether "that which we call goodness in creatures" is in itself to be taken to be, ontologically speaking, nothing more than an item in some thinker's biography (as in an anti-platonist understanding), or instead to be identified with something in God's eternal knowledge, and hence with the divine nature (as in a Platonist understanding of a type acceptable to Christians), Aquinas's analysis leaves matters open. Increasingly, I think that, like Albert, he preferred the anti-platonist understanding, but so far as I am aware he did not reject the possibility of a platonist or even Platonist understanding of it. Both in this analysis, implying as it does a distinction between option-tied and option-neutral goodness, and in his parallel treatment of the Power Distinction, Aquinas appears to leave the ontological question open.

THE COMMENTARY ON THE SENTENCES (BOOK 3 REVISION: 1256–7?)

8. Aquinas appears to have begun his academic lectures on the Sentences at Paris in 1252: a year in which a quarrel flared up between the secular masters, whose predecessors had made the University what it had become, and the friars, who were increasingly appropriating teaching positions and excluding the seculars from them. The quarrel was intensified by the irony that the friars, who professed a commitment to a more frugal life— sometimes arrogantly expressed—were getting corporately richer and better known as a result; and the seculars—who depended more on the money they received from teaching—were seeing not only jobs being barred to them, but avenues to careers which had long been among those held open to clerics. The record of the steady monopolisation of Parisian teaching chairs confirms this. So does the increasing use of religious, especially friars, as cardinals, inquisitors, papal legates, and so on.

There were academic and pastoral issues as well as economic ones. The new religious orders had a declared mission towards evangelism and propaganda, not towards academic inquiry.

There was some reason to fear that increasing influence from religious orders in university matters could mean in practice more powerful executive control, consequent tampering with academic integrity, and almost certainly growing restrictions of the (restricted enough) academic freedoms which the Masters of the previous century had succeeded in winning.[11] The campaign spearheaded (years later) by Bonaventure in his famous series of Lenten sermons, shows the sort of thing to be feared: most notably in the ensuing condemnations of which friars and seculars alike—Aquinas among them—fell foul. On the other hand, the pious activists ought not to be dismissed as intellectual Luddites, seeking above all to destroy important means for academic inquiry. As bulls of foundation etc. insist, the official Church's primary interest in the universities was in the instruction of clergy for an ordinary parochial ministry. Disinterested academic inquiry was not the official aim for which the funding had primarily been committed, whatever the reality may have been. To the official Church, universities were more important for the many who did a few years of study, and returned to become Poore Persouns in ordinary parishes, than for the relative few who proceeded to doctorates in theology or law. This was a priority accepted very widely, not least by the secular masters in the universities. And in the event some of the most outstanding in academic inquiry were friars. At the beginning of this dispute, therefore, regardless of what happened later, the parties in dispute were not drawn up on simple religious versus secular lines.

In 1253, however, the (then three) friar professors in Theology blacklegged during a strike called in response to yet another act of police brutality against members of the University. This sharpened divisions, and was resented by the ordinary Parisians too. At the beginning of 1256 the Dominicans were in such bad odour with the populace that the King had to place an armed guard in front of their convent.

At this point Aquinas was still a bachelor lecturing on the (first two books of the) Sentences under the supervision of his master. Shortly afterwards, however, with interventions not only from the Chancellor but from the Pope, Alexander IV (who had

---

[11] See the judgements of Denifle, Coulton, Halphen, and Walz himself at Walz, *Saint Thomas* (1962), 81.

reversed the pro-masters policy of his immediate predecessor Innocent IV), Aquinas was hurriedly accepted by the Chancellor as a master in Theology. This decision was resented by many in the University, as demonstrations against his inaugural lecture witness. But it was vigorously supported by the Pope in June 1256 and, out of turn or not, it left Aquinas in a position to begin his lectures on Book 3 of the Sentences as a master, and so entitled to revise and publish his work as he wished.

9. It is towards the very beginning of Book 3, in a smoothly revised text, that Aquinas's most detailed exposition of the Distinction comes. Even in the older editions we have a text incorporating the author's corrections and revisions. These can be seen for later parts of the book in MS Vat. lat. 9.851,[12] in Aquinas's own hand. The earlier part of this copy—including the article treating the Power Distinction—is in a fair copy in a scribal hand, practically without corrections. From this I would infer that the treatment as we now have it in the editions, is the treatment Aquinas wished us to have. I would also infer that the treatment is not (as I once thought, in *Atti* 1974) from a time when he was still a bachelor; but from his earliest work as a master, and thus master of what he was entitled to put into the public domain without magisterial supervision.

The context in *In 3 Sent.*, d. 1, qu. 2, art. 3 is a discussion of the Incarnation, and of whether God the Father could have taken flesh. (Lombard had maintained that any of the Trinitarian Persons could have done so.) The question is in the line of those

---

[12] See G. F. Rossi, 'L'autographo di San Tommaso del Commento al III libro delle Sentenze', *Div. Thom.* (Piac.) 35 (1932), 532–85; A. Hayen in *RTAM* 9 (1937), 219–36, rev. A. Dondaine in *Bull. thom.* 6 (1940), 100–8. Also A. Dondaine, *Secrétaires de Saint Thomas* (Rome, 1956), 279 pp. + fasc. of plates, 41–53, who shows that from the work of the scribe responsible for this section of *In 3 Sent.* the text can be dated firmly to 'tres tôt dans la carrière professorale de saint Thomas: au cours de son premier enseignement parisien' (53). On the question of a revision of *In 1 Sent.* a scholarly debate has not yet been closed: see esp. A. Dondaine in *Med. St.* 42 (1980), 308–36; L. Boyle in *Med. St.* 45 (1983), 418–29, rev. *Rassegna di letteratura tomistica*, 19 (ann. 1983), No. 73. More generally, P. Glorieux, 'L'Enseignement au Moyen Âge: Techniques et méthodes en usage à la Faculté de Théologie de Paris au xiii[e]s.', *AHDLMA* 43 (1968), 65–186; and the introductory parts of L. Boyle, 'Peciae, apopeciae, and a Toronto MS of the *Sententia Libri Ethicorum* of Aquinas' in P. Ganz (ed.), *The Role of the Book in Medieval Culture*. Proceedings of the Oxford International Symposium 26 Sept.–1 Oct. 1982, (2 vols.; Turnhout, 1986), 2: 71–82. For the passages from the *Scriptum super Sententiis* I have used the Mandonnet–Moos edn. (vol. III ed. Moos (1933) for *In 3 Sent.*); the Vives edn. and that of Venice, 1481, for *In 4 Sent.*; and the texts reprinted in R. Busa (ed.), *Opera* in 7 vols.

on whether the Redemption might have been brought about otherwise, and 'authorities' from Anselm are cited on either side of the question. The context is one of quite narrowly Christian theology, and is the sort of context in which Aquinas's predecessors had been using the Distinction. Yet it may be worth noting that he has taken practically the first opportunity available to him, as a master teaching in his own right, to give the most explicit account provided by him anywhere, of the Power Distinction. He must not therefore be taken—as he sometimes has been taken—to be a desultory or unwilling user of the Distinction.

10. He begins his account of the Distinction by setting it within the scope of what can or cannot be done 'by agents acting out of freedom of will'. Since it is agency which is in question, it has to be God's power to accomplish things external to his own nature which is going to be treated. Since the agency is voluntary, there is room for attributions to such a power to be intended in either of two ways.

(1) Things can be attributed to that power to accomplish things ad extra, as considered in itself. When they are, the "things" to be attributed are being considered only in their intrinsic descriptions—in their Avicennian essences—and in isolation from whether, in extra-mental reality, they will ever exist, or not. In this first way the "things" in question are said to be being attributed to God's option-neutral power.

(2) The same things may, on the other hand, be attributed to God's power to accomplish things external to himself, when they are being considered not abstractly but concretely, 'in an order directed towards (God's) wisdom and fore-knowledge and will'. In this way of making the attributions, we are considering the things, not merely in their abstract Avicennian essences, not merely in their intrinsic descriptions as elaborated and understood in our thought, but additionally and crucially in their actual relationship to God's will (as Aquinas and his fellows understood this to be executed): as willed by God to exist, or as not willed by God to exist.

11. Aquinas's exposition of the option-neutral arm of the Distinction begins: 'to (the) option-neutral power itself, since it is infinite, it is necessary to attribute every thing which is something in itself, and does not sink into a failing in power' (ed. Moos, par. 116).

Any option-neutral power—not only God's—will be infinite in its kind: like a form considered in itself, or the intrinsic content of a concept, an option-neutral power is something *formale*. But God's option-neutral power cannot be thought of as restricted only to certain kinds of object, as the option-neutral powers of creaturely agents may be: this, because that power held identical with the divine nature—for which God's option-neutral power is to serve as a kind of surrogate—cannot be thought to be restricted in any way. So no matter what comes under the concept of something brought about by a power, no matter what sort of power, has to be ascribed to the kind of option-neutral power which God's will have to be, if it is to be of use in answers to the range of questions on what God could or could not do, on which it was typically deployed. For it to be useful for the whole range of such questions, the notion of option-neutral power could not be restricted to any one kind or any given set of kinds. No matter what comes under the concept of something brought about by a power, must be allowed for within the (infinite) set of things which God can do in option-neutral power. This is the infinity appropriate to sets, it is not the kind of infinity which alone may be appropriate to any actual infinite.[13] Already, it is worth noting in passing, we have an indication that Aquinas does not intend to identify God's option-neutral power as such, with the divine nature. What counts as "something brought about by a power" is treated by him next.

1. Only *id quod in se est aliquid* can satisfy '*x* is not impossible to be done in an option-neutral power', if this is to come out true. *Quod in se est aliquid* covers both (*a*) entities which exist in extra-mental reality, and substantiate our true assertions concerning what is the case in that reality, and (*b*) the compositions of forms which substantiate our other

---

[13] On notions of the infinite generally see A. W. Moore, *The Infinite* (London [1990]), xiii + 268 pp., though the chapter on medieval treatments is a little disappointing. In some ways the same author's 'Aspects of the Infinite in Kant', *Mind*, 97 (1988), 205–23, is more pertinent to present purposes than that chapter. On Aquinas see J. Isaac, 'Le quodlibet 9 ... l'article sur l'infini en acte ... ', *AHDLMA* 16 (1947–8), 145–85.

true assertions. It rules out such bogus entities as not-being-the-nine-o'-clock-news, or privations generally. *Id quod in se est aliquid*, in other words, is either an individual of some kind (an individualised form), with *esse in re extra animam*; or a form (or ordered set of forms) abstractly considered, with *esse intentionale* merely. These two kinds of "thing" are the anchors of Aquinas's ontology generally: the *id quod in se est aliquid* requirement is not anything brought in ad hoc, as for some theological special pleading. As for the insistence on only "integral" things, not privations or open exclusions, that no doubt came to him with the commendations of Avicenna and of Neoplatonists before him. But it has the merit of excluding one important source of vagueness of reference, which is an important consideration for anyone developing his theory in a language which is at bottom semantically closed, and in need of conscious regimentations and restrictions, if trouble from such things as vagueness of reference is to be avoided or limited.

What the "something", or *ens* requirement also excludes appears from what Aquinas adds without delay: the conjunction of an affirmation and a denial is nothing; neither is anything being said, if it is being "said" that something is a man, and is not a man, simultaneously taken, as though in the force of one utterance (*dictio*). For that reason 'the power of God does not extend to this, that there should be simultaneously the affirmation and the negation of something. And the same reason holds concerning all things which include contradiction'.

Both difficulties, we may note, are put as concerning things conceivable by us as impossible to be done. In the first case, simultaneously affirming and denying the same thing is what cannot be done. In the second, the difficulty is that a contradiction cannot be asserted so as to generate an understanding in anyone's mind. The components of the contradiction 'This is a man', say, and 'This is not a man', do severally generate such an understanding. This is what makes it a *contra-dictio* in the first place: each component is, considered in itself, a significant *dictio* or utterance. ('This is a man, and it is not the case that bligs blags blugs' would not be so much as a contra-diction.) It is for that reason doubtless that Aquinas does not rule out the use of contradictions in reasonings; as in the antecedents of hypotheticals. It is not important that the proposition in antecedent position should be true rather than false, for the whole hypothetical to be true; but it is essential—for there to be a hypothetical proposition at all—that the antecedent should have some truth-value.

Perhaps it is useful to add that, because contradictions do not generate any understanding, even in the way in which a composition of concepts (forms abstractly considered) does, contradictions cannot be said to exist in any manner, even with *esse intentionale*, as objects of someone's understanding. No composition can be had, in anyone's act of judging, of being a man and not being a man. The latter is no "form" in the first place, and cannot be com-posed in any judgement. We cannot therefore, within the possibilities of Aquinas's metaphysics and philosophical logic, so much as coherently suppose contradictions as somehow existing, and "able to be done by God", until someone tries to assert their existence, or until God tries (!) to instantiate them. Contradictions cannot have *esse intentionale* in anyone's judging thought, never mind "existence in the mind of God". Things are indeed known to God—Rangers winning the Cup next year, and Celtic doing so—which would imply a contradiction, if asserted 'as though in the force of one utterance (*dictio*)'. The several things satisfy Aquinas's *ens* condition, their simultaneously holding, does not. Some examples of this sort of thing were seen in Albert above.

2. Every thing which *in defectum potentiae non vergit*—everything, we might say, which does not amount to a failing in power—must be allowed; cannot be excluded from the extension of God's option-neutral power.

By 'amounts to a failing in power' he means to include any concept which introduces a reference to being-at-the-receiving-end (anything to be assigned to the Aristotelian category of *passio*), whether or not it betrays such a reference on all its surfaces; in all the expressions in which it may be expressed. Nothing in the passage suggests that Aquinas thought it would always be easy, or even practically possible, to know beyond reasonable doubt whether a given expression (as used on some occasion) does or does not conceal a lurking reference to categorial passivity. What concerns his argument is that, once the expression is held to be passive, certain things follow.

His general example—being soft's implying liability to be easily divided—was already commonplace. So was his theological example, an allusion to the suffering and death of Christ, where the *pati* has its more everyday sense of suffering pain or suffering damage to one's well-being. It is for the reason that suffering and dying imply a reference to being-at-the-receiving-end, that 'we do not say that God can *in natura divinitatis* suffer or die or anything of the sort; just as we do not say that he is impotent' (ed. Moos, par. 116).

By indicating that he is speaking *cum determinatione* when saying 'can *in natura divinitatis* suffer and die', Aquinas obviates the rather silly candidates for counter-instances to divine power which even some modern writers who should know better have tried to raise; on the basis of a too sketchily presented version of traditional Christian doctrines on the Incarnation. By having specifiable rules—which he does not need to mention to his audience here—for when it is or is not appropriate to proceed from an assertion made *cum determinatione* to one made *simpliciter*, he is not open to the supplementary objection sometimes heard, that someone interjecting phrases like *in natura divinitatis* has to be trading on some ad hoc procedure which cannot be integrated into a coherent and honest dialectics. The insertion of *in natura divinitatis* is of specifically theological significance only to the extent that the matter of the example is specifically theological. The logic of *cum determinatione* arguments—what kinds of inference are licensed by *cum determinatione* assertions—is topic-neutral, as it should be. It is not the semantics of the predicates asserted *cum determinatione* which is crucial, but rather certain ranges of formal properties: for example, whether the predicates are weakened by the modification, or strengthened by it.[14]

[14] On assertions *cum/absque determinatione*, and arguments involving them: G. Klima, '*Libellus pro sapiente*—a Criticism of Allan Bäck's Argument against St Thomas Aquinas's Doctrine of the Incarnation', *New Schol.* 58 (1984), 207–19; which in the course of its argument to the topic of the title provides much that is of value for an appreciation of medieval treatments of arguments involving determinants. (I prefer 'determinant' to Klima's 'qualification' in translation of *determinatio*, because a qualification, strictly speaking, is only one species of determination.) G. Sinkler, 'Roger Bacon on the Compounded and Divided Sense', in O. Lewry (ed.), *Acts of the Sixth European Symposium on Medieval Logic and Semantics* (Toronto, 1983), 145–71; and A. de Libera, 'Référence et champ: Genèse et

More generally, it is not strictly because God's option-neutral power is God's (is a power ascribable by a/the being which is or ought to be worshipped, or whatever), that attributions which meet the criteria have to be ascribed to God's option-neutral power. It is because that power—that set of things abstractly considered, conceived by us as existing in a certain possible relation to God's will—is infinite; without even the restrictions of kind which creaturely option-neutral powers, infinite within their kind, must have. No doubt Aquinas believed both

- (*a*) that an active power which is not liable to any of the restrictions familiar in our own experience of acting, is at least conceivable,
- (*b*) that there is some such active power in extra-mental reality, and
- (*c*) that no power distinct from the divine nature makes (*b*) to be true.

But what he has been saying in par. 116 concerns only what can be and has to be attributed to an option-neutral power (to do things) as such, an option-neutral power conceived as being without any manner of restriction (in its totally active kind). What he has been saying in par. 116 then, necessarily concerns (*a*), and does not necessarily concern (*b*) or (*c*).

Since (*a*) could quite conceivably be held consistently with a denial of (*b*) and (*c*), or with a complete scepticism about their truth or falsehood, it follows that acceptance of the option-neutral arm of the Distinction—for which (*a*) has to be true, but not necessarily (*b*) or (*c*)—is not necessarily bound up with a particularly religious world-view. It is consistent with scepticism towards worship, prayer, etc. and even with what in an everyday sense would be accounted atheism: atheism of the old-fashioned and thoroughgoing Rationalist Press variety indeed.[15] It is of

structure des théories médiévales de l'ambiguïté (xiiᵉ–xiiiᵉ siècles)', *Medioevo* 10 (1984), 155–208, prepare the ground for an account of the matter on more general principles. See too the remark on the place of concern for systematic 'désambiguïsation d'une langue semi-formalisée: le latin 'technique' de la disputatio scolastique et des genres littéraires qu'elle commande'; and the judgement that 'Si certaines de ses théories… font place à une réflexion de type explicitement pragmatique, leur objet linguistique reste chez cet idiolecte technicisé, non la langue naturelle comme telle' (de Libera, 207).

[15] Calvin was to recognise the fundamental "secularity" of the Power Distinction, but saw this as grounds for disapproval. See *Inst.*, Fr. 1560, Bk. 3, ch. 23, par. 2, ed. Benoît, 3: 435.

some interest that the option-neutral arm of the Distinction is presented by Aquinas in this austere and metaphysical manner; though he does add a narrowly theological example, indicating to his audience that it was nevertheless the God of Abraham and the rest that he had in mind.

12. Aquinas then proceeds (in par. 117) to expound the option-tied arm of the Distinction, beginning with a reference which needs careful identification:

To this power, considered absolutely, when something is being attributed which it wishes to do and its wisdom has it in it that it should do the thing, then it is being said to be capable of that something in option-tied power. When, however, the power extends as far as in it lies, towards that which is being attributed to it, although his wisdom and will do not have it in them that it should be done, then it is being said to be capable of the thing in option-neutral power. (Ed. Moos, par. 117.)

I have deliberately used expressions like 'it wishes' rather than 'he wishes' in translating that passage, even where it is certainly the divine nature which is being referred to. I have done so, since the reference of some of the occurrences of 'it' is not beyond contest. The *Huic*, the 'this' in the opening phrase, 'To this power, considered absolutely' refers grammatically to the *Deum* of *Deum in natura divinitatis* which has just been mentioned, and to the *potentiae divinae* of the *quando potentiae divinae aliquid ascribitur* of par. 115, at the opening of the article's treatment of the matter. It was that power—namely God—which was being said in the same par. 115 to be capable of something either *de potentia ordinata* or *de potentia absoluta*. And it is that same power, namely God, to which Aquinas refers later in the sentence which *Huic* opens, when he again contrasts 'is said to be capable of *secundum potentiam ordinatam*' and 'is said to be capable of *de potentia absoluta tantum*'. But what must not be missed is that the *Huic* which opens par. 117 is not to be referred grammatically to the *ipsi potentiae absolutae*, in the sense of option-neutral power as such, with which par. 116 opened.

In par. 117, then, Aquinas is not concerned with attributions considered for membership of the set of things which God can do *de potentia absoluta*. (He had been concerned with these in par. 116.) In par. 117 he is concerned, as he had been in par. 115, with ascriptions to the divine power itself, namely God, whether the ascriptions in question are to be determined 'in option-tied power' or 'in option-neutral power'.

With that in mind, we can better appreciate what he wishes to say in expounding the option-tied arm, and may resolve some further ambiguities.

1. 'This power, considered absolutely': the divine nature, namely God, when we consider it only in itself and pre-scinding from what it may or may not have decided to bring about ad extra.

2. 'Which... its wisdom has it in it that it should do' or, less artificially, 'which... his wisdom has it in it that he should do': it is not the classical attribute of divine infinite wisdom which is in play here, but the "wisdom of God" which we have met often enough already, in Albert and others: the wise, providential order decreed by God; the actual order of things, as Aquinas believed it to be. 'His wisdom' here is on a par with 'Caesar's forces' in 'Caesar's forces crossed the river, while he remained in the camp'. 'His wisdom' refers to God's wisely ordered *ordinatio*, his creature.

When what is being attributed to God's power is to be identified with some or all of this actual *ordinatio dei*, God is being said to be capable of the same *secundum potentiam ordinatam*. But when we use 'God's power' in an extended sense, to refer not only to the actual *ordinatio dei*, but to any or all of what we can conceive to be included within a power of that sort, considered abstractly, and 'although God's will and wisdom does not have it in it that it should be', then God is being said to be capable (of whatever is being attributed to him) *de potentia absoluta* merely.

3. 'Although God's will and wisdom does not have it in it that it should be': in other words, although it is not something which ever is or ever will be any of the actual *ordinatio dei*. It is attributions made with an option-neutral determination which are to be seen as exceptional, 'iffy': *quamvis*, or in some manuscripts *licet*. Attributions made with an option-tied determination are apparently not exceptional, not iffy. If God can in option-tied power make pigs to be grunting, then he can do so sans phrase.

13. Aquinas next makes explicit a point which had previously

been in obscurity: that among the things which God's will and wisdom does not have it in it to bring about, are very different kinds of thing.

1. 'There are some things which have, inseparably conjoined in themselves, something repugnant to divine wisdom and goodness: sinning, lying, and the like. And we also say that God cannot do these things.'

The *in se* refers to the intrinsic "essences" of the things in question. In the very nature of sinning, or lying, is something 'repugnant to divine wisdom and goodness'. This is a quasi-definitional point about sinning and lying, and can be conceived to hold even if no one ever sins or lies. Here therefore we have certain "things" distinct from the divine nature, yet such that 'we say that God cannot do them'. Aquinas does not repeat here the condition which permits him to be consistent. Sinning and lying are not integral, individualised forms, as walking and being good are. There is no "form" of sinning or of lying. Sinning, for example, is a defective action, implying an action defectively ordered. The related integral actions—my activities in regard to my neighbour's wife, or my enunciation of 'I have no funds in any bank in the Channel Islands'—need not themselves be at all defective in their proper genre.

What of *divinae sapientiae bonitatis*? It might seem to refer to divine infinite wisdom and goodness, as held identified with the divine nature. But the *quando ... potentia se extendit quantum in se est ad illud quod sibi attribuitur* opens up a different possibility. This is that the wisdom and goodness in question are the kinds of wisdom and goodness which we can in some way understand, and which, if God so chose, could be manifested in some other order of things, though not necessarily in our own. They would in other words be option-neutral wisdom and goodness, *sapientia dei absoluta, bonitas dei absoluta*, as opposed to the option-tied wisdom and goodness manifested in the actual order of things. As was seen at Section 7 above, this possibility was allowed by Aquinas for independent reasons.

But in that case such expressions as 'God can lie/sin' will have to be understood as being systematically misleading. Like living, lying and sinning are not strictly things which our servants can do on our behalf. Our lying/sinning is by definition the lying or sinning for which we have a direct actorial responsibility. Our servants can of course go to the antipodes and perjure themselves at our behest. They can pack people into cattle trucks at our behest, and send them to Treblinka, or to Stalin's death squads. Our servants may well then be lying or sinning. If they are, though, they are doing it on their own head, in their own right. If on the same occasions we too may be said to be lying or sinning, what will then be our lies or sins are not going to be of precisely the same kinds as theirs. How curious that something so individualistically personal should, on the theory, be ident-ifiable with strictly nothing in the world.

In what concerns present issues 'God can lie/sin' cannot be understood attributively, within the assumptions of Aquinas's metaphysics and philosophical logic, but can very well be under-stood as a systematically misleading way expressing something like 'God can order lying/sinning to be done for his ends, or at his behest'. 'Dieus le volt!' used to be a crusaders' cry, and I am told that during the belligerency in Vietnam some Americans went round with buttons proclaiming 'Kill a Commie for Christ!'

On this kind of analysis Aquinas will be understood to be saying that ordering—lying/sinning—to-be-done-at-God's-behest is one of those things of which we are to say 'God cannot do that'. But this is because a notion of disorder is being understood to be implied in 'lie' and 'sin'. The difficulty is about the ordering of something inherently or quasi-definitionally disordered: which is not the sort of thing which can be done in anything ordered by a power unrestricted in any way.

His treatment of individualisable forms, signifiable and express-ible in merely descriptive terms, is quite different. He shows this in the same paragraph, when entertaining the possibility that God could not make a man with his head below and his feet on top. Things of this kind 'do not of themselves have an *incon-venientiam* towards divine wisdom', but are merely of a kind not scheduled for instantiation in the actual order of things (par. 117, ad fin.). Albert had made a similar point, with a robust vulgarity which Aquinas does not choose to emulate.

14. In par. 118 Aquinas lists four kinds of things.

1. Things which are not attributed even to (an) option-neutral power.

Examples of these are 'being on the receiving end' and 'for contradictories to hold simultaneously'. Of all such things it is to be said *simpliciter* that God cannot do them. The accent here would seem to be on the 'attributing' or on the 'saying', on the assertion's being made with truth. It is as though there is a kind of ascent envisaged, so that what is being denied *simpliciter* is that a proposition of the type exemplified in 'God can *in natura divinitatis suae* suffer' could for any case be true. The type of proposition in question is one in which the purported composition is of things which cannot be com-posed, so grounding a true proposition.

The crucial grounds for rejection here, are grounds of philosophical logic.

    2. Things which *ex se* are repugnant to God's (*eius*) wisdom and goodness.

The crucial grounds for rejection here are in metaphysics. The "things" in question are things which cannot be instantiated in any order willed by God, or possible to be willed by God. God's power to do things external to his nature is a voluntary power, the power of one *agens per intellectum et voluntatem*, as was indicated at the beginning of the *Solutio*, and governs all discussion of that power of God's. So we do not say that God can do the things of this kind, 'save under a condition, to wit, if he willed to'. The 'saying' that God can do these things is not ruled out in the way in which it was ruled out in regard to things of type 1: 'it is not *inconveniens* that in a true conditional the antecedent should be impossible'. The (fanciful) ordering-by-God of something inherently disordered, is what is being envisaged here. 'God can lie, if he wills to' can be said with truth, for the reason given, and the *dictio* in the antecedent, a *contra-dictio*, contributes to the whole hypothetical's having the truth-value which it then does have.

Aquinas does not repeat the examples here, but lying and sinning, allowed their strongly evaluative loading, are evidently the kinds of thing in play. And the very mention of 'repugnancy' which implies some kind of relationship between semantic contents, should alert us not to take the wisdom and goodness mentioned for the wisdom and goodness held identical with the divine nature. They can, however, be taken as in the alternative proposed above. Consistently with a rigorously negative theology, and in Aquinas's theology in particular, 'wisdom', or 'goodness', or any other appropriate filler of 'God's___' can be understood by us only in either of two ways: (*a*) improperly, as in metaphor or some other figure, or (*b*) when standing for something other than God, but viewed as being in some way dependent on God. If there is to be repugnancy, therefore, between, on the one hand, the concept of lying, say, or of sinning, and, on the other, the concept of God's wisdom or goodness, the wisdom or goodness named as being God's cannot be that wisdom or goodness of God which is to be identified with the divine nature. That is not something which can be understood in our true assertions, when we are predicating something properly of the divine nature. The possibility which remains is the one which has been proposed.

Like 'God's power', when this is to be understood of God's power to do things external to his nature, 'God's wisdom' and 'God's goodness' in the present matter must be referred either to the goodness/wisdom of God manifested in the actual order of things, or to the kind of goodness or wisdom abstractly considered as manifestable, if God so chose, in comparable possible orders of things.

3. 'Some there are which do not in their own natures (*de se*) contain a repugnancy.'

On these Aquinas's policy is: 'It must be conceded absolutely that God can in option-neutral power do these things; neither are they to be denied, save under a condition, to wit, one amounting to saying 'He cannot, if it clashes with his will'. These are things whose intrinsic natures contain no repugnancy in themselves (as square circles might be said to do) and no repugnancy to the kind of wisdom or goodness (or anything else) which could be manifested, if God so chose, in some or other order of things (as ordering lying or sinning to be done might be said to do).

No doubt the things under heading 3 include such things as "having one's feet above and one's head below", or the "golden mountain" which would become common in later discussions. 'God cannot bring about a golden mountain, if it clashes with his will' is true, if it is, for the reason that what God is being envisaged as bringing about is not the bringing about of a golden mountain, abstractly considered. It is the bringing about of a golden mountain whose bringing about clashes with God's will as to what shall be brought about. And this would be the bringing about of a "thing" which cannot be brought about; since to say of something that it can be brought about, is to imply (according to substantive views held by Aquinas and many others on the matter) that it can be brought about if God chooses to bring it about. By contrast 'God can in option-neutral power bring about a golden mountain' is to be conceded without reservation, since—in virtue of what the 'in option-neutral power' tells us—what God is being said to be able to bring about is the golden mountain, abstractly considered. The difference between the denial and the concession depends fairly evidently on the scope of what is being talked about. That the scope is indicated in the one case by the expressed condition, and in the other by the expressed determination, is worth noting towards a fuller understanding of the Power Distinction, but creates no particular difficulties.

4. 'Some things... which are attributed to [divine] power are such as are congruent with his will and wisdom.'

On these his policy is: 'it must be said *simpliciter* that God can do these, and in no way that he cannot do them'. Bringing it about that Paris should be the largest city in France in 1900, is the kind of thing in question here. It must be said *simpliciter* that God can bring it about for Paris to be the largest city in France in 1900, or for that matter, that the Lisbon earthquake should have occurred when it did. And it must not be said 'in any way'—under no matter what determination or condition—that he cannot do such a thing. It is those things which God can do in option-tied power which are to be treated in this matter.

15. Having outlined the Distinction, Aquinas finally applies it to the question from which he had started. This was whether God the Father could have taken flesh in an incarnation, as Lombard had said. In applying it Aquinas adds nothing new, but by going through his list of four kinds of "thing" attributable to divine power, he permits a measure of confirmation of the exposition given above.

(1) For the Father to be made flesh 'is not among those things which do not come under God's option-neutral power', since 'neither (a) does it imply a contradiction [and so be unable to be brought about], nor (b) does incarnation imply any defect in an incarnate Person' [and so be unable to be said to be able to be brought about].

(2) 'Neither is it among those things which are intrinsically inconsistent ('which *ex se* have an *inconvenientiam*'), but

(3) it is among those things which have an *inconvenientiam* on account of another order's [than the one being envisaged, containing an incarnation of the Father] having been instituted by a wise providence of God's (*a dei sapientia*). But

(4) for the Son to take flesh is in the fourth class'.

Aquinas then adds: 'for this reason it is to be conceded *simpliciter* that the Father could have taken flesh, and the Holy Ghost likewise; speaking [with the determination] "in God's option-neutral power" '.

Some might think that the 'conceded' in the final reply, and the choice of a double negative rather than a more simply affirmative assertion when eliminating possible objections under (1), would suggest a certain unwillingness on Aquinas's part to say straight out that the incarnation of the Father did come under God's option-neutral power. The suggestion is not supported from the passage. The 'concession' in the final reply is due simply to the form of the original *oppositum*. And the nature of the list practically required that since the first of the four classes was 'of those things which do not come under God's option-neutral power', an elimination had to be done by a second negative. In Aquinas's day, and even in the period of the celebrated condemnations of the 1270s, the dominant fear in any case was not that assertions of what God could do might be too wild, but that they might suggest less than ought to have been suggested.

16. For comparison, a related view, involving a different but apparently related distinction in which the terms *potentia absoluta* and *potentia ordinata* are used, may be considered. The related distinction is to be seen in a

use of the pair [*potentia absoluta*, *potentia ordinata*] that does mark a genuine distinction: namely, it will be said that e.g. absolutely speaking it is within God's power not to save Israel, this is within his *potentia absoluta*, but *given that he has promised* he cannot leave Israel to perish, it is not within his *potentia ordinata*. (P. T. Geach, *Providence and Evil* (Cambridge [1977]), 31, italics from Geach.)

The author insists:

The distinction, I say, is a genuine one; but I submit—though I should have Aquinas against me over this—that it has somehow got twisted the wrong way round. What we can say God can do *simpliciter* is what God can do in the actual state of affairs: and thus we ought not to say 'God can leave Israel to perish' but only 'God *could*, *would* be able, to leave Israel to perish *if* he had not promised otherwise.' (Same ref.)

It is not clear from the context whether Prof. Geach has merely devised his 'genuine distinction' to make certain points, or has found it in some other writer. He prudently does not ascribe it to Aquinas, and it is not to be identified with the Power Distinction as understood either by Aquinas or indeed by any other medieval examined in this book.

As was seen in Section 15 above, it follows from Aquinas's understanding of the Power Distinction that

What we can say God can do *simpliciter* is what God can do in the actual state of things;

which appears to be what Geach wishes, in his example of saving Israel. When things are 'congruent to God's will and wisdom', then 'it must be said *simpliciter* that God can do these' and moreover 'it must be said ... in no way that he cannot do them' (Aquinas, in the *In 3 Sent.* passage examined above). (In Geach's use of his 'genuine distinction' we were allowed to say 'God could, would be able, to leave Israel to perish if he had not promised otherwise': this is something Aquinas expressly rejects in the *In 3 Sent.* passage.)

Nothing in the Power Distinction as understood by Aquinas lends itself to a 'wrong way round' reading. For one thing, as has been emphasised more than once above, both the option-tied and the option-neutral arms of the Distinction are worded for being asserted *cum determinatione*. Yet results very similar to those obtained by understanding the 'genuine distinction' as Geach does, could be obtained from confusing 'God can do A in his option-neutral power (*de potentia absoluta sua*)' with 'God can do A' asserted absolutely (*absolute, simpliciter, absque determinatione*, sans phrase). A reader confusing the two could well go on to imagine that some assertion of the option-neutral arm (a *cum determinatione* assertion) were instead an *absque determinatione* assertion of the core-proposition, and that only the option-tied arm were to be understood as being worded for assertion *cum determinatione* (with 'provisos, sub-intents, or saving clauses', as Geach put it). Such a reader could then easily come up with a misreading of the Power Distinction to obtain results remarkably similar to results obtainable from a correct application of the 'genuine distinction' as expounded by Prof. Geach.

The *absoluta* in the *de potentia absoluta dei* of the option-neutral arm of the earlier medieval Power Distinction occurs *within* the modification in which the "determination" is expressed (*Deus potest F-ere de potentia absoluta sua*). It thus cannot rightly be confused with the *absolute* which could occur instead of that specific determination, to indicate that the core-proposition was to be understood as asserted *absolute, absque determinatione*, etc. (*Deus potest F-ere, absolute*).

It is perhaps better, however, to think of the 'genuine distinction' as quite different from the Power Distinction: useful for permitting contrasts, and to show some of the advantages of a terminology such as 'in option-neutral power', for avoiding at least some of the confusions which 'absolute' may invite.

UNDERSTANDING AND USE

17. All the essential elements of Aquinas's understanding of the Distinction, are available from that passage in *In 3 Sent*. It was an understanding which remained essentially unchanged throughout his later works. Before providing a synthetic statement of that understanding, it will be useful to take into account some features of his use of the Distinction. It is in its use, after all, that any tool is seen to best advantage. In the case of the Power Distinction in particular, as has been indicated already, some of the most elusive difficulties connected with it are not in its semantics, but in its pragmatics, in the relations between its appreciated content, and its users. Some of Aquinas's later uses of the Power Distinction show features which that in the relatively early Sentence Commentary does not. These may be worth marking: so in the Chapter now following, a couple of the more revealing later uses are examined.

7

Aquinas: Using the Distinction

The Power Distinction is used by speakers situated in the world. This is inevitably going to colour their grasp of the things around them, and so limit what they can with justice affirm of those things:

my knowledge of the world is going to remain eternally marked by this perspective-bound and "historically involved" character pertaining properly to the unreflective awareness of the world which precedes the taking up of positions about it. Truth involving humans is never fully complete or definitive; never delivers up to me the last word on the enigma addressed. It remains ever a kind of truth that is "provisional": 'there is absolute truth about the world in general', Merleau-Ponty will say, 'but not about any thing in particular'... (A. Dondeyne, *Foi chrétienne et pensée contemporaine: Les problèmes philosophiques soulevés dans l'encyclique 'Humani Generis'* (Louvain, 1961), VIII + 224 pp., 28, quoting M. Merleau-Ponty, pp., 28, quoting M. Merleau-Ponty, *Phénoménologie de la perception* (Paris, 1945), XVI + 531 pp., 344.)

Moreover, the Distinction is used either of things themselves situated, or of "things" which situated makers of judgements get round to having in mind. Limitations arise under all these heads, but they are after all limitations of a kind to which any useful tool is subject.

1. Option-tied assertions at least, if they are to be true, presuppose the truth of certain propositions about the world, or things in it. They at least are purported to be about what actually is the case, and to that extent are "indexed". What kind of world is the user situated in? What are his indexed assertions indexed to? On this, Aquinas and his academic contemporaries were in agreement: they lived in a God-ordered universe. Nor was this an academic doctrine merely, it was behind the received piety of the times. Aelred of Rievaulx (d. 1167) had put it:

God has spread out his heaven like a curtain, and there his stars shine, to give us light in our dark world, where the forest beasts roam about, seeking to devour us. Above the heavens are the great waters, from whence the rains come to soften the parched earth, which is the soul of man... We would labour in vain without the help of God who gives us our daily bread... My soul, unproductive through dryness, thirsts for thy gentle rain, so that there may spring up in it that heavenly bread that feeds the angels. (*Mirror of Charity*, ad init.)[1]

That—give or take a few degrees of warmth in the cause of virtue—was the received description of the God-ordered world in which the schoolmen as much as the writers of piety saw themselves as situated. Their very faith, they thought, required as much. So whereas—as appeared in Chapter 6—the core of the Distinction should be seen as something "secular", something holding or not, independently of any faith professed by the user, we might expect the use of the Distinction within a world so described to be governed by at least some ad hoc rules inviting acceptance because they seemed to favour orthodox rather than heterodox conclusions in applications of the Distinction.

In fact no such ad hoc rules appear in the uses of the Distinction examined, and in particular in those examined in the present chapter. To the extent that the rules for application can be discerned (from the results obtained by Aquinas from applying the Distinction, with the latter understood as in Chapter 6 above), they are the ordinary rules of kinds followed at the time for analysing and drawing inferences from *cum determinatione* "predications" made in unanalysed speech; to the extent that these can be discerned.

I mention this, because at one time I thought mistakenly that without some special ad hoc rule, the received doctrinal content of 'God has sworn and will not repent' could not have been accommodated; and it fairly evidently was being accommodated.[2]

[1] From G. Webb and A. Walker, tr. and arr., *The Mirror of Charity. The* Speculum Caritatis *of St Aelred of Rievaulx*, (London [1962]), XV + 159 pp., 1. Aelred, an Englishman educated in Scotland, is not a canonised saint, and the story of his canonisation is bogus; but in the 15th cent. the Cistercians found it politic to find a local cultus within England. Aelred's text, including some blood-curdling passages on the fate of unbaptised infants, which the arrangers mentioned omit, is in CCCM 1 (1971), ed. C. H. Talbot.
[2] It is always useful to keep in mind that medieval Christian users of the Distinction were as Christians committed to the content of 'God has sworn and will not repent'; and sometimes convenient in discussion to give a name such as 'the Immutable Decree rider' to that content, as I have sometimes done in earlier studies. But by failing to give enough

As now appears, no more is needed to accommodate this than the ordinary rules for treating *cum determinatione* assertions such as the arms of the Distinction should be seen to be. The *inconveniens* to be avoided is that even something as slight as the falling of a leaf, viewed as ordered by God, within an order viewed as ordered to be executed punctiliously and without fail, might seem to come under the ordinary Aristotelian definitions for strict logical necessity. (If it did, there would then seem to be no way in which 'God has disposed thus, but might have disposed otherwise' or the like could be said without absurdity.) In fact no such *inconveniens* arises in the case of the earlier medieval Power Distinction, and the reasons are not without interest.

AQUINAS'S USES, AND THE TYPE OF AUDIENCE TO WHICH THEY ARE ADDRESSED

2.   Aquinas introduced the Distinction into his academic *œuvre* at the earliest point in his career at which he was entitled to publish on theological matters in his own right (in *In 3 Sent.*, as was seen above). He used it in later parts of the Sentence Commentary, and in a number of narrowly theological works thereafter, up to his latest period. Some thirty or more uses of the Distinction can be found, nearly all of them already listed in *Atti* 1974. Those found in the traditional theological contexts of possible alternative manners of redemption—traditional among users of the Distinction by the middle of the thirteenth century—include some which could raise eyebrows among readers fed on expectations that Aquinas should be so much narrower in his envisaged domain for option-neutral power than, say, Ockham or Holcot.

In frankly philosophical works such as the commentaries on Aristotle, where the *opus redemptionis* was not formally under

---

weight to the two-type analysis of scientifically serious assertions, I formerly imagined in addition that commitment to the Immutable Decree rider would have to be accommodated in arguments either by a stipulative definition (of 'willed by God', for example), which is expressly rejected by Aquinas; or by some special methodological rule governing the drawing of certain inferences. In fact, if due weight is given to the implications of a two-type analysis, acceptance of the Immutable Decree rider need pose no special dialectical problems.

consideration, the Distinction is not in evidence; even in some passages where the metaphysical or logical issues were the same as those to be found in passages of theological works where he does use the Distinction. It does not appear in its canonical dress in the *Summa contra Gentiles*, even though (as was noted in *Atti* 1974) it is there that some of the clearest expositions of what lies behind the Distinction are to be found. And it should be seen as being used at *SCG* III, ch. 98, though with the option-tied and option-neutral determinations expressed respectively as *quantum ad rationem a principio dependentem*, and *quantum ad res quae subduntur ordini* (or again, as *si absolute consideretur eius potestas*). This was correctly identified in Gál 1976 as a use of the Distinction, though before it can be appreciated as such the text may need more commentary than either Gál provided or can be given here.

The works in which the Distinction is found—save occasionally where Aquinas is apparently deferring to the terminological preferences of some objector in a disputation—are the following: the Commentaries *In 3 Sent.*, and *In 4 Sent.*; the disputed questions *De Veritate*; the *Contra errores Graecorum*; the disputed questions *De potentia*; the *Summa theologiae*; and *Quodlibet IV*.

What these works have in common is not any one literary genre, but an envisaged audience of working theologians already presumed masters in Arts, among whom doubtless the use of a technical shorthand—jargon, if you wish—is justified, and can be expected to be no more than minimally troublesome. I shall concentrate on a couple of particularly significant cases, and especially on a passage from one of the disputed questions in the *De potentia*.

DE POTENTIA, QU. 1, ART. 5 (a. 1268)

3.   As has been remarked before, the text we can expect to find in the published *ordinatio* of a disputed question is a reflected version, reviewed by the disputant in a cool hour, perhaps years after the original occasion. It was accepted that this might result in substantial revision, or at least in notable rearrangement: often to bring out features within questions, or connections between questions. *De potentia*, qu. 1, art. 5 shows a reflected *responsio*, and some rearrangement within the objections and the replies to these. It is said that the rearranging was completed at Rome for the most part (Chenu, *Toward* (1963), 282: 1259–68; Van Steenberghen, *La Phil. au XIII*ᵉs. (1966), 587: with a query, 1265–8). The substance of this particular article would seem, however, to have come from an earlier disputation, at Paris, since a parallel passage in the *SCG* is from a part thought to have been composed before Aquinas left there in 1259.

In *De potentia*, qu. 1, art. 5, as it now stands, there is some tension between what is emphasised in the objections and the replies to these, and what is emphasised in the body of Aquinas's answer. In the objections of the original disputation (and in the replies) the Power Distinction had evidently been used. In a couple of places the objector had at least purported to have been dissatisfied, and had raised a tell-tale supplementary objection.

In the body of Aquinas's considered answer in the *ordinatio*, the Distinction is not so much as named; yet the intellectual context within which alone it can be sensibly used, is clarified.

4. The question in *De potentia*, qu. 1, art. 5 is the seminal one contributed by Abelard: Whether God can do things he does not do, and leave off things he is doing. It is a question which links earlier with later patterns of use of the Distinction. It covers the detailed questions on whether this or that element of the Redemption of the human race could have been otherwise than it was, in the context of which the Power Distinction seems first to have been introduced. It lays bare central issues which neither philosophers nor theologians can ignore, and which the more specifically theological dressing of the earlier discussions might even have obscured.

Aquinas begins the body of the answer with a bald summary, making plain his own stance on the matter:

It is to be said that this error—to wit, that God cannot do [anything] save what he is doing—has been the error of two sorts of people. First, it has been the error of certain philosophers saying that God acts out of a necessity of nature (*agere ex necessitate naturae*).[3] If this is how things

---

[3] In the context—in the very next sentence—it is the necessities ascribable to things in virtue of their "nature" which are in question. So in *agere ex necessitate naturae*, the qualification *naturae* would seem to be signifying here God's acting in creation by means of the natural capacities of things, as in the generation of pigs from pigs, in the case where the nature of pigs is seen to be acting without let or hindrance. Elsewhere, when denying that *res* proceed from God by any natural necessity, he spells out that that denial

were—since a nature is determined towards one thing—divine power might not be able to extend (*se extendere non posset*) towards other things apt to be done (*agenda*) rather than towards those things which it is doing. Secondly, it has been the error of certain theologians, considering the order of divine justice and wisdom according to which things are made to be by God, and in respect of which they were wont to say that God could not have left it aside; and they tended to fall into this, as if to say in consequence that God cannot do [anything] save what he is doing. (*De pot.*, qu. 1, art. 5; as ed. P. M. Pession (Turin, 1949), 17–20, or at R. Busa (ed.), *Opera*, 3: 189–90.)

A few comments are in order. Aquinas is careful to speak of the view he plainly rejects, as an *error*. (Albert and Bonaventure had done likewise.) St Bernard, the professional inquisitor, had not shown himself to be so nicely conscientious in characterising his chosen adversaries' position on the question. Aquinas records that he considers it an error, not only in the case of the philosophers, but in that of the theologians he mentions. He locates the theologians' view historically: 'this view is laid at the door (*imponitur*) of Master Peter the Virgin-snatcher (?*Almalareo*)'. He distinguishes what the holders of the view were actually wont to say (*dicebant*) from what they tended to fall into (*incidebant*), which would as it were have come down to saying (*ut dicerent*) something further, and apparently objectionable in a way in which what they had been actually saying, did not have to be.

He does not locate the philosophers' view so plainly. It seems to me, however, that the Leonine editors of parallel passages in *SCG* II, chs. 22 ff. are correct, and Avicenna is the philosopher primarily in view.[4] Avicenna was one of the greatest of metaphysicians, and Aquinas owed some of his central metaphysical notions to him: not least, the Avicennian essence, its instantiability by the will of God, and the ways in which necessity or impossibility might or might not arise from any of this.

5. In *De potentia*, qu. 1, art. 5 Aquinas argues "dialectically"

is to cover either any acting on God's part out of any imagined necessity of his own nature, or as if constrained by the nature of any created thing (*SCG* III, ch. 98: *res ipsae quae a deo sub ordine ponuntur, provenerunt ab ipso non sicut ab agente per necessitatem naturae, vel cuiuscunque alterius . . .*). And cf. *ST* I/19/4c: *dicendum est quod necesse est dicere voluntatem dei esse causam rerum, et deum agere per voluntatem, non per necessitatem naturae, ut quidam existimaverunt.*

[4] The Leonine editors at *SCG* III, ch. 98 are also justified in referring to Avicenna as the supposed source of the doctrine, even though the formula used is the formula widely ascribed to Abelard.

against the Philosophers (Avicenna notably, as has been remarked), from assumptions which he and they evidently shared. These assumptions included Aristotelian positions about the nature of action; and the older position, cited with approval at the beginning of the *Ethics* (*EN* i. i, 1094ª3), about all things aiming at good. But at bottom they were rooted in a refusal to concede that the world around us is from chance. Aquinas (like the Philosophers, if his argument is going to be even dialectically persuasive) refuses to see it as a sequence of ultimately mindless activities, one damned thing after another, in the manner of the ancient atomists, and in the opinion of many today.

Aquinas's support for the repudiation of such a view—if we discount a not entirely worthless prejudice against ultimately mindless activities—would seem to be essentially from Christian theological positions: most notably positions on Providence. His quarrel with the Philosophers is not that they have been rejecting it, through rejecting the position that Whatever comes about, is ordered (by God). That would have been his quarrel with the ancient atomists, or with a Hobbist position. His quarrel with the Philosophers here is that, while professing a doctrine of providence, of things' being ordered, they are in effect excluding the possibility of a freely imposed order, and thus of the kind of providence taken as implied in the faith of the Church. There is no call to delay on Aquinas's case against the Philosophers. It is unlikely to impress any but those already converted to his Aristotelian principles. Yet for the dialectical purposes which should be seen behind the arguments, no more was needed.

6. A more important reason for not delaying here, is that it is precisely on the assumption that the received Christian view of providence is preserved—that God is indeed 'an agent through will and intellect'—that the arguments of the Theologians have their force.

The question under dispute was Whether God can do what he does not do, and leave aside what he is doing. Taking it that behind the question is a concern that God's power may not be up to demands on it, Aquinas begins his treatment of the Theologians' objections with:

it should be known that someone (*aliquis*) is said not to be able to do something or other, in two ways.

In one way, without qualification (*absolute*): when some one of the principles—one necessary to an action—does not extend to that action. (As, if a foot should be broken, a man cannot walk.)

In another way, in virtue of a supposition (*ex suppositione*). Given that the opposite of some action is put as being the case, the action cannot be done. (I cannot walk while I am sitting.) (*De pot.*, qu. 1, art. 5c, ed. Busa, *Opera*, 3: 189.)

As the *aliquis* may insinuate, these two ways are relevant to the case of common agents. In God, the *principia* necessary for action, and their bearing on action, make the case importantly different from that of common agency. Aquinas explains that in God's case, since he 'is an agent through intellect and will', three principles are to be considered (for possible failure to extend to some action): the intellect, the will, and the power of the nature involved. Since 'an understanding does not move, save in so far as it proposes to the will that which is naturally desirable to it', any shortcoming will show either as a shortcoming in power, or a shortcoming in what is willed to be done.

Aquinas takes it that the concern behind the question is that there might be a shortcoming of the kinds mentioned apropos of common agency. Without further rehearsal of the differences between common and divine agency, he goes straight to the reasons for which something might have to be denied outright to divine power: 'there are two ways in which God is said outright (*absolute*) not to be able to do something'. In one way, when the power of God does not extend into it. (As, when we say that God cannot bring it about that an affirmation and a negation should be simultaneously true, as appears from what was said above.)

Now in this way it cannot be said (*non potest dici*) that God cannot do [anything], save what he is doing; for it is established (*constat*) that the power of God can extend itself to many other things. The 'power of God' mentioned here cannot be the divine nature, for it is power to do things, in agency ad extra, which is in question. It is a power which already extends to things, and can be 'extended to many other things'. It is thus God's option-neutral power. Aquinas's first reply is then not about a possible shortcoming in the (supposedly actually infinite) power which God was held to be. It is about kinds of case in which "something" is being imagined to be of the (potentially infinite) set of "things" of God's option-neutral power—a 'power of God' which indeed 'can extend itself into many other things'—and which, for either of two kinds of reason, has to be accounted ineligible for the set.

No matter how great the number and variety of things we may suppose to be included in this set, it indeed 'extends to many other things'. But when "something" is understood not to satisfy the basic condition for membership—not to count minimally as an *ens*, and an *ens factum*—then it is for us (Aquinas says) to say outright that God cannot do it. (His example is "bringing it about that an affirmation and a negation should be simultaneously true".) On the other hand, "something other than God is actually doing"—for there to be flying pigs, perhaps, or a golden mountain—can well be of the set, satisfying the *ens* and *ens factum* conditions. If it is judged to be of the set, then it cannot consistently be said (on this first type of grounds for refusing attributions to divine power) that God cannot do it.

The second way in which God is to be said outright not to be able to do something is 'when the will of God cannot extend into it' (same ref.). The 'will of God' here refers to some volitum of God's, actual or envisaged, and the 'cannot' carries weight. The grounds for denial are not just that the will of God does not extend into the thing envisaged; not just that the thing envisaged is not a part of the actual *ordinatio dei*, is not a member of the set of things God can do in option-tied power. It is that no volitum of God can include it, that no "thing" of the sort envisaged can be instantiated as part of any *ordinatio dei*.

Aquinas gives part of the explanation of this in a way which takes up the point at issue in the question under discussion in the disputation, which is whether God's goodness does not necessitate him to confine what he does to the best he can do. Since what is concerned here, incidentally, is the goodness of some envisaged doings of God, it is not the goodness which is to be identified with the divine nature which is to be imagined to be in play here. It is the goodness of the kind we may judge to be in creatures, used in Aquinas's favoured analysis of 'God is good': God's "operant" goodness, we might call it, extending the application of an expression of Albert's, to stand disjunctively for his option-tied or option-neutral goodness.

Of these last, which is in question in the second grounds for outright denial of things to divine option-neutral goodness? If I have understood the text so far, the grounds for denial are that the putative "thing" envisaged is not of the set even of God's option-neutral goodness. What he says is:

> The end... of divine will is its goodness, which it cannot not will. But to this end creatures are not to be made commensurate, to the point that without them divine goodness could not (*non posset*) be manifested. For just as divine goodness is being manifested by these things which now are, and through this order of things; just so it could be manifested through other creatures, even creatures ordered in another way.

Yet if his intended doctrine in the question is plain enough, his expression is by no means plain throughout. Towards the end of the body of *De potentia*, qu. 1, art. 5 he says: *absolute deus potest facere alia quam quae fecit*. An unsuspecting hearer might be inclined to think that Aquinas here was (1) deliberately addressing a contention made by an objector (*absolute loquendo, non potest facere alia quam quae fecit*, arg. 2), and that like the objector he was (2) using *absolute* to refer to the mode of assertion, to wit *absque determinatione* as against *cum determinatione*. From a rhetorical point of view Aquinas's words could well have been chosen to counter, rhetorically, the force of the objector's conclusion; and he may well have been acting as in (1). What should not be missed where, as here, our concern ought to be with the logical relationships, is that in his reply to the objection (whose conclusion he indeed rejects, in line with the view he maintains consistently elsewhere) he ignores the objector's formulation, implying a reply by invoking instead a distinction between *potentia faciendi* [in effect, God's option-neutral goodness] *de qua est quaestio*, and *divinae actioni* [in effect, God's option-tied goodness]. In any case he is not to be seen acting as in (2), as though using *absolute* to refer to the mode of assertion; and hence need not be seen as reneguing on the policy set out by him in his first and most explicit account of the Distinction, and followed by him elsewhere. Likewise, he need not be imagined to have suddenly switched allegiance from the Power Distinction to the 'genuine distinction' expounded in modern times, and used for purposes of contrast towards the end of Chapter 6.

The contrasting expressions in play here are:

(1) absolute deus potest facere alia quam quae fecit, *and*

(2) ex suppositione potest dici quod deus non potest alia facere quam quae fecit.

But a clue not to be missed is in the reason cited by Aquinas for allowing (2): 'because [God] cannot [sans phrase] make contradictions to be simultaneously true'.

The trouble is with the phrase *alia quam quae fecit*, and it is of this phrase that Aquinas is speaking in the words with which he concludes the body of the present question. When the things mentioned in the phrase are taken *composite*, so that the phrase means (in effect) 'things taken as willed by God to be, being other than the things willed by God to be', a contradiction manifestly arises. For that reason, in view of what had been said earlier, *alia quam quae fecit* are merely putative 'things', which God must be said not to be able to do, sans phrase. But when the things mentioned in *alia quam quae fecit* are taken *divisim*, so that the phrase means in effect 'Avicennian essences of things, considered prescinding from their being willed by God or not, being other than the things willed by God to be', no contradiction appears, and *alia quam quae fecit* are not necessarily things which God *absque determinatione* cannot do.

Again, as at Chapter 6, Section 16, part of the difficulty is from the word *absolute*, which out of context can be equivalent either to *absque determinatione*, said of assertions, or *divisim*, said of concepts usable within assertions. In the present context in the *De potentia* it is harder than it was in the passage referred to there, to appreciate which sense is in question. Yet it is not quite so hard as it has been left to be, with (2) reported in the form given above. In the passage (2) is expanded with the helpful gloss,

supposito enim quod ipse non velit alia facere, vel quod praesciverit se alia non facturum, non potest alia facere [quam quae fecit], ut intelligatur composite, non divisim.

With that expansion—showing just how the "things" at bottom in question, the Avicennian essences, are being taken *composite*—it becomes clearer that the *absolute* in *absolute deus potest facere alia quam quae fecit* is to be taken to signify that the things being referred to in *alia* are to be taken *absolute* or *divisim* from their (not) being willed to be, or foreknown (not) to be going to be done.

The contrasting expressions in play can then be seen to amount to,

1(*a*) On the supposition that *alia quam quae fecit* is taken *absolute*, i.e. *divisim* from their not in fact being willed by God to be, or foreknown by God to be, God can do them, and

2(*a*) On the supposition that *alia quam quae fecit* is taken *composite*, i.e. here, being considered as not willed by God to be or not foreknown by God to be going to be, God cannot do them.[5]

In any case we have what amounts to a contrast which has by now become familiar, between

1(*b*) God can in his option-neutral power do things other than the things he has been doing (or is doing), and

2(*b*) God cannot in his option-tied power do things (not willed by him to be) other than the things he has been doing (or is doing).

In this passage in the *De potentia*, where Aquinas tackles the central Abelardian question by spelling out the *composite/divisim* move, perhaps the central move in his reply, he is also bringing out the central place of the *composite/divisim* move in the use of the Power Distinction. It is because such a move can be carried out, and not unless such a move can be carried out, that uses of the Distinction are not necessarily futile from the outset, in the way in which 'This is the case, yet this might not have been the case' may have to be seen as either futile or absurd (because of 'this').

7. Aquinas adds that the error of the Theologians was their in effect supposing that the actual order of things was commensurate with the divine goodness.

I rejected above the reading in which the divine goodness in question would be thought that which was identified with the divine nature, and the error imagined to be that of confounding creature and creator. A little more should be said, as Aquinas's

---

[5] 'On the supposition that' in either case here may have not only the sense of 'supposing that' which has survived in common speech, but in addition a connection with the more technical sense of assigning a particular type of *suppositio* to a term already taken to be carrying its ordinary signification. Cf. the use of *supponit absolute* in the text of Hugh of St Cher quoted at Ch. 3, n. 13 above.

use of the Distinction here confirms that his understanding of it was as portrayed in Chapter 6 above.

The goodness identified with the divine nature has an infinity which, if it can be spoken of at all, has to be spoken of as the infinity of a class, not of a set. And nothing mensurate, however great or small—no set, however great or small—can properly be said to be 'commensurate' with it (with its actual infinity).[6] Thinking that something might be, would certainly involve error. But it would be a particularly gross error on the part of the Theologians. They would have had to believe either that the divine nature was capable of being measured up to (and thus was not actually as against potentially infinite), or that something ordered by God was actually infinite (and thus not an ordered multiplicity, which is absurd), which would mean either that there was more than one actual infinite (which is absurd), or that God is not actually infinite (which is absurd, if 'God' is to stand for something which exists, though not in any determinate way). Absurdities quite so obvious tended to be avoided by theologians; in those days, at any rate. In addition, the error involved would not have been an error to do especially with freedom or necessity in God's action, as is called for by Aquinas's argument. So although the first reading would result in something true, and consistent with Aquinas's formulas, it would not seem to be the one to pursue.

On a second reading of the contention that the error of the Theologians was in effect supposing that the actual order of things was commensurate with the divine goodness, 'divine goodness' is taken not to designate the divine nature, but to express divine option-neutral goodness, *bonitas absoluta dei*, as at Chapter 6, Section 7 above.

On this second reading the error of the Theologians is to suppose that the set of things actually willed by God is commensurate with the set of things which could be willed by God, without prejudice to preserving a goodness etc. in them, of essentially the same kind as is (supposed) manifested in the actual order of things. Two sets are in question, so talk of their being 'commensurate' or not is to the point. And the error here does

---

[6] 'If something is potentially infinite,... then it is not even possible for it to be actually infinite' (A. Moore, *The Infinite* (1990), 39, following Aristotle).

have something to do with freedom or necessity in God's action. If only what now is, is good, and God can do only what is good in that sense, then of course it is going to look as though God can do nothing save what now is. An error very close to that was the one which the adversaries of Abelard had feared.

If it is in order to avoid that kind of error that Aquinas is deploying the Power Distinction here, then the understanding of the Distinction as being between two ways of understanding God's power to do things external to his nature, would seem to be confirmed.

8. Replies to objections provide both confirmation of the interpretation argued, and connections with related notions, from earlier authors especially.

In ad 11 he makes use of *nosse* to claim for God *nosse* both of (1) all his own power (*totam potentiam suam*), and (2) whatever he is capable of ad extra (*quidquid potest*). By (1) he apparently wishes to refer to that power of God held identical with the divine nature. By (2) he apparently means what he calls in the same reply 'the excogitated schemas of all the things which he can do', and what are to be identified with the "things" he can do in option-neutral power.

In St Augustine *nosse* is used for knowledge which a human knower has in a quasi-habitual manner, and without epistemic recourse to anything external to his own *homo interior*.[7] Are we to take it that Aquinas is here using *nosse* for something like Bonaventure's knowledge *in habitu*: the knowledge which God may be supposed to have, whether or not he ever does execute anything ad extra. God's *nosse* will then be that (purely speculative) knowledge which Aquinas elsewhere calls *scientia simplicis intelligentiae*, as distinguished from *scientia visionis* (the analogate in God's case to '*cogitatio*' in Augustine's humans), which concerns only the actual created order. But if this is so, it means that more must be said on 'the excogitated schemas of all the things which he can do'.

In the same objection it had been asserted that 'God does not

---

[7] See G. Verbeke, 'Connaissance de soi et connaissance de Dieu chez s. Augustin', *Augustiniana*, 4 (1954), 495–515; and 'De ontwikkeling van het menselijk kennen', *Tijdschrift voor Filosofie*, 15 (1953), 195–22. Cf. G. B. Matthews, 'Augustine on Speaking from Memory', *Am. Phil. Qu.* 2 (1965), 89–92; and L. Moonan, 'Word Meaning', *Philosophy*, 51 (1976), 195–207.

have ideas, save of those things which he has made, or is making, or is going to make'; or 'do', in each case. With some hesitation ('It seems to have to be said... ') he replies that if 'idea' is meant to name the individualised form of some artefact, then indeed 'those things which neither are, nor were, nor will be, yet which God can do' do not have any idea corresponding to them. But if 'idea' should be taken as an unfulfilled schema, such as is merely excogitated in the intellect of an artisan, in this way they have an idea' (ad 11). But if 'idea' should be taken as an unfulfilled schema, such as is merely excogitated in the intellect of an artisan, then in this way the "things" which neither are, nor were, nor will be, yet which God can do, indeed have an idea corresponding to them (ad 11). The "things" of God's option-neutral power are to be seen as being precisely "unfulfilled schemas" of this sort, such as the ideas or designs which may be elaborated and entertained by us without even being intended for execution.[8]

9. The only "excogitations" spoken of here, as should not be missed, are in the mind of the creaturely artisan who is being referred to for purposes of comparison. The point of comparison lies in the fact that a creaturely artisan can know the contents of "ideas" he may have elaborated, without necessarily putting the ideas into execution, or even having any intention of doing so: 'For it is obvious in the created artisan', Aquinas adds, 'that he excogitates some operations which he never intends to put into effect.'

There is no "excogitating" in God, just as there is no capacity for arguing stepwise or telling the time. In such activities partial fulfilment and reference to embodiment are of the essence. I recall this here, because of an interesting feature of God's option-tied power, implicitly recognised by Aquinas but worth spelling out a little.

You and I and other intelligent creatures can excogitate "things" which God can in option-neutral power do. At any given time the set of such excogitates will be determinate, finite. But in principle we could go on excogitating the like. Even without supposing, with Aristotle and Avicenna, the perpetuity of the

---

[8] For Aquinas on Ideas and exemplars see *ST* 1/44/3c and 1/15/1c, and cf. J. Bittremieux, 'Ideae divinae de possibilibus', *ETL* 3 (1926), 57–62.

world of generation and change, but supposing, with the medieval
schoolmen generally, that God maintains intelligent creatures in
perpetuity *a parte post*, the set of things doable by God, and
excogitated by intelligent creatures, can itself be indefinitely great.
The creaturely excogitations in such a case are part of the
(ordered) set of God's option-tied power; which in that case must
itself be indefinitely great in its extension. If we suppose, therefore,
that intelligent creatures, maintained in perpetuity *a parte post*,
continue to excogitate in this way, it will follow that not only
God's option-neutral power but even his option-tied power is
potentially infinite (in respect of its extensive).[9]

In their specific content, however, these "excogitates" of
creatures have as such no existence outside of their excogitator's
mind. Hamlet's device to betray his uncle into confirming the
ghost's message could have been excogitated by someone as
being the sort of thing instantiable by God, if he wished. Even
so, God's knowledge of the contents in question is knowledge
simplicis intelligentiae only—the "things" excogitated by creatures
are known to God only as any other "things" of his option-
neutral power are known. Merely by being excogitated by some
intelligent creature, a "thing" does not become instantiated as
an item in the world of the categories; even if specifically the
same "thing" could be so instantiated, if God so wished (whether
through execution by the same creature responsible for the
excogitation, or otherwise). Creatures do not as it were take
God's hand and show him what to write into creation.

10.   Another objection permits him a comment on 'the reasons
by which God acts', which according to the Pseudo-Denis are
'productive of the things which exist' (obj. 10). We are to
understand these 'reasons', Aquinas says, not as notions serving
as exemplars of actual existents, but as notions or recipes which
could serve, if God so chose, as such exemplars. These instantiable
notions of things, abstract recipes of a type according to which
things could be brought about are the "things" of the set of
God's option-neutral power. They are *rationes productivae entium*,

---

[9] Tamen, si diligentius consideretur, necesse est dicere quod deus etiam scientia
visionis sciat infinita. Quia deus scit etiam cogitationes et affectiones cordium, quae
in infinitum multiplicabuntur, creaturis rationalibus permanentibus absque fine. (*ST*
1/14/12c.)

as Denis (or his translator) had said, but only on condition of understanding *productivae entium* in that abstract way. In yet another reply the same "things" are called *hae quae facienda sunt* (ad 13): in the sense not of "things which are to be brought about", like tomorrow's sunrise, but of "things of a nature fit to be brought about", like the unicorn.

What all these varied descriptions permit is a clearer idea of the elements of God's option-neutral power. 'Recipes capable of being dispensed', 'abstract ideas of things capable of existing', 'unfulfilled schemas', 'merely entertained contents or plans of things, not necessarily intended for execution, analogous to the plans excogitated but not intended for execution by creaturely artisans': all of these can be taken as pointers to a better understanding of the Power Distinction. At a later stage these, and other pointers, will be exploited.

SHIPMENTS OF DIVINE POWER?

11. Aquinas's strategy here shows the Power Distinction in use in one of its most typical ways. The question asked was whether God has it in him to do anything other than what he is actually doing. The questioner's interest is thus analogous to that of the anxious parent who enquires whether the newly qualified surgeon is up to operating successfully on the child's tumour. It is not to be understood as "really" being about actual outcomes: Will God do something that is not scheduled for doing, Will the surgeon operate successfully, important as such questions may also be to the questioner. Equally, it is not to be understood as the question of an impartial, scientifically curious biographer. It is a question from an interested questioner. Is this colleague really the sort of woman to go tiger-hunting with? Is the surgeon really up to that sort of operation?

Faced with Abelard's question as to whether God can do what he is not doing, Aquinas is put as an exponent of Negative Theology in the kind of embarrassment noted at Chapter 1, Section 4 above. He cannot, as a consistent exponent of Negative Theology on the divine nature, know anything about the divine nature: not the least glimmer. On the other hand, it could be evasive to pretend that Abelard had "really" been asking about outcomes. The anxious parent is not "really" asking whether the operation will be successful: he may have been assured already that that sort of knowledge is not available. Abelard was certainly not asking whether God was going to do what God was going to do. (Neither was he asking whether God could do something such that God could do it and not do it.) He might well have liked to have had the kind of information sought by a scientifically curious biographer. Critics reproached him for "curiosity" of a type not too far removed from that. Aquinas, however, cannot as an exponent of Negative Theology on the divine nature, either provide that sort of information, or expect to have it in the actual state and situation of man. In view of his views on divine simplicity, and on the absence of a *quid est* in God's case, it is rather Aquinas's opinion that that sort of information is not there to be provided on God. On his own admissions he can say nothing intelligible (literally significant) about divine power itself, the power to be identified with the divine nature. He can label it 'divine infinite power', but if the questioner wishes to know whether this is infinitely great, infinitely puny, infinitely nugatory, or whatever, Aquinas is apparently bound to be unhelpful. Even when asked whether divine power is less unlike the kind of power that comes out of the barrel of a gun, or the kind expressible in the smile of an infant, or of a Marilyn Monroe, he evidently cannot say. Deists and their successors, by contrast, would like to tell us all if not more than can be known about it.

12.   What Aquinas can provide, thanks to the Power Distinction, is an answer to an "interested question"—analogous to the questions of the prospective tiger-hunter and the anxious parent. The kind of move which this sort of answer involves, is worth looking at more closely. A comparison may be instructive: with a move entertained rather flippantly by Quine, and dismissed by him, for overcoming a problem with some analogous features. There is a difficulty, from Quinian starting-points, about the question: Did Heraclitus step this morning into the same water he stepped into yesterday? The difficulty is that 'water', like 'sugar' is a "mass term", and does not lend itself to that kind of use of 'same water'. Prof. Geach had raised a difficulty on such grounds, and Prof. Quine considered the following possible response:

A mass term like 'water' or 'sugar' does not primarily admit 'same' or 'an'. When it is subjected to such particles, some special individuating standard is understood from the circumstances. Typically, 'same sugar' might allude to sameness of shipment. Now in the sense in which one resists saying that Heraclitus bathed in the same water twice, a water is the aggregate only of molecules that were near a man when he once bathed. But a river is not such a water. (W. V. O. Quine, in *Phil. Rev.* 73 (1964), 102.)

A cynic might wonder how "sameness of shipment" came so quickly to mind, rather than sameness of kind, for example, and whether Professor Quine's imaginary puzzle-solver might not have been trading to some extent on the fact that shipments of sugar fairly typically discriminate between kinds of sugar: demer-ara in the forward hold, muscovado in the after, or whatever. The same cynic might also wonder why Heraclitus is bathing, rather than stepping into his river, and whether it had anything to do with the likelihood that 'an aggregate only of molecules that were near a man when he once' stepped into a river, would not necessarily be 'a water' in the relevant sense: it could just as well be "an air", "an air and water mixture with a weed or two and the odd guppy", or something of the sort. Cavils apart, though, there is a suggestion of value here. For certain reasons to do with the limitations which using mass terms in certain kinds of context involve, there are times when we might not seem able (as good Quinians) to offer a sensible reply using 'sugar' or 'water', yet we do wish to make a reply, since there is something in what is being put to us, or in leaving it unchallenged, which we might wish to resist. On some such occasions at least, we can sensibly reply: talking not about sugar or water, but about shipments of sugar or dollops of water. For a Quinian's purposes, what makes 'shipment of sugar' attractive is doubtless that (unlike 'sugar') it is a term of divided reference, admitting 'same' or 'an' readily. Quine, as is worth repeating, rejects the solution he has envisaged, but it can suggest something to the point here.

When Aquinas answers a questioner, referring to God's power to accomplish things either in option-tied power or in option-neutral power, he is making a parallel move: as though to reply in terms of shipments of divine power, or possible shipments of it. Parallel, but not the same. A shipment of sugar, in the sense which interests Quine here, is of the sugar kind. It is also (unlike sugar, this time) one and one only shipment of the sugar kind. Any or all of God's option-tied or option-neutral power is not necessarily of the divine kind. (In narrower sense of 'kind' nothing is, in Aquinas's view: the divine nature is in no species or genus.) God's option-tied power, like God, exists in extra-mental reality. Unlike God, it exists dependently, and may or may not be potentially infinite. God's option-neutral power is potentially infinite, and (unlike God) is not, considered in itself, any actual infinite. (Saying of a child that he is a potential footballer implies that he will be an actual footballer later, or has it in him to become an actual footballer. Saying of something that it is a potential infinite, or is infinite potentially, is not to imply that it will be an actual infinite when it grows up. It implies rather that it is not and can never become an actual infinite.) Rather like the perpetuity of the motion of the spheres in the *Timaeus*, which is 'a moving image of eternity', God's option-neutral power presents us with "an image of infinity", a reasonable surrogate of divine infinity; one we can reason with stepwise, in the way proper to rational animals. And what can be done in God's option-neutral power, unlike God, does not—considered in itself—exist in extra-mental reality, but like our understanding of God, and of the divine attributes, is a fiction of our understanding, with *esse intentionale* merely.

Yet not just any question asking what God can do, is necessarily one which the Power Distinction can particularly help the person asked, to answer. Take the questions 'Can God save my family from the plague?', 'Could God have saved my family from the plague?' These are unlikely to be the questions of a disinterested scientific inquirer, though they conceivably could be. They may still be of either of two importantly different types. In one the words are used to express an immediately practical question, susceptible of being answered with truth only as some corresponding factual question is to be answered. If the plague is a current threat and I ask 'Can God save my family?', out of human ignorance of outcomes, it is hardly surprising if I receive the same answer 'I do not know either' which I might have expected in reply to something like 'Will my family escape the plague?' If I ask out of doubt or ignorance as to whether any such escape ought to be attributed to God, I can expect the answer which the same speaker could give to 'Will God save my family... ?': 'Yes, if he chooses to; No, if he does not', if the person answering subscribes to Christian views on Providence. The past-tense question shows parallel possibilities, save that (if I am speaking about my family) I cannot be in ignorance about the fact of my family's survival. From both past-tense and future-tense questions of this general type, we can reach hypothetical answers which in turn invite questions of a different type.

We may have answers of the form

God can do A, if he chooses to, or
God can do A, whether or not he chose to.

If 'But can he?' is now raised, as it can be, the question no longer even can concern either the factual matter of whether A is (going to be) done, or the related, supervenient matter of whether A is (going to be) willed by God. These are expressly set aside. What remains is a question about whether God is strong enough to do A, regardless of whether he chooses to do so. The answer here has to be, Yes: provided that A satisfies the conditions for belonging to the set of things God can do in option-neutral power, and provided in the first place that some God exists. If, as for Aquinas, the conditions for belonging to the set are satisfied by any integral form, or ordered set of such forms, i.e. anything which could count as both a "thing" at all in the metaphysics he followed, and as instantiable, there could be literally nothing which God could be said not to be strong enough to do.

Of course an answer of this kind—say, 'God can in option-neutral power save the family from the plague, whether or not he chooses to do so'—is not going to answer the concerns of someone asking 'Can God save my family?' as an immediately practical question. What such a person would need to know, to have his concerns satisfied, is whether God can in option-tied power do so.

Yet these are not the only concerns which a questioner can be thought to have. We ought to resist the move to say here that what the questioner "really wants" to know in all cases is the answer to the question about what God can do in option-tied power. We ought to, in part, from a general resistance to the suggestion that someone else can tell me what I "really want" to know. I may need to know something other than I am asking, in order to be able to do something further; but that is not the same thing. And we ought to, because the questioner almost certainly does want to know whether God is strong enough to save his family, whether or not he has the slightest intention of doing so. Ordinary questioners like to know what sort of person they are dealing with, whether or not any limiting characteristics seem to be in play in a given transaction. This is not always because it can make any difference to the particular transaction, but sometimes for what it permits them to take up as a more general stance about things. On the range of things on which they are interested questioners, this is certainly so. Compare: 'The landlord couldn't renew the barrier in time, so when exceptional floods came they destroyed half the village', and 'The landlord could easily have finished the barrier. He refused, the swine!'

13.   Aquinas must as a consistent exponent of Negative Theology reply to the questioner: 'I cannot tell you of what sort God is', but may add 'I can tell you of what sorts God is not, and in addition I can tell you endlessly about the sorts of things of which he is capable; will that do?' By being able to say what God can or cannot do in option-neutral power, Aquinas can tell us of the sorts of things of which God is capable. We can then know how we might wish to respond to things.

If my desires are for something impossible—a not unheard of phenomenon, and something of a cliché in certain genres of romantic literature—then the knowledge that even God's power cannot satisfy them might induce me to be more realistic. If they are for something involving *inordinatio*, I might be open to persuasion that at any rate it would hardly be reasonable for me to expect much positive assistance from God in the matter. But where they are perfectly reasonable, and where I was assured that, for example, God could perfectly well save my family from the plague, and was just determined not to do so, then at least my response is in my control, and is informed through the knowledge I have gained. It is in my control, for example, to choose some variant or other of the *Quid hoc ad aeternitatem* approach, or 'let not my will but thine be done'. It is equally in my control to reject the supremacy of morals—as in the 'brief

Galilean vision'—and submit to God's determination none the less;[10] or indeed to choose what might be the only way for someone who wished to stand on strictly moral principle: some variant of the advice of Job's wife, 'Curse God and die'.

In much of modern philosophical theology this rather elementary point—that, in general, people like to know what sort of transagent they are dealing with—has been systematically obscured. Our practical concern is with what has to be done next, with what we need to fear or hope for. (This could be true, perhaps true by definition.) Never mind anything beyond what is called for in satisfaction of our hopes or fears. (Even if commands could follow logically, this one would be a non sequitur.) In philosophy generally the modern period has been marked by a shift of interest from metaphysics to epistemology, and in some quarters a readiness to take our "ideas" as the bounds of all our knowledge. In "natural theology" the narrowing is marked in a detectable shift from viewing God on the model of the Homeric Householder portrayed in Aristotle's *Politics*, to viewing God as the Great Testator (*ordinator*) whose character is none of our business but whose dispositions for us are crucial. This has been noted in Luther:

When Luther said we cannot know God but must have faith, it is clear enough that the inability he speaks of is a logical one: there is not some comprehensible activity we cannot perform, and equally not some incomprehensible activity we cannot perform. Our relation to God is that of parties to a testament (or refusers of it); and Luther's logical point is that you do not accept a promise by knowing something about the promisor. (S. Cavell, in 'The avoidance of love', at *Must we mean what we say? A Book of Essays* (Cambridge [1976; reissue of 1969 text] xxix + 365 pp., 324.)

A la limite, this makes philosophical theology somewhat pointless, and later writers in post-Reformation traditions were not blate in saying so. (Even when, like Barth, they were engaged in what, to an observer's view, was rather sophisticated philosophical theology.) In the present connection this narrowing typically

[10] 'The brief Galilean vision of humility flickered throughout the ages, uncertainly.... It dwells upon the tender elements in the world, which slowly and in quietness operate by love... Love neither rules, nor is it unmoved; also it is a little oblivious as to morals.' (A. N. Whitehead, *Process and Reality: An Essay in Cosmology* (1929; repr. New York, 1960), xii + 544 pp., 520–1.)

takes the form of saying that the only "real" meaning of 'Can God ___' is 'Can God in option-tied power ___'.

This was not Aquinas's way. He allows a move analogous to the "shipments of divine power" move, in a manner typical of his approach to attributing things to God generally, and consistently with a Negative Theology. He insists on the importance of our option-neutral assertions: only an option-neutral denial ('God cannot in option-neutral power do A'), not necessarily an option-tied denial, licenses the denial sans phrase of a putative attribution to divine power ('God cannot do A'). Yet he does not deny that only what is the case in option-tied power—whether past, present, or future—should govern our fears and hopes: only 'God can in option-tied power do A', not 'God can in option-neutral power do A', may license 'God can do A' sans phrase. His dispute with the moderns here is not so much over theology as over what the world is, and in particular what people are. What I can know, what I ought to do, what—if I do what I ought to do—I can hope for, does not necessarily add up to what is man in a God-ordered universe. Parties to a testament can be discontent with the dispositions made for them. Their discontent, like their role, need be of no more than what Heidegger called merely 'ontic' significance. Aquinas's people can have a discontent of 'ontological' significance: discontent not just because things are distressing (or pleasing), but because things can always be distressing (or pleasing); and from something independent of the natures of the things considered in themselves.

SUMMA THEOLOGIAE 1/25/5 (1266–8).

14. In the *Summa theologiae* the Power Distinction is addressed to the same Abelardian question faced in the *De potentia*: Whether God can do things which he is not doing. Within that question, it is addressed to the solution of an objection which runs:

God cannot do things which he has not foreknown and foreordained that he will do;
But he has not foreknown or foreordained that he will do [anything] save the things which he is doing;

Therefore he cannot do [anything] save the things which he is doing.

This sets the scope: it is God's power to bring about things external to his nature which is in question. Aquinas begins his answer by contrasting God's operations and ours, and arguing:

In God, power and being, will and understanding, and wisdom and justice is the same thing;
Whence there can be nothing in a divine power which cannot be in a just will of his, and in a just understanding of his.

Out of context, the first line might be taken as concerning the divine nature, with *in deo* then meaning "in the divine nature". It is not given out of context, however, but within the scope noted. Also, *in nobis* concerns a point not about our nature but about our operations; *in deo* likewise is to be understood to concern a point about God's operations, not his nature. As for the second line, it quite plainly refers to divine operations, and could be taken, even out of context, to do so; save perhaps by a reader labouring under the impression that Aquinas is some kind of Deist. The explication he gives, therefore, should be understood along the lines:

In the case of divine operations ad extra, what the operant power is, what is done, what is willed, what is understood, what is wisely ordered, and what is justly done, is the same thing;
Whence there can be nothing... (as above).

Aquinas then explains how he is taking these here (in themselves, or in relation to actualisation). 'Because the will is not determined of necessity to this or that, save perhaps *ex suppositione*, as was said above (qu. 19, art. 3); and [because] neither are God's wisdom and justice determined to this order, as was said above (in the body of the present question): there is nothing to prevent there being something in God's power which he does not will, and which is not contained within the order which he has established in things.'

The will which is not determined to this or that is precisely what might be called God's option-neutral will, the set of things which are apt to be willed by God. This is the same set (in

extension) as the set of things which God can do in option-
neutral power, so of course 'there is nothing to prevent there
being something in God's power [i.e. in the set of things which
he can in option-neutral power bring about] which he does not
will'. Even 'contained within the order' is worth noting. Each of
the things which God can be said to be able in option-neutral
power to bring about, is an 'order' in itself, and may contain
orders within itself which themselves could be considered as
things which God can in option-neutral power bring about.
Instantiable orders can thus contain orders themselves instantiable, without either the contained or the containing order ever
being actualised, or 'established in things'. So of course 'there is
nothing to prevent there being something in God's power [i.e.
in the set of things which God can in option-neutral power bring
about] which . . . is not contained within the order which he has
established in things'.

We have already seen *potentia exsequens* used (in Alexander of
Hales) for power over things. In the present question of Aquinas's
Summa, God's 'exsequent power' is equivalent to God's 'operant
power' in Albert's usage, for all or any of the power attributed
to God to bring about things external to his nature, whether
such power is being considered in its intrinsic content, or in its
being actualised in extra-mental reality within the actual order
of things. Likewise, God's *voluntas* is being understood as *imperans
(aliquid)*, his *intellectus* and *sapientia* as *dirigens (aliquid)*. We are thus
concerned here with different aspects of God's operation ad
extra, and confirmation for the interpretation argued for above
comes from Aquinas's own words. Because this is how 'power'
and the others are to be understood here, he continues,

what is attributed to [divine operant] power considered in itself, God
is said to be able to do in option-neutral power (*dicitur deus posse secundum
potentiam absolutam*).

The *secundum potentiam absolutam* "determines" *posse*, and the *dictio*
concerned in the *dicitur* is an assertion *cum determinatione*. What is
it that is attributed to divine operant power considered in itself,
and which God is said to be able to do in option-neutral power?
He tells us:

Of this description is everything in which the schematic notion of a
something-which-is is satisfied, as was said above (art. 3).

Everything, in other words, which satisfies the *ens* condition, just as in *SCG*; every Avicennian essence.

He balances his brief explication of option-neutral power with one of option-tied power:

What is attributed to divine [operant] power in so far as it executes the command of a just will, God is said to be able to do in option-tied power (*hoc dicitur deus posse facere de potentia ordinata*).

From all this, he says, 'it must be said that God can in option-neutral power bring about things other than the things which he has foreknown and foreordained that he will bring about; but it cannot be that he should do some things which he would not have foreknown and foreordained that he would do'. The logical point about scope which he is using there, is straightforward enough, but he adds a rationale for his choice of scope:

Because the bringing about of something lies subject to foreknowledge and foreordination, but not the being able to, which is natural [i.e. holds, if it does hold, in virtue of what is in the nature of the thing in question], for that reason 'God brings something about because he wills to' is true, but it is not true for the particular reason 'God can [bring it about], because he wills to', but [for the reason]'... because it is as it is in the nature [of the thing in question]'. (1/25/5c.)

Both the *naturale* there and the *in sua natura* are to be understood as referring to the thing's own nature, not the divine nature.

Any volitum of God's has to be immutably willed by God, whether the things contained in it are immutably willed to be executed within it in a contingent or a necessary manner. The conclusion of *ST* 1/19/3 runs:

Whence, since the goodness of God is complete (*perfecta*) and can be without other things (since nothing in the way of perfection accrues to him from other things), it follows that it is not absolutely necessary for him to will things other than himself. And yet it is necessary *ex suppositione*: for if it is supposed that he has willed, he cannot not will, because his will cannot change. (*ST* 1/19/3c.)

What he could have willed, however, speaking purely abstractly, with a 'could have' in option-neutral power, is an order in which all the Avicennian essences—or at any rate all the ones which concern us—are willed first to be actualised, then not: and all for God's own goodness. Such an order, if willed, would have been willed just as immutably as the actual one, or as any other order willed by God. It is not strictly the immutability of the willing, any more than the intrinsic nature of the order, which is crucial in accommodating such beliefs as 'God has sworn and will not repent', that the actual order will not be abandoned or supplanted.

AQUINAS'S USE OF THE DISTINCTION

15.   Aquinas uses the Distinction more than a score of times— quite a few more, depending on how you count uses—from the earliest work of his career as a master in theology, to works of his last years. In view of the pother raised in later times over how Scotus, Ockham, Holcot, Woodham, and others would be seen to use it, it may be of interest to list the various things which Aquinas was prepared to assert that God was able in option-neutral power to do:

He could have brought it about that the Father, and the Holy Ghost, might have taken flesh (*In 3 Sent.* d. 1, qu. 2, art. 3, ed. Moos, par. 119);

that the head of a (typical) man could be lower on his body, and his feet higher (same, par. 117);

that the nature assumed by the three divine Persons in the event of their all taking flesh could be one by the unity of a single (created) nature (*In 3 Sent.*, d. 1, qu. 2, art. 4, ed. Moos, par. 131);

that God can take on, in an incarnation, any creaturely nature he wishes to, no creature being inherently more "assumable" than any other (*In 3 Sent.*, d. 2, qu. 1, art. 1, Moos, par. 17);

that God could have taken on an irrational created nature (*In 3 Sent.*, d. 2, qu. 1, art. 1, Moos, par. 22);

... an angelic nature (*In 3 Sent.*, d. 2, qu. 2, art. 1, Moos, par. 25);

... a human nature of the female sex (*In 3 Sent.*, d. 12, qu. 3, art. 2, Moos, par. 86);

that God can reveal someone's damnation to him (*De verit.*, qu. 23, art. 8 ad 2);

that God can do things other than those which are [in the actual order of things] subject to his providence (*SCG* III, ch. 98);

that the perfection of grace [roughly: the benefit brought by grace in the actual order of things] could have been conferred on the human race otherwise than by the Incarnation of Christ (*Contra errores Graecorum*, I, ch. 16);

God can do everything in which the notion of a being can be satisfied (*ST* 1/25/5 ad 1);

God could have done other things than those which he has foreknown and pre-ordained that he will do (same *ST* 1/25/5 ad 1);

God could change the will of the demon to good (*De malo*, 16, art. 5 ad 13);

God can return the whole of creation into nothing (*Quodlibet IV*, qu. 3, art. 4c).[11]

The range of possibilities entertained is wide enough, but Aquinas takes care not to encourage unsatisfiable expectations. In the *In 3 Sent.* passage in which he introduced the Distinction, and answered that in God's option-neutral power the Father could have taken flesh in an incarnation, he also added: but it is not to be expected. And in the body of his response at *In 4 Sent.*, d. 45, qu. 2, art. 1a, ed. Busa, *Opera*, 1: 653, where he alludes to the Distinction, saying that things possible to be wrought by prayer extend to all the things which come under option-tied power, he is careful not so much as to mention any balancing option-neutral consideration. He thus shows himself aware of the rhetorical force of the Distinction.

In the later uses of the Distinction there is a perceptible shift to more general applications, rather than the narrowly theological applications prominent in the Sentence Commentary. God can in option-neutral power do things other than those which are

---

[11] The passage from *Quodlibet XII*, ad 2, dating from towards Christmas of 1270, which appears in Busa (ed.), *Opera*, 6: 1 as '*potentiae dei absolutae*', is to be read as '*potentiae dei, absolute*', as the context requires; and is not to be thought an omission from the present list.

[in the actual order of things] subject to his providence (*SCG*), things other than those which he has foreknown and pre-ordained that he will do (*ST*), indeed everything in which the notion of a being can be satisfied (*ST*). From the narrowly theological applications inherited from the pioneers of the Distinction, as seen at Chapters 2 and 3 above, he has moved perceptibly to an emphasis on application in issues of higher generality. Even there, however, he remains conscious of rhetorical niceties. The *SCG* mentions 'providence', an essentially philosophical topic, and of possible interest to audiences well outside the theology schools, and perhaps outwith Christianity. The *ST* retains 'foreknow' and 'pre-ordain', with their more narrowly theological resonances, more at home in the theology schools.

16. A point which remains to be spelled out is what (pragmatic) rules Aquinas is using, to permit him to use the Distinction, while acknowledging that whatever is ordered by God for execution is executed punctiliously and without fail, and that the actual order of things is ordered freely by God not to be supplanted or replaced.

In fact, no special rules are needed. If the arms of the Distinction are to be analysed as he has indicated, and as will be spelled out in Chapter 9 below, then no problem need arise. Both arms are to be seen as at bottom about Avicennian essences, considered in themselves in the option-neutral arm, and *divisim* from any instantiation; considered as instantiated in extra-mental reality (ordered by God) in the option-tied arm, and *composite* with either being willed by God to be, or not being willed by God to be. Moreover, when the arms are analysed into the narrowly predicative or composing-apt propositions which each demands, it can be seen that the insistence that the basic Avicennian essences should be taken *composite* in the one case, *divisim* in the other, is not settled arbitrarily in each case. It is settled in accordance with general principles for taking the terms concerned in their proper contexts within narrowly predicative or composing-apt propositions, and in accordance with general principles for drawing inferences from 'mixed' conjunctions, where the conjuncts are propositions not of the same type.

By his ordinary principles for analysing and using scientifically serious assertions, Aquinas has no difficulty in accommodating the force of the option-tied assertions of the Power Distinction. He might, if he wished, accommodate 'Necessarily, There are grunting pigs' or 'It is impossible for there to be flying pigs'—in unanalysed speech. If they are to be supposed to some scientifically serious purpose, their analyses will need composing-apt propositions, just as assertions generally do, where strictly logical modalities are understood to be in play. Any truth-making specific content which composing-apt propositions may have, is an object of some creature's judgement, with *esse intentionale* merely. As such, it is therefore not among those things—all the things of extra-mental reality—which can be seen as ordered to God's will. Being willed by God to be, is not itself an intrinsic feature of the sort of thing which even can be willed by God to be. To say that something is willed by God to be, is to imply that (*a*) it is being considered in relation to a cause of its existence in extra-mental reality, and (*b*) is so caused. To say that something is not willed by God to be, is to imply that (*a*) it is being considered in relation to a cause of its existence, and (*b'*) is not so caused. So considered, it is necessary, and Aquinas has no reason to dispute that. But the "it" or "something" which is being considered here, is in itself an object of creaturely thought, and consideration is surely a species of creaturely thought. The necessity may indeed be absolute, and not mere *ex suppositione* "necessity", but is to be located in our intelligent speeches, not in the things of God's ordering. Aquinas's use of the Distinction thus raises no special perplexities, invokes no special ad hoc rules to avoid such perplexities, and is consonant with his use of significant speech to scientifically serious purpose generally.

8

Beyond Paris's Theology Faculty

The Power Distinction developed within the Theology Faculty of the University of Paris; flourishing there at a time when that Faculty dominated academic theology in the Latin West. Some of the earliest users were men who played no slight part in the final establishment of the University and of the Faculty. Even those who, like Aquinas or Roland of Cremona, had come to Paris with already formed views in academic matters, or the many who went on to play a part in non-academic life, had it in common that they studied or taught within the Theology Faculty there. In the fourteenth century some commentators would suggest that the Distinction itself was something peculiarly Parisian. By then, that might not have seemed convincing. If anything, the Distinction had come to be of less obvious interest in Paris than in, say, Oxford or Cambridge, where Scotus, Ockham, Holcot, and Woodham had taken it up with some enthusiasm. I can recall being sceptical of the commentators' claims, at a time when I was more familiar with the later Power Distinction texts than with those of the period covered in the present book. It would now appear that the fourteenth-century commentators were amply justified. The problématique to which the Distinction was addressed had been made more acute by the man who had done more than anyone to establish an inde-pendent, inquiring spirit on the Montagne Ste Geneviève, Peter Abelard; it was transmitted to later generations by an academic object-text composed by a bishop of Paris, Peter Lombard; and it was addressed as part of the regular programme of study only by men already schooled in dialectics, and exposed to the Avicennian metaphysics favoured not least by some of the Faculty's own founders. The earliest uses so far recorded are indeed from the narrow entourage of the very same men, secular priests all, who were also pioneering institutionally, in setting the

Faculty of Theology and the University itself on a firm footing. There is surely room for an anthropologically informed study of this creative group and its doings. In any case, and at the very least, the specifically Parisian ambience of the Distinction's early uses, in the period dealt with in Chapters 2–8 above, cannot be ignored.

In the present chapter we see the Distinction move beyond the homogeneous community and sub-culture within which it had been flourishing. We see it alluded to in a discussion addressed to canonists, in a use foreshadowing later, political uses. We see it used to make a point in natural philosophy, which after the Black Death was to take up increasingly the attentions of the best thinkers, who in the period of this book had tended to do their chief work in theology. We see it used by a conservative theologian, in a prima-facie traditional theological context; but with a formula anticipating one made current by the greatest of the *novatores* of the sixteenth century. In sum, we see it begin to spread into the regions of politics and science where—historians have often suggested—it should be seen as seminal in the formation of the modern world.[1] The suggestions have never yet been proved entirely convincingly, for all the necessary steps, and will remain far from being proved when the necessary step provided in this book is completed. But they can be seen to be at least capable of being made good. The contributions from Robert Kilwardby and Roger Bacon in Oxford, and that of the canonist Hostiensis on the fringes of the papal curia, demonstrate that much. Not least interesting historically, however, is the reference to the Distinction in a frankly unscientific work by Hugh of Strasbourg, much used, it would appear, by pious writers and literary people and non-academic preachers: an early bridge, perhaps, from the Distinction's narrowly scholastic origins to a wider (and less prepared) audience than any that could be looked for in the schools. More than a century would pass between the deaths of Aquinas and Bonaventure, and the disturbance caused in the entourage of Chaucer by the narrow

[1] A. de Libera, 'Le Développement de nouveaux instruments conceptuels et leur utilisation dans la philosophie de la nature au xiv^{e}s.', *Acta Philosophica Fennica*, 48 (1990), 158–97, 179, does not hesitate: 'La distinction de la *potentia Dei absoluta* et de la *potentia Dei ordinata* est sans aucun doute la pièce centrale du dispositif conceptuel de la science de la nature'; adding: 'Sa signification n'en est pas moins problématique'.

augustinianism of 'the hooly bishop Bradwardyn'. But long before that, Hugh of Strasbourg's *Compendium* was playing its part in spreading some knowledge of the Power Distinction to an intelligent but non-academic audience.

FROM THEOLOGY TO LAW

Hostiensis (a. 1200–1271) 1.

Enrico Bartolomei, Henricus de Segusia (Susa), studied civil law in Bologna and taught in Paris by 1239. A bishop from 1243, he was made Bishop of Embrun, not far from his native Susa, around 1250. His archdiocesans of Embrun, mountain people in high Alpine valleys on what are now the borders of France and Italy, had independent views, and a reputation (sustained over centuries) for a predilection for "heresy" of one kind or another. Over centuries too they had experienced savage persecutions for their "heresies", from one source or another.

Hostiensis remained on good terms with Innocent IV, a fellow-student at Bologna, and cultivated the acquaintance of Henry III of England. He was joint legate with Hugh of St Cher in the delegation in Germany (1251) which was to lead to Aquinas's going to Paris. In 1262 he was appointed Cardinal of Ostia: hence 'Hostiensis', by which name he has since been known.

He began his long-popular *Summa* while teaching at Paris in 1239, completing it while Archbishop of Embrun, by 1253. His more detailed *Lectura in quinque libros Decretalium* began in his Paris teaching period too, and is said to show some influence from theological writers, Hugh of St Cher especially. It was completed only in the year of his death, 1271, and is one of the most important works in canon law to come from the Middle Ages. Dante honours him in the *Paradiso*.[2]

2. It is in the *Lectura* that some passages to present purpose are to be found. They cannot be taken, as some reports have suggested, as evidence of a use of the Distinction among canonists

---

[2] On Hostiensis see C. Lefebvre, *Dict. de droit can.* 5: 1211–27; and arts. of N. Didier cit. G. Le Bras, 'Théologie et Droit romain dans l'œuvre d'Henri de Suse', in *Festschrift N. Didier* (Paris, 1960), 195–204, 195 n.

of earlier times (than 'about 1250'). Since by 1250 the Distinction had been in use by theologians for some thirty or more years, it would not be particularly surprising to find such evidence anyway—for a use dependent on one by theologians, and not vice versa (as has formerly been suggested).[3] What the passages do serve to witness, is rather that the audience of canonists envisaged by Hostiensis (at whatever time the passage was added to the *Lectura*) could be expected to be familiar with both the terminology and the general content of the Power Distinction. It is as though it had become by that time an element of the intellectual ambience, which could be appealed to in order to make an expository point to an educated audience of non-specialists. (Non-specialists in theology.) It has no more significance in the history of the Distinction itself than a passing reference to DNA or to Carnot's Law by a modern theologian to an audience of theologians need have in the history of microbiology or thermodynamics.[4]

3. The main passage is from *In 5 Decret. libb.*, Comm. III. 6, 'De statu monachorum', 29–32, c. *cum ad*; Venice 1581, 134ra. What is in question in the context, is what a pope could or could

[3] J. Marrone, 'The Absolute and Ordained Powers of the Pope: An Unedited Text of Henry of Ghent', *Med. St* 36 (1974), 7–27, 19: 'The canonists had... defined the popes' absolute power as the right to act outside the ordinary course of law to meet emergencies'. In a note the same author adds 'This is the meaning reported in earlier canonists by the Decretalist Hostiensis (d. 1271) in a work... written about the year 1250'. That is not quite what Hostiensis in the passage cited was reporting the earlier canonists as saying: as should appear from the present treatment. Neither was he reporting that they had been 'identifying' *plenitudo potestatis* [*pontificis*] and *potentia absoluta* [*pontificis*], pace W. J. Courtenay at Ritter, *Wörterbuch*, 7 (1989), 1159. The second passage cited by Marrone, from 5.31.8, Venice 1581, fo. 72ᵛ, is obscure in its detailed significance, and does not reveal a 'definition' (pace Marrone, ibid.). Enough of it is clear: 'Neither is the pope wont to expedite these things, or other cases specially reserved to him in the foregoing verses, without the advice of his brothers, that is, the cardinals. Nor can he do this *de potestate ordinaria*... although it may be done otherwise *de absoluta*'. It appears indeed to be the post-medieval *ordinaria/extraordinaria* contrast which is in question here; but whether *ordinaria* or *ordinata* was originally intended, either reading provides an innocuous enough sense. I have been unable to find the text in the 1477 edn., and do not know whether *ordinaria* comes from Hostiensis, or from the 1581 editor.

[4] It is as a *vulgarisateur*—important in canon law, where 'common opinion' of authors carries some interpretative weight—that Hostiensis is still admired: 'Hostiensis, savant plutôt qu'original, eut grand poids dans la constitution de l'opinion commune' (G. Le Bras, 'Théologie et Droit romain' (1960), 196 n., as at n. 2 above). As a rule he is content to cite *theologi* anonymously, but mentions by name Hugh of St Cher, William of Auvergne, and Philip the Chancellor (Le Bras, 201 n.): all of whom had texts examined in Ch. 2 or Ch. 3 above.

not dispense from. Writers cited had maintained that a pope could not dispense a monk from something proper to being a monk, or (*vel*) the vow of chastity. Insisting, on the one hand, that the pope could not dispense a monk from being any of these, while the monk remained a monk [as then understood], they conceded, on the other, that the pope can make of the monk, a non-monk (*potest tamen facere de monacho non monachum*).

What the writers had been saying is straightforward enough, and is not peculiar to the powers of popes. Any spinster of this parish can make of a bachelor, a non-bachelor. What she cannot do is make a bachelor not to be a bachelor, or not to be an unmarried man, while he remains a bachelor of the kind understood. If being a monk implies being F, or cannot be true of anyone, without that person's being F (the case of the *proprium*), then it is logically impossible for anyone to be a monk without being F. And if that is so, the pope will no more be able to make someone to be a monk and yet not F, than he is able to make a Euclidean triangle not to be rectilinear. This is a theologically uncontentious point, unlikely to be disputed in even the most ultramontane of circles; given only the ability to follow an argument.

It is after citing the views of the writers that Hostiensis reports the opinion of others—*alii*, unnamed and perhaps therefore still alive—to the effect that although the vow of chastity is of the essence of being a monk (*licet ... sit de substantia monachatus*) the pope can *de plenitudine potestatis* dispense from the vow. It is in explaining what he means by 'in virtue of the plenitude of his power' that Hostiensis adds the gloss: 'which is to say, not in virtue of option-tied, but of option-neutral power; in virtue of which he can change the *substantiam rei*'.[5]

It should be noted that Hostiensis is not necessarily attributing a use of the Distinction to *alii*. It is he who is himself alluding to it, making use of its terminology in order to explain to his

---

[5] The text runs: 'de plenitudine potestatis, q.d. non de potestate ordinata, sed de absoluta, secundum quam potest mutare substantiam rei'. On *plenitudo potestatis*: W. Ullmann, 'Leo I and the Theme of Papal Primacy', *Journal of Theological Studies*, 11 (1960), 25–51, esp. 40, 46; Y. Congar, 'L'Ecclésiologie de St Bernard', *Analecta sacri ordinis Cisterciensis*, 9 (1953), 136–90, esp. 159–65 and 181–90; J. Cantini, 'De autonomia judicis saecularis et de Romani Pontificis plenitudine potestatis in temporalibus secundum Innocentium IV', *Salesianum*, 23 (1961), 407–80, esp. 464–74. The Cantini study is also germane to *potestas de iure/ de facto* discussions.

audience what (in his judgement) *alii* had meant by *de plenitudine potestatis*. The latter expression had already had a long, and at times no more than dubiously honest, career in ecclesiastical circles. It stood therefore in need of clarification and explanation. What is to the point here is not so much whether what Hostiensis is saying is a good explanation, as that he is using the Distinction to make one. For if he had had no reason to believe that his audience was already familiar enough with a firm enough concept of the Distinction, he could not have expected his gloss to be able to serve as an explanation.

Yet it is worth asking at least what sort of an explanation was being given. A hasty twentieth-century reading of *potest mutare substantiam rei*—unlikely to occur as a serious possibility to a thirteenth-century canonist—might lead someone to suppose that Hostiensis was attributing to the pope a power which Aquinas and others would routinely deny to God: a "power" on a par with making Euclidean triangles not to be rectilinear. Some reflection, however, allows for the thought that this is a lawyer's text, and that the *substantiam rei* is to be understood to signify the material content, enforceable in canon law, of the state or condition of monkhood: something analogous to the material content of a contract. Even today, English lawyers speak of a material change in a contract as being a 'substantial' change in it.

The point which *alii*, thanks to the gloss, can now be seen to be making, is the relatively innocuous one that the pope has some kind of ultimate say, in the Western Church, as to what is to count as being either essential or narrowly proper to being a monk (as that is to be understood within the canon law of the Western Church). As Hostiensis—or rather *alii*, as understood by him—understood things to be, the popes of the time were still working on the notion that you could not be a monk while simultaneously excluding in principle the content of the vow of chastity. In other words, he thought we could say, a pope maintaining an institution of monkhood so understood, could not consistently with the decree maintaining that institution concede that there could be anyone who was such a monk and yet could exclude in principle the vow of chastity.[6] The pope

---

[6] Since what is in question here (as Courtenay, 'The Dialectic' (1985) already

could not do so *de potestate sua [scil. pontificis] ordinata*. But he had as pope, so Hostiensis recognised, the power to decree otherwise. Prescinding therefore from the canonical order he had decreed, and considering only the content of "being a monk"—a content not including the having of a vow of chastity—the pope could indeed in option-neutral power, *de potestate sua [scil. pontificis] absoluta*, make being a monk in the Western Church not necessarily to imply having a vow of chastity, and so make it possible for there to be a monk, under the canon law of the Western Church, without a vow of chastity.

4. The disanalogies between divine and pontifical option-neutral power are of course important. That which can be brought about in divine option-neutral power is any thing which can, considered in its intrinsic content, be brought about; anything satisfying the *ens* condition and the *factum* condition, as Aquinas put it in passages seen in Chapter 6 above. That which can be brought about in divine option-tied power is what actually exists in extra-mental reality, as ordered by God. The scope of papal option-neutral power, as in the gloss given by Hostiensis, embraces not things of extra-mental reality, but ways of understanding or classifying such things, with a view to regulating juridical or quasi-juridical effects: ways of binding and loosing, as might more plainly be said. This scope is finite in important ways, and its generality is open to debate and challenge. Both in the nature of the "things" of the sets of option-neutral and option-tied power, and in the width of the scope (the extent of the sets), papal powers diverge importantly from divine ones. So great is the divergence, that even to use the same terminology

---

recognised) is whether vows of chastity or poverty could be held to be of the essence of monkhood, it is hard to see how 'the case under consideration entailed a possibly inherent contradiction' (same ref.). Given either decision (by pontifical stipulation doubtless) on the definitional point, what is or is not entailed is fairly clear. Moreover, even if there were an analogy with the alleged possibility (referred to in Courtenay) of God's undoing the virgin's undoing, I have yet to see evidence of a historical connection between the virgin case (a hare started by Jerome, unsuccessfully split by Damian) and the Distinction, on anything like a par with the connections which can be shown from discussions of the necessity of the mode of the Redemption, in Anselm's period. As is plain from Chs. 2 and 3 above, the present passage in Hostiensis takes us nowhere near the historical origins of the Distinction. On the virgin case see L. Moonan, 'Impossibility and Peter Damian', *AGP* 62 (1980), 146–63.

could be dangerous.[7] When a uniform rhetoric of despotic power becomes established, as in later medieval or early modern times, crucial diversities in the logic of the expressions (when used with reference, on the one hand, to divine power, and, on the other, to creaturely power), can begin to be overlooked. Favourable rhetoric is attractive to despots and their flatterers. Over time, the rhetoric begins to interfere with the understanding of the logic. Either the applications to creaturely cases inflate the understanding of creaturely power—in this case papal power— until the sustained rhetoric gives reason to fear, as Reformers feared, that the exaltation of papal powers has crossed the boundary from gross flattery to literal idolatry. Or we are invited to let man be our measure, and be sensible, and reduce our notion of God to that of an unimaginably powerful despot of a general kind we can only too well understand; as in the amalgam of Deism and emotive Reform which opposed Hume in the eighteenth century. Or we do both, and create Hobbes's monstrous God-state, neither God nor honest creature.

Yet the rhetoric does not have to get out of hand. The very important disanalogies between the Power Distinction, and the analogous distinction applicable to humans, do not necessarily interfere with the point Hostiensis was making. He was explaining something of the meaning of *de plenitudine potestatis [Romani pontificis]* as used in an opinion defended by *alii*, by means of a comparison with a distinction applicable to papal power and analogous in certain significant respects to the Power Distinction (which of its nature may not itself be applicable to creaturely power). So far from introducing the Power Distinction to his audience—as some historians appear to have thought—he is taking it as being familiar enough to them, for him to be able to use an analogous distinction to it, in explaining a legal notion. Had the Distinction not been already familiar enough to his audience, such an allusion to it could not have been explanatory, and might well have been gratuitously mystifying.

5. This pedagogical or expository use of the Power Distinction

---

[7] Dangers of a related shift have been noted: as when 'the realm of *potentia absoluta*' comes to be conceived not 'as a simple capacity or total possibility but as a course of action, albeit occasional'. In such a case a disturbing element is introduced into the dialectics, as noted in Courtenay, 'The Dialectic' (1985), 252.

—the first such use, perhaps, in a non-theological context—shows that by the time Hostiensis was writing, an acquaintance with the general content of the Distinction was something which could be presupposed in at least some educated audiences outside the theology faculties.[8] What is not so clear is how far outside theology faculties the *Lectura's* intended audience may have been. The work could well have been addressed to theologians as well as to canonists. Yet this does not greatly weaken the argument. If you address two types of audience, you are unlikely to go out of your way to use anything positively mystifying to the one, merely on the grounds that it will be plain to the other.[9]

FROM PARIS TO OXFORD

Kilwardby and Roger Bacon invite attention first. Among historians Kilwardby, a Dominican who became Archbishop of Canterbury, is remembered chiefly for his condemnations of views of Aquinas and others. He is often thought of as the establishment man. Bacon, by contrast, is still portrayed in less critical accounts as a Morning Star of sturdy empirical inquiry, whose experimental activities brought condemnation on him. To their contemporaries the two men may have appeared less of a contrast. Both had made their academic mark by teaching in Arts, not Theology, at Paris: and by teaching the "new" Aristotle of the wider corpus which by then had become available, including the "natural" treatises and the *Ethics*. Both knew a purer Aristotle than their predecessors had known, an Aristotle freer of the Avicennian (and hence on occasion Neoplatonist) associations with which Aristotle had come to the generations whose development of the Power Distinction has been seen already. The opposition of the newer Aristotelians to views of such people as Albert the Great and Aquinas—a measured opposition—owed

---

[8] In later times notions analogous to those of the Power Distinction can be seen even in official, legislative texts. (See J. Holub, 'Ordinaria potentia—absoluta potentia', *Rev. d'hist. du droit français et étranger*, 28 (1950), 92–9.)

[9] What remains uncertain is exactly when this particular passage was added. It cannot have been later than 1271, but could have been as early as the 1250s, when work on the *Lectura* began. The Distinction had already been in the intellectual ambience in Paris in the 1230s, when Hostiensis was teaching there.

something to the irritation which the more careful interpreter can hardly avoid when hearing readers' impressions or ingenious reinterpretations passed off as interpretations *tout court*. There is evidence that in their own day they were often seen rather as natural fellow-travellers of a quite narrowly Aristotelian tendency: Kilwardby's *De ortu scientiarum* and Bacon's *Summulae dialectices* often travelled in the same codices.[10]

Robert Kilwardby, OP (d. 1279)

He had already been lecturing in Arts at Paris before joining the Dominicans. Like so many of the friars considered above, he had first undertaken academic studies as a secular cleric. While at Blackfriars, Oxford, around 1250, he compiled 'the most interesting introduction to philosophy produced in the middle ages' (Van Steenberghen), his *De ortu scientiarum*. Only some time after that did he turn to lecturing on the Sentences, often continuing to reveal an Artist's preoccupations. As a theologian he was notoriously conservative: 'Chronologically speaking, he belongs to the same generation as Saint Thomas Aquinas; intellectually, he lived in a different doctrinal world' (Gilson). Yet the same historian's last word on Kilwardby in the same account, should also be recalled: 'Conservatives sometimes get ahead of progressives simply by anticipating progress without moving from the spot'.[11]

[10] See A. de Libera, 'Les *Summulae dialectices* de Roger Bacon. I–II: De termino, De enuntiatione', *AHDLMA* 53 (1986), 139–289, 142: 'Fidelity to Aristotle is here the mark of a particular inquiry which contributes to the conduct of the sciences and not simply to that of the *disputatio*. In this respect the *Summulae* constitute a counterweight in logic to the *De ortu scientiarum* with which the manuscript tradition has so narrowly associated them.' One of the codices which contain these two works (and others of an Oxford provenance) was owned by the son of Christopher Columbus. Columbus himself acknowledged, in a letter addressed from Haiti to the King of Spain, that (through verbatim quotations in Pierre d'Ailly) he had studied Bacon's suggestions of going west to India. (*DTC* 2: 18–19.) For Oxford theology at the period: J. Catto, 'Theology and Theologians 1220–1320', in *The History of the University of Oxford*, 1 (1984), ed. Catto with R. Evans, 471–517; P. Raedts, *Richard Rufus of Cornwall and the Tradition of Oxford Theology* (Oxford, 1987), xiii + 272 pp.

[11] References are to F. Van Steenberghen, *Introduction à l'étude de la philosophie médiévale* (Louvain, 1974), 611 pp., 478; E. Gilson, *History of Christian Philosophy in the Middle Ages* (London [1955]), xvii + 829 pp., 359. The question examined here is edited in E. Gössmann (ed.), *Robert Kilwardby: Quaestiones in librum tertium Sententiarum*, 1. *Christologie* (Munich, 1982), 64 + 260 pp. Other substantial parts of the Sentence Commentary are edited in the same series by G. Leibold (1985) and J. Schneider (1986).

6. At *In 3 Sent.*, qu. 7 he introduces the Distinction, and uses it repeatedly in that question. In the rest of the Commentary he appears to ignore it.[12] The question in which he uses it is whether the human soul of the nature taken on in the Hypostatic Union was 'united to the Word through a necessitating habit of grace'. Was it necessary, in other words, for the soul of the human nature taken on in the Hypostatic Union to be informed with habitual grace. Could some soul not so informed, have thus been united? Or, as one of the objections put it, Could Christ have been *simul iustus et peccator*?

It is to this question especially that Kilwardby chooses to address the Power Distinction. He begins his reply:

There is a distinction to be made concerning divine power, according as we are speaking of it as option-neutral (*loqui de ipsa absoluta*), or (*aut*) as modified *per congruentiam*.

Kilwardby is telescoping here. As the *modificata* shows, he is concerned with two determinations of *potentia divina*: one expressed in *absoluta*, the other in an adverbial expression signifying a reference to *congruentia*. That it is indeed the Power Distinction which is in play here, is confirmed from the very next sentence, in which he gets down to questions of content:

it is to be said that, so far as option-neutral power is concerned (*quantum ad potentiam absolutam*) God can unite a man to himself in unity of person, with respect to his body and with respect to the soul too (from the union of which, his nature is given), without a habit of grace. But (God) cannot do this, in so far as congruent power is concerned (*quantum ad potentiam congruitatis*). (Ed. Gössmann 1982: 33.)

The congruency here is congruency to God's will, it is the Power Distinction which is in question. Even if the terminology had puzzled us, we need not have waited long for Kilwardby to make his own identifications. 'I say that he can do this in option-neutral

[12] A slight allusion is made at *In 2 Sent.*, d. 1, qu. 2, and is quoted by Dr Randi from MS Merton 131, fo. 38ra: 'licet in perpetuis non differant esse et posse quoad ultimam potentiam, differt tamen agere et posse agere; sed tum distinctione aut enim intelligitur "de actione dei primaria et absoluta" (cuius est intelligere), et verum est; aut "de actione secundaria sive relata" (cuius est creare), et falsum est...'. (E. Randi, 'La teologia post scotistica', 92–3 n., in L. Bianchi and E. Randi, *Le verità dissonanti. Aristotele alla fine del Medioevo*, prefazione di Mariateresa Fumagalli Beonio-Brocchieri [Bari, 1990], xv + 194 pp., 87–118.) Punctuation from me, and 'differt' retained from the MS. It is the case of *agere/posse agere* which is being said to differ from the other case mentioned.

power (*de potentia absoluta*)...' he emphasises, giving reasons. He also recognises the consequences to which he has opened the door:

If you say 'Then God would be simultaneously a sinner, or at least an unjust man, and the just one (*simul peccator, vel iniustus saltem, et iustus*), the most vile, and the best (*vilissimus et optimus*)', what should be said is: Even this does not seem *inconveniens* in relation to option-neutral power (*potentiae absolutae*). For just as we concede opposite attributes (*opposita*) to God by reason of the diverse natures [of the incarnate Word], to wit that he should be capable of suffering, and not capable of suffering, dead, and not dead, and the like; so it would seem able to be said in the question now proposed. And an *inconveniens* does not in fact arise from the fact that opposite attributes are being said of the same thing.

He then immediately insists, as though to obviate any mis-understanding which might have been feared to be forming in his hearers:

I say, however, that this cannot be, in so far as congruent power is concerned (*quantum ad potentiam congruitatis*), because it is not fitting that he should be called a sinner or even an unjust man... [With the determinant] 'On this power' consequently an *inconveniens* would follow, and in consequence something impossible, to the extent that the 'im-' of the 'impossible' there marks a privation in the congruent power. (Same, p. 33.)

In that last sentence I translate Kilwardby's sense rather than his too compressed *littera*. From what he has said 'it is obvious what is to be replied if it is asked whether Christ could have taken on a sinful flesh. For even if he could have done this in option-neutral power (*de potentia absoluta*), he could not do so in option-tied power (*de potentia congruitatis*).' And therefore, he adds, he did not do so; because whatever is either *incongruum* or *indecens* is an *inconveniens* to him, and in consequence is something impossible in the way in which impossibles arise by that route (*per illam viam*).

This calls for some spelling out. When something was said to be impossible to God, in the discussions with which Kilwardby was au courant, it could be on either of two diverse kinds of grounds. There were two diverse routes, as it were, or *viae*, to impossibility; but at the end of either, a strict logical possibility was to be had. In the first, some imagined "thing" was no thing at all, even at the level of the truthmakers of composing-apt propositions; or, like the divine nature itself, was not the sort of thing which could be brought about, by no matter what imagined power. An example of a "thing" that is no thing, might be a triangle that is not a triangle, or is not rectilinear. A second route to strict impossibility starts from a genuine thing, and of a type that can be brought about: a unicorn, perhaps. But this second route proceeds by the supposition that no such thing is in fact to be actualised within the actual order of things; and depends on the thing envisaged's being taken in the judgement *composite* with its (not) in fact being willed by God or foreknown by God to be in extra-mental reality.

It is whatever is not in fact to be actualised in extra-mental reality which is being called *indecens* or *incongruum* here in Kilwardby. We need not imagine that it is being thought of as necessarily indecent or incongruous in itself, taking these terms to carry the pejorative connotations they commonly carry nowadays. It may merit no description stronger than 'not fitting in any place within the (unique) order disposed to be actualised' or 'not congruent to what God has willed'. If that is the (technical or quasi-technical) sense they carry in Kilwardby's argument here, then the additional, aesthetically or morally pejorative connotations which the same words could carry in uncoded modern uses, ought not to be seen as playing a part in the logic of the argument; but no doubt would have done no harm to its persuasive force as a piece of rhetoric.

Yet this does not mean that there is nothing in the logic of the argument which calls for attention. Consider:

For something *incongruum/indecens* to be brought about by God, is *inconveniens*,

for it can be taken in more than one way. First, it may be taken so that the thing envisaged—which might be as harmless in its intrinsic content as a unicorn or a golden mountain—is taken *composite* with its being *incongruum/indecens* in the technical sense noted. The assertion then concerns something-not-being-brought-about-by-God's being brought about by God: which is manifestly *inconveniens*, in the strong sense of being an absurdity. Such a thing—the innocent core-content taken *composite* with its not being brought about by God—is of course strictly impossible to be brought about by God (in any order of things brought about by God). Our route to this impossibility has involved an innocent core-content (a unicorn, perhaps), and a merely *ex suppositione* "necessity" (to wit, that our actual order of things is not to contain a unicorn), but the impossibility ultimately reached is a strict, logical impossibility. Even so, it is an impossibility which, like Kilwardby's logical impossibilities quite generally, is the impossibility of some putative *ens rationis* in the judgement of some thinker; not some alleged impossibility fancied to hold with strict logical impossibility of something in extra-mental reality.

The second way of taking,

For something *incongruum/indecens* to be brought about by God, is *inconveniens*,

can make it to be false. In this second way the thing envisaged (a unicorn again, perhaps) is being considered in its own intrinsic content, *divisim* from its (not) being instantiated, as may again be supposed, in extra-mental reality. The speaker following this second way need not deny that in fact there are no unicorns in the actual order of things, and may well suppose that the actual order of things does not contain any. He prescinds from that, however, when considering the intrinsic content of the unicorn, to ask whether such a content is (prescinding from what may or not be the case in the actual order of things) capable of being instantiated by God. If there is no reason why a unicorn, considered in its intrinsic content merely, and prescinding from what may or may not be willed by God or foreknown by God to be in extra-mental reality, could not be instantiated by God, then in this second way of taking, 'For something *incongruum/indecens* to be brought about by God, is *inconveniens*,' the assertion (that it is absurd for a unicorn to be brought about by God) may be false. The thing at bottom envisaged (the abstract recipe of a unicorn) is, considered as in the second way, not at all impossible to be instantiated by God; in which case we have something (in fact not to be instantiated by God, and hence something *incongruum/indecens*) which, to be brought about by God, is not at all *inconveniens*.

In Kilwardby here, the divine Word's taking on a sinful flesh was not within what was decreed by God for the Incarnation, and was therefore *in-congruum* and *in-decens*. Whatever is *incongruum* and *indecens*, for whatever reason, is in addition strictly impossible to be done by God, and strictly *inconveniens*. It is by this indirect route that it is (strictly) impossible for a sinful human nature to have been taken on in the Hypostatic Union; just as it is impossible for the leaf which did not fall a few moments ago, when considered as something-not-to-be-instantiated-within-the-actual order-of-things, to have fallen a few moments ago.

Despite the striking verbal similarities with Luther's formulas, which can hardly escape a modern reader, we must not imagine that Kilwardby was concerned with a particular case—that of Christ—of the same question with which Luther was concerned more generally. In Luther the question was whether the same man—the same "individual human nature" as Kilwardby but not Luther might have been inclined to put it—could be *simul iustus et peccator*. And in Luther the *simul* indicated logical "simultaneity" of two attributions envisaged as holding of the same individual suppositum of its (human) kind. (In some passages, Luther's *simul* may carry in addition a note of temporal simultaneity, but this does not interfere with the points being made here.)[13] In Kilwardby the question was whether an incarnate Word could in God's option-neutral power have been a sinner in his human nature while "simultaneously" being the Just One of the Scriptures in his divine nature. Kilwardby's *simul* too indicated logical simultaneity, but between two attributions holding *cum determinatione* of the same (divine) suppositum. (The determinants 'in his human nature' and 'in his divine nature' express this.) Luther's *iustus* and *peccator* were understood to be predicated *absque determinatione* of a suppositum of a human kind. Kilwardby's were understood to be predicated *cum determinatione*, in different predications containing different determinants, of the same (divine) suppositum.

In order to have been addressing Luther's question, Kilwardby would have had to make his *simul* apply (like Luther's) to a particular human being, to wit, to apply to Christ in his human

[13] A variety of related formulations are listed at A. McGrath, *Luther's Theology of the Cross: Martin Luther's Theological Breakthrough* [Oxford, 1985], 134 ff. Neither here nor in R. Hermann, *Luthers These 'Gerecht und Sünder zugleich'* (1930; repr. 1960), 314 pp., to whose further discussion we are referred, nor in half a dozen recent general or introductory works on Luther, have I found whether he was taking his formula here from some earlier writer.

nature. And then he would have had to ask whether Christ could in his human nature have been *simul iustus et peccator.* To the best of my knowledge that is not a question which Kilwardby ever asked. And there is reason to believe that, if he had, he would have rejected the suggestion as being logically absurd. The reason, however, has to do not necessarily with any theological differences between him and the Reformer on the point, but rather with their different views on philosophical logic or metaphysics.

Kilwardby's use of the Distinction is straightforward enough, and is in a question of the type to which it had traditionally been addressed: could the means of redemption for the human race have been different? It is of only mildly historical interest, from its appearance at that time in a work composed in Oxford. In Oxford Sentence commentaries composed earlier, I have not so far seen the Distinction used. Even the striking formula is interesting chiefly as a cautionary example of not putting too much trust in formulas taken out of context, and from different periods.[14] Yet it does witness to the fact that Kilwardby, by no means sympathetic to everything being done by his Parisian contemporaries in theology, would appear to have had no particular objection to the use of the Power Distinction.[15]

Roger Bacon, OFM (d. 1292?)

Legend ties Friar Bacon to Oxford, where he is almost the only medieval Franciscan thought Memorable by the tourist-guides. He did live in Oxford, at more than one period apparently. Yet Bacon's only known university teaching was in Arts, at Paris,

---

[14] For a further suggestion, see L. Moonan, 'Could Christ have been *simul iustus et peccator*? Kilwardby's Answer', in D. A. Boileau and J. A. Dick (ed.), *Tradition and Renewal: Philosophical Essays Commemorating the Centennial of Louvain's Institute of Philosophy* (3 vols.; Louvain, 1993), 2: 143–54.

[15] Kilwardby's successor at Canterbury, John Peckham, OFM, followed him not only in condemnations of doctrines favoured in the schools, but in using the Power Distinction. In the question *U. caritas potest diminui* Peckham wrote: 'Deus enim... posset si vellet, quantum est de potentia absoluta, additum subtrahere' (MS Florence, Nat Bibl. G4/854, fo. 60c, cit. J. Auer, *Die Entwicklung,* 1 (1942), 108 n.).

and as a secular cleric: years before he became a Franciscan.[16] No earlier than 1266 he tells us that although he had written much, in his secular days, for teaching purposes, he had not put an *ordinatio* into the public domain in any philosophical discipline.[17] Unless the *Physics* Commentary—from which comes the passage to be examined here—was completed later than that, it was not recognised by him as a *scriptum* ordered for publication. This could have been a tactic, of course, to disarm dismissal of his newer work by readers who might have been familiar with the earlier work, remaining unimpressed by it. But there is no reason why it should not have been straightforwardly informative. The substance of the *Physics* Commentary surely came from the Paris period anyway. Bacon boasted that he had commented repeatedly on Aristotle's works, 'more than any other master'.[18] The *Physics* is the anchor-text of the *libri naturales*, and the very suspicion in which these works had earlier been held by the authorities might not have been unattractive to Bacon. In any case his academic interest in its contents is not in doubt.

---

[16] On Bacon see *DTC* 2: 7–31 (G. Delorme); *New Cath. Enc.* 12: 552–3 (J. Weisheipl); and Emden, *Register... Oxford*, 1: 87–8. T. Crowley, *Roger Bacon: The Problem of the Soul in his Philosophical Commentaries* (Louvain, 1950), 17–78, ch. 1, 'Bacon's life and works', and S. C. Easton, *Roger Bacon and his Search for a Universal Science: A Reconsideration of the Life and Work of Roger Bacon in the Light of his own Stated Purposes* (Oxford, 1952), are also of importance. Crowley helpfully marshals the evidence from Bacon's writings, and eliminates the inauthentic *De retardatione*. Easton (237–40) gives a useful critique of earlier biographies. Introductions to the editions should also be seen. F. Alessio, *Mito e scienza in Ruggero Bacone* (Milan, 1957), 328 pp., gives in his Introd. further critique of biographical accounts, besides much commentary of importance. Émile Charles, *Roger Bacon, sa vie, ses ouvrages, ses doctrines d'après des textes inédits* (Paris, 1861), xvi + 416 pp., is still invaluable—though only after reference to corrections in the more recent works mentioned. To the editions listed at Easton 1952: 236–37, should be added Pierre Duhem's edition of a scientific fragment, with a commentary still worth reading: *Un fragment inédit de l'Opus Tertium de Roger Bacon précédé d'une étude sur ce fragment* (Quaracchi, 1909); also the edition of the *Summulae* by A. de Libera, as at n. 9 above; and E. Massa (ed.), post Ferdinand Delorme, *Rogeri Baconis Moralis Philosophia* (Zurich [1953]).

[17] Bacon appears to include himself among *nos theologi*, in the letter addressed to the Pope to accompany the *Opus minus* (cit. T. Crowley, *Roger Bacon* (1950), 26); and cf. *Multa in alio statu conscripseram propter iuvenum rudimenta* (*Opus tertium*, 13), and *In alio statu non feci scriptum aliquod philosophiae*; both cit. Delorme in Introd. to *Opera hactenus inedita*, vol. 13, p. xxiii.

[18] Bacon's editor has no doubt but that the works in the Amiens MS, including the *Physics* Commentary, are 'a most instructive specimen of the intellectual work he was carrying out in the Street of Straw, around 1250'. The mention of the Seine in an example (cited by the editor) is hardly evidence for the work's being composed in Paris, but the references to things in the classroom as aids to teaching can be taken as reflecting the circumstances of the work's use. (See Introd. to *Op. hact. ined.*, vol. 13, p. xxiv.)

The editor dates the *Physics* Commentary to 'around 1250' (*Opera hact. ined.* vol. 13, p. xxiv), and argues that the text now available is one compiled by Bacon for teaching from, at Paris. He notes that the copyist of Books 1–4 has had before him a source with many gaps: but a source taken not from notes taken continuously and annotated as for a student's use, but one put in order by the lecturer in a cool hour from his own notes (and those of students, apparently), as for future use, whether in future teaching or in the preparation of an *ordinatio* for publication. (See *Op. hact. ined.* vol. 13, p. xxvi.) The order in which commentaries on different Aristotelian works succeed each other in the manuscript (p. 13, vol. xxvii) would seem to confirm that the Amiens manuscript indeed represents such a text, and by a teacher who was teaching according to the programme imposed by the succession of object-texts laid down for treatment at due times within the academic year; and who was doing so over more than one year—repeatedly, as indeed Bacon himself claimed. In short, the text we now have in the edition is from a master's *lectura*, for a course given by the master (Bacon) repeatedly, under regulations specifically identical with those of Paris.[19]

7. Roger uses the Distinction in his Commentary on Book 4 of the *Physics*, when considering the question of the vacuum which, he was arguing, could not be had in the real world. In reply to an objection, to the effect that a vacuum could be had, because disembodied dimension could be had, he said:

To what is objected I reply that it is not true, because dimension is an accident and accident cannot be without a subject, and to make an accident without a subject is not an ordered effect.

So (*unde*) in the option-neutral power of the First (*de potentia primi absoluta*) it could well be, and it would thus exceed every finite effect?

But speaking in terms of that power which is due, and in terms of the actual ordering of power (*loquendo de debito potentiae et ordinatione*

---

[19] As Delorme politely but firmly indicates, it is by no means 'une simple glose', as Émile Charles had concluded after an examination made brief through no choice of his; and it is quite mistaken to say, with Victor Cousin, 'Malheureusement ce n'est pas ici un commentaire régulier, c'est un assemblage de notes, une simple glose et encore dans le plus grand désordre.' (Both cit. Delorme at Introd. to *Op. hact. ined.*, vol. 8, p. v.) Duhem recognised it for 'les leçons de R. Bacon, jeune maître à la Faculté des Arts de Paris', though it is not a mere *reportatio*, as Duhem had suggested in addition. (Delorme, same ref.)

potentiae), then its power [the power of the First] does not exceed every act, but is convertible with the acts and effects ordered and possible to be, in accordance with real possibility.

And thus it is obvious that to make a vacuum would be to make a substance, and thus the opposite of the position put forward by the objector, follows. (*In Physicam*, ed. F. M. Delorme, with the collaboration of R. Steele, in *Opera*, 13 (Oxford, 1935), 224–5.)[20]

The Power Distinction is plainly being used here. God is referred to as 'the First (*Primum*)', as in the translations of Avicenna.[21] Perhaps, with its less overtly religious connotations, it seemed more appropriate to Roger in discussing questions of natural philosophy. 'Real possibility (*possibilitatem rei*)' is in effect the *de re* possibility relating to the *res* in virtue of which a narrowly predicative proposition is true, in the case where it is true. "There being a possible vacuum" in the actual order of things, would imply there being a possible accident (which of its nature is "accident of") which would not be an accident of anything. Hence there could not be such a thing, for us to be able to assert truly to be the case in the extramental reality of the actual order of things.

Roger makes it quite clear that what he is allowing to be possible in divine option-neutral power, is not disembodied dimension, or accident which is not accident-of, but a vacuum which would be itself a substance; and thus capable of being said truly to be had, by anyone placed to do so. His doctrine here thus anticipates and avoids what some of Stephen Templar's condemnations of 1277 had in view; particularly those grouped as articles 196–9 in R. Hissette, *Enquête sur les 219 articles condamnés à Paris le 7 mars 1277* (Louvain, 1977), 340 pp., and 138–41 in the *Cartularium*. Consider, for example, art. 196/140:

Quod facere accidens esse sine subiecto, habet rationem impossibilis implicantis contradictionem.

Roger had been careful to emphasise that what God could do in option-neutral power was not that, but rather to create a

---

[20] This text was treated by Duhem, albeit in a different connection.

[21] Avicenna was no doubt also behind the distinction between *esse* and *essentia* which Delorme records at many places: 'l'*essentia* représente l'état absolu et abstrait d'une chose, et l'*esse* son état concret' (Introd. to *Op. hact. ined.*, vol. 8, p. viii). It is Bacon's terminology, not the terminology followed by Aquinas in his *De ente et essentia*, which has endured among philosophers.

vacuum which would be a substance. What this brings out is not merely that Roger was not heterodox on the matter, by the standards of his time. More interestingly, it brings out that he was no British empiricist born out of due time. Hissette is no doubt correct to suggest that the propositions interested the censors of 1277 for their possible implications for Eucharistic doctrine. But only a page or so later, he cites as germane to the Condemnations this text from an anonymous work:

Cum Primum sit omnipotens, poterit conservare accidens in esse sine subiecto. (Hissette 1977: 289, citing the edn. by A. Zimmermann.)

The *poterit* there suggests that an option-neutral possibility—one which Roger had been careful to reject—is being entertained by the anonymous writer, and asserted. By taking this text, and its Avicennian wording, along with Roger's, we might have to ask whether Templar or his scrutineers could not have been interested (also) in implications for natural philosophy.

Roger's terminology is worth noting in passing, particularly for the option-tied arm, where he uses *loquendo de debito potentiae et ordinatione potentiae*. The *loquendo* insinuates that it is a determinate mode of speech which is in question—as in a *cum determinatione* assertion, for example. The 'debit of power' suggests a measure that is due, neatly expressing two important features of *potentia dei ordinata*, or at any rate of what is specific to it, and not shared with *potentia absoluta dei*: that it is not necessarily infinite in the way divine option-neutral power is, and that it is justly ordered. Had these insinuations left Roger's intentions in any doubt, the gloss he promptly adds should have removed them. The debit of power, the ordering of power in question, is convertible with the 'acts and effects ordered and possible to be done according to real possibility'. Roger's is a straightforward and a knowing use of the Distinction, of interest—given its date—chiefly for its occurrence in a definitely physical context, rather than a theological one. I have not found another in such a context, from within the period covered by this book.

Richard Rufus, or Richard of Cornwall, OFM (fl. 1250)

It is commonly taken to be established that these two names refer to the same person. For arguments identifying one Richard

Rufus of Cornwall as author of both works to be quoted from presently, and assigning both to one of Richard's sojourns in Oxford, see P. Raedts, *Richard Rufus* (Oxford, 1987), chs. 2 and 3. The use of the Distinction recorded in one of them appears to be essentially straightforward, and in line with the generality of those which have been seen above; yet it is possible, if the famous strictures of Roger Bacon on Richard are to be understood as some have suggested, that a point at issue between the two Franciscans, not in theology but in philosophical logic, may presage conflicting ways of understanding the formulas of the Power Distinction, in certain types of argumentative context, and may demand in consequence even greater care in applying the Distinction than has been seen in the users examined so far. Yet even if this is so, it is not apparent in the use to be recorded from Richard, where no consequences calling for anything methodologically controversial are being drawn. When it comes to pursuing the career of the Power Distinction into its next phase, lasting roughly from the decade of the condemnations (the 1270s) to the Black Death (in the middle of the fourteenth century), the cases of Bacon and Richard may have to be reopened in the light of the new context. In the light of present knowledge, however, nothing like that is called for.[22]

[22] Details on the Raedts book are at n. 10 above, and see also R. Wielockx, 'Richard Rufus et la théologie à Oxford: A propos d'une nouvelle monographie', *ETL* 65 (1989), 136–44. It is Dr Raedts's opinion that 'A. G. Little, The Greyfriars in Oxford (Oxf Hist Soc, xx, 1892), p. 142 n. 1, established once and for all that Richard Rufus and Richard of Cornwall are one and the same person'. Roger Bacon's vigorous denunciations of Richard, which served to keep him in mind, have often been quoted: Et optime novi pessimum et stultissimum istorum errorum ⟨auctorem⟩, qui vocatus est Richardus Cornubiensis, famosissimus apud stultum multitudinem. Sed apud sapientes fuit insanus, et reprobatus parisius propter errores quas invenerat ⟨et⟩ promulgaverat quando solemniter legebat Sententias ibidem, postquam legerat Sententias Oxoniae, ab anno Domini 1250. The conjectural readings are from the editor. (T. S. Maloney, ed. and tr., *Roger Bacon: Compendium of the Study of Theology*, edition and trans. with introd. and notes, par. 86, p. 86.) More than one scenario accommodates both this, and the other evidence which Raedts adduces. Worth considering is the possibility that the earlier Oxford course on the Sentences had been within the convent, and not in the University's programme; that the Commentary in the Balliol MS represents the substance of the lectures given at Paris; and that whether or not Richard ever used the Commentary in University lectures in Oxford, he completed his *ordinatio* after his return there. If the copy now extant (prepared for consultation within the convent in Oxford) was made there, that would be enough to explain features of the copy which have been identified as typical of copies done in Oxford rather than in Paris. The precise nature of the issue(s) dividing Bacon and Richard on the signification of voiced sounds is unlikely to have been so straightforward as the views reported by Raedts apropos of Bacon's strictures would have us believe; and

In his important article on Peter de Trabibus, in the *I. Brady Festschrift* of 1976, at 285 n., Friar Gideon Gál reported that Richard Rufus of Cornwall had 'repudiated the distinction', or at any rate a 'misunderstanding' of it, as found in an option of Alexander of Hales. The work to which Gál was referring, is in fact an *abbreviatio* made by Richard, of Bonaventure's Sentence Commentary, at *In 1 Sent.*, d. 43. The key part of the reply, quoted by Gál from Vat. lat. 12 993, fo. 117rb, '*Sed haec distinctio... posse peccare*', is almost verbatim from Bonaventure. As was seen above in Chapter 5, Bonaventure is not, at that place, to be seen as repudiating the Power Distinction. He is to be seen as (correctly) denying its applicability to an objection entertained, in precisely the way in which it had apparently been used by someone. I have not yet seen the context within the *abbreviatio*—which, like many examples of its genre, is reported as not beyond deviating at times from the doctrine of its source—but I would be surprised if Richard's intentions at the point in question, should turn out to have been significantly different from Bonaventure's.

One reason for this opinion is that Richard, like Bonaventure, would seem to have used the Distinction in his own Commentary on the Sentences, and with no great air of reluctance. This was already reported by Dr Randi at p. 177 n. of 'Armonia...', from 1990, as at Chapter 1 above, n. 13. On the same fo. 96rb of MS 62 of Balliol College, Oxford, from which Randi quoted 'so this "ability to ___" seems to be contrary to the divine order and wisdom, because [God] does whatever he does, wisely and in an ordered manner', Richard contrasts what might be done out of power, sans phrase (*de potentia, absolute*), with what God could not do out of justice (*de iustitia non posset*); and adds 'Just as, in other words, he can do things out of power, sans phrase (*potest de potentia simpliciter*), but cannot out of the power put into service (*non potest de potentia convenientiae*)'. That last phrase replaces an earlier *de convenientia*, expunged in its favour. There would seem to be no great puzzle about Richard's meaning here: *sapientiam et ordinationem divinam* names the actual order of things, viewed as willed by God; *convenientia* refers to the same thing, and the connecting use of *conveniens* has been seen more than once above,

in any case its consideration here would call for an anticipation of considerations which themselves are more appropriate to developments of the Power Distinction in the period from the 1270s to the 1340s.

and in Franciscan writers. The first contrast, of '*de potentia, absolute*' with '*de iustitia*' would seem a conscious acknowledgement of continuity with the long established *de potentia/iustitia* distinction, with its echoes of Augustine. The second, in its substitution of '*de potentia convenientiae*' for '*de convenientia*' at the very least suggests an acquaintance with the newer terminology (i.e. with '*de potentia ordinata*'), and might suggest a determination to provide an alternative, in line with it, and meaning essentially the same, but recalling the connotations and associations of *conveniens*. (Did *conveniens*, like *decens*, find particular favour among Franciscans?) So here, at fo. 96rb of the Balliol manuscript, at *In 1 Sent.*, d. 42 of the Commentary attributed to Richard, we have at the very least a willed allusion to the Power Distinction.

From a few folios later, in the other passage which Randi quoted in the same note, may be read:

And the answer will be that when 'God could have redeemed otherwise, or created another world, either greater or lesser' is said, it is true [when asserted under the determination] 'out of bare power (*de potentia nuda*)'; but if the speaker's determinant (*sermo*) is 'out of a power of God clothed in a most ordered mode of acting (*de potentia dei vestita ordinatissimo modo agendi*)', then he could not. For if he had made several worlds, he would have destroyed the order of things, and then would not have made all things in a most ordered manner. (*In 1 Sent.*, d. 44, at MS Oxford, Balliol College 62, fo. 99rb.)

This would seem to be a fairly straightforward application of the Distinction: to the Anselmian problem of the possibility of a different mode of Redemption, and to the more general Abelardian problem of creating a world different from the actual world. Richard implicitly recognises that the Abelardian problem is more general, by letting his solution to it serve for the more specific one too. He also recognises, in the context of the passage quoted, the Anselmian background. I have not noticed Richard's terminology, contrasting *de potentia nuda* with *de potentia dei vestita ordinatissimo modo agendi*, in other writers from within the chronological limits of the present book. To theologians of a Franciscan bent, familiar with the story of the "conversion" of Francis, stripping off his father's clothes, it is a terminology which just could suggest the picture of a naked power behind the clothed one, ready to come out and get down to serious business; and hence just could dispose some hearers towards a very different understanding of the Distinction's formulas from the one in general currency, by Richard as much as by others, during the period covered in the present book.

THE DISTINCTION LEAVES THE SCHOOLS

Hugh of Strasbourg, OP (fl. 1265)

From a Strasbourg family, Hugo Ripelin de Argentina entered the Dominicans. For some time he was prior in Zurich. Returning to Strasbourg, he composed the Compendium beginning with the words *Theologicae veritatis*. (Hence the title *Compendium, 'Theologicae veritatis . . .'*, often written *Compendium theologicae veritatis*: something of an optimistic exaggeration.) The *Compendium* enjoyed a success out of all proportion to any strictly theological merits, not least by travelling under the name of famous writers. One of these was Albert the Great, and we have that to thank for being able to find the *Compendium*—already the beneficiary of some fourteen editions by 1500—in volume 34 of the widely accessible Borgnet edition of Albert's works.[23]

The plan of the work is like that of Bonaventure's *Breviloquium*. The content—not to be compared with Bonaventure's—is frank compilation, unevenly digested from a variety of sources. It is often entertaining, a Good Read; and will tell you how to tell a man's character from the thickness of his lips. Its potted erudition, listed by numbers, was evidently seized on eagerly by preachers, littérateurs, and pious writers. It is therefore of unusual interest in the present connection, not for any academic contribution some might look for in it, but as an indication of what non-academics were evidently prepared to copy or buy, and read. Its chief value in the present connection, as a potential transmitter, may not appear fully until the history of the Distinction in later medieval times is itself more fully related.

[23] For Hugh, see Kaeppeli, 2: 260–9; *Dict de Sp.* 7: 894–6; G. Boner, 'Über den Dominikanertheologen Hugo von Strassburg', *Archivum Fratrum Praedicatorum*, 24 (1954), 269–86. Paternity of the *Compendium* was established in L. Pfleger, 'Der Dominikaner Hugo von Strassburg und das *Compendium theologicae veritatis*', *Zeitschr. f. kathol. Theologie*, 28 (1904), 429–40. See also K. Schmitt, *Die Gotteslehre des Compendium theologicae veritatis des Hugo Ripelin von Strassburg (Eine deutsche theolog. Terminologie des 14. Jahrh.)* (Münster, 1940).

This is worth emphasising, for the real significance of Hugh's contribution arguably cannot be appreciated if we mistake it for an academic treatment, in tacit competition with those which have preceded.

Considerations of genre are in place not only for complete works, but for professedly complete treatments within works. Hugh's two-column chapter on the power of God (Bk. 1, ch. 27) is an omnium gatherum of diverse things said by people about divine power which Hugh has presumably selected as noteworthy. He lists these not uncritically, but without clear enough contexts or connections. The chapter is not to be taken as a unified, critical account of divine power. To take it as one—even as a poor account of the sort—would be a mistake of the same general kind as could be made by taking a humourist's division of murder into simple, blue, and holy, as a critical piece of moral reasoning, even a poor one.

8. Early in the *Compendium* Hugh transmits a Negative Theology view on the divine nature (ch. 24 passim, ed. Borgnet, 34: 27–8). Nothing is said of God attributively and properly (*digne et proprie*), in an attribution made on account of his own excellence. Not even pronouns will serve us: God cannot be pointed to, either in a *demonstratio ad sensum* (for God is incorporeal) or in a *demonstratio ad intellectum* (for God is unknowable, *incognoscibilis*). Because of the connection with "understanding", the *incognoscibilis* can be taken to imply a denial of knowledge of any *quid est* of God's, and need not be taken to imply that it cannot be known that there is a God, *quia est*. We cannot make God known by any definition, but can do so in a certain kind of respect (*qualitercunque*) through a circumlocution. The way in which this is done in practice, he shows by (in effect) benignly interpreting a text from St Bernard as being intended as systematically misleading, much as Aquinas in Chapter 6 above was seen to wish 'God is good' to be analysed. (Out of context, Bernard's text could instead have been read as a reduction of the divine nature in terms of something in creation, along the lines suggested by Hobbes for analysing 'God is omnipotent'.)[24] I mention the

---

[24] Bernard's text runs: 'Quid est Deus? quo nihil melius cogitari potest. Quid est Deus? voluntas omnipotens, benevolentissima virtus, lumen aeternum...' (cit. Hugh of Strasbourg, *Compendium*, ch. 24).

Negative Theology and the apparent willingness to analyse certain ranges of attributions to God as systematically misleading: to emphasise the substantial continuity on these matters between Hugh and the Dominicans (and others) who have been examined already, and because the information on the matters mentioned is provided by Hugh in what there is of a context for his chapter on divine power; to which I now turn.

9. The chapter headed *De potentia dei* (Bk. 1, ch. 27, ed. Borgnet, 34: 30–1), begins:

The power of God (*potentia dei*) is twofold, to wit absolute (*absoluta*) and ordered (*ordinata*). He can do many things in the first way which he cannot do in the second way, because many things come under his power (*subsunt suae potentiae*), which do not accord with him (*non conveniunt sibi*) ... (Borgnet, 34: 30.)

It is a little unusual in this period to find *potentia dei...absoluta/ordinata* used in the nominative; though not so unusual as I once thought. Philip the Chancellor, for example, had used *potentia ordinata* in the nominative, contrasting it with *potentia prima simpliciter*. (See Ch. 2 above, and *Summa de Bono*, De fide, ed. Victorius a Cena, 79.)

In Hugh, two ways of understanding *potentia dei* are in question. But are they the ways distinguished in the Power Distinction? Comments on some of the expressions used in the text quoted are in order. In Hugh's usage *congruentia* appears to refer to the intrinsic coherence of the "things" considered in themselves— the Avicennian essences. And *convenientia* (as in a number of those seen already) appears to refer to *convenientia* to the divine actualising will.[25]

Two reasons obtainable from the context might suggest otherwise, and will need to be accounted for. The first is what—on the understanding of *convenientia* just identified—could be a puzzling assertion on Hugh's part. Many things (*multa*), he says, come under God's power to bring about things external to his nature, which he could bring about (*posset facere*), but which *non conveniunt sibi*. On the reading in which *convenientia* is an envisaged relationship of an Avicennian essence to the divine, actualising will, that

---

[25] Kilwardby, as may be recalled, had called this relationship to the actualising will by the names of *congruitas* and *convenientia* alike.

would be straightforward. It would indeed refer to things which God could do in option-neutral power, but not in option-tied power: unicorns, perhaps, or golden mountains in Ecuador.

That would not be at all puzzling, but Hugh immediately gives an example which, on the face of it, is not of that type, and could suggest an *inconvenientia* of a more profound kind. The example is *facere mala*, commonly thought more profoundly incompatible with divine action than beasts or geographical features which (as may be supposed) God has simply not decided to actualise. How could *facere mala* signify something to be counted among things which in themselves come under God's power and could be done, and yet (merely) do not *conveniunt sibi*, are not to be found within the order of things actually willed?

One way can be appreciated if we recognise that Hugh is compressing, telescoping what he is reporting in this chapter. If we understand *facere mala* as 'doing things which are to be adjudged evil in the actual order of things', the puzzle can readily be dissolved. Let us suppose that fornication is such a thing. If fornication is to be adjudged evil, then there is some determinate kind of activity so to be adjudged. If there is, there will be an Avicennian essence for the activity of the kind in question. If there is, it could well be that the Avicennian essence of the activities concerned might be actualised in some order of things in which such activities were not, when identified, to be adjudged evil. In such a way God could readily bring about things which, if brought about within the actual order of things, we might have to adjudge evil, in an order in which no such evaluation need be called for. In such a way God *posset facere mala*, which yet would be things which do not *conveniunt sibi*.

The second reason from the context, for querying the identification of *convenientia*, can also be accounted for. It comes from a few sentences later, where Hugh had been saying:

> Although God is omnipotent, culpable acts are not attributed to him—like lying, or willing wickedly.
> Neither are acts that are in anything's debt (*poenales*), like fearing and suffering pain.
> Neither are corporeal acts, save perhaps in an extended sense (*transumptive*).

In all these cases what is in question is not just something which

God might or might not be able to bring about (*facere*), as had been the case at the opening of Hugh's ch. 27. It is something of which God is taken to be the immediate agent (*agere*). Others had regularly made the point that whereas God could bring it about that walking, or fearing, or growing tired could be done, he could not himself be said to be able to be the immediate agent of any of these. A less awkward way of putting this will be seen presently.

10. Hugh, in the meantime, is adding the text which needs attention:

> Neither are unsuitable acts (*inconvenientes*), which can be had in three ways:
> First, if anything contradicts divine power, as is "making something greater than itself";
> Secondly, if it contradicts his truth (*eius veritati*), as in 'making something simultaneously to be and not be', or 'making it to be that something past should be future';
> Thirdly, if it contradicts his goodness, like 'damning Peter and saving Judas'.
> Anselm on these: 'Any *inconveniens* whatever, even the smallest, is impossible with God'.

What is under consideration here are envisaged *actūs* of God, not (as earlier) envisaged *facta* which God might be able to bring about. That walking should be done by someone, is a possible object of God's power to bring about things. That walking should be done by God (walking as God), is not. Hence,

> God can bring it about that (some *x* of some kind is walking)

is true, whereas

> God can bring it about that (God is as God walking),

is not. The 'as God' is inserted merely to obviate trifling objections based on supposing a doctrine of the Incarnation, and ignoring the unexceptionable ways in which it was routinely accommodated in such contexts in the Middle Ages.

The *inconveniens* in the first of Hugh's three types of *actus inconvenientes* is thus not in "making something greater than itself" (not necessarily in itself an *inconveniens*), but in "God's making something greater than himself'". In the second, it is not merely "making something simultaneously to be and not to be" (which is already an *inconveniens* in itself), but "God's making something to be and not to be". In the third, the example indicates that 'contradicts his goodness' is referring not to that goodness of God which was identified with the divine nature, but the *bonitas* providentially disposed in the actual order of things; as has been encountered in a number of medievals already. What is left inexplicit is that what is *inconveniens* here is not just "damning Peter and saving Judas" (which in itself is not *inconveniens*), nor even "God's damning Peter and saving Judas" (which in itself is not *inconveniens* either), but "God's damning Peter and saving Judas within the *bonitas ordinata* of the actual order of things", in which order, so Hugh is evidently supposing, Peter is for saving and Judas for damning.

In the opening passage of Hugh's ch. 27, then, there is no reason why *convenientia* should not have its otherwise expected meaning of *convenientia* to God's actualising will. That being so, Hugh's contrast of *potentia dei ordinata* and *potentia dei absoluta* can be taken as an intended reference to the Power Distinction. Given the nature of the work, we could hardly have expected much more than an illustrative use anyway.

TOWARDS WIDER HORIZONS

In Kilwardby the Distinction leaves Paris for another theology faculty, that of Oxford. It was a slight enough move. Kilwardby's use of the Distinction was straightforward, and addressed to the kind of question to which it had regularly been addressed: on whether the mode of redemption of the human race could have been different. The formula, adumbrating Luther's historically unconnected (?) *simul iustus et peccator* formula, but in such a notoriously different kind of theologian, may catch a reader's attention. But Kilwardby was no innovator in the manner of the *novatores* of the sixteenth century, as the Reformers used to be called. Even the suggestion that Kilwardby introduced the Distinction to Oxford could not be sustained. It is not apparent in Oxford theology before that date, but can hardly have been unknown there. People in Oxford do often read, and in the

Middle Ages generally there was much sub-cultural intercourse between universities. Works in which the Distinction was used had been well enough known to earlier Oxford men. Kilwardby's own use confirms that he did not see himself as introducing a novelty. He is clear enough, but concise; making no effort to explain the Distinction, as to an audience to whom it might have been unfamiliar. One point could be worth marking. It is noted more than once in this book that the famous condemnations of the 1270s do not condemn or reprove the Power Distinction. In Kilwardby, even if it was some time before he became Archbishop, we see one of the ecclesiastical authorities chiefly responsible for the condemnations, himself using the Distinction in a manner typical for the time, and without any reluctance.[26]

In Hostiensis the Distinction left not only Paris but the ambience of the theology faculties. For a canonist, it is true, he had unusually strong theological concerns; but the *Lectura* was surely addressed in the first instance to men formed in that other higher faculty, of Canon Law. In Hostiensis, moreover, the Distinction itself is only being alluded to (albeit as something with which the audience was expected to be familiar). What was being used, to explain what *alii* had been saying about the expression *de plenitudine potestatis*, used of the pope, was a distinction applicable to creaturely power, analogous to the Power Distinction and acknowledged as derived from it. Alexander of Hales, and Aquinas too, had at least hinted that an analogous distinction, applicable to creatures capable of acting *per voluntatem et intellectum*, could be made. Hostiensis, perhaps as early as 1250 or thereabouts, can expect his audience of academic (but not necessarily theologian) hearers, to be familiar enough with the broad sense of the Power Distinction, to permit them to take his analogous distinction in their stride, and find it more readily graspable than the explicand, the expression *de plenitudine potestatis*. In later times, use of related distinctions applicable to creaturely power—both within political discussion and for pedagogical purposes—was arguably to interfere with the understanding of the Power Distinction itself, as maintained with fair constancy

---

[26] Kilwardby's successor at Canterbury, the Franciscan Peckham, who is also remembered for some condemnations, was also to show no particular unwillingness to use the Power Distinction; as was noted at n. 15 above, where the references are given.

during the period of this book. But that goes well beyond what can be treated here.

In Bacon the Distinction remains in the university, and almost certainly in that of Paris, but leaves the higher faculties for Arts. Bacon's use is the first I have yet noticed in a work of natural philosophy, or in academic lectures addressed to students engaged in a university course in Arts. In its content, however, it is not so very different from one or two of the uses noted above from Albert the Great and Hugh of St Cher, who were engaged in professedly theological works.

In Hugh of Strasbourg the Distinction is not used, but is recognisably referred to. In Hugh it has left not only the theology faculties but the schools, for the *Compendium* is not an academic work. It depended on academic works, but found a substantial welcome, throughout the Middle Ages and a little beyond, outside the schools. Poets and preachers welcomed it: were they always able to follow its too compressed reference to the Distinction?

At this point in the progress of the Power Distinction, as it prepares to make its way outside its alma mater, it is useful to review its understanding and use within the period examined. In the light of nuances and corrections provided by the various texts from the period, I set out in the Chapter following a more specific account of the Distinction than was possible in the working notion of Chapter 1 above.

9

The Earlier Medieval
Power Distinction

Elements of an appreciation can now be put together. This
involves locating the Distinction in its genre, drawing attention
to salient features of the circumstances in which it was used, and
providing the bones of an analysis. It concludes the account
of how the earlier medieval Power Distinction was understood
and used. Brief queries are added on its aptness alike for purposes to which it was addressed, and others to which it might
yet be.

THE DISTINCTION RECONSIDERED

1. *Locating the Distinction in its genre*

It is surely no accident that the earliest users to appear are pupils
of the Masters who brought philosophy back from the groves
and cloisters to the (publicly regulated) market-place. For the
Distinction is to be understood as at bottom a dialectical device,
an element in the regimented or stylised speech of the informal
but disciplined inquiries in which the Masters of the twelfth
century had brought back the spirit of Socrates.

The very nature of dialectical debate makes it hard to identify
authorship of dialectical devices:

Dialectic is a co-operative and progressive polemic—a polemic not between persons, but between theses and counter-theses. Theses are not personal property, nor arguments.[1]

It is for such reasons, incidentally, that anyone hoping for a unique and correct answer to 'Who invented the Power Distinction?' may have to remain disappointed. Yet some clues which have appeared from earlier chapters should not be ignored.

Philosophical discussions in our day too are carried on at this level of strictly informal discussion, disciplined by shared standards of rigour, and made easier by shared techniques or shorthand forms. By using such techniques or forms in the approved ways we may tell ourselves—justly or not—that it is reasonable to think that at least the substance of our arguments could survive and indeed benefit from a more formal treatment. An example of such a shorthand is 'systematically misleading expressions', a coinage of Ryle's which has been used more than once in the present work. And the detection of such expressions is at least sometimes a useful move still in our modern equivalents of dialectical discussions. From the middle of the twelfth century the Latin West was provided with the most famous collections of "fallacies" to be detected or avoided in dialectical discussions: Aristotle's *De sophisticis elenchis*. By no means all of the "fallacies" of that work are strictly logical fallacies, and some can hardly occur outside dialectical discussions. The Power Distinction, at bottom, is a device which enables a dialectical disputant either to unmask one of Aristotle's "fallacies"—that known as Secundum Quid—or to show that he is avoiding the like himself.

The fallacy of Secundum Quid, or more explicitly the fallacy *A dicto simpliciter ad dictum secundum quid*, or *a dicto secundum quid ad dictum simpliciter*, has been called 'one of the subtlest and most common sources of error'. It consists, as the same writer put it, 'in using a principle or proposition without regard to the

---

[1] G. Ryle, 'Dialectics in the Academy', in G. E. L. Owen (ed.), *Aristotle on Dialectic: The Topics*, Proceedings of the Third Symposium Aristotelicum (Oxford, 1968), viii + 346 pp., 76. And see J. Isaac, 'La Notion de dialectique chez saint Thomas', *Rev. sc. ph. th.* 34 (1950), 481–506. On how the practice of disputation in the medieval schools almost inevitably led to complications of the logical issues see I. Angelelli, 'The Techniques of Disputation in the History of Logic', *J. Phil.* 67 (1970) 800–15; and cf. Aquinas's remarks on *dialectica docens* and *dialectica utens*, at *In 4 Metaph.*, lect. 4, as at Busa (ed.), *Opera*, 4; 420, col. 2, n. 7, and related remarks at *In An post.*, lect. 1, nn. 5–6, and lect. 20, n. 5. These last are now available in the revised first volume of the Leonine, 1*, 2, (1989), but were already discussed by Isaac in the article just referred to.

circumstances which modify its applicability in the case or kind of case before us'.[2] It is worth noting that it was by theologians as a rule, and in theological contexts, that the Distinction was seen in the foregoing chapters to have been used. And it has often been noted that although it has perhaps the least strictly logical importance of any of Aristotle's logical works, the *De sophisticis elenchis* nevertheless appeared to make the greatest impact (of any of the logical works) on theologians in the earlier thirteenth century. This is unsurprising. It gave them practical assistance in conducting their enquiries on the level of regimented but not necessary formal argument. It gave them graspable examples and convenient ways of putting things. And it gave them models for providing more of the like, for their own discussions.

Medieval schoolmen were able to treat the fallacy of Secundum Quid as one arising where the rules for arguing from predications *cum determinatione* or *absque determinatione* were being disregarded. The arguments and rules in question were at precisely the level of regimented discussion. The "propositions" in premisses and conclusions were not being taken as yet analysed in a manner appropriate for more strictly "scientifical" purposes. H. W. B. Joseph's way of putting the difficulty, with its explicit reference to 'applicability in the case or kind of case before us' brings out that the underlying problem here is one of "pragmatics" rather than of syntax or semantics. In drawing inferences from *cum determinatione* or *absque determinatione* "predications" generally, this is also the underlying problem. When assessing 'The Ethiopian is white in respect of his teeth, therefore he is white' or '... is curly in respect of the hair on his head, therefore he is curly', what is crucial is not strictly the semantic content of 'white' as against 'curly'. Their being licensed or not in an individual case does not depend directly on the specific content of 'white' or 'curly', but upon certain formal or topic-neutral properties which stand to the specific contents much as transitivity stands to the specific content of 'to the right of ___ in a straight line', or 'father of'.

For both 'God can in option-tied power ___' and 'God can in option-neutral power ___' were being used in the period of

[2] H. W. B. Joseph, *An Introduction to Logic* (Oxford, 1916; repr. 1950), 7ll. + 608 pp., 589.

this book as *cum determinatione* "predications" on the unanalysed but regimented level of speech appropriate to the 'dialectical' discussions in which so many of the schoolmen's inquiries were made. Someone reasoning from either to a simple conclusion of the form 'God can ____' tout court, or from a denial of the latter to a denial of one or other of the former, stood in danger of a Secundum Quid fallacy, if he was not being careful. The Power Distinction made it easier for people to be careful about such things, and easier to show that they were being careful.

2. *A discussion for theologians?*

Throughout the period covered by this book, the period covered by the Faculty's own great flowering, up to the condemnations of the 1270s, the Distinction flourished in the Theology Faculty of Paris. It was used while the Faculty was still finding its feet: from before 1219 by Geoffrey of Poitiers, and from the same period it would seem by the still unidentified *Quidam* reported by William of Auxerre. William himself used it, and was held in great respect within the University. So did those other respected pioneers in academic theology, Philip the Chancellor and William of Auvergne; though in expressions which did not find the same favour among their successors in the schools. In the crucial period when the Distinction was passing to the schools of the friars, it appears (in its now familiar expression) in Hugh of St Cher, Roland of Cremona, and Guerric of St Quentin among the Dominicans, and in Alexander of Hales (including a passage arguably from Alexander himself) among the Franciscans. It is used and clearly expounded by Albert the Great, and even in the contentious days of condemnations and mutual recriminations, around 1270, it was used alike by Aquinas and Bonaventure. It was not itself called in question in the condemnations of the 1270s.

Among the users mentioned it is to be found alike in Sentence commentaries, in Summas of theology, and in disputed questions: in works, that is, of academic theology addressed to academic theologians. It is rarely found outside of such works: in commentaries on Aristotle, for example, or in works of apologetics or of pious instruction. In Aquinas, where logically similar puzzles about divine power are raised in commentaries on Aristotle, there are barely hints of the Distinction. Yet in his own theological works, from earliest to last, he uses it a score and more times, and contributes greatly to its understanding.

Outside Paris's Theology Faculty it was not much in evidence. Neither, for that matter, was theology in those days. Oxford, for example, whose time would come in a marvellous period between the condemnations and the Black Death, was up to then barely a satellite of Paris in theology. At least two Oxford men of the period did use it: Roger Bacon the Franciscan and Robert Kilwardby the Dominican. Both had done earlier work in Arts at Paris. Yet both point forwards rather than backwards. Bacon uses it in a context of natural philosophy, in a discussion on the vacuum; Kilwardby on an intriguingly worded objection, concerning whether Christ could have been *simul peccator, vel iniustus saltem, et iustus*. Hostiensis, Henricus de Segusia, the influential Enrico Bartolomei from Susa, introduced the Distinction, or an adaptation of it, into jurists' discussions; but he too had had Parisian connections. The belief that he had introduced the Distinction from jurisprudence to theology has been shown (above) to be mistaken. So both in respect of the people using the Distinction, and of the works in which it is to be found (in the period covered in the present book), it was very much a theologians' device, and one largely restricted to discussions within academic theology.

3. *A theological terminology?*

Even the terminology of the Distinction has a theological and recognisably 'Christian' tone. It was not expressed in the Platonic dress of the Calcidian translation of the *Timaeus*, which had been favoured by the "scientifically" minded of the earlier twelfth century. Perhaps the fate of Abelard, and the effects of Bernard's cleverly angled distortion of Abelard's views on what God could do, had been noted. Neither was the Distinction expressed in the language of Aristotle, whose views on matters other than logic were provoking such concern from ecclesiastical authorities in the earlier half of the thirteenth century. It was expressed in a developed version of a distinction which had been used by Augustine, to somewhat similar purpose: the distinction between what God could do *de potentia* as against *de iustitia*.[3] Albert the Great at one place appeared to identify the Power Distinction with the earlier one, though perhaps he meant no more than that Augustine should be understood as having "really meant" the same by his formulas. Since at another place Albert seems to identify Plato as an early user, it may be that strict identification of the distinctions was not Albert's intention.

One rather interesting antecedent was provided by the Fourth Lateran Council of 1215, in whose large shadow much of the theology of the thirteenth century should be seen to lie. This had emphasised that God *sua omnipotente virtute* had created from nothing, *de nihilo condidit creaturam*. It had then contrasted *haec sancta Trinitas* with that creation, executed *iuxta ordinatissimam dispositionem temporum* (Consitutio I, De fide, ed. Alberigo *et al.* 1973: 230). The reference to creation makes it clear that it is God's power to do things extrinsic to his nature which is in question in *sua omnipotente virtute*, and the *haec sancta Trinitas* is referred grammatically to the subject of *condidit*. God's "almighty power" here is thus not to be identified with the divine nature, and in the context nothing more than God's option-tied power need be in question. This would be a traditional way of using *omnipotens*, appropriate in a conciliar document of the kind, but a way which was already becoming less common in the West.[4] I have not found reference to this text in close association with early uses of the Distinction, and am not suggesting that we should see in this text a historical antecedent. (Also, it is by no means excluded that the Distinction will yet surface in texts anterior to 1215.)[5] But a green light from the Council for speaking in that way of God could hardly have been unwelcome to theologians of the time. Some might see further encouragement to the *modi loquendi* in which the Distinction was already being

[3] *Contra Gaudent.* 1, ch. 30, CSEL 53; 233–4, PL 43; 727. Cf. J. Plagniaux, 'Le Binôme "*iustitia-potentia*" dans la sotériologie augustinienne et anselmienne', *Spicileg. Becc.* 1 (1959) 141–54; R. Crouse, 'The Augustinian Background to Anselm's Concept of *iustitia*', *Can. J. Theol.* 4 (1958), 111–19.

[4] See A. de Halleux, 'Dieu le Père tout-puissant', *Rev. théologique de Louvain*, 8 (1977), 400–22, and works referred to there. The Conciliar texts are cited from J. Alberigo, J. Dossetti, P.-P. Joannou, C. Leonardi, P. Prodi (eds.), with H. Jedin, *Conciliorum oecumenicorum decreta* (Bologna, 1973), XXIV + 1135 + 1–169* pp.

[5] As was noted in Ch. 2, the text from PL 175; 457, cited at Courtenay, 'The Dialect of Omnipotence' (1985), 247, 261, and again at Ritter, *Wörterbuch*, 7; 1157, ought not to be counted among these.

put, from Gregory IX's bull of 1228, supporting a measure of academic freedom for the students and masters of Paris. That bull commanded the theologians to avoid the fictions of the philosophers (*figmentis philosophorum*: in the first instance, a veiled reference to Abelard's *involucrum* taken from Plato's World Soul?) and keep their speculations 'contained within the bounds established by the Fathers'.[6] The very terminology of the Distinction insinuated that nothing significantly more adventurous was being done, than had been done from at least Augustine's day with the *de potentia/iustitia* distinction.

4. *The topics of discussion*

The earliest uses of the Distinction which have so far come to light are addressed to a narrowly theological problem: whether this or that means of redemption providentially ordered by God could have been otherwise. Problems like this take their rise within a tradition of quite narrowly Christian theology, and are of a type widely canvassed in Anselm's day. Could God have given to Christ power over all things, and in particular the power of justifying and saving (Geoffrey of Poitiers, a. 1219); Was another manner of redemption possible to God (*Quidam*, cit. William of Auxerre, a. 1229); Can God damn Peter or save Judas (William of Auxerre, a. 1229; Hugh of St Cher, OP, *c.* 1225); What is the power, concerning baptism, which according to Augustine God could have given to men, but was not willing to give them (W. of Auxerre, a. 1229; H. of St Cher, *c.* 1225)?

Contemporary with all save the very earliest of these are uses of the Distinction in connection with problems which are not theological in quite such a narrow fashion. Hugh of St Cher, OP, who continued to ask questions of the narrower type, also asks the following. Can God dissolve angels and souls out of existence; Can he make a man to be an ass, while the nature of each remains; Can he bring it about that two things opposed contradictorily could be true together (all, *c.* 1225)? To the same type we might assign the question reported by Roland of

---

[6] *Ab Aegyptiis argentea vasa* of 7 July 1228. With others, I read *contenti* for *contempti* at Paris, *Cart.* 1, No. 59. The Rahner edn. (1955) of Denzinger signals this bull as being 'De terminologia et traditione ecclesiastica servanda' (No. 442, p. 206).

Cremona, as canvassed by unspecified *philosophi*: Could God have done better than he did? Roland's *philosophi* here are surely Abelard and his platonic sources. This question resurfaces in St Bonaventure.

In a third type are narrowly theological questions given sophistication, or a particular slant, by some complication from sources which may have to be sought elsewhere than in narrowly Christian discussions about the means of redemption. Roland of Cremona, for example, used the Distinction in connection with the question: Could the human race have been redeemed otherwise than it has been, in view especially of (legends of) the means of redemption having been shown to Adam and the prophets in ecstasies. The complication there concerned consequences of supposed revelations about the decreed order future to the recipient of the revelations. It was a complication which had already enjoyed a vigorous career within Islam, and was to take the fancy of poets in the West, not least of Chaucer, both in the tale of Chauntecleer, and in *Troilus*. Alexander of Hales asks whether the Incarnation could take place now. The complication here is from considerations of tense. Discussions involving these had already been undertaken by theologians, independently of Power Distinction questions; not least in Peter Lombard.

Some of the complications arise in connection with speculations about angels. (Here too there may be some echoes of discussions within Islam.) Bonaventure uses the Distinction in a number of questions betraying this sort of complication: Can the will of an angel confirmed in grace (or rebellion) change; Could God have condoned punishment to the rebellious angels? Albert the Great was unhappy about a whole genre of questions concerning angels' purportedly moving masses around. These were among the 43 questions on which he (with Kilwardby and Aquinas) had been consulted by the Master-General of the Dominicans. Albert's unhappiness was not about angels as such, but about the idea of their moving masses around; perhaps also about the propriety of putting weight on (non-physical) speculations in constructing thought-experiments in natural philosophy. On the question, however, of whether an angel could move the mass of the Earth as far as the sphere of the moon, he did use the Distinction. Even so, he could not resist adding: This is a showman's question, not one for a philosopher. It may be worth noting that the

Cartesians of later times took to asking questions about what angels might be able to do, where earlier inquirers had asked about what God could bring about. No doubt the shift was both piously and cautiously intended: but assertions about creaturely option-neutral power are in fact problematical in (additional) ways in which assertions about God's are not.

5. *Progress to a more general question*

What a review of the topics confirms, is that while the original impulse to deploy the Distinction was provided by narrowly theological discussions, it was soon recognised as applicable to questions of wider generality, in philosophical theology. It was at the widening phase, rather than the initial one, that Abelard's seminal question on whether God could do other than he does, makes its appearance. It was also at the post-initial phase that complications from classical or Islamic backgrounds begin to be noticed.[7] The initial impulse to deploy the Distinction would thus appear to be from a modest ambition to deal with the kinds of question canvassed by Anselm and his contemporaries about the "necessity" of this or that means of redemption: and to do so in a dialectically usable way, graspable quite as readily by a Poore Persoun as by a Clerke of Oxenforde. It was not long, however, before schoolmen realised that it offered a like means for two questions of higher generality, which went straight to the heart of the established Christian view of the world as at bottom a universe of God's ordering, rather than the sum of things understood by the ancient atomists. More precisely, the challenge is raised by one question, in two stages.

The question is, Can God do what he is not doing? The first stage of the answer is Yes, because there is nothing in God to

---

[7] I do not find evidence in the writings examined for Chs. 3 and 4 for the claim that the Distinction had first been used by 'theologians attempting to gloss or reinterpret authoritative statements about divine immutability'; if that is what is being claimed at W. Courtenay, 'The Dialectic' (1985), 247. At a period before the Distinction appears, theologians (Lombard, Hugh of St Victor et al.) had certainly been addressing such problems, and Courtenay, 244, is no doubt correct in seeing Damian as addressing a problem of the sort. But it is rather in discussions of whether the mode of Redemption could have been other than it was, that the earliest uses of the Distinction to surface so far, have appeared. Damian's concern in any case, in the famous letter (ed. A. Cantin (1972) in *SC* 191), was not that of an academic theologian.

necessitate him to do what he is doing, and nothing in the intrinsic nature of something done by God, in virtue of which it has to be as it happens to be. Rather, what there is in the actual order of things is willed by God; and there is nothing in the nature of being willed by God (nothing necessarily implied in the meaning of 'It is willed by God that ___') in virtue of which that which is willed by God is eo ipso necessary (that the propositions which satisfy 'It is willed by God that ___' are eo ipso logically necessary). At a second stage, the answer just mentioned has to be shown to be both coherent dialectically and not inconsistent with anything shown to be implied in the faith of the Church.

In the first stage the rival views are from philosophers. The most radical of these rival views was that of the ancient atomists, in which there is no universe; only a sum of things, and in effect a closed, mechanical system in which everything which can happen within the system inevitably does happen, and inevitably recurs in every possible manner. This view was familiar to the schoolmen, if only because it was rehearsed in their own Scriptures:

Vanity of vanities, said Ecclesiastes, vanity of vanities, and all is vanity.... What is it that hath been? The same thing that shall be. What is it that hath been done? The same that shall be done. (Eccl. 1: 2 & 9.)

They were not faced with that view, however, in a form which they could (psychologically speaking) envisage as a serious intellectual challenge to their own world-view at that time. It did not present itself to them as a "live option" for acceptance as a world-view, but rather as an *inconveniens* to be avoided. If some apparently different philosophical position could be shown to be reducible ultimately to that view, the apparently different position would have to be rejected.

One philosophical position of the kind had come with impressive support, and was very much acceptable psychologically at the time as an intellectually "live option". This was, as Aquinas summarised it, 'the opinion of some Philosophers, saying that God acts out of the necessity of [his] nature. And if that were the case, since a nature is determined to one [kind of] thing, divine power could not extend itself towards other things than those which it is doing' (*De potentia*, qu. 1, a. 5). This is a view imputed to Avicenna by Algazel, in a less than sympathetic critique from some forty years after the former's death. The view was imputed to him also by Dominic Gundisalvi, one of Avicenna's translators, in a work which owed much to Avicenna. And it has been imputed to him by historians since, almost universally. In fact Avicenna can be shown to have held an importantly different view, and it is to Gundisalvi's honour as a translator, that one sufficient argument to show this can be obtained from the very parts of the *Shifa* translated by Gundisalvi.[8] More to the point here, is that the view passed for Avicenna's in the medieval schools. No medieval academic, to my knowledge, challenged the attribution. So the view passed to the schools with the prestige of Avicenna behind it.

Much of Avicenna's thought was expressed in ways particularly welcome to devotees of Augustine, and the translations sometimes emphasised the apparent similarities. Avicenna (after Aristotle) also provided some of the greatest of the thirteenth-century schoolmen—Albert and Aquinas most notably—with the core of philosophical logic and metaphysics on which the latter's understanding of the Distinction depended. A view with those letters of credence had to be countered.

It was countered, by arguments to the effect that God acts out of no necessity of his nature, but that 'his will is the cause of all things' (as in Aquinas, *ST* 1/25/5c). Aquinas there added: Neither is what God wills determined naturally and out of necessity to these actual things. Being willed by God, that is, does not of its nature necessarily imply being necessitated.

This left untouched other doctrines important for them to hold: not least the doctrine of a God-ordered world, with which they were able to oppose the view that what there is, is no more than a sum of things. It left untouched the doctrines needed to protect a God-ordered world: that there was nothing in the nature of God, or in the meaning of 'willed by God', or in the intrinsic nature of the order of things held actually instantiated in subjection to God's will, to build any genuine necessitation

---

[8] See tr. 9c of the medieval Latin translation, ed. S. Van Riet in *Avicenna Latinus: Lib. de philosophia prima sive scientia divina*, V–X (Louvain, 1980), 500–1; where the role of First Governor must not be misunderstood, and where the First Governor itself is not to be confounded with the First, sans phrase, to wit, with God.

into the actual things of our world. What there is in our world, they held, is indeed not to be said *simpliciter* to be possible not to be: but that is only because of the particular end imposed on it. An order of things descriptively indistinguishable from ours, to any degree of approximation we might wish, is (when considered in its intrinsic content only) quite possible to be ordered so as to be first instantiated, and then not.

If the logical and metaphysical means to reconcile a God-ordered world with a rigorously negative view on the divine nature were coming from Aristotle and Avicenna, the same cannot be said about the positive motivation. Where the view that the world was ordered by God was in contention, the positive support invoked by medievals seen above was seen to come, typically and for the most part, from dogmatically Christian sources: Scripturally warranted beliefs as expressed in the "authorities" accepted in their discussions.[9]

Just as typically, it was being emphasised that that was where the support was coming from. It was natural enough in a theology faculty, after all, and we have seen in Chapters 2–8 more than one admonition from ecclesiastical authorities to the effect that theologians ought to keep their academic disputes to domains where the disputes could and ought properly to be settled ultimately by appeal to dogmatically Christian sources. All the more interesting, then, that theologians working within such constraints should have found themselves forced, in order to settle in a comprehensive enough manner their narrowly "Christian" disputes about whether the means of redemption might have been otherwise, to keep the more general question in mind.

6. *A shift in the choice of topics addressed*

In the period covered in this book a certain movement can be discerned. First the Distinction is used ad hoc, on the kinds of problem which had already been attracting discussion among the theologians of Anselm's time. Moreover the mode of theology in which it was being used was ostensibly the same mode as the

---

[9] See, in indexes to the Quaracchi editions, for example, uses of texts such as 'O Lord, Lord, Almighty King, for all things are in thy power: and there is none that can resist thy will,... Thou art Lord of all, and there is none that can resist thy majesty' (Est. 13: 9–11); Job 37 (passim); Rom. 9: 19 ff.; Wisd. 12: 13, 8: 1, 9: 1; 11: 12 ff.; Eph. 1: 11).

one used by Anselm: with the *opus redemptionis* as the central theme, and dialectics as very much the *ancilla*. The Distinction is then used in questions of wider generality, in philosophical theology. Even then, however, the central question—Abelard's seminal question on whether God could do otherwise than he is doing—remains at its core a generalisation of the questions canvassed in Anselm's day on the *opus redemptionis*. In Abelard's own statement of the question the importantly non-Christian input, which indeed contributed to the perplexities, was from Plato; and indeed from the Plato slanted by Macrobius and others, which had been so much admired by Christian writers in the earlier twelfth century, for its apparently "scientific" reinforcement of the Christians' world-view. As against the view of the ancient atomists, the view of the Plato understood in the earlier twelfth-century West was a "scientific" view emphasising the *universitas*, and eagerly welcomed by Christian apologists. Even there, the Platonic input was as an *ancilla* (to an apologetics addressed to non-Christians taken to be sophisticated in Greek philosophy), and intervened in the (rhetorical) complications of the issues, not in their (broadly logical or analytical) core.[10] Yet by the end of the period covered, in both Bonaventure (*In 1 Sent.*, d. 43, at *Op. theol. sel.* 1 (1924), 615, 616) and Aquinas (*ST* 1/25/5 ad 1), the Distinction is being used in a question where the philosophical theology (the input which is not essentially "Christian") is central, and the specifically "Christian" input is more in evidence in the motivations for addressing the central question with such emphasis.

UNDERSTANDING THE DISTINCTION

Within the period of this book, the Power Distinction itself—the dialectical device—was understood in a uniform manner. By that I mean that application of the Distinction by different users to like cases yielded like results. By that criterion there was only one distinction in play in the applications examined in Chapters 2–8.

If the contrasting arms of the Distinction are taken, as they

[10] See L. Moonan, 'Abelard's Use of the *Timaeus*', *AHDLMA* 64 (1989), 7–90, 72–4.

have been taken throughout, as putatively significant utterances, then they are open to being justified in accordance with more than one theory. What is it that is true, when it is true that God can in option-tied power do this, or cannot in option-neutral power do that? Not surprisingly, the users can be seen to diverge on this point: in line with their views on the content of utterances generally, and in effect in line with their views on universals. For the earliest users in Chapter 2 not enough material is yet available to permit a sure enough opinion. For the users of Chapters 5–7, ample material was seen above. From it a synthetic and provisional analysis, representing in intention the core of the earlier medieval Power Distinction—the Distinction as understood by the medievals examined above—is now put forward. The terms in which it is put forward are sometimes ours rather than theirs, for the analysis is meant not only to represent a historical position, but to present it so as to be understandable within our own culture; whether or not we may wish to view it as of purely historical interest, or as in some ways a serviceable position still. Even as a historical position its interest is considerable: given the part it played in discussions central to theologians in its own period (one of the most productive in the history of systematic theology), and the key which it provides to an understanding of shifts within theology and beyond, in the later medieval period in which so much of the warp of our own culture's canvas was added.

7. *Making the option-neutral arm true*

As used in the period examined, option-neutral assertions—for example, 'God can in his option-neutral power make there to be flying pigs'—are to be understood as conjunctions of a proposition of composing-apt type, and one of narrowly predicative type (though with some unique features). The composing-apt component may be considered first.

The option-neutral assertion cannot be true where the core expression ('flying pigs' here) fails (as 'bligs blags blugs' fails) to express any putatively significant utterance. Neither can it be true where the core expression implies a contradiction (as 'square circle' does). It can be true where, as I am supposing in the case of 'flying pig', the intrinsic content satisfies both the *ens* and the *ens factum* conditions as demanded by Aquinas above; or where there is an "Avicennian essence" of flying pig; or where it might be said that the intersection of being a pig and being a flyer is not empty.

Where those conditions are satisfied, as for 'flying pig', what is further necessary if the option-neutral assertion is to be true, is that the intrinsic content in question, considered in intrinsic content merely, and prescinding from any relations in which it might be seen to stand either to comparable intrinsic contents or to instantiation, should be asserted to be contained within the (non-ordered) set of "things" which can satisfy the conditions mentioned. In terms of the composing-apt analysis the intrinsic content of 'flying pig', considered in the abstract manner mentioned, is to be 'composed' with the concept of such a set, by means of the necessary relation appropriate; in this case, that of containment of subsets in a set.

The wider set envisaged here is the (non-ordered) set containing any intrinsic contents which can satisfy the conditions noted, and no other elements. The 'any but only' condition identifies the set, or more precisely distinguishes it from any set of such things which might be finite, no matter how extensive. If I might have had a holiday in Morocco last year, but did not, it might perhaps be said that it was within my option-neutral power to have brought about such a holiday, and also that it is in God's option-neutral power to have brought about such a holiday. Even if both could be said with truth—creaturely option-neutral power raises complications which divine option-neutral power does not, and I leave the question open here—the 'any but only' condition would distinguish the set envisaged, not only from that of any option-neutral power of mine, but from that of any agent finite in any way whatsoever.

If the *ens* and *ens factum* conditions are as straightforwardly specifiable as they appear, and the infinity appropriate to the set of things of divine option-neutral power is potential, then a more formal analysis of the composing-apt element of the option-neutral arm, would not seem to involve any peculiar difficulties, or even to demand particularly recherché formalisms.

With an analysis of only that component, however, we have not yet caught that it is precisely God's option-neutral power which is in question. We have not yet excluded that 'God can in option-neutral power make there to be flying pigs' is just a rather fanciful way of making the point that although there are no such things, there need be nothing inherently absurd in the notion that there could have been such things. We have excluded that what has been explained under the name of 'God's option-neutral power' could be attributed to any being finite in any way; but we have not excluded that for anything—call it a superfact—which satisfies the conditions for something within "God's option-neutral power" as understood so far (with only the composing-apt component of the analysis in place), we can further envisage a finite agent—call it a superfactor—which likewise satisfies the conditions for something within "God's option-neutral power", and is powerful enough to produce the superfact envisaged. We have not excluded that for any super-factor envisaged within "God's option-neutral power", a superfact equally within "God's option-neutral power", and which our superfactor cannot produce, can be found. In short, we have as yet only "God's option-neutral power", some pure fiction of ours, and not *God's* option-neutral power sans phrase.

To make the difference, between fictions of "God's option-neutral power", and *God's* option-neutral power, no more is needed than to conjoin with the composing-apt component of the analysis, a proposition expressing the truth, if there is a truth there, of God's existence; in the way open to proponents of a rigorously negative theology on the divine nature. Of course the 'no more is needed' invites an ironical smile, at the enormity of what is needed, and its contentiousness. Yet it was something which the medievals examined above were prepared to assent to anyway; and for that matter it was something against which Hume was prepared to concede, not necessarily only with irony, that his destructive arguments were not able to prevail.

What is needed, in any case, is to be able to conjoin a proposition (of narrowly predicative type) to the effect that something exists, and not everything which exists in some or other determinate manner.

The very expression of a proposition to that effect raises difficulties, some of which will be considered presently. If it is true, however, there is no time at which it is not true; and hence no time at which its falsehood could make a conjunction of which it formed part, to be false. In order to reason from an analysis of the option-neutral arm, therefore, we need only be able to reason from (the truth of) the composing-apt component of the analysis. If that is so, and if the utterance of that component is an utterance of a declarative sentence in which specifiable elements are being said to belong to an identifiable set of such things, then any difficulties about expressing the assertion of the narrowly predicative proposition about God are beside the point; provided it can be expressed in at least some reliable way, so as to be able to be asserted with truth.

8. *Making the option-tied arm true*

The importance of some features of God's option-tied power will appear fully only where attributions not only to divine power but also to divine wisdom (providential wisdom especially) can be taken more fully into account: it is characteristic of the wise to set things in order (*sapientis est ordinare*, Arist. *Metaph.* A2, 982^a 17–19), and 'the name of being the wise one sans phrase is reserved to him alone whose consideration bears on the end of the totality of things; and he furthermore is the origin of that totality' (Aquinas, *SCG* ad init.). For present purposes the following ought to be said.

Even at the stage of detecting, say, 'God can in his option-tied power make there to be grunting pigs' as systematically misleading, and reformulating it in preparation for analysis, a difference between option-tied and option-neutral assertions appears. Option-neutral assertions, being seen when regimented to be about abstract contents of things, considered in themselves, had to be analysed primarily as composing-apt propositions. There is no room for a true assertion about *abstract contents* of things, *considered in themselves*, to be expressed in an analysed proposition, save in one of composing-apt type. Option-tied assertions are to be seen rather as being about *abstract contents* of things *considered* not in themselves, but *as instantiated in extra-mental reality*. They are thus to be seen as being about some item in the world, and to be analysed primarily as narrowly predicative. A necessary condition will be,

  (1) There being grunting pigs, belongs to the order of things willed by God to exist in extra-mental reality,

which needs to be spelled out in various ways. The force of the naming-expression in subject position may be caught in the existential (narrowly predicative) proposition,

(2) There are grunting pigs.

The predicate of (1) implies belonging to a certain class, 'the order of things willed by God to exist in extra-mental reality'. Bearing in mind that the Negative Theology views of the medievals examined above are to be taken into account, what is to be made of 'the order of things willed by God'?

9. *Two types of order*

The order is twofold: internal, between elements (sub-orders) of the whole order, and external, by which all the things of the order are ordered towards the end imposed (by God).[11] That the whole *ordinatio dei* is to be thought an imposed order, not necessarily a perceived order, is to be noted; and it may be useful to say a little more on how the types of order mentioned are to be distinguished.

A perceived order is the sort of thing which excited William Paley, and still seems to excite many. In a watch 'we *perceive* (what we could not discover in the stone) that its several parts are framed and put together for a purpose...' (*Natural Theology*, ch. 1, emphasis added). Of course, as Hume had already argued, we perceive nothing of the kind. But I wish to note that what some people have in mind, some of the time, when they speak of an order, is a "perceived order" or 'display of intelligence' (Hume, *Enquiry... Understanding*, sect. XI; *EUN* 135): a sequence which, to an intelligent observer, though not necessarily to a critical one, may suggest a deliberate placing of the items in sequence.

That there should be a perceived order is consistent with the world-view in which whatever happens, happens by necessity, or by "chance". A perceived order coming about by "chance" can be seen on a small scale, when players of word-games draw

[11] Cf.: Est autem duplex ordo considerandus in rebus. Unus, quo aliquid creatum ordinatur ad alium creatum: sicut partes ordinantur ad totum, et accidentia ad substantiam, et unaquaque res ad suum finem. Alius ordo, quo omnia creata ordinantur in Deum. (Aquinas, *ST* 1/21/1 ad 3.)

seven letters at random, and discover that the sequence of letters, placed left to right in order of arrival, coincides with the sequence of letters in an English word. There seems no reason of principle why this should not happen on a larger scale. If the world is a closed mechanical system, as in views such as the old atomists favoured, then if some sequence can happen within the possibilities of the system, it has to happen, indefinitely many times.[12]

It would seem to follow that Paley-type arguments, commonly thought of as directable against views such as that of the old atomists (or of Hobbes), are apologetically worthless for such a purpose. If successful, Paley-type arguments argue to a perceived order. Views such as that of the old atomists can accommodate a perceived order, of no matter what complexity. Hence successful Paley-type arguments leave views to the effect that whatever happens, happens by necessity, undamaged.

Quite different is what may be called a deliberately imposed order, a sequence understood to have resulted from intelligent disposition.[13]

For an order to count as an imposed order in this way, it is neither necessary nor sufficient that any intelligence other than that of the imposer should recognise or "perceive" it for what it is. Some writers have desks which are highly ordered in this imposed manner, yet not all observers appear to recognise it for the order it is, or any order at all. And a mistaken hypothesis, in science and in detective work alike, often arises when an order is "perceived" in the phenomena, only for subsequent events to show that the "perception" was not really justified. This sort of hypothesis can be mistaken either because there was no one order to be seen in the phenomena, or because there was one, but not the one taken from it. If the world is an imposed order, views to the effect that whatever happens, happens by necessity (strict, logical necessity) will have to be false.

As for being an order 'willed by God', it is necessary (but not

---

[12] Aquinas noted: 'quidam totaliter providentiam negaverunt, sicut Democritus et Epicurei, ponentes mundum factum esse casu' (*ST* 1/22/2c).

[13] That Paley recognised the possibility of imposed orders too, would appear from his reference, in his letter to the Prince Bishop of Durham, to 'the completion of a regular and comprehensive design', at *The Works of William Paley, D.D., Archdeacon of Carlisle . . . Complete in one Volume* (Edinburgh, 1828), xxviii + 712 pp., 434.

sufficient) that (1) the order is in itself (including any internal ordering) instantiable punctiliously by a power unrestricted in any way; which is to say that its intrinsic content, considered abstractly, should be one of the things of God's option-neutral power, treated in Section 7. To obtain a further necessary condition, a concept sometimes used for relationships within the order may be brought into play. The truthmaker of (2), 'There are grunting pigs', from Section 8 ad fin. above, may stand as an item in the world in (non-necessary) relationships with comparable items. Given certain circumstances, for example, it may be unpreventable that there are grunting pigs; and given the grunting of the pigs it may be unpreventable, in other circumstances, that the burglar alarm will sound. People sometimes speak of such outcomes as 'necessary', or 'necessary in the sense of being unpreventable', or *ex suppositione* "necessary"; but as the scare-quotes are intended to indicate, the "necessity" involved here in the core-propositions is not that of the strictly modal necessities to be displayed in composing-apt propositions.[14] The assertion that given the loss of a horseshoe nail, the loss of the kingdom is unpreventable might be true, and even 'The loss of the kingdom is unpreventable', uttered at that time, might be true. In that case, however, 'The loss of the kingdom is unpreventable' ('It is now unpreventable that the kingdom is lost') does not necessarily imply 'Necessarily, The kingdom is lost', but may imply 'The kingdom is lost' (a narrowly predicative proposition) and 'Necessarily, If it is unpreventable at some time that the kingdom is lost, then at some other time the kingdom is lost' (to be understood as composing-apt). ('The kingdom's being lost' in the composing-apt proposition has to be taken *divisim* from its instantiation, whereas in the *res propositionis* of 'The kingdom is lost' (in effect, when designating that proposition's

---

[14] See Prior, *Formal Logic* (1962), 184–5 and refs., on *de re* "necessities". For Avicenna: 'Les propositions dans lesquelles il y a nécessité par une condition non essentielle se voient parfois attribuer en propre le nom d'absolues, parfois le nom de réelles comme nous leur avons attribué exclusivement, bien que sans chicaner sur les mots' (*Isharat*, tr. Goichon (1951), as at n. 17 below, 137). On 'réelles' Goichon notes: 'Cf. *Najat*, 31. Cette nécessité non essentielle est une nécessité non métaphysique'. On 'absolues' she notes: '*Wujūdiyya* signifie littéralement relative à l'existence, existente, réelle. Une telle proposition constate que dans l'être, dans le réel, les choses sont ainsi; elle constate le fait, sans plus.... Cette nécessité de fait s'oppose, chez Ibn Sina, à la nécessité logique de la modale, qu'il appelle la nécessité vraie; cf. *Lexique*, no. 588, § 35.' (Same, 137 n.)

truthmaker) it has to be taken *composite* with its instantiation.)[15]

If the whole *ordinatio dei* is one of the things which God can in his option-tied power bring about, and is an *ens factum* existing in extra-mental reality, then it too ought to be in principle able to be said to be unpreventable or not. But if it is to be said *simpliciter* and with truth to be unpreventable, then there must be no conceivable way in which it can be prevented, and no conceivable kind of entity by which it can be prevented. (Being prevented, being preventable, and being unpreventable are all to be understood as said of existents, not of concepts or any other intentional entity.) No matter how great the actual order of things may be, a superfact within which it was possible but prevented, or within which it should be executed, but not punctiliously, by a superfactor, is possible in God's option-neutral power. No matter how slight the actual order of things might be, its punctilious execution is unpreventable in any way, by no matter how powerful a superfactor... —only if its execution is due to something itself not determinate in any way in its being. So a second necessary condition for something's being 'willed by God', is that (2) the order's punctilious execution is unpreventable, *simpliciter*. With a further condition, that (3) the order of things is something in extra-mental reality, we have a set of conditions severally necessary and jointly sufficient for excluding something's being willed by anything other than God. With the condition already needed to make it God's option-tied power which is being explained,

(3) Some God exists,

understood as in Section 7 above, we have what was lacking in the jointly sufficient set for 'willed by God'.

10. *Avicennian essences*

These were referred to more than once in the analyses, as the abstract contents of things, capable of receiving existence in

---

[15] The *res propositionis* is a linguistic item, designating the *res realis* in virtue of which the narrowly predicative proposition is true, if true. In his short *De propositionibus modalibus* (Leonine vol. Aquinas gives grammatical transformation rules for getting between *res propositionis* and *dictum propositionis*, thus indicating what sort of thing he understood the *res propositionis* to be.

extra-mental reality, given an actual cause of the appropriate kind; and capable equally of not receiving such existence, should no such cause be present. They are called Avicennian as a gesture of recognition towards Avicenna, the great Persian meta-physician,[16] but chiefly as a reminder that the "essences" in question are not limited to Aristotelian essences, though they would include these. A passage from Avicenna's *Isharat*, which could serve to introduce the notion, is worth quoting here for what it permits us to see by comparison, more of what the medievals examined above should be seen to be doing in the Power Distinction, with related notions:

Every being, if you consider it according to its essence without con-sidering another being, must be in so far as existence is necessary to it in itself, or else it is not. If it is necessary to it, it is truth in itself, the one whose existence is necessary by its own self. It is the subsistent. And if it is not necessary, one cannot call it impossible by essence, after having supposed it existent. On the other hand, if such *a condition* as 'lacking a cause' is *joined in consideration to its essence,* it becomes impossible; alternatively, such a condition as 'its cause existing', and it becomes necessary. But if *no condition* is *bound to it,* neither the realisation of a cause, nor its inexistence, it remains in itself the third thing, and that is possibility [contingency]. It is then, in relation to its essence, the thing which is neither necessary nor impossible. Thus every being is necessary by essence, or else possible [contingent] by essence. (*Isharat,* tr. after Goichon, 357–8.)[17]

Every being other than God, on this view, has an essence which might be instantiated or not. Considered in itself—'if no condition is bound to it, neither the realisation of a cause, nor its inexistence'—it is contingent to be or not to be. Considered in relation to whether or not there is something which makes it unpreventable, 'if such a condition as "lacking a cause" is joined in consideration to its essence, it becomes impossible; alternatively, such a condition as "its cause existing", and it becomes necessary'. The phrase which should be marked is 'a condition . . . joined in consideration to its essence': this is the

---

[16] Avicenna, or Abū 'Ali al-Ḥusayn b. 'Abd Allāh b. Sīnā, b. 370 AH/AD 980 in Afshanah near Bukhara, now in Uzbekistan; d. Hamadan 428 AH/AD 1037 See s.v. 'Ibn Sīnā' (A.-M. Goichon), in *The Encyclopaedia of Islam,* new edn. III (1971).

[17] A.-M. Goichon, tr., *Ibn Sīnā (Avicenne): Livre des directives et remarques (Kītāb al-'Išārāt wa l-Tanbīhāt)* (Beirut, 1951).

Avicennian essence, taken *composite* with the condition in question. When the same Avicennian essence is considered 'with no condition bound to it', it is being considered *divisim* from such conditions. In the option-tied arm of the Distinction, because of the narrowly predicative elements of the analysis, the Avicennian essence has to be understood as being considered with a condition to the effect 'its cause existing', joined to it in the very consideration. In the option-neutral arm, where the Avicennian essence is being considered as an object of thought, and hence *divisim* from whether it has anything like an instantiating cause or not, the implications are very different. It is in their making use of the notion of Avicennian essence, of the notion of something's being 'joined in consideration' to such an essence, or not, and more generally of the two-type analysis for assertions of scientifical importance, that the medievals examined above can instructively be compared with Avicenna. If the 'cause' of the schoolmen was a free disposition of God's, and that of Avicenna was present, where it was present, by necessary emanation from the First Governor at least, it will not be surprising to find differences in understanding the diverse "impossibilities" involved in their case and his. Because both the nature of the "impossibility" which Avicenna should be seen to intend here, and the scope of the necessary emanation to which he is committed, no instructive comparison on the 'impossibilities' is yet available. Fortunately, it was not on those that comparison was desirable.

11. *The "things" which God can do in option-neutral power*

These are to be understood as Avicennian essences considered in their intrinsic content only, prescinding from (1) any necessary connections with other "things" of the same kind, and from (2) whether or not they are instantiated. So considered, they are susceptible of two-way possibility. And so considered, they can serve as truthmakers of composing-apt propositions which are true. This is already an indication of their ontological status.

They were called *entia*, and I call them 'things', but the only kind of existence they have is *esse intentionale*. That is all that is needed, of course, for the way in which 'any identifiable thing concerning which an affirmative proposition can be formed can be said to be something (*ens*), even if the thing in question is not something which has any place in extra-mental reality' (Aquinas, *De ente et essentia*, ad init.). This class of "thing" is wider than that of the "things" which God can do in option-neutral power, as will appear. But because that which holds of higher kinds necessarily holds of subordinate kinds, nothing which fails the conditions for an *ens* in this weaker way of understanding it can be held to be among the things God can in option-neutral power do.

The *ens* condition—as it may be called, following Aquinas in *SCG* II, ch. 25—requires the Avicennian essence to be such as to ground a true affirmative proposition. It requires therefore a *compositio* to be had. The first way in which something can fail to satisfy the very notion of an *ens*, is by taking it away through postulating something opposite to it: just as the very notion of *x*'s being human is taken away by postulating that *x* is not human, or not rational, or not animal. 'Human non-human' and 'Human non-animal' are not things of the kind required, or indeed of any kind. The opposite of something is nothing, *non ens*. So (in what follows I list the examples rejected in *SCG* II, ch. 25) (1) 'for one and the same simultaneously to be and not to be', and hence (2) 'for contradictories simultaneously to hold' is not among the things God can do. Contradictories are involved both in con- traries and in opposites by privation, 'for it follows, If it is white and black, that it is white and not white; and If it is sighted and blind, it is sighted and not sighted'. So (3) 'making opposites simultaneously to be in the same thing in the same respect' will not meet the *ens* condition. Moreover, by the removal of an essential principle, the removal of the thing itself comes about. 'So if God cannot make a thing simultaneously to be and not to be, neither can he bring it about that any one of a thing's essential principles should be lacking, while the thing itself remained; as if it could be that a man should not have a soul.' This permits (4) 'bringing it about that an essential principle of some thing should be lacking, while the thing itself remains' and more specifically (5) 'bringing it about for someone to remain a man and not have a soul'. 'Besides, since the principles of certain sciences, like logic, geometry, and arithmetic, are taken from the formal principles of things only, it follows that God cannot bring about the contraries of those principles, that the genus should not be predicable of the species, say, or that lines drawn from the centre to the circumference should not be equal, or that a rectilinear triangle should not have three angles equal to two right angles.' We may thus list (6) 'there being contraries to the formal principles of things whose being is constituted by these', and specifically (7) 'there being a genus not predicable of its species', (8) 'there being lines drawn from the centre to the circumference, without being equal', and (9) 'there being a rectilinear triangle which does not have three angles equal to two right angles'. Aquinas then added, 'From this it is obvious that God cannot bring it about that the past should not have been, for this too involves contradiction; it is of the same necessity that something is when it is, and that something was when it was.' So we may add (10) 'the past's not having been' as failing to meet even the *ens* requirement.

Because the object and effect of an active power is an *ens factum*, a *factum* condition has to be met, in addition to the *ens* condition. Aquinas's *factum* is Albert's *opus*, and Avicenna's *ens* necessary *ab alio*: what is in question is something analogous to an artefact. *Factum*, here as often in medievals' usage, is a loaded term, implying teleology, internal structure, and dependency on intelligent disposition of some kind. Not surprisingly, the loading of *factum* has often been isolated as contentious in the views of the world put forward by Christians. Sartre repudiated it as the 'vision technique du monde', Hume attacked it by his insistence that the atoms of experience do not come pre-connected, and his acceptance of the ideal of the Way of Ideas, in which only what can be backed by experience is 'intelligible' in the 'philosophical use of language'; and only what is "intelligible" in that (technical) sense can be allowed in any discourse with scientifical pretensions. A la limite, any discourse which does not merit to be cast into the flames, as so much sophistry and illusion.

The following fail to meet the *factum* condition. (1) God. This is because it is of the essence of a thing done that its existence should depend on some cause outside itself. "Something brought about" (*factum*) is of its nature determinate, and what exists in a determinate manner exists up to a point, and thus problematically. God exists in no determinate manner, and thus cannot meet the *factum* condition. (2) Something equal to God. This, for the same reasons. Equality is between determinates, and if anything exists indeterminately, there cannot be more than one of it. (3) Something's being conserved in being without God: 'for the conservation of each thing's being depends on its cause, whence it has to be that, if the cause is removed, the effect is removed. If therefore there could be some thing which was not being conserved in being by God, it would not be his effect.' This is a very different way of looking at things from that which is common today, even among professing worshippers of God. The idea that there might be a sum of things, and no God, is looked on nowadays as at least a serious possibility. It is often looked on as the view in possession, the presumption to be overcome. It is hard to appreciate that among medieval school-men it was a view held to be not merely false, but implying the possibility of something in principle impossible: that God should not be God. What gives force to this is that 'God' here, as in the usage of the medievals examined above quite generally, is taken to stand for something existing unrestrictedly, a necessarily existing simple. The modern way of looking at things takes leverage from abandoning this fundamental way of using 'God', and in effect providing "God"—what nowadays may be imagined to be God—with some kind of essence.

All of these, (1)–(3), are excluded because there is something—determinateness, and hence perhaps ontological dependency—involved in the notion of an *ens factum*, which logically cannot be reconciled with the divine nature. Whatever the divine nature is, it cannot be ontologically dependent on anything. But a further series of things is excluded on the grounds that God is—as was supposed—a voluntary agent, if acting at all. From that came (4) something which cannot be willed by God. On what comes under this heading Aquinas has this to say:

Quae autem velle non possit, considerari potest, si accipiamus qualiter in divina voluntate necessitas esse possit; nam quod necesse est esse, necesse est non esse. (*SCG* II, ch. 25.)

If the *in voluntate divina* here means 'in a divine volitum'–and both the examples which follow, and the scope-setting *'quia est per voluntatem agens'* which has preceded would suggest as much—the sense then seems to be:

The things which he cannot will, can be considered if we take in how there can be necessity in a divine volitum. For that which is necessary to be [in the case where it is actualised in a divine volitum], is necessary not to be [in the case where it is not actualised in the divine volitum].

Under the heading of things which cannot be willed by God, as then appears, are both (1) things which cannot be willed tout court, and (2) things which cannot be willed in the sorts of volitum ascribable with truth as possible to God.

Among the first are (5) for God not to exist, (6) for God not to be good, (7) for God not to be happy. Aquinas had already argued (in *SCG* II, ch. 80) that 'of necessity God wishes himself to be, to be good, and to be happy'. This is a point worth marking by those concerned with theological problems of evil. God's own 'goodness' and 'happiness' have nothing logically to do with evils or miseries in the world, or goodness in the world. To argue that there is more good than evil in the world is as much beside the point (of whether God is good or not) as to argue from the Lisbon earthquake or its latest horrific counterpart. This in itself could be a more disturbing thought for some than anything in Hume or Voltaire. But it is not something which can even be begun to be treated here.

Among the things which cannot be willed in the sorts of volitum ascribable with truth as possible to God are (8) anything evil and hence (9) sinning. In addition, God's will is immutable, and some consequences flow from that. But a word on what is being asserted here will not go amiss. 'It is one thing', says Aquinas, 'to change one's will, and another to will a change in things. For someone, with the same will immovably persisting, can will that now this should be done, and later the contrary. But a will would be being changed if someone were to begin to will what formerly he did not will, or were to leave off willing what he had been willing. And this cannot happen without some change presupposed either on the side of the knowledge [available to the one willing] or bearing on the disposition of the substance of the one willing.' (*ST* 1/19/7c.) Since in God's case both are immutable, he concludes, the will has to be immutable too. Because of that we can list (10) not fulfilling what has been willed by him. But from that it does not follow that the same has to be said about willing that first something and then its contrary should not be immutably willed.

So whereas any volitum of God's will have to be immutable, in the sense explained, not just any volitum of his has to be free of an immutable will for first something and then the contrary. If the latter holds true of our actual order of things, it will not be from the kind of thing which anything might be thought to have to be, in order to be "something willed by God". It will not be in virtue of any imagined requirement that just any volitum of his has to be such that whatever it first is, it can never be the contrary. In particular, not just any volitum of God's has to be such that its Avicennian essence cannot first be instantiated and subsequently not instantiated. Not just any volitum of God's, therefore, is eo ipso guaranteed against annihilation. It could in principle have annihilation built immutably into it from the outset.

The medieval schoolmen quite generally took it that although the actual order of things was not unique and enduring in virtue of anything in its intrinsic nature, or even in virtue of being something immutably willed by God, they equally took it that, as it happened, God had freely ordered it so as to endure and be unique. By considering the use of the Power Distinction by the medievals examined, we are perhaps placed to understand better how creation can be said to be freely ordered by God.

In the practice of the schoolmen seen above, only Avicennian essences considered in themselves—only the things of God's option-neutral power, in other words—are susceptible of two-way possibility (contingency) vis-à-vis existing sans phrase or not existing sans phrase. (At least some of the schoolmen seen allowed to what lay in the power of creaturely agents, an analogous contingency vis-à-vis existing in this determinate mode or that. I am not concerned with this here.) For this reason it could be said that, for anything at all, considered in itself, God is free to will it to be, or not to do so. For this reason, therefore, we can justify the (anthropomorphic) way of speaking in which God may be said to have (something analogous to) 'liberty of indifference' in respect of things (Avicennian essences) considered in themselves, and to have it unrestrictedly. What philosophers have called 'liberty of indifference' can be set out, following Molina, a seventeenth-century Spanish Jesuit, as

An agent is free if, given all necessary conditions for ϕ-ing, it both can ϕ and not ϕ. (A. Kenny, *Will, Freedom and Power* (Oxford [1975]), vi + 170 pp., 123.)

God cannot in any proper way be said to have 'liberty of spontaneity', that other concept familiar in philosophers' discussions of human agency. 'Liberty of spontaneity' is defined in terms of an agent's wanting something which it lacks. If, as the schoolmen were agreed, and as follows if God is something which exists, but not in any determinate manner, God cannot be said to lack anything, he cannot be said to be able to want anything in the ways needed to make sense of 'liberty of spontaneity'.

12. *The "things" which God can do in option-tied power*

These are Avicennian essences considered as actually instantiated (by God's voluntary ordering). So considered, they are not susceptible of two-way possibility. If they actually are, they necessarily are. If they are not, it is impossible for them to be. Yet if, ontologically speaking, they are nothing other than the things of our ordinary categorial world—roses, coloured surfaces, grunts, and so on—it is none the less important that what "they" should at bottom be seen to be, in a Power Distinction connection, are Avicennian essences considered not in themselves but as instantiated. It is they, the Avicennian essences, which in option-tied assertions are being taking *composite* with their instantiating cause, their being willed by God; and in the corresponding option-neutral assertions are being taken *divisim* from an instantiating cause, or whether there ever is to be one.

The things of God's option-tied power thus coincide with Albert's *opera*, Aquinas's individualised forms, which are to serve as ultimate truthmakers for true, narrowly predicative propositions. At least two difficulties arise here: both through the narrowly predicative condition of the analysis ('There are grunting pigs', above), which might have seemed the least problematical of the conditions, and is of a kind which is most familiar.

The first difficulty is that we may never know precisely what we are talking about, when we say with truth that God can in option-tied power do something or other. If the things around us are both really structured, and given their structure by God's will, there can be no guarantee that we know or will ever come to know this true structure of things, or even what manner of things the real things are. There is nothing to prevent us, for example, from believing that things around us are so ordered that in chemical reactions oxygen is given off, when all the while the things around us are "really" so ordered that on the same occasions it is rather that phlogiston is being added, or for that matter that something is going on which no one will survive long enough to understand, never mind believe.

The second is that when we say that God in his option-tied power can do such and such, we may never know whether what we are saying is true. A remark made in a different connection is worth comparing:

When there is an external reality to which our statements relate, then they may be regarded as possessing determinate truth-values whether we in fact know these or not. (M. Dummett, *Elements of Intuitionism* (1977), 386.)

When we say that God can in his option-tied power make there to be grunting pigs, it may be in reality that not grunting pigs but pig-parts or pig-phases have been instantiated by God, together with providentially ventriloquist parasites of amazing persistence. It will then be determinately true that God can in his option-tied power make there to be ventriloquist-bearing pig-phases, or whatever, and that what we are saying is false.

Different responses to these difficulties are possible. At least two are worth noting, in view of historical developments which might be connected with the later history of the Distinction. The first response is to retreat to the metaphysical high ground, to rest content with assertions of high generality: about the world consisting of structured *opera* (Albert) or individualised forms (Aquinas). This permits a principled negative critique of scientific work: what conflicts, for example, with the view of the world as consisting of ordered individualised forms, will be rejected from the outset as a tenable explanation of what there is for science ultimately to explain. This may be a more modest role in the *critique des sciences* than some might have wished, but it may equally be as much as any metaphysician can legitimately claim. Historically, the retreat to the metaphysical high ground has been taken, not least by self-professed followers of Aquinas or other medieval or ancient metaphysicians. At its best, it has produced negative work of good quality.[18] More often, it has invited the scorn it has at least sometimes merited: if not in Molière's jibe at a *vis dormitiva*, then at least sometimes in Galileo's *Dialogues*.

This kind of response concerns not only natural science but theology too. The philosophical theologian's role becomes a negative one, excluding (only) theological views entailing inconsistency with how things, in general terms, can be held to be. Constructive systematic theology will then be able to look to philosophy only for tools or expressive vehicles, not for any assumptions of substance.

In neither case, of science or theology, is such a restraint on metaphysicians' ambitions likely to prove unwelcome: to genuinely scientific inquirers. And in science at any rate, the suggestion that any scientific explanation is going to have a provisional character anyway, is unlikely to cause offence.

Another response is that God has revealed how the world is. Not necessarily down to particulars, though history is familiar with 'fundamentalist' attempts to read Genesis or other Scriptures as a scientific textbook, and with dated predictions of the world's proximate end. Yet at least down to the level of assertions to the effect that God has ordered all things, and orders them ultimately to good, despite appearances. The Achilles heel of this response—even were it invulnerable otherwise—is in 'despite appearances'. In empirical inquiries, what can we go by, if not by appearances? We do not have to be particularly Empiricist to recognise that much: 'There can be no doubt that all our knowledge begins with experience' is the first sentence, not in Hume, but in the *Critique of Pure Reason*. There is more than one way to go by appearances, of course. But sooner or later all ways seem either to reduce to making them the only originals of all our knowledge, or to postulate realities ineluctably ungraspable in the grasp of appearances.

The first way can produce perplexities of paralysing force. The second—in its religious or theological forms—is liable to leave the door open to a Holy Office or a committee of mullahs to overrule the evidence of our own senses, as though by decrees

---

[18] e.g. the critiques of mechanism in P. Hoenen, *Cosmologia*, ad usum auditorum (Rome, 1931).

which can somehow escape the strictly provisional character of our science. When that sort of overruling is allowed it remains possible to uphold God's ordering of the world doubtless; but at the cost of cheapening our science and encouraging scepticism even concerning what we taste and feel. In one way or another 'human reason precipitates itself into darkness and contradictions; and while it may indeed conjecture that these must be in some way due to concealed errors, it is not in a position to be able to detect them. For since the principles of which it is making use transcend the limits of experience, they are no longer subject to any empirical test.' (I. Kant, *Crit. of Pure Reason*, Pref. to 1st edn., A viii, tr. Kemp Smith, repr. 1964.) I shall return to that point, since Kant was concerned there with precisely the kind of metaphysics which he thought the metaphysics of the genre to which the Power Distinction is central, to be. For the time being it is not the "dogmatism" of metaphysicians with which I am concerned, but the surrender of the metaphysical pass to the professional dogmatists, the Holy Office and the mullahs. The danger thence ensuing (to the rest of us) is not dogmatism but fideism of some kind; and more than a chance of scepticism by that route too, when the mullahs' and assessors' intellectual clothes begin to get threadbare. I mention this, because both scepticism and fideism used to be supposed to have grown and flourished pari passu with the Power Distinction itself; in the heyday of the Distinction, which lay in the fourteenth century, and beyond the scope of this book. And I mention it, because although there is good reason to fear both ensuing from a problem built into the notion of things God can do in option-tied power, it has nearly always been the use of the option-neutral arm which has been supposed—by twentieth-century historians—to have had that effect. If fideism and scepticism really did flourish pari passu with the Distinction or its successor(s) in later medieval times, as its applications burgeoned within the schools and as impressions of its content spread far beyond, it might be profitable to historians to attend more narrowly to how not the option-neutral but the option-tied arm was then being used.

13. *Use of 'can' in the Distinction*

What work is the 'can' doing in 'God can in option-tied/neutral power ___'? Where is its work to be accommodated in the analyses? Answers have already been implied, but are worth spelling out.

When '___ can do such and such' is completed with a personal name, like 'Stalin' or 'Fischer-Dieskau', we are likely to expect that "powers" inherent in the person referred to are in question. When told that Fischer-Dieskau cannot sing this evening, and having no reason to believe him otherwise impeded, we are likely to be concerned for him, if we are at all sympathetic, and to hope that the presumed impairment to the exercise of his powers will soon be remedied. When reflecting that Stalin can no longer massacre his own people, we may be permitted a measure of *Schadenfreude*. None of this is applicable in the case of God, though we could well imagine it to be.

In schoolroom grammar—and perhaps in some pulpit catechesis—'God' is treated as a personal name. Initially, therefore, we might expect 'God can do greater things than he has done' to tell us at least something of God's powers, and 'God cannot make a wall he cannot knock down' to be reason for concern.

In the usage of the medievals examined above, 'God' was not to be used—as 'Stalin' might well be used—in subject position in an analysed proposition, so our initial expectations on hearing personal-sounding names are already under challenge. Now it is to be noted that the 'can' is not to be taken in the same way in the contrasting arms of the Distinction.

In the option-neutral arm what is to be caught from the 'can' is the contingency of the existence of creatures on a divine will that is free in the way in which something willed by an unrestricted being can be said to be free: with 'liberty of indifference'. This is caught in the analysis by making the option-neutral assertions to be "about" not any imagined "powers" inherent in God, but some set of Avicennian essences, to which two-way possibility (contingency) to be is to be applicable, without restriction as to type of being or quantity of beings. Option-neutral assertions are thus to be seen to be about the contingency of all determinate things without restriction, given the existence of something with unrestricted existence, by which the determinate existence of all besides can be explained. That fundamental contingency of determinate beings is what the 'can' in the option-neutral arm should be seen to capture.

In the option-tied arm, the 'can' is to be seen to be doing (in addition) significantly different work, because the things which God can be said to be able to do in option-tied power are not susceptible of two-way possibility (contingency). Option-tied assertions are then "about" not God but determinate actual entities: which of their nature are the way they are, and no other way. Of course this actual green leaf can become an actual red leaf, but that is because being a green leaf does not exclude being in addition possible to become red. Being actually green does exclude the possibility of becoming green: 'What is, necessarily is, when it is; and what is not, necessarily is not, when it is not' (Arist. *De int.* 9, 19ᵃ23).

The "necessity" which attaches to instantiated Avicennian essences is related to the family of *ex suppositione* "necessity", and is not to be mistaken for a strictly logical modality, expressible only in propositions to be analysed as composing-apt. If a terminology favoured by Anselm, is preferred, we might say that we have here a *necessitas consequentiae* ('Necessarily, if pigs are grunting, pigs are grunting'), not a *necessitas consequentis* ('If pigs are grunting, then that pigs are grunting is necessary'). But on the strength of 'Necessarily, On the supposition that pigs are grunting, pigs are grunting' if that is true, one is not entitled to assert 'Necessarily, Pigs are grunting'.

So whereas what God 'can' in option-neutral power do was to be understood as what may (contingently) be done in relation to one type of thing (an Avicennian essence) other than God, what God 'can' do in option-tied power is to be understood rather as what must (*ex suppositione*) be, in relation to another type of thing (an instantiated Avicennian essence) other than God. One way to picture the latter should probably be avoided: to picture God as the ultimate in despots and everything else as the ultimate in complaisant subjects. What the despot 'can' do, on this picture, is (concretely) what the subject "must" do.

The main reason here for avoiding this picture as a guide to understanding how creatures stand in relation to God, is not that it is unpleasing to men and women of sensibility and honour, or makes a mockery of Christian doctrines on the point: though it is unpleasing, delineating not the God of Abraham, Isaac, and Jacob but Holy Willie's God writ large. The main reason here is that it misrepresents in a crucial respect the logic of the relationship between the being of God and that of things. For there to be despotism and subjection, in the concrete, there must be at least something (in despot and subject) which each is, and which the other is not. But there is strictly nothing in created things which God is not. Whatever there is in creatures, is in God, and without the restrictions under which it is found in creatures. So whereas a very powerful being, even an unimaginably powerful being, could be a despot, something literally infinite in its being simply cannot (logically cannot) be one. The thought behind this can also give sober content to Augustine's well-known slogan to the effect that God is *intimius me mihi*; and a content which permits it to apply not only to thinking creatures but to creatures of literally every kind.

If the 'can' in the arms of the Distinction does have the use(s) mentioned, it becomes clear why the users regularly accepted that 'God can in option-tied power do *A*' implies 'God can do *A*' sans phrase, but that 'God can in option-neutral power do *A*' does not necessarily imply 'God can do *A*' sans phrase; and why they regularly accepted that 'God cannot in option-neutral power do *A*' implies 'God cannot do *A*' sans phrase, but that 'God cannot in option-tied power do *A*' does not necessarily imply 'God cannot do *A*' sans phrase. The three possible cases can be set out thus.

ord T	abs T
ord T	*abs F*
ord F	abs T
ord F	abs F

The italicised second line does not represent a possible case, as 'God can in option-tied power' can never be true where 'God can in option-neutral power do A' is false.

If we go on to ask why the users accepted this, the following may be said. By the meaning of the terms, 'God cannot do A' *simpliciter*, is true if, and only if, 'God cannot in any determinate mode x do A' is true, for no matter what determinate mode x. But for no matter what determinate mode x may be envisaged, if God can in that mode do A, then he can in his option-neutral power do A. Hence, working back by the *modus tollens*, if God cannot in his option-neutral power do A, he cannot do it in any determinate mode whatever, and hence cannot do it, *simpliciter*.

If 'God can in option-tied power do A' is true, then by the analyses 'God can in option-neutral power do A' is true. But if that is true, 'God cannot in option-neutral power do A' is false, and hence (as argued above) 'God cannot do A' *simpliciter*, is false. Also, we may say 'God can do A' *simpliciter*, only if it is true *omnibus modis* (ord T, abs T). Aquinas in the *In 3 Sent.* passage in which he expounded and used the Distinction for the first time in his extant works was content to say in such a case, where 'God can do A' was true, merely that it was true, and that it was not to be said in any way (in any determinate mode, including therefore 'in God's option-neutral power') that God could not do it.

WAYS OF EXPRESSING THE UNDERSTANDING

14. *Looser and stricter ways of speaking*

What is to be understood as being distinguished in the Power Distinction as used in the period covered, can be expressed to varying degrees of precision: though not always in ways usable in a serious explanation.

Speaking loosely and anthropomorphically we might say that what was being distinguished are alternative ways in which God's 'operant' (Albert) or 'exsequent' power (Alexander of Hales, Aquinas) can be understood by us. By 'God's operant power' is intended here not that power of God held identical with the divine nature, but that power of God held (capable of being) exercised in subjection to a divine will. In the Distinction, as we might accordingly say, we are meant to distinguish, on the one hand, the power actually exercised under God's will, in the actual order of things; on the other, the power judged available to be exercised under God's will, if he chose to exercise it (or, judged available to have been exercised under God's will, had he chosen to exercise it). Those last alternative expressions, alternative *modi loquendi*, are to be seen as no more than that. If a rigorously negative theology on the divine nature is to be respected, the differences of tense and mood in such *modi loquendi*, are to be taken as stylistic merely.

Even from passages seen above it is noticeable that a number of the medievals examined used this loose way of speaking at times, and I am not aware that any of them rejected it. Why, in any case, should it not be used in circumstances in which it is unlikely to mislead, and where the speaker has no pretensions of offering a serious explanation? Even in contexts where serious information needs to be put quite precisely at certain points, loose ways of speaking at other points need not be held objectionable. We need not reproach almanac-makers, for example, on whose accuracy a navigator's life may depend, if they speak of the sun setting or the tide turning; though we could be justified in reproaching them if they were either loose where they should have been precise, or precise but inexact where they should have been both, as in giving times or places. Moreover the schoolmen could plead precedent: their worship, their Scriptures, their creeds, the writings of their *sancti* generally abounded in loose and anthropomorphic ways of attributing things to divine power.

Where, however, a rigorously negative theology on the divine nature is to be maintained—and not one of the writers examined above shows an attempt to maintain any other type of view—anthropomorphic ways of attributing things to divine power are to be accounted not merely loose but incapable of being tightened without failure of one kind or another. Three types of treatment remain available.

(1) They may be understood to be about the divine nature, their terms retaining the significance which they usually have; but to be improperly said, so as to be "true" not as a proposition but as a figure or a narrative may express something true. (Cf. Nathan's parable of David's adultery with Bethsabee and his executive murder of her husband; or for that matter the J-tradition account of creation in Gen. 2.)

(2) They may be understood to be said properly, and with truth; albeit not of the divine nature, but of something else, considered in relation to it. (This is how the intelligible,

composing-apt components of the analyses of the arms of the Power Distinction were to be seen above.)

(3) They may otherwise be taken as said properly, and of the divine nature; but at the cost of their terms being evacuated of the signification they usually carry, and of being literally unintelligible (lacking in signification), if they are to be true of the divine nature. (This is how the assertions of divine existence in the analyses given above, are to be seen. It is also how *Deus est unus et trinus* and *Deus est sapiens* were seen to be taken, in passages quoted above from Aquinas.)

No harm need be done by taking approach (1) in giving an initial exposition of the Distinction, or where no more than an identifying description is needed, for a passing reference. But if the analyses given above are in substance correct, a genuine explanation of the Distinction cannot avoid both approaches (2) and (3), in their place. If we reconsider approach (2), however, the one most narrowly concerned in the Power Distinction in particular, we ought not to omit recognising that it in turn is susceptible of being understood in more than one way.

15. *A linguistic approach to understanding the Distinction*

If we take a linguistic approach, we may construe talk about things which can be done in God's option-neutral power as talk about logical products of certain propositions of composing-apt type, together with a proposition in which God's existence is asserted (this, to spell out that it is God's option-neutral power which is in question, even though God is referred to no more than obliquely in the composing-apt propositions).

We may likewise construe talk about God's option-neutral power itself as talk about the logical sum containing all the logical products just mentioned (and no others); together with the assertion of God's existence.

Correspondingly we may construe talk about things which can be done in God's option-tied power as talk about conjunctions of logical products of composing-apt propositions and logical products of corresponding propositions of narrowly predicative type; together once more with the assertion spelling out that it is God's option-tied power which is in question.

We may likewise talk of God's option-tied power itself as any or all such conjunctions. The conjoints here will be consistent (if the things in question are indeed to be said with truth to be instantiated by God's will), but need not be maximally consistent in their own types. If the things of God's option-tied power are to make up an ordered whole, not in virtue of their intrinsic content, but by God's will, it is difficult to see how this could be seen to be done, if it is not at least possible that others could have been instantiated, consistently with them, but have not been instantiated.

16. *A conceptualist approach*

If we take a conceptualist approach, we may construe talk about things which can be done in God's option-neutral power, as talk about a way in which we can conceive of the intrinsic contents or "Avicennian essences" of things (as in Section 10): to wit, absolute, ignoring any necessary relationships in which they might be judged to stand with comparable contents or essences, and prescinding from whether the things ever are to be instantiated (by God's will) or not, in extra-mental reality. And in order to spell out the point that it is God's option-neutral power which is in question, we will have to spell out that this way of conceiving things is consistent with an assertion of divine existence.

In this approach talk of God's option-neutral power itself is to be construed as talk about the (non-ordered, and indeed inconsistent) set of (ordered) Avicennian essences of things; together of course with an assertion of divine existence. In this way the essences or contents of things are being considered *divisim* from any condition implying their instantiation.

Correspondingly we may construe talk about things which can be done in option-tied power as talk about another way of conceiving Avicennian essences: as instantiated (by God's will) in extra-mental reality; together with the assertion of divine existence.

Talk of God's option-tied power itself is then to be construed as talk about any or all of the (ordered) set of Avicennian essences held instantiated (by God's will) in extra-mental reality; together as always with the assertion of divine existence. In this way the essences or contents of things are being considered *composite* with a condition implying their instantiation.

17. *A realist approach?*

If we have a linguistic and a conceptualist way of intelligibly construing talk professedly attributing things to God's option-tied/option-neutral power, may we not expect also a "realist" way?

May we not, for example, speak of the things which God can do in his option-neutral power, not only as coinciding in content with the Avicennian essences, but as real, abstract entities existing wholly independently of our language or thought? Difficulties inherent in attempting to speak in such ways already became apparent in the course of expounding St Bonaventure's treatment of the exemplars, and had already been encountered by Christian thinkers impressed by Plato but unable to recognise a place for independently existing Ideas. Given a rigorously negative theology on the divine nature, there is no place for such entities. Even if they are allowed to be 'pre-existing in God' (as Aquinas was prepared to allow to the concept of goodness), or to be existing in the eternal knowledge of God (and hence not to be held anything distinct from the divine nature), this is not to present purpose, since in either case they can be said with truth to exist, only if they have to be in principle unknowable to us (by being identified with the *quid sit* of the divine nature).

Moreover 'pre-existing in God', or being known to God's eternal knowledge, is something which speakers favouring linguistic or conceptualist approaches to the matter can allow just as readily. They can readily allow the things of their respective inconsistent sets to pre-exist in God, or be known to God's eternal knowledge. If they can, they can as readily accept them as existing in extra-mental reality, as identified with the divine nature. Considered as existing in that way, however, they have to cease to be viewed as intelligible. A non-ordered set is nothing in reality other than the things of the set; and not being ordered, the set itself—a methodological fiction of ours—is not the sort of thing which can satisfy the *ens* condition for an Avicennian essence, and hence is itself not the sort of thing which, as such, can be said with truth to pre-exist in God, or to be known to God's eternal knowledge.

The nature of the difficulties faced by one attempting a realist understanding of the Distinction, appears in connection with the option-neutral arm. Since an option-neutral assertion is implied in the option-tied arm too, this is even more troublesome. What is needed, if we are to have a "realist" way of understanding the things of option-neutral power, comparable to the other ways envisaged, is that they themselves should be independently existing. What they have, from the possibility of pre-existing in God or being known to God's eternal knowledge, is that they should *as pre-existing in God*, or *as known to God's eternal knowledge*, be thought to have real existence (indistinct from that of the divine nature). But that does not necessarily imply that they should sans phrase be thought to have real existence; it does not give us anything which the conceptualist and linguistic approaches could not give us (in addition to what they provide more specifically); and most crucially it cannot give us what is being sought here: a way in which we can construe talk of God's option-neutral power as (significant) talk of some kind. It can provide us with (yet) another way of expressing (properly, with truth, but in literally insignificant speech) the truth about God, such as is had already in the analysis, in order to capture that it is God's operant power which is in question. But that is not what is needed at this point.

The sustainable objection, therefore, to a realist approach, balancing the linguistic and conceptual approaches, is not that it does not permit 'God can in option-tied/option-neutral power make there to be grunting pigs' to be true. It is rather that it does not permit a way for us to understand either arm of the Distinction better, and does not permit a way for us to understand the option-neutral arm at all.

It may be true to say:

(1) There are no flying pigs, and some God exists; and (2) Some God exists, and nothing more can be said here,

when and only when it is true that:

(1) God cannot in option-tied power make there to be flying pigs, but (2) God can in option-neutral power make there to be flying pigs;

but it brings no increase in understanding. Likewise it may be true to say:

(1) There are grunting pigs, and some God exists, and nothing more is to be said here,

when and only when it is true that:

(1) God can in option-tied power make there to be grunting pigs;

and both of the more modestly expressed equivalents may have piety as well as truth to commend them. But what is to the point here is that the more modestly expressed equivalents are unilluminating intellectually, if taken as analyses, in ways in which the corresponding equivalents in the linguistic and the conceptualist approaches need not be.

USING THE DISTINCTION

No special rules, peculiar to uses of the Power Distinction, appear from the uses examined. If the analyses given above are in substance correct, no special rules would be called for anyway (in order to avoid *inconvenientia* such as theologically reprobate conclusions, for example). That rather what they intended to achieve was in general being achieved, appears from the way in which schoolmen in the period concerned can be seen to respond to uses of the Distinction on the part of their fellows. Objections to such uses—in disputation, for example—are rare in the period, and those which are to be found are against incorrect or inappropriate applications of it, not against the Distinction itself.

So far as evidence one way or the other does appear, the rules under which the Distinction was being used in the period were the rules appropriate to applying distinctions made in this way, to wit, in contrasting *cum determinatione* assertions. I add the restriction because in truth the precise rules followed were not always the same in different schoolmen, and are rarely if ever spelled out in Power Distinction contexts. This is not surprising, as the nature of most of the surviving texts in which the Distinction is used, makes explicit indications unlikely. The texts are to be found for the most part in works of academic theology: in Sentence commentaries, in theological disputations, or in summas often owing content to both previous genres. Sentence

commentaries were addressed to an explicitly theological problématique, for the benefit of an audience fresh from studies in
the dialectics current at the time in the university. Explanation
of purely dialectical matters—such as the rules for drawing
inferences from *cum determinatione* assertions—was unlikely to be
needed; where it was needed, as where the commentator was
aware that his students had been instructed by someone who
was following rules different in some point of detail, it is not the
sort of thing which we should expect to find in a finished *ordinatio*,
or even in an approved *reportatio*. In the disputations of the
masters, participants were likely either to share the same rules,
or at least to be familiar with those of their colleagues. Only
where there might be occasion for objections where objectors
might hope to show that their colleagues' favoured dialectics
might lead to embarrassing positions in theology, is there any
reason to hope that some explicit information on dialectics might
be given. In summas and related works where a systematic
treatment with overall coherence was the aim, even some of the
incidental information called for in commentaries in order to
explain treatments of difficulties arising from the object-text, or
in finished versions of disputed questions in order to explain
certain treatments of objections, was liable to be omitted, or to
be implied so smoothly as to fail to be noticed. Readers familiar
with Aquinas know the value of going back from treatments in the
Summa theologiae especially, to parallel passages in commentaries
or disputed questions; where a less "seamless" account, more
instructive to us to whom his academic sub-culture is inevitably
distant in some ways, can often be found.

In the case where the incidental information concerns rules
for making inferences from *cum determinatione* assertions two quar-
ries have the richest veins: commentaries on the *De sophisticis
elenchis* (a work often remarked to have concerned theologians
more than logicians when it became available in the Western
schools); and questions on the consequences of the Incarnation,
where *qua*-phrases especially are often of importance. Even there,
it is not easy (or even always possible) to be sure just what is
going on.[19]

---

[19] The studies of G. Klima and A. Bäck, referred to at Introd. n. 17, show both what
can be obtained from an instructed reading of such sources, and the difficulties of
obtaining it.

As it happens, we do have enough information to appreciate what is going on in the *composite/divisim* move. If one dialectical move can be seen as particularly crucial to the successful use of the Distinction, it is probably that in which the Avicennian essence of a thing is taken in the option-tied arm *composite* with the thing's instantiation, and in the optional-neutral arm *divisim* from that. Now if the two-type analysis is indeed to be seen behind the arguments of the medievals examined, that is enough to show how the *composite/divisim* move here is no ad hoc sleight of hand, but is called for under appropriate general principles.

ITS POINT

The Power Distinction as used in the period covered—the earlier medieval Power Distinction—involved locutions in which things are professedly attributed to divine power.

18. It permitted its users to treat that range of locutions as 'systematically misleading'; in such a way as to enable theologians maintaining a rigorously negative theology on the divine nature, consistently to pursue an important range of the theology most typical of the theology faculties, and with reason to reject propositions which might seem of the same theological range, but can be shown to be inconsistent with a negative theology on the divine nature.

This is not something marginal to theology, though indeed it does not sound like the activities occupying working theologians most of the time. Of course even systematic theologians are likely to spend more time using a language much closer to the language of the foundation-myths, or revelation, or whatever, to which they may appeal as to an authoritative source. But where, as with the schoolmen above, theologians see themselves as professionally engaged, not in sophisticated propaganda or instruction, but in a scientific endeavour, they must be prepared to meet the standards appropriate. They may continue much of the time to use a language closer in its tone and in its evocative force to the language of their sources, but if their scientifical pretensions are to be made good they must be prepared to spell out their crucial arguments in more sober if less evocative ways.

They may be justified in giving importance to figures or narrative, for example, but if they cannot in principle make the connections needed between figure, say, and sober predication, or if they cannot even in principle set limits to what figures or what stories are to be taken as instructive in this or that type of matter, what becomes of the scientifical pretensions? Now the schoolmen had quite serious pretensions to science in theology, some of them seeing the theology of their schools as the very paradigm of Aristotelian science, the "hard science" of the day. The Power Distinction provided them with both a means and a model for crucial parts of the connections needed between the language of the sources and that of sober, scientific arguments. If that is important, it could be unwise for theologians to dismiss the following more specific results obtainable from applying the Power Distinction, as something of only marginal importance to the working theologian.

The Distinction provides:

(1) Two ways in which 'God is powerful' can be said significantly and with truth: when it means either 'At least something is contained in God's option-tied power' or 'At least something is contained in God's option-neutral power'. How these in turn are to be spelled out was seen above and need not be repeated here. It also provides:

(2) Two ways in which 'God is omnipotent' may likewise be said: when it means either 'For any Avicennian essence, if it is considered as instantiated, that essence is, so considered, of the (ordered) set of God's option-tied power' (this is "almightiness" over creation), or 'For any Avicennian essence, if it is considered in its intrinsic content merely, and prescinding from whether it is to be instantiated or not, is (so considered) of the (non-ordered) set of God's option-neutral power'.

It likewise provides:

(3) Two ways in which assertions of the form 'God can do A' can be said significantly and with truth: when it means either 'God can in option-tied power do A' or 'God can in option-neutral power do A'; and consequently:

(4) Two ways in which 'God can do everything' can be said significantly and with truth, at least when it means 'There

is nothing which God cannot do': where 'everything' covers
everything existing determinately in extra-mental reality
(this coincides with the "almightiness" version of omnipotence above), and where it covers anything satisfying the
conditions for an Avicennian essence (this coincides with
the other version of omnipotence).

By the same tokens it provides means for a justified rejection
of various bogus ways in which the same locutions might be
imagined to be used: where 'God can ___' might be imagined
to be completed by just any form of words making recognisable
English. It provides means for rejecting necessarily false ways, as
where 'God can ___' might be completed by such expressions
as either purport to name, or else are to be seen as implying,
some inconsistency. And it provides means for rejecting inap-
plicable ways, inattributable in principle to something existing,
but existing not in any determinate way.

Besides what it thus provides directly, the Power Distinction
also provides something of a working model for a strategy of
wider application, for attributing things to God more generally.
This wider strategy can embrace attributions not only to divine
power, but to divine wisdom, justice, and indefinitely many
others of the sort. It thus allows not only for the Power Distinction,
but for a comparable Wisdom Distinction, of evident relevance
to thorny issues of divine providence, and indefinitely many
others.[20] As was seen already in Chapter 1 above, a willingness
to use a strategy of the sort can be seen in Origen, and in the
author of Romans 1: 20. The Power Distinction, therefore, while
apparently a product of the medieval schools, and for long of
particular prominence within those schools, is not something sui
generis, but of a piece with a wider strategy, and that a strategy
to be placed in a theologically traditional and enduring pattern
of thought.

In its own day, the Distinction's theological point was para-
mount: its aptness for addressing certain limiting-questions on
the *opus redemptionis*.[21] In Anselm's day such questions as 'The

---

[20] On the strategy see 'Attributing things to God', *Ephemerides theologicae lovanienses*, 68
(1992), 86–116.
[21] The central place of the *opus redemptionis* in theologians' theology is more than a
passing medieval vogue, and may follow from any serious attempt to do justice to the
content of affirmations of (Christian) faith. 'Mais à y regarder de plus près, on s'aperçoit

mode of redemption actually willed by God is so and so, but might things not have been willed otherwise by him?' had given rise to much discussion. In the period covered in this book they were being answered, thanks to the Power Distinction, almost routinely.

19. Beyond theology narrowly conceived, the Distinction and the world-view which came with it enabled at least some of the medievals examined above to maintain in the face of what can now be seen as a considerable challenge in the early decades of the thirteenth century, an appreciation of the world as an ordered whole: an imposed order, not due to chance or necessity, but to be held an order at bottom due to the will of God.

If such an order could be supposed, not only could an Aristotelian science of the natural world be looked for, but the challenge could be met of those who would say that the world is no more than a sum of things, and no real order—a view to be seen behind the 'error of the philosophers' attacked by Aquinas in the *De potentia* passage examined in Chapter 7— without having to fall into the 'error of the theologians' attacked in the same place. The combination of the Power Distinction and the imposed-order view at once preserved the possibility of an (autonomous) Aristotelian science concerning the things of the world around them, and offered an apologetical defence against intellectually informed challenges. That such challenges were being encountered at the time is apparent from the effort put by Aquinas into the *Summa contra Gentiles*, which would have been largely otiose, had no such challenges been in view, or had all of them been seen as something in the past, like the views of the ancient atomists.

Beyond such still broadly academic purposes, the Distinction— once given currency through such widely copied works as Hugh

que le contenu des affirmations de la foi est relatif non aux propriétés de Dieu, considéré comme une sorte d'objet étranger, ou au rapport Dieu-homme, considéré comme une relation objectivée, mais à ce qui, tant de côté de Dieu que du côté d'homme, concerne précisément la réalisation d'un plan de Dieu sur l'homme, l'alliance annoncée aux patriarches et scellée dans le mystère du Christ, l'assomption de l'humanité dans la vie de Dieu. Autrement dit, les affirmations de la foi portent sur ce qui est en train de s'accomplir dans l'être même du croyant. Mais elles ne sont pas pour autant de simples propositions descriptives: elles ne sont pas une 'théorie' du salut, pas plus qu'une théorie de l'être de Dieu.' (J. Ladrière, *L'Articulation du sens: Discours scientifique et parole de la foi* (Paris, 1970), 228.)

of Strasbourg's *Compendium*—lent itself to a different kind of use. It lent itself to being used in a kind of "cognitive therapy" for people who, when asking 'Can God . . . ?' questions, were asking neither as casual enquirers nor academic inquirers. They may be called "interested inquirers", as their interest in the answers to the questions is to be thought of as in some way personal, existential, practical rather than speculative. The questions envisaged here are of the 'Can God save my family from the plague?' variety, which can be of so much more than merely academic interest to the questioner.

Yet 'lent itself' above was used advisedly. The Distinction lent itself, was of a nature apt, to this kind of use; but I am not aware of any evidence from the period to prove that it was being used in such a way at the time. There is certainly evidence from Chaucer's period, but that was much later. In the period examined the Distinction was essentially an academic tool, used by an academic in-group (largely within the Theology Faculty of the University of Paris) for academic purposes.

Not only had it not been 'calculated to be used' for pastoral purposes, in the sense of not having been devised or even given currency for such purposes. It might be queried whether it is 'calculated to be used' for pastoral purposes, among a wider, non-academic population, even in the sense of being of a nature apt for such uses. In a wider population we cannot count on only a received, technical or semi-technical understanding of the device being uniformly maintained. We might rather expect that, sooner or later, the technical or semi-technical notions are going to become obscure to many, to the point where suggestions built into the terminology—even suggestions contrary to the original semi-technical notions—re-emerge, making impressionistic, novel interpretations of the terminology a real danger. If a modern philosopher, reading the *absoluta* of *potentia absoluta*, can run together the *absolute* appropriate to a mode of assertion (not used in the Distinction) with the *absolute* appropriate to the way in which the abstract contents of things are to be considered by one asserting the option-neutral arm of the Distinction, why may not anxious, non-academic users in medieval times, be liable to like impressions or worse? If a modern academic historian, reading *ordinata* in the option-tied arm, can entertain seriously the thought that something 'inordinate' might have been in question in medieval uses of the option-neutral arm, why may not anxious non-academic medievals have entertained interpretations as wild—and, in a "pastoral" context, more damaging perhaps?

Yet despite that reservation about the appropriateness of extending the Distinction's application in a "pastoral" direction, it can be said in sum that the earlier medieval Power Distinction— the Distinction as understood in the period examined—was of a nature apt to provide thinking Christians with a way of giving reason for the faith that was in them: whether in respect of scientifical inquiry (in theology especially), in respect of apologetical or polemical defences against reasoned attacks on the faith or doctrine of their Church, or even (if it ever was so used in the period) in a more broadly "pastoral" manner. And if that is even in substance true, the earlier medieval Power Distinction cannot be dismissed as either frivolous or idle, or worse; as some later uses of the same terminology sometimes have been, whether justifiably or not.[22]

In addition to its aptness to serve those purposes of reflective Christians, the Distinction may also prove apt for application to

[22] One distinction using the contrasting terms of the Power Distinction has been cited under the phrase 'the Scholastic distinction between God's *potentia absoluta* and *potentia ordinata*' (P. T. Geach, 'Omnipotence', *Phil.* 48 (1973), 7–20, 16). Since in that distinction *potentia absoluta* 'is God's power considered in abstraction from his wisdom and goodness', *potentia ordinata* is 'God's power as controlled by his wisdom and goodness', and Prof. Geach is apparently considering the expositions of *potentia absoluta* and *potentia ordinata*, not as they might be used in expounding the Power Distinction, but in a manner purportedly permitting a speaker to say of God something analogous to 'This man "has the bodily and mental power to do so-and-so, but he certainly will not, it would be pointlessly silly and wicked"', it cannot be the Power Distinction as understood in the period covered in this book (or, I would suspect, the distinction(s) used by scholastics fairly generally for the rest of the Middle Ages), which is being referred to successfully here. I once mistakenly thought that a medieval Power Distinction was intended—see 'Why can't God do everything?', *New Blackfriars*, 55 (1974), 552–62—but subsequently learned from Prof. Geach that by 'the Scholastic distinction between God's *potentia absoluta* and *potentia ordinata*' he had had in mind not the earlier medieval Power Distinction, or the corresponding distinction(s) to be found in Scotus, Ockham, and many later medievals, but a distinction expounded by a late 19th- or early 20th-cent. Irish neoscholastic. When reprinting the earlier passage in *Providence and Evil* (1977), 19–20, Geach added: 'There are various acceptations of this distinction; I am here considering only one'. The distinction as reported and expounded by Geach could well be 'wholly frivolous', as he says at the place mentioned; or even perhaps 'bogus', if it should be the same distinction he has in mind in *Phil.* 48 (1973), 328, or *Providence and Evil* (1977), 31. But the historically important Power Distinction as understood and used by the medievals examined above— the earlier medieval Power Distinction—is neither frivolous nor bogus.

academic puzzles of a genre still found of some interest in philosophy: Can God do everything, can he make an uncontrollable creature, an irresistible cannonball, a wall he cannot break down...? It is by considering puzzles of the genre that such devices as the Distinction stand to be specified and refined anyway, so it is not surprising to have seen some of them addressed by medievals, in the passages examined above. Already in Hugh of St Cher, an interest in such puzzles was to be noted. Yet from the period there is little evidence to suggest that omnipotence-puzzling was being cultivated as an end in itself (still less as a means towards choosing between concepts of God, in the modern fashion). Even in series of disputed questions, a genre of discussion which might seem to invite puzzles of the type, no great penchant for omnipotence-puzzling appears in the period.

The Distinction would certainly seem apt for application to puzzles still currently addressed by philosophers, though this is not the place to demonstrate as much. What should be given here is a caveat. On the one hand, the Distinction might seem particularly apt to such purposes, as it does not rest on particular conceptions of a divine nature, on a par with conceptions which may be had of natures of determinate things generally. (Within Negative Theology assumptions, "concepts of God" can be no more than heuristic, or something of that sort.) On the other hand, the contentious assumptions in the Distinction are not of that philosophy-of-religion kind. They are rather in metaphysics (at a high level of generality), and in theory of language and of argument. In metaphysics what is chiefly contentious in the Distinction is that not everything which exists, exists in some or other determinate manner. In theory of argument the most contentious issue is how, or even whether, that metaphysical contention can be expressed so as to be usable in reasoned argument. Previous to those questions are others: how things may be said to exist in a determinate manner, what limits may have to be respected on what may count as a thing to be referred to in a scientifically usable expression ... Why, for example, should blindness not count as some kind of thing? Why should Don Juan's adulteries not count? Were not even some among the *mille tre* to count as something real, even as punctiliously executed? What is wrong with a "nature" of bindweed, consisting of not knowing that it is not bindweed? And so on. If I do not go into such questions here, it is not because I do not think them important, or because I cannot think how they might be argued. It is rather that this is not the place for such arguments. Such questions, in any case, were not greatly in contention among the medievals examined above: Albert did not much argue for his structured *opera*, or Aquinas for his individualised forms. Or if either did, scholars might wish to bring the arguments more plainly to our attention. The questions are not greatly in contention today either: views such as Albert's or Aquinas's are regularly not argued against but simply ignored. Yet if the views are as contentious as they appear, they could well be put more explicitly in contention.[23] Also contentious, and still not even stated as fully as might be desirable, if it is to be put in informed contention, is the two-type analysis which was argued to lie behind the use of the earlier medieval Power Distinction.

So although it need not be false to speak of the Distinction as apt for applying to the range of puzzles mentioned, we might be better to say rather that it is apt for clarifying and dissolving the puzzles, but only in virtue of principles very different from those more commonly addressed in our day to such puzzles. Can such principles themselves be defended? The chief benefit to philosophy, to be looked for from attempts to apply them in the ways envisaged, could even lie in their aptitude for exposing as deeply contentious, issues in metaphysics or in the theory of argumentative language, which either in medieval times, or in modern times, or in both, have arguably not yet been put seriously enough in contention.

SUMMARY OF MAIN CONCLUSIONS

The following have been established.

1. Specifically the same distinction was being used by authors

---

[23] On the question of individualised forms, however, see P. Geach, 'Form and Existence', *Proceedings of the Aristotelian Society* (1954–5), slightly revised in A. Kenny (ed.), *Aquinas: A Collection of Critical Essays* (London, 1970), 29–53; and A. Kenny, *The Heritage of Wisdom: Essays in the History of Philosophy* (Oxford, 1987), ch. 3: 'Form and existence in Aquinas'.

of the period considered, both when using the terminology which was to become canonical, and in some cases when using different terminologies.

This conclusion has not been able to be made good in earlier studies, as no analysis correctly identifying the Distinction had been provided in them, on a basis of examining a comprehensive range of comparable texts in the different authors.

2. The Distinction was regularly used by authors of the period as though understood in the way outlined above, and not in any incompatible way.

The analysis of the Distinction given above should be taken as stated here, and will not be repeated, although it is perhaps the chief progress made to an understanding of the Power Distinction quite generally, in the present study.

So far as I am aware, no comparably detailed analysis has been attempted in the critical literature, for uses of the Distinction in this period. Where incompatible ways appear in analyses of later uses, it may be worth checking first whether the texts really do support an analysis incompatible with the one given above, now that it is available for comparison. Where particular later texts are found really to reveal an incompatible understanding of the distinction used there, yet in (speciously) similar terms; and where the basis of the discrepancy appears to be systematic, rather than a simple slip on the medieval user's part: it should now be easier to explore the nature of the systematic basis for discrepancy (e.g. a different way of understanding terms of the kind used, or incompatible rules for drawing inferences from the kind of assertion used). In sum, if the understanding of the Distinction outlined above is correct, it is applicable not only for interpreting Power Distinction passages in writers from the period examined, but can provide in addition a heuristic tool not previously available to interpreters of (at least speciously) similar passages in later writers, from later medieval or early modern times.

3. As a dialectical device, the earlier medieval Power Distinction is neither bogus, nor frivolous, nor idle.

By 'the earlier medieval Power Distinction' I refer to the distinction used in the period examined, leaving open the question whether device(s) used in similar terminology in similar contexts in later times should be understood as specifically the same distinction, used in those later times, or as specifically different. The question cannot be settled until comparisons are made; and only the first term of such comparisons is provided above.

4. Positively, the Distinction is of its nature apt for more than one kind of purpose.

5. During the period examined, however, it was used predominantly within academic theology, and especially within the Theology Faculty of the University of Paris, being addressed to questions of whether or how it might significantly and with truth be said that the actual mode of Redemption was so and so, but might have been otherwise; first to questions concerning this or that particular element of Redemption, then more generally.

Two remarks might be in order here. To some extent the shift from particular to general may amount to a shift from a narrowly theological to a more broadly apologetical use: appropriate at the time to meet challenges arising from impressive statements of necessitarian views of things. To what extent the shift to a more general question came from such challenges (as in the Platonic optimism attributed to Abelard, or the necessary-emanation views attributed to Avicenna), and to what extent they were already invited by Damian's abrasive denunciations or Anselm's excessively smooth, almost evasive analyses, is a question which historians might now usefully consider.

Secondly, uses of the Distinction do seem to appear earliest in academic texts by theologians of the Theology Faculty of Paris. Even when uses or allusions appear elsewhere, they appear rarely if ever (in this period) in authors without Parisian connections or academic origins. Later medieval authors remarked on the Parisian connections of the Distinction, even at a time when it appeared to be being used more in other universities.

6. By permitting answers to such questions to be treated as 'systematically misleading' in the ways specified above, the Distinction was of such a nature as to be accommodated within a wider strategy for treating locutions professedly attributing things to God; embracing not only the Power

Distinction but also comparable distinctions involving locutions professedly attributing things to divine wisdom,
divine goodness, and (though it is not argued above, indefinitely many) others.

Some hints of these others, in the expressions *sapientia ordinata*,
bonitas absoluta, were already to be seen in texts examined.

7. This made it of particular importance to users intent on
   maintaining, together with a way of understanding such
   apparent attributions, a rigorously negative theology on the
   divine nature.

8. Wherever a user examined above expressed a clear answer
   one way or the other, he showed an intent to maintain a
   rigorously negative theology on the divine nature. No
   user examined above showed an intent to maintain any
   incompatible view.

Both points 7 and 8 are of importance, and do not seem to
have been made in connection with the use of the Power
Distinction within the period examined. I emphasise this, as a
failure to appreciate the Distinction's aptness for use within
assumptions of a rigorously negative theology on the divine
nature can lead to a failure to recognise either the nature or the
point of the Distinction.

9. During the period the Distinction does not appear from
   the evidence to have been addressed to the "pastoral"
   purposes ('Can God save my family from the plague?') to
   which it might also be thought apt; though of course most
   of the surviving evidence appears in narrowly academic
   discussions. By contrast, it was occasionally used in a genre
   of omnipotence-puzzling which still exercises academic
   philosophers.

10. If the two-type analysis is indeed to be seen behind the
    medievals' use of the Distinction, then the *composite/divisim*
    move sometimes spelled out by medieval users when defend-
    ing or explaining a use of it, can be seen not as some ad
    hoc chicane, but a move required in the circumstances
    under more general principles.

11. On the same condition, and if the 'can' in the option-tied

arm of the Distinction is to carry inter alia the force of a disguised *de re* "must", then the insistence that 'God can in option-tied power do A' (but not '... in option-neutral power...') implies 'God can do A' sans phrase, and that 'God cannot in option-neutral power do A' (but not '... in option-tied power...') implies 'God cannot do A' sans phrase, is likewise to be seen not to be arbitrary, but to be required under more general principles.

The main assumptions still in need of substantiation are as follows.

1. Most obviously a matter of contention: That not everything which exists, exists in some or other determinate manner.

This is in need not only of proof, but of a way in which it can be expressed, so as to play a part in a reasoned argument.[24] This makes for a wider kind of ontology than is commonly accepted today, though if it is correct it adds no more individuals of any kind, no more kinds of individual, and at most one existent which, not being determinate in any way, cannot be thought of as being added to what there otherwise is, in any way at all. It does perhaps imply, however, that not everything which can be said with truth to exist, is a possible object for our science.

2. That nothing exists in a determinate manner in extra-mental reality, save what can be seen as the instantiation of an integral 'form' or class of forms.

Arguments are not easy to find in Albert, for his *opera*; or in Aquinas, for his individualised forms. And arguments are not much easier to find in modern writers for allowing arbitrary individuals as values of bound variables. Simple dismissal is not an argument.

3. That a two-type analysis for assertions on which scientifical weight is to be put, is indeed to be found in the schoolmen, and in particular is to be seen behind the uses of the Power Distinction.

Even to state the thesis for arguing, more is needed than either

---

[24] Arguments against expressing it as in 'Something exists, and not everything which exists, exists in some or other determinate manner', are countered in 'On Saying that God's Being is Infinite', forthcoming.

Prior's concise statement,[25] or the working notion in Chapter 1 above sets out. Substantiation, both for Aristotle and for schoolmen, will need to overcome some genuinely arguable objections.

PROSPECTS

The main prospects opened up are of two kinds. For historians' purposes the more precise notion of the Distinction now available, permits both the "fortune" of the Distinction in later times, and its origins and antecedents, to be pursued more knowingly. If the "fortune" of the Distinction includes the stimulation of challenges to received medieval ways of thinking, not only in theology but in politics and in the natural sciences, then the importance of that need not be laboured.

In reopening a long-obscured way in which at least some theologians' theology can be pursued consistently with maintaining a rigorously negative theology on the divine nature, the earlier medieval Power Distinction as expounded above opens prospects of a different kind. For while it has needed considerable exhumation, the Distinction ought not to be taken for an archaeological curio, reconstructed from the remains of dead men's psyches, and of no application outside its own century. Whether or not God has any option-neutral power, or any option-tied power, or even whether there is any God of which such assertions can be made, is not a religious but a metaphysical issue. It is a matter of how things ultimately are, or are not; only derivatively if at all a matter of what, if we get this right, we can hope for. If it is true that things are as the earlier medieval Power Distinction requires them to be, if its assertions are to be true, then it is important that it is true. If it is false, or nonsensical, or a deception, it is then important that that is so. Perhaps, someone may say, things are such that the world really is a world without God—not just in this or that religious or philosophy-of-religion sense, but as 'God' was at bottom meant by the users of

---

[25] Prior, in the passage quoted in an earlier chapter, including in particular: 'A division of propositions which is given some prominence in the logic of Aristotle and the Schoolmen is that into (a) propositions simply asserting that something is or is not so, and (b) ones asserting that something must be, may be, need not be or cannot be so.' (*Formal Logic* (1962), 185.)

the Distinction. If that really is so, then sooner or later it will not take any peculiarly religious insight, or any critique of one, to bring the consequences to our attention.

INDEX NOMINVM

Abelard, Peter (Petrus Abaelardus)
53, 78, 90, 113, 115, 116, 126, 168,
186, 199, 269, 270, 281, 296, 331,
333, 379
Abumacer (Albumasar; Abū Ma ʿshar
Dja ʿfar b. Muḥammad b. ʿUmar
al-Balkhi, d. 272/886) 103
Ackrill, J. L. 37
Adams, M. McC. 13
Adamus Woodham, OFM
(Wodeham, Goddam) 11
Ælred of Rievaulx 265–6
Alanus ab Insulis (Alain de Lille) 141
Alberigo, J. 332
Albert, St (Albert the Great, OP,
Albertus Magnus, *doctor universalis, d.
expertus*) 56, 115, 148–92 (esp. 148–
51), 195, 201, 334, 337, 362
Alessio, F. 312
Alexander IV, Pope 246
Alexander of Hales, OFM 57, 79, 80,
99, 128–44, 144–7, 152, 173, 175,
194, 217–20, 334, 362
Alfarabi (Avennassar; al-Fārābī, Abū
Naṣr Muḥammad b. Muḥammad
b. Turkhān b. Awzalagh, d.
339/950) 103
Algazel (Ghazali; al-Ghazālī, Abū
Ḥāmid Muḥammad b. Muḥammad
al-Tūsī, 450/1058–505/1111) 103, 337
Alii, cit. Hostiensis 300
Aliqui, reported by Bonaventure 202
Allard, B. 87
Almagno, S. 12
Angelelli, I. 43, 328
Anselm, St (Anselmus, Anselm of
Aosta, of Bec OSB, of
Canterbury) 50, 54, 58, 80, 141,
151, 248

Aristotle 29, 35, 36, 37, 41, 47, 59, 66,
103, 105, 131, 173, 174, 175, 183, 271,
312, 328, 331, 337, 338, 343, 370
Auer, J. 10, 11, 119, 311
Augustine, St 58, 72, 84, 195, 278,
331, 332
Averroës (Ibn Rushd; Abū 'l-Walīd
Muḥammad b. Aḥmad b.
Muḥammad b. Rushd, al Ḥafīd,
520/1126–595/1198) 103
Avicenna (Ibn Sina; Abū ʿAli al-
Ḥusayn b. ʿAbd Allāh b. Sīnā,
370/980–428/1037) 37, 54, 59, 81,
83, 84, 93, 103, 118, 121, 250, 270,
314, 337, 338, 346, 348, 379

Bäck, A. 15, 36, 43, 252, 369
Bacon, Roger, OFM 54, 305, 311–15,
316, 326
Bannach, K. 10
Barnes, J. 41
Barth, K. 287
Bataillon, L.-J. 13, 159
Benoît, D. 4, 253
Berkeley, G. 127
Bernard, St 53, 90, 270, 320
Bérubé, C. 221
Bettoni, E. 132, 198
Bianchi, L. 13, 17, 306
Bissen, J.-M. 221
Bittremieux, J. 279
Bochenski, J. M. 17, 56
Boethius 58, 119
Boileau, D. 311
Bokyngham, *see* Buckingham
Bologna, University of 102
Bolzano, B. 35
Bonaventure, St 115, 193–228 (esp.
193–5), 317, 319, 334

INDEX RERVM

364; holding true of the divine
nature, with significance, but
improperly 363; holding true in
a "systematically leading
expression", properly, but of
something other than the divine
nature 363; many, but expressing
at most one truth 34
providence, foreknowledge,
foreordaining 337
"shipments" of divine power,
wisdom, etc. 281–8

illustratio veritatis aeternae 209–10
Immutable Decree rider 64, 266–7
"imposition of names" 233–4
impossibilia 180
in patria, in via 153
indecens 307–10
indeterminacy of reference, not
possible in Power Distinction's
uses of 'God' 32–3
individualised forms 40, 355
instruments de travail, incl. indexing
systems, codifications, 12th–13th
cent. 52–3
interested questions, interested
inquirers 281–2, 374
Islamic backgrounds 334
iustitia/potentia 57–8, 83, 89, 117, 119,
137, 179, 332
de iustitia/potentia 69, 72–3, 113
per iustitiam/potentiam 58, 119

Laws of Contradiction, of Excluded
Middle 182, 191
liberty of indifference, of
spontaneity 354–5
licentia docendi 103

manuscripts 59, 60, 80, 87, 91, 115,
128, 129, 147, 152, 247 and n.,
306, 311, 316, 317, 318
mass terms 282
masters, Masters, 11th–12th cent. 50–
2, 96
modal logic(s) 54, 58
claimed for Theology Faculty 189–
90

"names", common 39–40
of God, *see under* God
necessity:
necessary emanation (attrib. to
Avicenna) 336–7
necessary *secundum potentiam dei,*
necessary *ut ordinatum est secundum
sapientiam dei et non dependens ex
singulari arbitrii alicuius* 131
*necessitas consequentis, n.
consequentiae* 360
necessity *ab alio, per se* 83
negative theology 21–3, 68, 107, 123,
132, 144, 152–9, 220, 239–45,
320, 344, 376
turn away from (Hugo de
Novocastro)? 139–40
Negative Theology 239

omnipotence:
acc. to: Bonaventure 206–7;
Fourth Lat. Council 332; Hugh
of Strasbourg 322–3; William of
Auxerre 75; *see also* "absolute
omnipotence"
Power Distinction 371–2
opera, structured 40, 162–3, 355
operant power, *see under* God
opus conditionis 114
opus redemptionis 1, 114, 239, 372–3
oratio (molecular utterance) 33–4
ordinare (Bonaventure) 208–10

plenitudo potestatis 300
posse:
p. de facto/de iure 140, 204; see also
potestas: de iure/de facto
p. per potentiam/per iustitiam 58
p. potentiae/impotentiae 141
*p. secundum perfectionem, sec.
imperfectionem* 134–6
possibile:
p. absolutum 91
p. in se 88
possibilitas (for a capacity) 59
possibilities:
"real", abstract 65
secundum causas superiores
(Albert) 180

169, 202, 290; *potentia exsequens,*
vs. *potentia absoluta* 169; *potentia
exsequens* vs. *potentia potens* 137;
potentia in habitu, vs. *potentia in effectu*
137; *potentia operans* 24; *potentia
ordinabilis dei* 140; *potentia ordinata
(dei)* 81; *potentia potens,* see *potentia
exsequens; potentia prima, sive
simpliciter,* vs. *potentia ordinata* 82;
*potentia quae non est determinatum ad
aliquem effectum,* vs. *potestas [sic]
calefaciendi determinata ... ad
calefacere* 75; *potentiae absolutae*
(dat.) 307; *potestas conditionata rebus*
107; *potestate absoluta,* vs. *potestate
ordinata quae respicit ordinem rerum*
128; *quantum ad potentiam
absolutam,* vs. *quantum ad potentiam
congruitatis* 306–7; *quantum ad
puram potentiam dei* 63, 64; *quantum
erat de potentia absoluta* 109; *quantum
est de se,* vs. *quantum est ex parte
ipsorum [quaecunque ... potuit et nunc
potest]* 215; *quoad potentiam
decentem,* vs. *quoad potentiam
absolutam* 130; *(potest deus aliquid)
secundum quod habet comparationem
ad res,* vs. *sec. quod habet
comparationem ad potentiam
ordinatam* 86; *secundum potentiam
absolutam,* vs. *exsequens* 290; *sua
omnipotente virtute,* vs. *iuxta
ordinatissimam dispositionem
temporum* 332; *supponere absolute,*
vs. *supponere rem subiectam divinae
potentiae, retorquendo ad deum
tamquam ad subiectum* 125; see also
composite/divisim distinction;
possibile-in se
understanding 16–17, 96, 145, 339–
62, 364–8; Albert 170–2, 178,
180, 185, 191–2; Alexander of
Hales 141–2; Aquinas 245, 247–
61, 276; Bonaventure 205–6;
Geoffrey of Poitiers 61; Hugh of
St Cher 118–23; Philip the
Chancellor 84; Quidam,
reported by William of Auxerre

63–4; Roland of Cremona 110–
13; from William of Auvergne
94–5; William of Auxerre 71, 75
use 96, 146, 333–9, 368–70, 373–7,
379, 380; Albert the Great 162,
163, 166, 169, 170–1, 174–5, 179,
182, 190, 191; Alexander of Hales
130, 131, 138, 140–1; *Alii,* reported
by Hostiensis 300; *Aliqui,*
reported by Bonaventure 202;
Aquinas 229, 254, 260–1, 265–
95 (esp. 292–3); Bonaventure
202, 203, 204, 205, 215; Geoffrey
of Poitiers 57, 60–1; Guerric of
St Quentin 128; Hugh of
Strasbourg (illustrative use
merely) 321; Hugo de
Novocastro 139–40; John
Peckham 311 n.; Odo Rigaud
147; *Quidam:* reported by Albert
the Great 168–9, reported by
William of Auxerre 63, 64;
Richard Rufus 318; Robert
Kilwardby 306–7, 311; Roger
Bacon 313–14; William of
Auxerre 69, 70, 71–2, 74
use suggested, but doubtful or
contested: Anon., cit. W.
Courtenay 61–3, 299 n.; Anon.
modern, cit. P. Geach 375 n.;
Hostiensis, or 1581 editor, cit. J.
Marrone 299 n.; *Philosophi,*
reported by Roland of Cremona
110; *Quidam,* reported by Albert
168; William of Auvergne 95; *see
also* Hugh of Strasbourg, *under*
P.D. use *above*
predicables 45–6
predicate expressions, taken *formaliter*
44
predicates, predication 36, 44–6, 58
propositional functions 55, 56
propositions 35–9, 235
as used 35
broadly or narrowly
understood 36, 329
cum modo ("necessary", composing-
apt) 36, 41–3, 81